LISTENING TO THE PHILOSOPHERS

LISTENING TO THE PHILOSOPHERS

NOTES ON NOTES

RAFFAELLA CRIBIORE

CORNELL UNIVERSITY PRESS
Ithaca and London

Copyright © 2024 by Cornell University

All rights reserved. Except for brief quotations in a review, this book, or parts thereof, must not be reproduced in any form without permission in writing from the publisher. For information, address Cornell University Press, Sage House, 512 East State Street, Ithaca, New York 14850. Visit our website at cornellpress.cornell.edu.

First published 2024 by Cornell University Press

Library of Congress Cataloging-in-Publication Data

Names: Cribiore, Raffaella, author.
Title: Listening to the philosophers : notes on notes / Raffaella Cribiore.
Description: Ithaca [New York] : Cornell University Press, 2024. | Includes bibliographical references and index.
Identifiers: LCCN 2023035822 (print) | LCCN 2023035823 (ebook) | ISBN 9781501774751 (hardcover) | ISBN 9781501774768 (paperback) | ISBN 9781501774775 (epub) | ISBN 9781501774782 (pdf)
Subjects: LCSH: Philosophy—Study and teaching. | Note-taking—History. | Education—Philosophy.
Classification: LCC B52 .C79 2024 (print) | LCC B52 (ebook) | DDC 107—dc23/eng/20231128
LC record available at https://lccn.loc.gov/2023035822
LC ebook record available at https://lccn.loc.gov/2023035823

To Stefania and Ottavia

Contents

Foreword by Roger Bagnall   ix
Acknowledgments   xi
A Note on References and Abbreviations   xiii

Introduction: Orality and
Note-Taking   1

Part I: Ancient Annotations in Context

1. Notes and Notetakers   17
2. Taking Notes in Class   38
3. Students' Annotations
   in Philosophy   47
4. *Notae* of Stenographers   70

Part II: The Voice of Epictetus

5. Epictetus as an Educator
   and a Man   87
6. Epictetus and the World of Culture   118

Part III: Recording Lectures of Philosophers

7. Introduction: Ancient
   Commentaries   163
8. Notes from Athens: Philodemus
   On Frank Criticism   170
9. Taking Notes in the School of
   Didymus the Blind   200

10. Listening to Olympiodorus 227

Conclusion: The Authentic Philosopher's Voice 245

References 251
Index 271

Foreword

Raffaella Cribiore's accidental death while this book was in press deprived her of the chance to put the final touches on the book as edited, and I have had to try to discern how she would have responded to the queries that are an inevitable part of editing or given the text a final revision before typesetting. I ask the reader's understanding on her behalf and mine. Her distinctive voice throughout remains unmistakable, as it was throughout her scholarly work. When she came to graduate study at Columbia University, after an interruption in her education as the result of a move to New York and years of raising her family, it was with a first-rate training in the classical languages at the Università Cattolica del Sacro Cuore in Milan and the beginnings of a knowledge of papyrology from her work with the great scholar Orsolina Montevecchi.

Her passion for studying ancient education was there from the outset, and it defined her entire scholarly career. Her revised dissertation (*Writing, Teachers, and Students in Graeco-Roman Egypt*) was published three years after she received the doctorate in 1993 and quickly achieved classic status. (She was proud of the large number of copies stolen from libraries!) It was a revolutionary achievement, the first study of school texts based on an investigation of the materials of these texts and their handwriting. She showed in it the attention to practical detail that marks all of her work, but also an ability to enter sympathetically into the world she studied; she could envisage the students' hands as they moved with the pen across the surface of a papyrus or potsherd. At the same time, she understood that this down-to-earth approach needed a broader context in the theory and practice of ancient education. There followed over the next twenty years four more single-author books, beginning with *Gymnastics of the Mind*, which won the Goodwin Award for 2004, and continuing with three books on Libanius. There was also a joint volume of ours collecting and studying *Women's Letters from*

Ancient Egypt. She had an acute eye in looking at handwriting; I learned much from working with her even if I could never achieve the same level of insight.

Listening to the Philosophers: Notes on Notes is the logical continuation of these investigations, moving from the focus on rhetoric that occupied her attention for many years to look at philosophy and philosophers; advancing in wisdom, Epictetus would doubtless say. The reader familiar with her earlier work will perceive the imaginative ability to see what is really going on in a text, particularly at the boundary between document and literature; for this is where student notes belong, just as the school papyri fall into a zone between documentary and literary papyrology. It is not to be her last book: a volume of school texts in Coptic, preserved on ostraca in the Columbia University collection and coedited with Jennifer Cromwell, is currently under review. With it she returns to the raw materials that sparked her interest thirty-five years ago as a graduate student, the original products of teaching and learning.

One further result of her insistence on understanding concretely the situations in which students learned is also still to appear. Her death occurred just before a colloquium at the Fondation Hardt of which she was the co-organizer with Daniel Anderson, devoted to the spaces of education. Her contribution to the resulting volume, which her co-organizer will edit, looks at three physical contexts for late antique education that still exist, all of which she knew firsthand: Apollonia in the Cyrenaica, Kom el-Dikka at Alexandria, and the school at Amheida, ancient Trimithis, in Egypt's Dakhla Oasis. She was a member of the excavation team there, enjoying, perhaps unpredictably, the inelegant life of a member of an excavation team in the desert. Her range of engagement with ancient education was unique and irreplaceable.

—Roger Bagnall, New York University,
September 2023

Acknowledgments

When examining ancient societies, I have always been interested in how people obtained an education, how teaching and learning functioned, and how individuals progressed to become members of their communities. In my previous publications, I inquired about the general levels of instruction from the elementary stages to learning literature and then rhetoric. This was the *enkyklios paideia*, the "circular" and general education; if an individual completed all its stages, it was assured they would have acquired a substantial knowledge that somewhat reflected their power. Philosophy was not part of this system. Those who wanted to follow a philosopher, listen to his words, and learn to practice a different way of life might or might not have covered the previous levels of education. And yet, not much is clear about the classes taught by philosophers. I found it irresistible to try to find out more.

First of all, I would like to thank the three readers for Cornell University Press; their advice has helped me improve my work very much. I am very grateful to all those who have read parts of the manuscript. Among the friends who gave me precious advice are Phillip Mitsis, Michael Peachin, and David Konstan. I also thank Craig Gibson and Stephen Kidd. I owe the title of this book to Sean Gurd, who has been enthusiastic about the project from the very beginning. Hans Teitler has been extremely helpful regarding stenographers, and I owe him a great deal. Richard Sorabji and Michael Griffin have responded to crucial questions that illuminated a period with which I needed to familiarize myself. Paul Zanker has also been very helpful in showing me how to obtain from the Louvre the image for the book's cover. In the section on Philodemus, it will become very clear that my debt to Daniel Delattre is great.

In spring 2021 I was asked to deliver three lectures at Washington University in Saint Louis as part of the Biggs Family Residency in Classics. Since COVID was a menace, unfortunately I could not be present and had to give my talks virtually. Yet my experiences with the questions that followed and faculty and student interactions were overwhelmingly positive. I am grateful to John and Penelope Biggs, Cathy Keane, and those who enriched my project, especially Peter Martens. Many thanks to all the others who also contributed to this book in different ways.

A Note on References and Abbreviations

Journals and works are abbreviated as in *L'Année Philologique*. Ancient authors and their works are abbreviated according to the fourth edition of the *Oxford Classical Dictionary*. In the notes, references are cited by author's name and date of publication.

Abbreviations for editions of papyri, ostraca, and tablets follow John F. Oates et al. (2001), *Checklist of Editions of Greek, Latin, Demotic, and Coptic Papyri, Ostraca, and Tablets* (Oakville, CT).

GMAW Eric Gardner Turner. 1971. *Greek Manuscripts of the Ancient World.* Princeton.

PLRE I, 1971 Arnold Hugh Martin Jones, John Robert Martindale, and John Morris. *The Prosopography of the Later Roman Empire.* Vol. 1. Cambridge.

LISTENING TO THE PHILOSOPHERS

Introduction

Orality and Note-Taking

Theodor Mommsen never completed his *History of Rome*. The first three volumes were published between 1854 and 1856, but Mommsen never published an account of imperial history up to the empire's decline. Though the scholarly world waited impatiently for the appearance of the volume IV that Mommsen continued to promise, he felt he had a problem with inscriptions and with sources in general and devoted himself to the *Corpus Inscriptionum Latinarum*. He also disliked the scandals and sexual anecdotes of what he considered a degenerate age; Mommsen lost his emotional commitment to write about this period. However, teaching imperial history radically differed from completing and publishing the history of the empire. Mommsen lectured on Roman history at the University of Berlin for a quarter-century. Half of the lectures dealt with late antiquity, and he declared that if he could live his life over, he would concentrate on that age.

His students also copied down his lectures. Though the drafts of Mommsen's lectures are not extant, in 1980 the German historian Alexander Demandt discovered a complete transcript of his lectures covering imperial history up to late antiquity in a secondhand Nuremberg bookshop. Part I consisted of three notebooks transcribed by his student Paul Hensel, who later became a professor of philosophy at Erlangen. Paul also took notes down for parts II and III, while the last two volumes (existing in book form) were copied over in a different hand—that of Paul's father, Sebastian—and contained cartoon drawings of father and son.[1] Both Paul and Sebastian attended the lectures from eight to nine in the morning. After a course of lectures, they both wrote to Mommsen to express their admiration for his magnificent teaching and to ask if he could reserve them seats right in the front. They declared that Mommsen reconstructed a lost world, bringing to life for them the events of the age of the emperors. Never in their student careers had they ever heard or experienced something so powerful. Using the notes of the two Hensels, Demandt effectively published Mommsen's *History of the Empire*.

Just as Demandt did for Mommsen, we can try to study the notes from students of ancient philosophy. Some philosophers in antiquity chose not to write down and publish many of their lectures but delivered their words only for the benefit of their students, who wrote them down. We will see that Aristotle produced works for publication written in a good prose style, but except for some fragments, these did not come down to us. Many of his treatises were instead transmitted as records taken down by students; their mistakes and repetitions point to live speech. Some scholars have contended that these works do not transmit Aristotle's actual words, but we can call them the "raw Aristotle," as with Mommsen's lectures.[2]

Aristotle, in those texts that reproduce his actual lectures, referred not to readers but to listeners who were present. The title of this book, *Listening to the Philosophers: Notes on Notes*, shows the implicit connection between orality and note-taking. It also refers to an essay of Plutarch, *On Listening to Lectures*, which was dedicated to a young man who was starting to study philosophy.[3] That essay's main theme was proper behavior in the lecture room, where some students did not have a true appreciation of their teacher's message. We will see that some of the students we will encounter in this book were also indifferent to their teachers' words and were deaf to philosophy. Yet others—for example, Arrian—listened with fervor and reported what they heard.

---

1. Cf. in part III the marginalia in the notes taken from Olympiodorus's lecture.
2. See the introduction of Beresford 2020, xi–xv at xiv.
3. *De recta ratione audiendi, Peri akouein. Mor.* 37–48.

From the first century BCE to the sixth century CE, notes written by students who recorded lectures of their teachers of philosophy are preserved on papyri and in various kinds of manuscripts. They provide information on the curriculum, the role and identity of teachers and students, their relationship, and the formation and use of books. All of these are subjects that have been explored only very cursorily; in this book I will analyze these issues in detail and shed light on ancient classes of philosophy in order to clarify the ways in which notes and notetakers functioned. The extant students' notes that I study in the following parts come from antiquity. They are notes taken down by Philodemus of Gadara from the lectures of his teacher Zeno in the first century BCE, notes of Arrian recording the *Discourses* of Epictetus in the second century CE, and notes of students of Didymus the Blind in the fourth and Olympiodorus in the sixth century. Working back from these notes, it is possible to understand the methods and practices of what was originally an orally conducted education, and in particular an education in philosophy.

First and foremost, this book is about education in philosophy. Secondarily, it concerns the formation of some philosophical texts, rather than philosophy per se. Here I am eminently interested in educational practices and in the oral and written methods followed in higher education, especially rhetoric and philosophy. Many aspects of ancient pedagogy, such as the role of oral delivery and the value of annotations in the course of classes, still remain obscure. Attention to these still-unexplored areas will enrich our knowledge not only of how classes were conducted but also of how lectures and commentaries were preserved. We will connect with the classroom through students' written notes and *not* through theoretical pronouncements such as those of Quintilian or Plutarch. This will complement what we know from the occasional texts on education and narratives that are part of rhetorical texts and epistolary communications. We will familiarize ourselves with learning methods and students' means of recording their teachers' voices and producing their own books and commentaries.

Written texts in the ancient Greco-Roman world were never free from the constraints of orality. They were sometimes composed by an author, dictated to a scribe, and then read and commented on, mostly aloud.[4]

---

4. The sophist Libanius, for example, always wrote his speeches by hand and had to employ a scribe only when his arthritis became unmanageable. *Or.* 1.232 shows that he always penned his texts until his old age; cf. also *Or.* 3.5.

The written and spoken worlds were closely intertwined, so that some philosophers who delivered lectures allowed listeners and students to record notes as Mommsen's students did. Ancient educational practices are associated with the way in which much philosophy has come down to us. From the time of Plato, Aristotle, and even before, people rushed to lectures to hear the philosophers' words, ask questions, and discuss. And not only philosophers: in the second century CE, audiences also attended the eminent doctor Galen's lectures and scientific demonstrations en masse; there, listeners took written notes that they sometimes published under their own names. Galen resisted that trend and even tried to stop it, to no avail. In short, this habit of taking notes at public lectures was widespread and did much to promote knowledge of the subjects in question.

In late antique philosophical teaching in particular, writing by the philosophers who lectured in class was a last resort that could never fully replace the living, spoken word. Education was based on the spoken word and the interactions of teachers and students, both of whom engaged in clarifications and questions and answers. Most philosophical production consisted of oral discussions put into writing as preparation for further classes or notes when philosophers-in-training and students recorded their teachers' words. Some texts that were initially written down were later read in class, producing commentaries and generating students' notes.

And yet it is important to keep something in mind: for Socrates, Plato, and the Stoic Chrysippus, philosophical instruction mainly consisted of preparing students for argumentation and methods of thought. In later times, when written texts acquired a new importance and commentaries became the usual basis for teaching, freedom of instruction and lively discussions endured as methods to inculcate paideia. Besides clarifying obscure parts of classical and authoritative texts, personal training in the classroom continued to focus on individual growth and spiritual progress, so that exegesis brought benefit to the soul. In this period, teachers and students continued to engage in discussions; extant questions and answers based on ancient authoritative works and communicated by notes give us the flavor of teachings and transmit the voices of the classroom. We will see that dialogues present in commentaries were part of daily instruction. The teachers' answers urged pupils to take full advantage of their words and of the texts on which they commented, also aiming to improve and change the students' lives. Epictetus's *Discourses*, which consisted of notes taken down during lectures, show vividly that young men's interactions with their teacher were supposed to lead to fundamental spiritual progress. While the urgent, exhortative words of Epictetus's teachings show a rare immediacy, it is more difficult to identify the personal voice of a philosopher through the commentaries of late antiquity that focused mainly on Plato and Aristotle.[5]

That said, it is fundamental to realize that education in the imperial period typically focused on a text, and reading and exegesis could also be highly technical. It is not equally clear in Epictetus whether this was also the case. His *Discourses* taken down by Arrian do not include discussions on texts; thus his theoretical teaching has not survived in transmission. It is possible that it was confined to afternoon classes that Arrian did not cover, but we also have to consider that the young Arrian of Nicomedia made some choices in how he portrayed the echo of the philosopher's voice. Reliance on a text will be evident in part III of this book. Over time, texts had become difficult to understand as the language barrier became stronger. Young, apprenticed philosophers needed to know the authorities, especially Aristotle and Plato.

Notwithstanding, "to learn philosophy, even by reading and commenting upon texts, meant both to learn a way of life and to practice it."[6] Texts were supposed to produce some transformation in young men's lives, and spiritual benefit had to derive from exegesis. The Stoics made a distinction between theoretical instruction and philosophy as the practice of virtues, logic, physics, and ethics. We know of the existence of manuals on spiritual exercises (*askesis*), but these are lost, and it is likely that these exercises were transmitted orally as part of teaching. Chrysippus addressed an attentive student who was carefully taking down his *hypomnemata*. He did not consider him ready for philosophy: "You also have to be ready to apply the teachings of philosophy to your

---

5. Thus, for example, to recognize the efforts of Olympiodorus to guide and inspire the future conduct of his wards is not easy. See part III.
6. P. Hadot 1995; 2002, 146-57 at 153. See also P. Hadot 1990, 496-98. Bénatouïl (2009), who maintains that his own approach is not theoretical or pedagogic but an application of doctrine to a life, does not mention Hadot but basically draws from him. Cooper (2012), who gave a major reinterpretation of ancient philosophy, also supported the view that philosophy was teaching how to live and explored this concept in Socrates and later thinkers. He disagreed with Hadot (pp. 11-14) on some points, especially about the existence and interpretation of spiritual exercises. The three topoi of Epictetus that I cite at the beginning of part II were the basis for a philosophy that was not theoretical and "philosophical" but taught how to live.

way of life and live by them."⁷ The eminent and pioneering French philosopher Pierre Hadot helpfully divided philosophy into three parts.⁸ The first two parts consisted of theoretical philosophy, but the third part, which did not exclude the other two, included a pedagogical dimension, the succession of steps needed to achieve mastery, and the various phases of paideia.

This book argues that the notes students made when listening to their masters' lectures communicate powerfully the notions of teaching and learning that we would otherwise only know cursorily. Notes recorded in class give us the possibility of listening to students' and teachers' actual voices and allow us to study contextual elements familiar to us from our own school days.⁹ We have all taken notes in the past, and we continue to do so in our own idiosyncratic ways. When notes are drawn from an ephemeral source, such as a lecture or a meeting, they often remain the sole testimony of that event; this is why they are precious. We shall see that this was a common characteristic of ancient notebooks, which derived not from any fixed text but from lectures, which could change course at any time and vanish. Far from being disappointing pieces of literature, these notes instead allow us glimpses of texts that were not yet edited, of writing habits, and of routines of everyday life. They are particularly valuable, moreover, because without them we would not know of important cultural practices.

First, a word of caution regarding concepts like the continuity of human experience, that is, attempts to recognize aspects of ourselves and our world in those who inhabited it so long ago.¹⁰ Among historic customs, practices, and behaviors that may confound us, we can recognize much that remains familiar. The seduction of recognition must be resisted to a degree, and likewise we must challenge the assumption that writing in all forms, then and now, is fundamentally similar. And yet, for centuries students have taken notes in class using various writing implements and materials, and for centuries readers have hovered

---

7. *Stobaeus* 2.7.11. Johannes Stobaeus, who lived perhaps in the early fifth century CE, was a compiler of extracts from Greek authors.

8. See P. Hadot 1979.

9. Sellars (2021, 20) considers the *Meditations* of Marcus Aurelius an ensemble of thoughts and quotations redacted in a notebook without order. Systematic note-taking was very popular in the eighteenth and nineteenth centuries and later started to fade. Notes have continued to exist but are drawn more sporadically.

10. Schoeler 2010, 1. See also Bagnall 2011, 1–5. There is a contemporary critique of presentism.

over books, giving their full attention to texts by marking them in some way. We now use asterisks and scribble observations (complete or incomplete) in the margins, establishing a personal rapport with—and sometimes defiling—something written. By mingling ourselves with a text and its author, we are choosing not to read passively. We are intrigued by the annotated books of famous figures, as if we could capture their souls through their meticulously handwritten notes. Michel Foucault believed that copybooks of notes were very personal and could give almost psychoanalytic insights.[11] Notes on ancient materials like papyri or ostraca are unique because they reveal the idiosyncrasies of those who wrote them, and yet each kind of note-taking has an attractive, personal flavor that does not equally emerge from finished texts. Writing in 2012, Mark O'Connell noticed an increased degree of contemporary interest in marginalia, stemming from nostalgia for tangible books; this resulted from the rise of e-books, which cannot easily be annotated.[12] Today, notes might consist of ink on paper or various electronic alternatives and might be placed in the margins of books, in notebooks, or on random pieces of paper.

Further, we generally consider ancient texts in the complete or fragmentary forms in which they were transmitted, but other types of texts such as drafts, alternate versions, and notes have also emerged from the Greek and Roman worlds. Genetic criticism, a fascinating theoretical discipline begun in France in 1979, can help us think about such texts.[13] Its adherents view literary and subliterary works not as static and negligible pieces of writing but as part of a writing process that starts at the moment a work is conceived.[14] Papyrologists inspect drafts, corrections, and different versions in hopes of understanding a writer's point of departure. The origin of a book in the author's mind is in itself unreachable, but the process of reconstruction in stages imbues the book itself with new meaning. When writing takes place, it may initially appear in different forms, such as notes or drafts, which may result in different versions of a text.

---

11. Blair 2004.
12. O'Connell 2012.
13. The main journal of the movement is *Genesis*. Literature in English is scarce; the best general book is Bryant 2002. See also Deppman et al. 2004. Cf. Cribiore 2019.
14. Genetic critics explore rare book and manuscript libraries and search for autograph manuscripts. So, for example, in order to study certain great nineteenth-century French writers, some scholars have composed genetic dossiers into which they have fitted every kind of writing by the author in question, including letters and notes.

It is reasonable to suppose that people usually used notes in their writing endeavors in antiquity, just as in modern times. One of the basic differences between ancient and modern annotators is how they store information. While reading neurologist Oliver Sacks's memoir, *On the Move: A Life*,[15] I was struck by the author's note-taking habits. He recorded information obsessively and produced multiple books of notes that helped him in the composition of his volumes, derived from reading or personal reflections. Once he suddenly jumped out of the water during his daily swim around New York's City Island to record a thought, and then he continued to swim. Taking down a large number of usable annotations requires an agile mind. As he grew older, Sacks started to trust his memory to a lesser extent and made use of a stenographer to keep a record of his thoughts.

Oliver Sacks is certainly not the only modern author to use notes as a memory aid and to compose books. Many scholars still do so, penciling their books so heavily that they produce miniature commentaries. When I purchased a Teubner edition of Dionysius of Halicarnassus's *Opuscula* online, I was pleasantly surprised to see that the front page bore the name of its previous owner, a renowned classics scholar, still living, who had heavily annotated the text. His notes filled expanses of blank space in the book, written in the margins horizontally or vertically, and like an ancient *catena* surrounded sections of text concerning certain writers such as Demosthenes, who was an object of great attention. Some of these notes contained references to other authors or made grammatical and syntactical points; others commented on a passage, while still others posed questions. We will examine ancient marginalia in part III. We will also see that ancient authors such as Galen and Augustine filled their margins with notes whose interpretation sometimes caused problems.

The topic of note-taking in antiquity encompasses a large quantity of materials. No comprehensive study of this subject for the Greek and Roman worlds has previously been undertaken. With some exceptions (especially that of Quintilian), I focus on Greek writers.[16] Roman writers were more prone to disclosing the articulations of their work, and this is a subject that has already attracted attention.[17] However, Greek writers also deserve to be taken into account, despite

---

15. Sacks 2015.
16. The translations of texts are my own unless otherwise specified.
17. Cf. Gurd 2012.

their tendency to be less generous with this information. For pragmatic reasons and to focus on the clearest examples, I have limited myself to select cases. For example, I will not include the second part of Libanius's *Autobiography* (*Or.* 1), which lacks unity and a guiding theme and takes the form of an ensemble of rambling notes in roughly chronological order.

Furthermore, the process of categorizing instances of note-taking into groups—such as notes that informed literary works and annotations that responded to traveling, reading, listening, or thinking—is also somewhat arbitrary, because these categories often overlap. I will not include in this work ancient doxography, a formal genre identified by modern scholarship that comprises descriptions of tenets and ancient philosophers' views. Originally, some doxographical texts were derived from notes that philosophers and would-be philosophers jotted down, but most doxographical literature depended on older doxographical literature. Diogenes Laertius cited many of the sources.[18] In areas other than antiquity, more attention is devoted nowadays to the practice of note-taking versus a finished work. A recent case concerns the sixteen thousand pages of Leonardo da Vinci's notebooks with doodles in the margins. They had been examined before but not with the same depth. This investigation has since revealed the connection between his painting and scientific endeavors.[19]

This book is divided into three parts, which are in turn subdivided. **Part I: Ancient Annotations in Context** comprises four chapters. Chapter 1, "Notes and Notetakers," explores the general use of notes in antiquity and introduces the subject, devoting initial attention to the value of note-taking as an informational tool and as a writing method. It is valuable for this study, even though the evidence is sometimes anecdotal. This topic is not well known, and finding mentions of authors' general use of notes requires a special alertness because authors rarely alluded to their working practices. Lucian and Plutarch are almost alone among Greek writers in explicitly stating that they gathered notes before engaging in writing endeavors, but their testimony suggests that ancient philosophers used this method, probably often.[20]

---

18. On doxography, see, e.g., Runia 2016.
19. Fiorani 2020.
20. Unfortunately, we have only one side of the equation because precise correspondence between a text and the notes that contributed to it is not at our disposal.

We also do not know exactly what the students, who are the protagonists of the rest of the book, did with their notes and whether these helped and encouraged them to produce their own texts, as Libanius's speeches gave birth to students' declamations.[21] It is a reasonable guess that those who had the ambition to become philosophers often did so. The aspiring philosopher who left the class of Epictetus thinking that he was ready to become a full educator must have used his notes from the lectures to produce new works. Some information about using notes taken in school to create further compositions comes in the chapters of part I, starting with chapter 2, "Taking Notes in Class." Notes were widely used in rhetoric for composing both declamations and speeches. Orators, moreover, brought notes into court and when they delivered *epideixeis*.

Chapter 3 covers "Students' Annotations in Philosophy." It illuminates the performances of some philosophers and philosophers-in-training who took advantage of notes. I will devote special attention to the school of Aristotle, since some of his works can be regarded as students' lecture notes. After that, I look at the evidence concerning other schools of philosophy. There is, however, an essential difference between the pedagogical evidence considered in part I and the rest of the book. The first part considers notes as they are revealed by the *literary sources* and as they inform the practice, without including an examination of actual texts that in fact are not extant. The rest of the book covers some philosophical texts that are transmitted and directly show the importance of notes in *teaching and learning*.

Chapter 4 examines a specialized use of annotations (*notae*) by stenographers, who became especially popular in the late antique Greek world. While stenographers began operating in the Roman world in the time of the Republic, in the Greek world it was only later in the period that people used them to take down dictated letters and treatises and to record sermons. An evaluation of stenographers' work is important on its own merits but also in light of what follows in the book. In two of the educational texts that I consider, those of the second-century philosopher Epictetus and the fourth-century Christian philosopher Didymus the Blind, a central question that needs to be answered is whether it was students or stenographers who recorded these lectures.

---

21. Cf. *Or.* 3.16.

Part II: The Voice of Epictetus is devoted to the notes that Arrian took while his teacher, the Stoic philosopher Epictetus, lectured at his school in Nicopolis, in Epirus. It is divided into two chapters: "Epictetus as an Educator and a Man" and "Epictetus and the World of Culture." It discusses the transmission and origin of the text that tradition attributed to the historian of Alexander, Arrian, when he was young and attending Epictetus's school. The question of whether Arrian had recorded the text himself by using stenography or with the help of stenographers, or entirely redid and composed the text in the manner of what Xenophon had done for Socrates, has been debated for a very long time without a satisfactory solution. I argue, however, that an answer to the dilemma exists, namely that stenographers were not involved in recording Epictetus's lectures, because the resulting text would look entirely different if they had been. As tradition has upheld, the text consisted of notes that Arrian had jotted down, although with some cuts. The text of the *Discourses* contains identifiable features that indicate it consists of notes that Arrian jotted down. Arrian recorded the lectures without excessive discomfort because the philosopher did not maintain a fast pace; he also employed various methods, one of which was abbreviations. The papyri show that abbreviations appear not only in documents but also in literary texts.

In part II my interest does not lie in specifically highlighting Epictetus's philosophy, although it will occasionally be necessary to mention some Stoic principles, particularly when referring to the school curriculum. Instead, I examine how Epictetus's school functioned, what kind of teacher he was, and how he tried to inculcate principles in his students that would persist beyond the classroom and highlight a way of life for them. In chapter 6 of part II, I describe how the school of Epictetus offers many angles of observation that have never been studied before, including his attitude toward the contemporaneous cultural world. Arrian's notes are unique insofar as they illuminate the philosopher's classes and his use of rhetoric, literature, myth, and the theater. Although he was polemical with regard to rhetoric and the Second Sophistic, Epictetus adopted some rhetorical features and approaches in his dialogues. The notes, which probably were never edited in antiquity, also reveal the nuances of Epictetus's often-harsh relationships with his students. The exacting "therapy" that Epictetus practiced was not forgiving toward young men who were still yoked to the type of mechanical education they had previously received and who seemingly made no effort to reach a true understanding of books and of themselves.

Part III: Recording Lectures of Philosophers has a composite nature and is divided into four chapters. After an introduction on ancient commentaries (chapter 7), this part looks at texts that were transmitted and recorded by students in the form of notes.

In chapter 8 I examine the text *On Frank Criticism*, which contains notes that Philodemus of Gadara took during the first-century BCE lectures of Zeno of Sidon in Athens. The papyrus roll, though lacunose, gives a powerful view of educational methods, including punishments and the psychagogue's method of exhortation. Teachers and students applied frank criticism to correct others; *parrhesia* was a duty that, in theory, did not involve jealousy or competition and was an expression of friendship. A new examination of more fragments of the text shows that this practice was quite troublesome.

In chapter 9 I take into account the fourth-century school of Didymus the Blind in Alexandria, in particular two commentaries consisting of notes taken down during his lectures and containing questions and answers. Didymus was not simply a grammarian, as has recently been claimed, but rather an educator who needed to cater to young men of various educational backgrounds and levels. In this case, too, I argue that stenographers were not involved; rather, a student (or students) of Didymus recorded his classes, in the process introducing mistakes and leaving spaces between words, a practice common in school settings.

Chapter 10 concerns records of philosophical lectures delivered in the sixth century. In particular, a course on Plato's *First Alcibiades* creates many questions, as the philosopher Olympiodorus allowed students to take down *apo phones*, from his own voice. Why did Olympiodorus, and philosophers like him, allow these lectures to circulate, in an apparent show of generosity? Are some of the mistakes and imprecisions necessarily the fault of students, or could they derive from Olympiodorus's own carelessness? Is the resulting text the work of a single student who recorded the voice of the philosopher, as scholars have claimed, or of many in collaboration? I argue that the reality that several students took down the philosopher's words is one of the reasons for the supposed "generosity" of Olympiodorus and explains why he preferred not to intrude. In the margins of the text of the commentary, many students' drawings and further notes are preserved, many of which are interesting and have never before been studied.

Listening to the Philosophers reveals why it is imperative to understand the fundamental question of what *makes* a book. Drafts of later published texts, incomplete works, and texts with annotations by students recording the spoken words of their teachers are all examples of what can be called "books." Thus the examples that follow will uncover how notes are not only objects of pedantic scholarly attention but also objects that illuminate cultural and educational routines in antiquity. They preserve works of great value that have come to us not as fixed texts but as texts in evolution and as more spontaneous pieces of writing, providing a uniquely vivid glimpse into daily life and the classes of ancient philosophers. It is captivating to explore texts that plunge us into ancient culture and to hear the voices of eminent ancient educators, especially when notes capture it all with authenticity.

PART I

Ancient Annotations in Context

Ancient testimonies, mostly literary in nature, provide evidence that a range of people extensively used notes that could assist them in their literary endeavors. Ancient notes, like modern ones, are ambiguous in nature, poised between writing and orality. They could be simple, brief records kept for later use, a collection of *Quellen*, or they might be sketches of thoughts, bridges conducive to formal writing. They could be added to a manuscript destined for wide circulation, or they could indicate a private interest, exclusively serving a personal need.[1] They might be collected to form a complete text, then eventually discarded when they became obsolete.

---

1. Zetzel 1980.

Chapter 1

Notes and Notetakers

A study of notes needs to consider that a scholarly disdain for annotations has been one of the most durable of clichés. Gerard Genette has mentioned "the inevitably disappointing nature of the genre" that consists of irregular and concise textual statements.[1] The disparagement of notetakers is similar to the bad reputation that has always been ascribed to excerptors for hiding behind their work and selecting certain authors.[2] With notes we are in a more favorable position, however, because they are more strongly connected to those who record them and those who use them. It is true that the precise identities of some of the student notetakers who appear in this book are unknown, but there is much for us to contemplate and surmise.

---

1. Genette 1997, 319. Yet Genette devoted much attention to notes, which he defined as elements strictly connected to a segment of text of a certain length and possessing a local character. This definition does not always apply to what will be discussed in this book.
2. Konstan 2011. Excerptors do a mechanical job that requires them to remain impersonal, something that is rarely fully appreciated, even as we owe a great debt to the collections that excerptors produce. The relationship between excerptors and the works of literature they select is mostly obscure to us.

Notes have already attracted some attention. In French criticism, for example, the note has achieved a prominent position.[3] French scholars exploring the sixteenth century and later have paid the most attention to the conversation between notes and a primary text, and they have examined notes' contents, style, and rhetoric. They have explored the "geography" of notes: their placement with respect to the main text.[4] The placement of the notes that we will consider, however, is more difficult to determine with certainty. Sometimes annotations were written in the margins (as Galen and Augustine did), and in part III, we will examine notes and doodles done by students and students' marginalia on papyri. These notes covered large quantities of texts and were extensive.

Very often, however, notes appear to have been separate entities, at least in the evidence that has come down to us. The limited knowledge we have of ancient works and of how manuscripts were written, as well as the apparent reticence of the sources in revealing technical details, keep us somewhat in the dark. In her great book on information management, Ann Blair focused on note-taking and collections of notes in the Middle Ages and the early modern period, particularly the sixteenth and seventeenth centuries. The materials that Blair examined, however, were richer; they offered the possibility of studying autograph literary manuscripts and of tracing the evolution from excerpts and jottings to various phases of drafts. This approach is not possible for antiquity, and we cannot readily compare periods that are so distant.[5]

A reader who might be initially confused by the diversity of the information that follows needs to realize that this chapter of part I is about a typology of contexts where note-taking is relevant. The information concerns various situations and different authors who found it necessary to compile notes that could assist them in their written projects. It is only through their testimony that we know of the existence of annotations which are no longer extant. A chronological order here is maintained only within the distinct categories but is present in the rest of parts II and III. In selecting a range of annotations, I have restricted my observations mainly to literary figures, rhetors, philosophers, some representatives of the medical profession, and some religious figures

---

3. Dürrenmatt and Pfersman 2004.
4. Lefebvre 2004. In those cases, notes acquire some independence from the whole and may even have their own titles or dedications. Notes in this case become a space of some freedom, where an author or a reader enters into a dialogue.
5. Blair 2008.

in late antiquity. I have also paid some attention to authors of miscellanies that originated from notes, which form a category in themselves. I have passed over lexicographers, commentators, and anything encyclopedic, as this would have required a different focus than that mainly concerned with students' annotations.

The annotations looked at in this study were selected and categorized with a sociohistorical filter, but with a few limitations. First, some notes and discourses about notes might belong to different groups simultaneously and have been divided somewhat arbitrarily. Other ways to consider the evidence exist, such as dividing notes into three groupings and considering a literary and cultural interpretation: (1) testimonia of notes and note-taking, (2) accounts pervaded by irony and claims dictated by different points of view, and (3) discourses about notes and note-taking. I will not particularly concentrate on strategies of communication, thorough identification of the authors who commented on note-taking, and audiences' expectations. Finally, I have considered notes taken during reading and through memory with a view to using them as material for composition. In later parts, notes drawn from the words of a teacher, which will be the proper subject of this book, will be taken into deeper account.

Terminology Used for Annotations

Clement of Alexandria defined his work made up of notes as *Stromateis*, "miscellanies, literary weavings," referring to the unorganized character of the collection: "This is not a piece of writing rhetorically shaped for display nor a systematic treatise, but my notes stored for old age, a remedy for forgetfulness, a mere reflection, an outline of vividly alive originals, words I was thought worthy to hear and blessed and memorable men" (*Strom.* 1.1). This term *stromateis* was not in common use, although Gellius cited it along with other works of the same kind.[6] Clement's definition aptly defines what notes were and were not—an ensemble of annotations that usually differs from a rhetorically wrought text or a treatise and implies that this type of work has a private character. Further, he indicates that notes were memoranda kept in order to safeguard against the failure of memory. The relationship between the power of memory and annotations was often put into relief, to the point that it became

---

6. *NA* Pref. 7. On Gellius, see Beer 2020.

a kind of cliché. Clement also insists upon the fundamental difference between real events and vividly pronounced words on the one hand and their pallid counterparts, the notes that recorded them, on the other.

As we will see later, the definition of notes and note-taking varies. Roman writers used the word *commentaries*, which denoted the raw material of prose or poetry that still needed to be revised and rearranged.[7] In this sense, Cicero most closely resembles Lucian when writing to Lucceius to request a favor. Hoping for a bit of immediate glory (*gloriola*) through the immortalization of his accomplishments, he asks his correspondent to embellish and expand upon notes that Cicero himself would eventually put together. In the correspondence, Cicero uses the Greek term *hypomnema* for a collection of notes or for a text that is without a complete form.

In Greek, a note is commonly called *hypomnema*. The first to use this term in the sense of its etymological meaning ("reminder" or "memorandum") was Thucydides.[8] Starting with Plato, the term develops the meaning "notation," but it could also refer to a literary commentary or sets of notes. It finds a place in historiography with Plutarch and Lucian, who use it to refer to notes, but for Eunapius it designates the historical commentaries that he used to prepare himself.[9] Marcus Aurelius calls the *Discourses* of Epictetus *tois Epicteteiois hypomnemasi:* that is, Epictetan notes.[10] In the case of Epictetus, the term maintains its original meaning, "jottings," and *hypomnemata* (in the plural) refers to a collection of annotations rather than a single one. Most Greek commentaries to the *Categories* (for example those of the late antique philosopher Ammonius) draw a distinction between works considered to be treatises, i.e., those called *syntagmatica* and those works called *hypomnematica,* in which only the principal things were written.[11] The Peripatetics lectured from notes called *hypomnemata*, and during classes their students would take down notes, which became texts.

Other terms that occasionally appear in the sources, παρασκευή, ὑπογραφή, and ὑποτύπωσις, refer more properly to sketches and outlines.[12] In Latin the term *hypomnemata* appears sometimes, but generally

---

7. Cic. *Ad fam*. 5.12.10. See Lightfoot 1999, 218–19.
8. Thu. 2.44.2 and 4.126.1.
9. Eunapius, *VS* proem 453.
10. *Meditations* 1.7.3.
11. On the *Categories*, cf. Sorabji 2016a, 5–8; Praechter 1909 (2016), 47–48.
12. Devresse 1954, 76–77. The term *Hypotyposis* was used about the "sketch" Albinus produced from the lectures of Gaius. Galen calls *hypographai* a set of notes, in *Hipp.Epid.iv comm*.17B 249.

adnotatio is used to designate a work added to something already written. *Commentarius* is also used, though not exclusively in this sense. The term *hypomnema*, however, could be employed for a monograph, as with Galen. The latter frequently used this term in reference not only to a single work, but also to the whole of his production, with the result that it is impossible to apply a single definition to his usage.[13] The etymological concepts of memory, memoranda, and aide-mémoire were always present.

Notes were also sometimes called *grammateia*, usually referring to writing on wooden tablets. Curiously, Lucian connects the term with amorous notes written by women. In *Toxaris* the term *grammateia* repeatedly designates the notes a married woman would have her maids bring to a young man in order to inflame him with love for her.[14] In Lucian's *Professor of Rhetoric* 23, the sophist of the easy road boasts of his popularity with women, showing to everybody the passionate notes (*grammateia*) they sent him. Lucian, of course, is being playful and pointedly deceptive.

In documentary papyri, the term *hypomnema* has been used since the third century BCE and is attested up to late antiquity (with a slightly different meaning). The archive of the third-century BCE businessman Zenon shows several examples. Notes consisting of a few lines that follow a letter and are called *hypomnema* appear to be postscripts, as in *P.Col.Zen.* II 107 (or *P.Col.* IV 107) which is in the hand of Zeno himself. At times, however, *hypomnemata* exist independently and refer to short communications, examples of which include directives about the destruction of certain trees or a lumber shipment.[15] It is clear that no single term existed to designate notes, and that the one that appears most frequently, *hypomnema*, always needs to be reevaluated. I will revisit this term in part III referring to self-standing textual commentaries.

Notes were habitually used in medicine, and Galen refers repeatedly to the fact that Hippocrates took notes on pieces of papyrus and parchment and on tablets. His son Thessalos had found his father's *hypomnemata*, which he put together in the *Epidemics*.[16] In another book Galen called the notes *hypographai* (sketches). To these Thessalos added "some

---

13. Boudon-Millot and Jouanna 2010, 95–96.
14. Lucian, *Toxaris* 13.3; 14.13; 16.25. In those notes the woman confessed her love and threatened to kill herself if her love was not requited.
15. *P.Col. Zen.* II 96 and I 47. There are also examples of whole letters designated in this way; see *PSI* I 106 from the same archive.
16. Galen, *in Hipp.Epid.iv comm.* 174a 922 and 796 and 17B 249; *De diff.resp.* 7 890.

CHAPTER 1

notes himself, not a few" (7 890). Some have taken this to mean that he added books two and five, but others have considered book four also interpolated and illegitimate (not *gnesios*).[17] Traditionally all the *Epidemics* have been wrongly identified as a collection of notes, with various parts appended and containing deficient language. Finally, in his edition of the text, Jacques Jouanna clarified that the text did not consist of notes.[18]

In the Roman world, Pliny the Younger used the term *commentarii* for the 160 volumes of notes his uncle left him (*Ep.* 3.5.17). The model of the elder Pliny must have counted as a great stimulus, but as Ilaria Marchesi remarks, "Peer pressure must have been strong."[19] It is possible that these contained some comments, and they must have observed some order. The volumes consisted of papyrus rolls, inscribed on both sides in a small and tight hand.[20] Notes were prone to being misplaced, discarded, or lost after being incorporated into a text, with the result that in general we are only informed that they had existed at one time; individual notes usually have not survived, except on papyrus.

Where did the students who recorded lectures write their texts? Writing notes on a papyrus roll required some ability. With the absence of tables and probably also a lack of boards to support the papyrus, writing notes was an act of dexterity.[21] It is conceivable that these students employed tablets. Nowadays, electronic media and keyword searching have alleviated the notetaker's burden, but in the Greek and Roman worlds storing and indexing notes required manual organization. Given the prevalent use of alphabetical order, which was enforced starting with primary education and was also used for numerical sequences, we may surmise that individuals employed it to manage abundant notes, probably taking advantage of readily available slave labor. Notes could be made on erasable writing surfaces and thus be inherently temporary,

---

17. Galen, *De diebus decretoriis libri* 3, 9 859. There was much confusion. Galen thought that when it was uncertain whether a work had been written by Hippocrates or by Thessalos, it was best to learn that text only summarily.

18. Jouanna (2016) accepted the conclusions of a dissertation by Hellweg (1985) that made careful consideration of the language. It clarified that the work was intended for a medical audience and therefore adopted a specific style, but that stylistically it was coherent. Books I and III were separated long ago. It is conceivable that the author had relied on reworked *hypomnemata*.

19. Marchesi (2008, 145) remarks that at any rate Pliny did not leave historical works.

20. Pliny the Younger appears to admire these capacious rolls. He was probably used to reading texts written on the recto. Dorandi (2007, 29–36) has commented in detail on the passage regarding Pliny and the terminology for notes.

21. McNamee 2007, 20–21.

or they might be written on more permanent materials, such as papyrus, parchment, ostraca (potsherds), or tablets. Reading widely, excerpting information, and assembling notes must have been part of the working methods of many writers, even those who never mention these activities.

The physical storage of notes is unclear. Many were lost or discarded, as they were only intended for short-term use, while others cannot be recovered because they were not deposited in locations designated for long-term storage. However, archival evidence suggests that preserved notes would have been stored together with other incomplete pieces of writing.[22] For example, Libanius makes a distinction between speeches he delivered and those he kept in a chest (*kibotion*) for emergencies, like delivering an impromptu oration.[23] The latter must have needed some finishing touches, and his notes for declamations were likely stored along with them (*Ep.* 877.3). His slave was in charge of the chest, with the result that the sophist found himself unable to locate desired notes in the slave's absence (*Ep.* 744.5). From Synesius's *Ep.* 154.62–63 we learn that the author's enemies assumed that the books he kept in this chest were incomplete and uncorrected (*adiorthota*). These chests, therefore, would usually have contained material that still needed work. Early Islamic historians used a similar chest to store annotations from both oral and written sources.[24] Other scholars, whether contemporary or later, could use the notes in the chest to compose their own works with no concern for plagiarism. Better organization featuring indexing and headings came later, at the turn of the eighteenth century, with the invention of a peculiar but handy "note closet" in which a great variety of notes could be stored.[25]

Writing Strategies

Here, I focus on the ancients' strategies of composing works by using notes derived from oral performances, the reading of texts, the jotting

---

22. For Pliny the Elder, Naas (1996, 328) supposes that there was an intermediate phase between collecting notes and utilizing them for composition and thinks of a *boîte à fiches* (index card box).

23. See *Or.* 18.118 on Julian taking out books from his chest. Cf. also Synesius *Epp.* 130.59 and 154.62–63.

24. Juynboll 1973.

25. According to Blair (2010, 92–95), this was a high-tech piece much admired. No examples of it are extant.

down of original thoughts, and memories of events like traveling. "Of course, the ancients made notes!" one might say. On the writing process, John McPhee says, "You begin with a subject.... You pile up volumes of notes and then figure out what you are going to do with them."[26] Writing them down to compose a whole text was the ultimate achievement. Ancient works of literature must in many cases have been derived from notes, because writers needed to construct and organize their texts and to record what they had read, and they likely did so often, as we do, from notes. Most of the time, however, the notes that writers took in antiquity are not extant as separate entities in their original forms unless they are preserved on papyri, ostraca, or tablets. Even though in some rare cases authors explicitly mention the ways in which notes shaped their work, many aspects and circumstances of note-taking, both inside and outside the classroom, are obscure. It is also important to recognize that sometimes we risk falling prey to anecdotes that are short and isolated, but it is the composite picture that counts.

The primary rationale for making annotations was to remember knowledge gained through reading, listening, and seeing to ultimately benefit people's ability to combine sources and put together written works. Students who recorded lectures did so not only to enrich their patrimony of knowledge but also to learn how to organize and create written works.[27] The narrations of our predecessors' prodigious memories that have come down to us are fabulous. Memory needed to be aided and stimulated, both in school and in real life. The students of rhetoric and philosophy whom we will meet later recorded portions of texts and discussions in order to retain this knowledge.[28]

A well-known letter by Pliny the Younger reveals precious information regarding his uncle Pliny the Elder.[29] A compulsive reader, the elder Pliny would isolate and preserve excerpts from any book—even bad ones (as we are told)—in case he might ever need them. He would have assistants make notes for him as he was basking in the hot Italian sun,

---

26. McPhee 2017.
27. Cf. the introduction. An excursus on writing strategies can be beneficial to illuminate students' later use of annotations, even though, in this case, we are only allowed to guess.
28. One should take into account, however, that a text written in somewhat disorderly fashion as an ensemble of notes and observations of events reported orally could displease some readers. See the remarks of Papias, a writer of the church in the second century, as reported by Eusebius of Caesarea *HE* 3.39.15. Papias had said that Mark, the writer of the Gospel, did not err when he "put down disorderly the things said and done by the Lord." Some people had not approved of that.
29. Pliny the Younger *Ep.* 3.5.10–11.

eating dinner, and being rubbed down after visiting the baths. Pliny did not write his notes himself but instead verbally responded to texts that others read to him. His note-taking therefore depended on listening to others, just as students would take notes when listening to their teachers. The elder Pliny also relied on note-taking when traveling, bringing along a secretary (*notarius*)—a stenographer who would take *notae* on tablets to later be "translated" into Latin or Greek words. I will describe in greater detail at the end of part I how stenographers were used at the beginning of the Roman imperial period but only appeared later in the Greek world. In Pliny's case, however, he was very concerned with productive work, and on frigid days he would take care that long sleeves protected the *notarius*'s hands.[30] Speed characterizes the entire passage describing Pliny's frantic literary habits, and we can almost visualize notes flying from his mouth straight to the tablets.[31] Clearly idiosyncratic to each notetaker, the practice of note-taking did not necessarily happen in the privacy of one's room.

The example of Pliny the Elder is certainly suggestive, but in general Greek and Roman authors showed some reluctance to discuss their writing methods and preferred to present only their finished product.[32] Authors such as Plutarch and Lucian, who like many others relied on note-taking, disclosed their methods only in part. Plutarch, who devoured "omnivorously works in all areas of ancient learning,"[33] wrote in a letter to a friend that appears at the beginning of *On Tranquility of Mind* that as a gift he "had gathered together observations from notes" that he had intended for his own use.[34] The word *hypomnemata* has aroused scholarly attention regarding Plutarch's sources, namely whether he relied on multiple sources or just one.[35] The friend had requested a treatise, instead of which Plutarch, in order not to appear unfriendly, sent

---

30. Pliny the Younger *Ep.* 3.5.15.
31. See Pecere (2010) where such practices are widely discussed.
32. Livy, for instance, never discussed his working methods. Scholars, however, paid attention to his use of Polybius in his later books and thought they could deduce aspects of his writing methods from that. See Luce 1977, 185–229. On other historians' presentation of their methods, see Marincola 1997, 63–86.
33. Stadter 1989, xliv–xlvi.
34. *On Tranquillity of Mind.* 464F–465a. Cf. 457d *On the Control of Anger* where he says that he always made an effort to collect information. On his writing methods, see Pelling *1979*, revised in Pelling 2002. See also Stadter 2014.
35. Pettine 1984, 95–102. *Hypomnemata* meant notes in general. It is likely that Plutarch used his annotations taken from his vast readings. In what follows I will consider the varied nomenclature used to distinguish notes.

this specimen. Thus, Plutarch was in the habit of first writing notes for himself on various subjects, then later combining them.[36]

In *De historia conscribenda* 47–48, Lucian recommends that a historian collect facts carefully, first producing a series of notes (again called *hypomnemata*) without concern for continuity or "beauty." The notes then needed to be properly arranged and ordered, then finally embellished with charm and proper style.[37] Every meticulous ancient historian must have started a project by randomly collecting material in the form of annotations, which he subsequently arranged. Thucydides's *History*, much admired by Lucian, is emblematic of the difficulty historians faced in accurately evaluating and ordering each piece of testimony.[38] Thucydides does not discuss his working methods, but in his *Vita* his later biographer Marcellinus[39] commented on his copious notes from the time the war started.[40] Even if we do not have the notes or the copies redacted under the supervision of Thucydides (or indeed any other Greek historian), editions of their texts that contain rather modest and literary marginalia survive, testifying to how grammatical and rhetorical curricula used these authors' works.[41]

Literary evidence from other poets and prose writers indicates they also used various note-taking methods. For example, Diogenes Laertius reports on the writing habits of the philosopher Timon, who was fond of wine and composed poems as a respite from philosophy.[42] Though difficult to take at face value, this anecdote still alludes to modes of note-taking that are not unrealistic and must have been frequent. His disorderly way of writing and preserving his creations may

---

36. If we examine Plutarch's statement, however, it does not seem to inform us only about his writing habit but needs to be read rhetorically. He wanted to warn his friend not to have many expectations in order not to attract any criticism.

37. This apparently objective statement needs to be read in the context of Lucian's bitter polemic against contemporary historians.

38. See, e.g., *Thucydides* 1.2, 20–22.

39. *Vita Thucydidis* 47.3. Marcellinus probably lived in the fourth century CE. Thucydides would note down speeches, discussions, and events without regard for style, later developing and embellishing what he had written down to preserve in his memory.

40. Centuries later, Gert Avenarius (1956, 85–92) agreed with Marcellinus and went further. He considered the historian's eighth book an ensemble of notes due to its lack of speeches. Thucydides did not have enough time to fully develop this book before his death.

41. McNamee 2007, 124–25. Prentice (1930) takes it for granted that Thucydides assembled notes before and during the war but wonders where they would have been kept.

42. *DL* 9.110. Dorandi 2013, 109–16. It seems that wine and poetry go together. Timon was not an enthusiastic teacher; he preferred to mind his own business, unlike his peers, some of whom pursued students (*DL* 9.112). Of course, this was Diogenes's opinion.

have depended partly on his state of inebriation. He would write here and there on a papyrus roll, producing poetic excerpts of which he subsequently would lose track.[43] Timon (*DL* 9.114) had great difficulty reciting his "half-eaten" poetic texts on request, and if a complete annotation escaped him, he sometimes would find half a poem scrawled somewhere on the roll. Diogenes commented that Timon was *adiaphoros*, "indifferent," and made no effort to preserve his notes, which were apparently all together on a single roll, in order. Some character traits may have facilitated his tendency to write annotations rather than to automatically conceive of a piece of writing as a whole. He would also cooperate with poets and tragedians by sketching plots and giving them material. Like Diogenes, he was very fond of quotations—or rather, fragments of writing.[44]

Notes were usually private, but they could be shared with personal assistants and other students and in rare cases passed from author to author as a "gift." This is the situation in which the poet Parthenius of Nicaea reveals a dedication of his *Erotika pathemata* (Sufferings in love) to the poet Gallus.[45] The teacher of Vergil and a favorite of emperors, Parthenius was famous in his day, but his poetry has mostly been lost.[46] All that survives is this little prose work that contains thirty-six love stories. Sending it to his friend to be rendered into verse, Parthenius describes it as "a little notebook" (*hypomnemation*). Parthenius was no different from other ancient writers who jotted down ideas and facts for later use. Here he had collected mythological stories that, in his opinion, had not yet been subjected to sufficient treatment. While he offered them to Gallus in hopes of receiving a poetic gift in return, it is conceivable that he had tried (or was going to try) to turn them into poetry himself as a challenge to his friend. It is inspiring to imagine Parthenius putting together a much larger collection of "sufferings."

---

43. *Epitulittein*, to open a book. So Timon composed different parts of poems. He marked a note distinguishing half a poem and then completed it later.

44. Dorandi 2013, 728–32; Goulet-Cazé 1986; see König and Whitmarsh 2007, 133–49. On the date, see Jouanna 2009.

45. Lightfoot 1999.

46. Pl.xxiii *P. Geneve* inv. 97. On Parthenius's fragments on papyrus, see McNamee 2007, 301–4.

Notes and Memory

We now rely heavily on computer memory, and a single transient glitch can render our memory storage unreadable. Therefore, we are confronted with sudden failure instead of a healthy, natural process of forgetting. Scholars have studied the art of memory, emphasizing certain ancient figures' incredible feats, and yet within the generally positive assessment of artificial memory there were, and still remain, some doubts.[47] The power of memory was essential to the orator, but it usually required a natural visual memory. As a result, I argue that students of rhetoric needed to write notes and concurrently work on their memory skills if they chose to become professional orators. Though aware of memory's importance, Quintilian had more modest goals, framing the system as useful for remembering a list of names but not for parts of speech.[48] Pseudo-Longinus's *On Memory* insisted that natural endowments, proper exercises, and personal application could remedy a faulty memory. His perception that many still had difficulty remembering shows that a good memory was not universal, and that the art was not infallible.[49]

We have already pointed out some examples of the use of notes to retain information. This is an important theme that deserves a longer treatment than I can give it here. My discussion will concentrate on certain examples while only mentioning others. The importance of memory is also relevant to the case of the students we will encounter in the rest of the book. Arrian and the pupils of Didymus and Olympiodorus took down the lectures of their educators not only because their memory was not sufficient to record them in their minds but also because a written text was a better and more secure voucher for credibility. Their teachers allowed the students' lecture notes to circulate under the students' own names. The notes recorded by the advanced students were full texts compiled by listening to their teachers' lectures, perhaps supplemented also with shorter annotations jotted down after conversing with their teachers and classmates and consulting texts. From the elementary level on, young people wrote notes, made doodles, and

---

47. Yates 1966; Cicero, *De oratore*, *Ad Herennium*; Philostratus, *Vita Apollonius* 1.7; Seneca the Elder, Preface and 18–19 on Latro; Xenophon *Symposium* 62; Aeschines, *De falsa Leg*. On Philip's great memory; Plato, *Hippias minor* 368d–369a on Hippias's art of memory; Lucian, *Dance* 74.
48. Quintilian 11.2.
49. Patillon and Brisson 2002, 125–232. The addendum on memory transmitted under Longinus's name is by an unknown author.

recorded passages written by various authors.⁵⁰ The papyri, however, can barely testify to the notes of older students because we do not have a way to distinguish these from those of adults. This is a part of an activity in class of which we are not informed but which is reasonably thought to have existed.

These young men were in a better position than other youths who placed their annotations unsystematically and ended up losing them. An anecdote of Diogenes Laertius concerning Antisthenes underscores both the value of notes and their ephemeral quality. In it, the philosopher refuses to console a very unhappy student who has lost his notes, with the admonition that he should have inscribed them in his mind and not on papyrus.⁵¹ The philosopher pointed to the superiority of natural memory, which the ancients cultivated and tried to enhance by using certain strategies of recollection. A well-known scene in Plato's *Theaetetus* reads like an example of meta-literature, the intersection of orality and writing. In it, Euclid confesses his inability to recall a speech of Socrates, showing that he instead must rely on annotations to reconstruct it. As soon as he had reached home after listening to the philosopher, he jotted down some notes as aide-mémoire (*hypomnemata*), writing more at leisure later as his recollection became clearer.⁵² Gaps remained in his memory, and he asked Socrates to clarify details whenever he went to Athens. On returning home, he would correct the whole. The resulting text was a different version of the original one.⁵³

The drawn-out process evident in this example shows that the transitions between memory, notes, and a definitive text were quite elaborate. Many other authors followed this system, even if they did not explicitly mention it due to the usual reluctance or lack of interest in describing writing methods. Many centuries later, Libanius's students (3.16) slowly reconstructed the orations he delivered over the course of several days. At times, however, the process of putting together a correct and plausible text would become so difficult that an author would abandon the task. Thucydides originally intended to insert transcripts of original speeches in his history (1.22.1), but he soon realized that his own

---

50. See part III.
51. Diogenes Laertius 6.5, Dorandi 2007, 409. For Antisthenes 5/4 BCE see McNamee 2007, 114–15 description of learned scholia. The word *gnorimos* is usually translated as "friend, acquaintance" but I think "student" is more appropriate since Antisthenes had a school.
52. *Theaetetus* 143a. Some hurry transpires from the passage. Notes could evaporate.
53. *Phaedr.* 274D–275 story of Teuth: writing cannot substitute memory but can only be an aid to memory.

recollections and the reports that others brought him—presumably in the form of notes, or oral reports—would not allow him to reconstruct speakers' words with enough accuracy. As a result, he wrote speeches that would express in the best way the speakers' original meanings.

Looking at Aulus Gellius and his notes can give us an idea of how memory worked. In his *Noctes Atticae*, Gellius[54] confirms the connection between note-taking and memory by saying that he recorded in his notes everything that was worthy of being remembered (*memoratu*).[55] Notes allowed him to retrieve things and books he had suddenly forgotten (*oblivio*). Sometimes he refused to include excessively long entries, instead opting for short ones (*adnotatiunculae*).[56] After Gellius jotted down the notes (*adnotationes*), he adjusted and polished them in his *commentarii*.[57] A few first-person plural pronouns reveal that Gellius used assistants in this work of storing and indexing; he distinguishes his own work by using the first-person singular pronoun. We can surmise that a scribe prepared a clean copy. His original notes were assembled in a somewhat disorderly and brief fashion, with no thought for style.[58] As in the case of the elder Pliny, note-taking was not a completely solitary experience but could be a pleasurable nighttime activity (19).[59]

There is no doubt that Gellius's collection is a sophisticated work that testifies to an erudite and refined act of reading and excerpting. Yet recent scholars have neglected, and even purposely disregarded, the fact that notes formed the basis of his work. Gellius's collection has been defined as a cultural artifact of "literary historicizing" subdivided into short articles.[60] It is important to consider both aspects.

---

54. *NA Praef.* 2–3.

55. Cf. W. Johnson (2010, 118–20), who points to the fact that the term *memoria* is not only personal memory but also what is worth remembering of the past. See Holford-Strevens (2020) for a new edition of the first ten books.

56. *Noctes Atticae* Pr. 1–3; 1.7.18; 15.14; 17.21.50. There are a few points to mention here. Where does this statement of Gellius lead us? In mentioning how the book originated, did he simply report it without any ulterior motive? Did he try to defend himself from eventual criticism concerning the nature of the work, as Plutarch may have done? Was he addressing the reader to point to the way the text was supposed to be read?

57. On the difference of the two terms, see Dorandi 2007, 36–37.

58. Cf. above what Lucian wrote. Yet Gellius uses the adverb *facile* (easily) to describe the work of the slaves who organized the material in order to retrieve it.

59. *Praef.* 19. It is unclear whether slaves were still present at night, but of course they could be invisible. These activities are called *lucubratiunculas* in Pr. 14, cf. Kerr 2004.

60. Howley 2018, 20. Exclusive consideration of the finished product, which requires ignoring the presence of notes per se and the ways in which these four hundred articles may or not relate to each other, is no doubt a legitimate reaction to past considerations of Gellius's book as no more than a mine of information to be cited. And yet one needs to be cautious.

It is true that Gellius himself wrote in a sophisticated literary world, but he was explicit about the genesis of his work, showing how it came to be. Perhaps he threw away his notes after he used them, as writers could land in trouble if their disorganized annotations were exposed to others, becoming precarious textual residues of doubtful veracity.

Awareness of possible loss of evidence, along with a desire to prevent future losses, motivated compilers to gather a large quantity of notes and lists of various characters that were not school exercises. In these works, the impulse to collect extracts from vast readings and to compile entire volumes of notes gave rise to some works that are only partially known.[61] A good example is the collection of a first-century CE Egyptian woman named Pamphila who compiled eight or ten volumes of *Notebooks*. Photius, the late ninth-century patriarch of Constantinople who wrote brief comments to about 280 works, mentioned that Pamphila gathered her miscellanies from what she directly learned from her husband and his learned male visitors.[62] Photius considered her style simple "because she was a woman" and commented on her choice to disregard genre in favor of producing a miscellaneous collection without order. In another entry about the compiler Sopater, Photius included fragments from Pamphila's works.[63] The notice devoted to her in the less trustworthy *Suda* lexicon contradicts that of Photius. Pamphila was related to the grammarian Soteridas of Epidaurus, who was probably her father, and the *Suda* credits her apparently numerous works to either Soteridas or her husband.[64] In this report, her *Notebooks* comprised thirty-three books. We do not know Pamphila's final aim or whether she had intended to produce a more ambitious work based on her annotations. In an age when most women were only partially educated, her awareness that evidence could be lost and her desire to prevent future losses are remarkable, even if they were dictated by personal and antiquarian interests. The ten fragments of her notes that are extant come from citations in sources such as Diogenes Laertius and

---

61. These texts are often impersonal, and the compilers concealed their own thoughts and identities, though something can be gleaned from the material they gathered.

62. While I have discussed men as notetakers so far, the patriarch Photius hands down an intriguing example of a female notetaker. See Henry 1959–67, 2:170–71. Women rarely had access to rhetorical education, and Photius rightly remarked that Pamphila's style did not show traces of that.

63. Henry 1959–67, 2:123–28.

64. Suda under v. Adler 1935, *Suidae lexicon* I 4 no. 139.

Gellius.[65] Was Pamphila drawn only to sensational and frivolous subjects? It is difficult to form an objective judgment on the basis of only ten fragments that may have survived on account of their playful tone. Her collection may have been more ambitious, and in fact it is telling that her *Notebooks* inspired the *Notebooks* or *Memorabilia* written by Favorinus of Arles.[66] Favorinus embodied the characteristic polymathy of the Second Sophistic,[67] but as was the case of many of his other works, his compilation *Notebooks* or *Memorabilia* did not survive and is known only by later quotations and descriptions.

Compilation of Notes and Lists

The students of Olympiodorus sometimes wrote lists of various items in the margins in addition to recording their teacher's lectures.[68] In general, some lists addressed beginners' needs. In these, words were divided into syllables for easy reading and learning how to write. Other lists were memorized, with subjects varying from months to rivers, famous historical or contemporary personages, and mythological figures.[69] Three examples of lists compiled in an educational setting elucidate these characteristics. First, Ammon, *scholastikos* of Panopolis, wrote in his own hand a list of philosophers, notes from a teacher's lecture or annotations on some readings that Ammon had made personally. A member of a distinguished Egyptian priestly family, Ammon must have had an education in rhetoric and philosophy.[70] His list includes Presocratics, Academics, Cynics, Peripatetics, and Stoics. At the beginning he ordered the list by teacher-student and then by schools of philosophy.

---

65. Cagnazzi 1997. In fr. 3 a smith uses a bronze axe to kill the son of Pittacus as he sits in a barbershop. Fr. 4 consists of a pretty riddle whose answer is "the year." Fr. 6 contains an anecdote about Alcibiades wanting to donate a piece of land to Socrates, and fr. 9 regards Alcibiades being encouraged by Pericles, his maternal uncle, to learn to play the double flute. Seeing his face so altered as he blew into the instrument, however, the vain Alcibiades broke it in a rage and threw it away.

66. Sandys 1997, 77–79; Barigazzi 1966.

67. Gleason 1995, 131–32.

68. Cf. part III.

69. See Legras (1997) who looked at the possibility that the *Laterculi* and other lists could refer to the teaching of history.

70. *P. Duke* inv. 178, *P.Ammon* I 1, Willis 1978, 140–53 at 145–51; Willis and Dorandi 1989. See van Minnen 2002; Cribiore 2019, 177–78. See also *P.Ammon* I 2 A, Maresch and Andorlini 2006: a codex with *Odyssey* 9 and 11 was found among the papers of Ammon. It testifies to his level of culture.

The second example is the so-called Anonymous Londiniensis, *P.Lit. Lond.* 165, an isagogic text on medicine and causes of disease that seems to consist of lecture notes taken by a student. The writer did not copy from a model but instead wrote down his uncertainties and thoughts with corrections and improvements, showing that the text was not static but fluid. The writer added numerous notes on top of the lines or in the margins, presenting two versions of the same text, the second of which should be considered an ensemble of notes as an aide-mémoire.[71]

Another text to be considered is a papyrus dating to the second to first centuries BCE, *Laterculi Alexandrini* (Berlin P. 13044r), which may have originated in Alexandria. It contains lists of painters, sculptors, architects, and technicians. In addition, it lists the Seven Wonders of the World, the largest islands, and the tallest mountains, as well as rivers, springs, and lakes.[72] This "list of lists" is anonymous but may have been the work of a teacher who wrote it, copied it, or had it copied to inculcate notions of general culture in his students. Whether this list derived from someone's original annotations is impossible to know. Diels compared it with the anonymous *Tractatus de Mulieribus*, which listed the names of fourteen notable women (including goddesses and women in myth) with brief notices.[73] Diels also mentioned Hyginus's *Fabulae*, which included lists of lyric poets, wonders of the world, the seven wise men, and many more prominent individuals, mostly from mythology.[74]

Annotations while Traveling

When traveling for pleasure today we favor taking pictures that can later revive our original impressions. Yet travel writers often also take copious notes, which they can later clean up easily and conveniently transfer to the cloud, an inbox, or a hard drive. In the ancient world, note-taking was of paramount importance for travelers who needed to

---

71. See Manetti 1999. However, Ricciardetto (2016, xli–xviii) considers the papyrus a draft.
72. Diels 1904; Cribiore 1996, 270, no. 380 plates LXVII–LXIX. The hand is graceful but irregular, not a book hand. Legras 1997, 591–93.
73. The text is of unknown authorship and should be dated to late second or early first centuries BCE. The purpose and genre of this work are unknown. Gera (1997, 60–61) made the hypothesis that Pamphila might be the author of the catalog, but this is only a suggestion with no proofs.
74. Rose 1933. Cf. Cameron 2004, 11 and passim. This work was probably published around the second century, but the existing copy is abridged and interpolated. See also the list included in *Joseph's Bible Notes*, see part III.

preserve information. Notes taken during travel are usually derived not from reading but from observing unfamiliar places or customs firsthand and formulating questions; nevertheless, they too could contribute to the composition of a text. Pausanias does not explicitly mention taking notes during his travels, but unquestionably he must have filled innumerable notebooks with his observations, which would have traveled with him throughout Greece along with his books and other equipment.[75] In the second century, the sophist Aristides had notes written up when he visited Egypt.[76] Making sure to see all the important sites—temples, the Labyrinth, the pyramids, and canals—he consulted books when possible, but when necessary he took his own measurements with the help of "the priests and prophets of each place." Aristides mentions that he had ordered his slaves to make notes (*hypomnemata*) but those containing measurements were lost, with the result that he could not send them to his unknown addressee. This treatise was supposedly occasioned by a scientific question regarding the rise of the Nile, but in saying this, Aristides's tone is unmistakably literary. As a rule, a notetaker's personal intervention is assumed whenever note-taking is mentioned in antiquity, as is the case nowadays. Literate slaves and assistants, however, could facilitate the task, as in the case of the elder Pliny. An example of a scholar who requested that a subordinate make annotations appears in Aelius Donatus's *Life of Vergil* 34. Eros, Vergil's secretary and freedman, reports that during an extempore recitation Vergil completed two lines that he had previously left unfinished. Vergil immediately ordered Eros to make note of the two half lines on the scroll.

The Annotations of Theophanes and the Geography of Notes

Illustrating travel note-taking during a later time period is a trove of papyri with notes taken during a fourth-century CE journey.[77] Theophanes of Hermopolis traveled from that city to Syrian Antioch and back.[78] Theophanes was a wealthy and educated man, and his notes

---

75. Pretzler 2004, 210.
76. Aristides, *The Egyptian Discourse* 36.1.
77. Other observations on notes on papyri will be presented occasionally.
78. He primarily used the *cursus publicus*, the imperial transport service, but sometimes also traveled by riverboat, spending on average more than eight hours a day in transit.

and accounts reveal intimate and curious details.⁷⁹ The information we can glean from his travels is so rich that with some imagination it can illuminate and supplement the unknown details of Pausanias's and Aristides's journeys.⁸⁰ The archive of Theophanes's papers is a priceless source of evidence for everyday social history. The diverse memoranda taken during his journey indicate not only that note-taking was necessary while traveling but also the manner in which it was done. The notes cover the whole period of the journey, from mid-March to early August, and offer precious information about several areas, including baths, the diets of officials and subordinates, different kinds of wines, and items of jewelry. Different hands appear in the documents, and different conventions of keeping records have been observed. Altogether, Theophanes's notes indicate that note-taking was not always systematic but needed to be "translated," that is, interpreted and put into chronological order. In the case of Theophanes, annotations were essential for organization and for rendering an account of expenses.⁸¹ In this archive, sometimes blank spaces in the papyrus attracted intrusive annotations.⁸² This practice is not unique to Theophanes. For example, the medical papyrus *P.Lit.Lond.* 165 mentioned earlier contains on the verso a letter and recipe in the hand of another writer, who took advantage of the empty space.

Notes in the Margins

Writing habits change with the passing of time. In classical antiquity an author could either write and compose a text in his own hand or dictate it to another person, but by late antiquity dictation came to prevail in the writing of texts and letters. At that point, authors entrusted others to pen their notes, a practice that might generate some confusion.

---

79. He preferred to be elegantly dressed, and on one occasion he purchased a very expensive hat as well as tickets for the theater and concert hall.

80. The papyri were published by Roberts in 1952, in vol. 4 of the *Catalogue of the Greek and Latin Papyri in the John Rylands Library* at the University of Manchester. More letters belonging to this archive were published by Rees 1964, 2–12, nos. 2–6, and 1968. See also Moscadi 1970. Matthews (2006) considered the whole archive.

81. An issue to be solved. In the *Third Discourse on Kingship*, von Arnim maintained that in *Or.* 62 Dio had put down common places (*loci:* that is, notes) that he could eventually use in speechmaking. Paolo Desideri (1992) refused to recognize that on the grounds that a short address to the emperor was included (paragraphs 1 and 3). Von Arnim was right here, in my opinion: *Oration* 62 is a conglomeration of various notes.

82. Empty spaces were often left at the end of a roll containing a literary work and were occupied by the name of the author and title. Cf. Del Corso 2022.

However, teachers and students themselves sometimes wrote notes in the margins of a text. In part III we will look at marginalia on papyri, some of which were the work of teachers and students.

Galen relied on notes, but only one instance is explicitly mentioned in his works. The notes that he wrote in the margins of some texts were apparently very extensive; he would fill these spaces with an alternative discussion of the same subject, allowing him to decide at a later time which of the two was preferable (*In Hipp. Epid. I CMG* v 10.1). The text in the notes therefore offered a different version. In one instance Galen had failed to give clear instructions to the scribe, who accidentally copied and combined both versions. Notes in this case acquired a different dimension and lost their identity as notes.

Further, we encounter Jerome briefly annotating a private translation of a learned letter of Epiphanius of Salamis by indicating its various contents in the margins.[83] An illustrious monk had asked him for a Latin translation that might simplify the argument. This translation was stolen and divulged by someone he defined as a "pretend" monk, and Jerome found himself the subject of accusations because of his free rendering of the text.[84] The brief notes in question were a service to the reader. Marginal notes were always in danger of being misplaced, and Jerome was not exempt from these accidents. In *Ep.* 106.46 he ranted against a stupid scribe (*nescioquis temerarius*) who erroneously incorporated his notes into the body of a text.[85]

Augustine similarly relied on scribes and stenographers. In the prologue to his *Retractationes*, he does not mention personal writing but only dictation and oral delivery. At the end of his life, he felt the need to consolidate his work, aware that he would leave behind a huge written legacy; he compiled the *Retractationes* in an attempt to shape his authorial legacy to the world.[86] He finished working on the text in 427, but it remained incomplete. It took the form of a compilation of notes that reveal the author's utter frustration in ascertaining what in his body of work had been lost and what had been manipulated

---

83. *Ep.* 57.2: *Ex latere in pagina breviter adnotans*.

84. Christian writers apparently found it difficult to accuse other monks and brothers. Cf. Tertullian *CPL* 14, preface to book 1. See Cribiore (1999, 273–74), where a dissenting brother is described as becoming an apostate. It is possible that the malicious "pretend monk" here was a regular monk who disagreed with Jerome.

85. See Arns 1953, 71–77.

86. *Retractationes* 1.2. A translation in *The Fathers of the Church*, vol. 60. (1999). See also Eller 1949.

and altered.[87] His annotations were of varying length, according to the number of corrections that he wanted to make.

The intrusive presence of his brothers, who insisted on disseminating incomplete works, is remarkable, despite Augustine's attempt to exonerate them by invoking their desire to please him. Two episodes concerning notes are curious.[88] Burning with desire to have his writings at any cost, his brothers went so far as to try to appropriate notes he had written in the margins of a work, and by so doing they created an entirely new text. In *Retractationes* (II 39) Augustine reveals that he did not recognize a particular text titled *Adnotationes in Iob* that had been circulating under his name. The text consisted entirely of his notes, which were unintelligible in the absence of the original work. He refused to emend it because it was defective. By editing the text, he would have acknowledged ownership of it—something he did not want to do. The situation, in any case, was not so unusual. Augustine's brothers had shown the same zeal when compiling another work, *Explanation of the Epistle of James, Retr.* 12.32 (58), which consisted of notes they had lifted from those that Augustine wrote to clarify that *Epistle*. These two incidents put into sharp relief the fact that annotations could have a valuable life of their own as the different voices of a single author.[89]

---

87. Altogether his *opuscula* numbered ninety-three.
88. Cf. Cribiore 2019, 276–77.
89. As an addendum, I would like to bring in an unusual parallel in the world of law. Expert jurists answered legal questions asked of them. Collections of such responses were one of the genres of legal literature. Thus for the jurist Paul there was a collection of *Responsorum libri XXIII* published around 220 CE. These responses were given in various contexts such as when somebody approached the jurist to ask a question or was in court or in a meeting of the emperor's consilium. But who then took down the answers? It is unknown where these "notes" were kept as well.

Chapter 2

Taking Notes in Class

The Papyri

Taking notes was a typical activity in school. From Plato's *Republic* to Plutarch's *How to Study Poetry* to Basil of Caesarea's *Address to Young Men on Greek Literature*, students were advised to discard or select certain passages for various reasons, mostly ethical ones.[1] In particular, papyrology reveals interesting information in anthologies written by students of various levels of schooling. One may guess that most of the time these students copied from books or from samples provided by their teachers, but when the mistakes are considerable it is possible that they jotted down what they heard. A few examples follow, proceeding in order of difficulty. First, *P.Köln* III 125 is a Ptolemaic fragment of a papyrus roll that underwent an unusual treatment—it was washed and erased.[2] The remnants reveal notes by two different students. The first, with his name Maron at the bottom, writes two Homeric verses and three unidentified iambic trimeters in a crude hand. The second

---

1. Morgan 2007.
2. See Cribiore 1996, 232, no. 250. It was extremely rare that a papyrus was washed before a different text was inscribed on it. If possible, it was preferable to write on the back.

hand is slightly more skilled but less competent and writes anapestic verses from a tragedy of Aeschylus.

Another example from a school anthology, *P.Yale* II 135, dated to the second to third centuries CE, contains brief extracts from authors like Demosthenes and Homer. In addition, the anthology shows a hexameter containing all the letters of the alphabet, which is sometimes present in beginners' texts in both Greek and Coptic. This kind of exercise, a tongue twister, was called *chalinos* (gag) and joined letters difficult to pronounce; these texts curiously later passed into Hesychius's *Lexicon*, where they received some pseudo-meanings.[3] Thus, school exercises were an important part of culture. This student had grabbed a papyrus with an account on the front and wrote his exercise on the back. He had a large, crude hand and curiously adorned some of his letters with decorative serifs and roundels.

Some papyri consisted of various fragments of notes, such as *P.Mich.* inv. 3498 and 3250a, b, and c.[4] A short roll originally cut from a larger one resembles a small school roll that is visible in a mummy portrait found in a student's household shrine.[5] Not only do both sides of the papyrus exhibit writing, but the front (recto) also reveals a previous text that had been erased. Shortly after the papyrus was manufactured, a patch was used to cover some damage on the back, where the papyrus is in some places dark and abraded. Students did not have many chances to get hold of high-quality papyrus, and therefore they would end up cutting a piece, relying on scraps of inferior quality, and using the verso, that is, the back of a papyrus where the fibers were vertical.[6] A look at the two different hands that inscribed the front and back confirms the suspicion that this papyrus is an example of notes written as schoolwork. The hand that wrote the text on the back is further hampered by having used a large Egyptian pen, but it is the uncouth penmanship on the front that fully displays the characteristic hallmarks of a student's hand.[7] The front of the papyrus contains a list of lyric and tragic first lines (*incipit*), many of which

---

3. *Anthologia Palatina* 9.538. Cf. Cribiore 2001b, 166, 179.
4. Borges and Sampson 2012. See *P.Mich.* inv. 3498 and 3250a, b, c. The date is second century BCE.
5. Cribiore 2001b, 155, fig. 23.
6. Cribiore 1996, 57–62.
7. The editors Borges and Sampson (2012, 16–17) are unsure and prefer to think of the private hand of a scholar, but the irregularities, clumsiness, inability to keep a straight line, and continuous dipping in the ink point to someone with limited schooling.

are unknown, while the back contains fragments of Euripidean lyric. The writer of the incipit had attempted to complete, but then abandoned, an alphabetical order. His idiosyncratic notes formed a small collection. The verses could have been merely a mnemonic exercise, or they could have led to a longer text.

Another list from the first century CE contains epigrams mostly by Philodemus (with some by Asclepiades), with the text written on both sides.[8] There are three different hands, none alike. Hand A wrote the first column, while hand C wrote the rest of the text. The first hand is rather irregular, including different interlinear spaces and corrections and showing endings of some lines that protrude on the right. The rather coarse handwriting suggests a student without much experience. Hand C is smaller and faster and appears quite accomplished, revealing some familiarity with documentary handwriting. On the top part, in a space between columns two and three, a third hand (B) wrote text that contains corrections, marked ink dipping, and poorly formed letters. This writer shows some ambition in style and inserts a few finials at the end of the vertical strokes. While the first writer tended to write complete texts, the second hand wrote incipits of epigrams. The text written by the third hand is a recipe for a cough remedy. This writer was interested in practical matters and greedy for any scrap of papyrus. All these texts are notes used as memoranda.

Among the attested school exercises from Greco-Roman Egypt, many prove to be annotations when the text stands by itself and is not fragmentary. A Ptolemaic papyrus scrap, recovered from mummy cartonnage and dated to ca. 250 BCE, offered the ideal canvas for an exercise in a grammarian's class.[9] It is unclear why he completely filled the margins with the closing chorus shared by several plays of Euripides. Perhaps he was reminding himself that the chorus was identical in each play, or perhaps he wanted to make note of an interesting teacher's observation. One Roman papyrus is fundamentally similar to the one with the incipits described above.[10] In this example, a student had created a "page" by using thick lines of separation, perhaps in imitation of a codex's layout. The two resulting columns contain incipits of verses from the *Odyssey*, and the student was preparing to prove that he knew

---

8. *P.Oxy.* LIV 3724.
9. *P. Yale* I 20; Cribiore 1996, 240.
10. *P.Ryl.* III 545, third century CE; Cribiore 1996, no. 291.

his Homer. Memorizing the beginnings of verses from the *Iliad* and writing them down would call to mind the second halves.[11]

Annotating in a Rhetor's Class

The practice of annotation in schools of rhetoric began early. Quintilian expressed strong criticism when describing the erratic behavior of some orators who, drawing on their annotations, only juxtaposed clichés and clever remarks instead of trusting in their natural skills. As a consequence, their speeches could not hold together. Quintilian compared them to notebooks in which students copied down passages that they admired and excerpted from other people's declamations and which were equally disorganized (2.11.7). The rhetor gave great importance to reading and listening as activities that would improve speaking and writing, but much attention had to be devoted to making a right choice.[12]

Theon, who composed his treatise on *Progymnasmata* in the first half of the first century CE, considered notes to be part of the composition process. When taking notes, a boy should aim to recreate an occurrence that happened to him or a public event, such as a tumultuous assembly, a procession, or a spectacle (p. 107).[13] Moreover, the activity of listening to declamations and speeches would produce annotations of various parts of them, so that, for example, a student would initially record as much as he remembered of a proem, returning to the task over the next few days until his recreation of the whole text was satisfying. Next, little by little, he would repeat this exercise for the narration and the rest of the speech, which he would now be able to write down.[14] This was only in part a mnemonic exercise; it recalls what Philostratus narrated about the students of Dionysius of Miletus.[15] Dionysius was an eminent rhetor who was said to have trained his pupils by means of mnemonics. People thought that these young men had peculiar and formidable memories and that Dionysius was employing the magical arts. The sophist, however, revealed his simple method. He gave his declamations over and over so that his students listened repeatedly and

---

11. Cribiore 1996, nos. 193 and 201, written in clumsy hands by novices.
12. Quint. 10.1.8 and 15–16.
13. Patillon and Bolognesi 1997, c–civ and 105–7 from an Armenian text.
14. Patillon and Bolognesi 1997, 106; the danger was that speeches taken down from auditors were considered authentic.
15. Philostratus *VS* 523.

memorized them. This was a common occurrence among sophists and philosophers who did not lecture only once on the same subject but instead repeated these lectures numerous times.[16] Engraving lectures in the students' memories was only part of his technique, while note-taking step by step formed another part for remembering and repeating the whole.

Libanius's "good" students remembered a speech by dividing it into sections (*Or* 3.16). The rhetor hinted at a teaching strategy by which his pupils, during and after his lectures, could collectively reproduce his orations, learning at the same time to make them their own. The young men would listen very carefully as he delivered a speech and—according to Libanius—memorize different passages. After the lecture, the students would assemble the parts, each one bringing his own contribution, and by trying to fit all the sections in order they would attempt to reconstruct the whole speech. It would take them several days to accomplish this. They would later continue to recite the whole text, even to their fathers at home.[17]

Taking notes during lectures and declamations and later transcribing them with better ordering and handwriting was time-consuming. We understand this from Marcus, Cicero's son, who was studying in Greece. He was not an exemplary student, however, and had landed in some trouble when he wrote to Tiro, his father's secretary. As he was studying literature (*philologia*) and practicing Greek and Roman oratory, he urgently requested that a *librarius*, who could save him time by copying his notes, be sent to him from Rome.[18] This librarius could be a professional scribe or perhaps was only a secretary, one of those at the service of prominent families. Most students took notes while listening to lectures to compensate for the lack of textbooks. Were they also in the habit of using stenographers? A well-known passage in Quintilian is interpreted as evidence that they were. Here, Quintilian explains that his urgency in writing his work on the orator's education was due to the fact that two books on the subject were already circulating under his name, even though he had not emended or published either one. It is reasonable then, to surmise that slaves had taken down a two-day lecture using stenography, a task they would have been assigned. The

---

16. Of course, there could be differences between the various lectures.
17. Compare the technique of Euclid Plato, *Theaetetus* 143a.
18. Cicero, *Ad. fam.* XVI.21.8. It is possible that Marcus was lazy or unable to use his notes efficiently.

other lecture course, spanning several days, had been recorded through notes and "published" by some of his students.[19] Stenography at that time was seen in the Roman world as a slave's task, and there are no examples of individuals with a liberal education using this skill.

Learning Note-Taking as an Aid to Declaiming

In addition to note compilation skills, students also learned oratory, in which note-taking was a fundamental part. Students learning oratory were encouraged and advised to take notes because they needed to have at their disposal some writing that reminded them of their teacher's words. The main issues underpinning what follows are, first, why notes figure so conspicuously in sources about the delivery of speeches and, second, whether they were universally agreed to have held such importance in an oratorical performance.

With respect to ancient note-taking, Seneca the Elder and Quintilian offer much food for thought.[20] Seneca's collection of *Controversiae* and *Suasoriae* has the appearance of an ensemble of annotations; in fact, the author himself presents it as such. As has often been remarked, this is a difficult text to parse. In the first preface, while vaunting his past feats of memory,[21] Seneca says that age had much diminished his capacity for recollection.[22] This protestation of a failing memory allowed him to exclude more recent examples from his list of prominent rhetors, instead concentrating only on those of his own age. Another of Seneca's statements colored by rhetoric is that he was yielding to the will of his sons.[23] He apparently asked them to permit him to put down his observations without order (*ne . . . certum aliquem ordinem*) as he traversed his memories. Even though this is a frequent feature of random collections

---

19. Book 1, *Proem* 7: *quantum notandum consequi potuerant interceptum, boni iuvenes.* I give *notare* the usual meaning of "take down notes." See Boge 1974; see also Teitler 1985 considering a later time.
20. On Seneca, see Fairweather 1981; Berti 2007; Migliario 2007.
21. Scholars such as von Arnim considered tales of the phenomenal memories of literary figures such as Seneca the Elder to be no more than some kind of topoi. Other strategies, like annotations, must have been used concurrently.
22. *Controversiae* 1, Preface 1–5. Seneca's declaration, for example, that he had not exercised his memory in a very long time seems contrived, even though he is probably alluding to the difficulty of writing everything down.
23. This could be regarded as a rhetorical dedication that appears in many texts, such as those by Plutarch or Quintilian.

of notes, Seneca was likely addressing his general readers and asking them to curb their expectations.

Seneca's observations about orators' preparation and styles of delivery are noteworthy because they show the Forum intersecting with the schoolroom. Seneca warmly lauded orators like Porcius Latro, with his strong physique and unfailing memory, who never needed to reread his notes because he memorized his declamations by writing them.[24] He also painted a commanding portrait of the declaimer Cassius Severus, who did rely on notes when declaiming. Tacitus and Suetonius were less enthusiastic: Tacitus regarded Cassius with disdain, while Suetonius cast his net much more widely and was able to put the man in perspective.[25] With the body of a gladiator, a passion for jokes, and a voice both sweet and strong, Cassius made a powerful impression, especially when he was angry. Seneca contrasted Cassius's written texts with those he delivered, concluding that his oral declamations were vastly superior: Cassius let his notes serve as set outlines and guide him, but he also trusted extempore speech. It seems that Cassius's public persona was so commanding that people sometimes became overwhelmed.[26] He never spoke without notes (*sine commentario numquam dixit*) and did not use cursory ones (those in which *nudae res ponuntur*), instead employing annotations so detailed that they included possible opportunities for wit (*salse dici*, *Contr.* 3, Pr. 1–18, at 6). It seems that the combination of abundant notes and personal charisma was irresistible.

The degree of reliance on notes was a contested issue among orators. Would Quintilian have approved of Cassius's long and colorful notes? Certainly not, as notes were auxiliary to a text. Instead, Quintilian allowed pleaders to bring short notes that they could glance at during delivery, but he was firmly opposed to those who brought whole summaries and full headings. Short notes could also be inserted into a written text in a moment of inspiration, thus strengthening a writing strategy (10.6.5). He observed that some pleaders often wrote brief annotations of their introductory statements beforehand and covered the rest through mental preparation (10.7.30). An inspiring mosaic at the supposed villa of Lucius Verus, located north of Rome on the Via

---

24. *Contr.* 1, Pref. 16–18. Those who write slowly, said Seneca, retain their compositions easily, but Latro, who wrote very fast, still kept his writing in his memory.

25. See Bloomer 2015, 121–22.

26. Some declaimers aroused incredible enthusiasm. Eunapius *VS* 101.1–108.4 (485–93) says that his own teacher, Proaeresius, had an adoring following with people licking his breast and kissing his hands and feet after a speech. Cf. Cribiore 2007a, 52–54.

Cassia, portrays a standing rhetor enveloped in an abundant toga. He is represented as in the act of oration, raising his right arm straight above in a dramatic gesture. His eyes are directed to a codex of tablets in his left hand. He is looking intensely at his notes.[27] Quintilian, speaking of hand gestures, reported that some did not approve of excessive gestures like raising an arm and a hand (2.12 9-10). Quintilian's account is confirmed by Plutarch, who refers to speakers as getting up from their high chairs (*thronoi*) when they were ready to lecture with lecture notes (*eisagogai*).[28] At times these notes circulated, as in the case of Cicero, who wrote *commentarii* of this sort that were later collected by Tiro (4.1.69). Other authors' notes were also disseminated, whether in the form in which they been composed, as aids for speaking, or even collected in book form (10.7.30–33).

Quintilian was a strong advocate for writing over improvisation and stated that it was best for a rhetor who was writing on tablets to maintain a blank one (*vacua tabella*) at hand for notes and additions (10.3.32)—an exciting example of literary and documentary evidence corresponding. The papyri from Greco-Roman Egypt show that this practice had become current. A first-century opisthograph papyrus roll from Oxyrhynchus (5093) contains notes for rhetorical *epideixeis* that were written informally by a rhetor preparing to declaim or teach. To the left of the single column on the verso, a large space was left blank for annotations. Other notes on rhetorical compositions are visible in some papyri (*P.Mil.Vogl.* I 20; *P.Köln* VI 250). A few documentary papyri contain presentations of legal cases. In all of these, a large space was left for the annotations of the advocate in court, who would select highlights from his material that might be useful while presenting. That this was the usual format for such documents is shown by an example in which the space for annotations was never filled (*P.Sakaon* 35).

The custom of bringing notes when delivering declamations and speeches continued in late antiquity, as the rhetor Libanius testifies. Weakening eyesight and crippling arthritis in old age could make it necessary to entrust others with that task. In Antioch in 385, Libanius, who had declared that he always took care of his writing duties personally, mourned the death of his secretary, who had at that point been

---

27. Caserta 2012. I thank Christopher Jones for bringing this to my attention.
28. These *eisagogai* were introductory sections. Orators could write them down as reminders or glance at them.

writing the notes Libanius brought with him when declaiming.[29] The secretary's highly legible and competent hand allowed the old rhetor to read them easily at a glance.

The evidence presented above shows that notes (whether shorter or longer) were considered indispensable when delivering a speech, serving as tracks on which a rhetor's speech could glide effortlessly. Seneca did not share Quintilian's sacred respect for the dignity of a rhetor's profession but cherished the flamboyant. For him, the use of abundant annotations might result in a more dazzling performance. For Quintilian, on the other hand, abundant notes infringed on the skill of a rhetor, exempting him from accurately memorizing a text (10.7.31–32). Notes were supposed to be brief, permitting the orator to show that he did not actually need them and to shine in all his bravura. However, were annotations adopted so much more frequently in court or at an *epideixis* than they were in preparing an individual text? Seneca and Quintilian were referring to public performances, where the presence of notes would be evident to the audience and therefore could be discussed and somewhat justified. A writer's private strategies were less on display, even though we assume that rhetors based their compositions on notes.[30]

---

29. *Or.* 1.232. See Festugière 1965, 632. Martin and Petit (1979, 267–68) follow this interpretation and presume that the scribe wrote down the whole text for the sophist to memorize but did not take into account that orators brought notes to the delivery.

30. Law commentaries of the classical period were a different matter. In nonjuristic works the text and the lemmatic commentary were located on separate rolls, and there was a connection between lemmata and the commentary. Not all parts of a text would need a commentary. Schulz 1946, 183–85.

Chapter 3

Students' Annotations in Philosophy

The School of Aristotle

Aristotle founded the school in Athens in the last twenty years of his life, calling it the Lyceum or Peripatos, referring to a portico where teachers and students used to stroll,[1] as Epictetus would do many years later. Carlo Natali remarked that the type of scientific and philosophical research commonly associated with Aristotle does not seem appropriate for discussion while strolling, but ethical lectures to students on pleasure, pain, or friendship could be suitable topics.[2] Diogenes Laertius (5.3) reported that "in time the circle of his students grew larger and he then sat down to lecture.... He also taught his pupils to discourse upon a set theme and trained them in oratory." Anton Chroust noted that Philodemus of Gadara berated Aristotle for abandoning philosophy for rhetoric and said that Aristotle's only reason for doing so was to antagonize Isocrates.[3]

---

1. Diogenes Laertius 5.2.
2. Natali 2013, 96–119. This book provides a secure bibliographical framework for Aristotle, bringing together all the pieces of evidence. Protagoras (Plato, *Protagoras* 315b) is a model for showing the sophist conversing and teaching while strolling in the midst of an attentive audience.
3. *De Rhetorica* vol. 2, 50–57; Chroust 2015, 105–16.

CHAPTER 3

Theophrastus, Aristotle's successor, described the school's various parts in his will. It had a museum with statues of the goddesses, a bust of Aristotle in the temple, and a statue of Nicomachus that was commissioned and paid for; the statue also had to be life-size. The school had tablets with world maps, a library, a garden, a walk, and houses around it in which groups of people interested in literature and philosophy could reside. Use of visual aids such as diagrams, maps, and lists indicate this teaching practice was fairly institutionalized and could not have been conducted entirely in an outdoor location. However, no documentation has survived, and it is unclear whether the lectures were delivered in a gymnasium, as is often claimed. Natali also argued that Aristotle preferred reading to lecturing, purchased many books to construct a large library, and based some of his teaching on these texts. Even though this may be correct in general, his teaching activity must have included lecturing.[4] The story of the Peripatos's decline after Theophrastus has often been related. The accounts of Strabo and Plutarch, who attributed the cause of the deterioration exclusively to the loss of the library, have been deemed simplistic, and scholars now take into consideration various causes of decline.[5]

Examining the various combined pieces of evidence concerning teaching and learning in the School of Aristotle proves fascinating. In antiquity, Aristotle's works were divided in two groups: exoteric and esoteric.[6] "Published" only in the restrictive sense of the word, the exoteric texts are known only from fragments. Written with some elegance and style, they were serious but not technical in tone and were destined to reach a larger public. By contrast, the esoteric works were used within the school and were not polished. Their unliterary style points to rough lecture notes or notes taken down by his students.

Scholars have debated for many years whether some of these works represented Aristotle's personal lecture notes. In 1920 Henry Jackson argued that Aristotle's informally written works were his memoranda for the lectures he was about to deliver.[7] Jackson confidently pointed to several characteristics that supported this theory. For example, in the *Metaphysics* phrases were strung together in a disorganized

---

4. Natali (1991) argues that it is important not to consider Aristotle like a modern professor as some scholars portray him. One of the reasons is that unlike the sophists (or modern academics), Aristotle was never paid for his classes.
5. Strabo 13.1.54; Plutarch, *Life of Sulla* 26. See Natali 2013, 102–4.
6. Guthrie 1981, 41.
7. H. Jackson 1920.

way—paragraphs were inserted from literary works and the text included repetitions, additions, omissions, instructions to himself, and a conversational tone uncomplicated by grammar and syntax.

Later in 1923, William David Ross reconsidered the question, maintaining that the stylistically rough works of Aristotle had the same style as the philosopher's own notes originally drawn up as a teaching aid.[8] The unpolished style of these works, complete with digressions and repetitions, was explained by the fact that Aristotle never intended to publish these notes. Ross describes a divided view among scholars—that either those works represented annotations done by Aristotle or instead were drawn up by his pupils as they recorded his lectures. Ross decidedly dismissed the second hypothesis: "The latter hypothesis is ruled out by various considerations. It is hard to suppose that the notes of pupils would have produced such intelligible and coherent results." It is not uncommon for students to be accused of being incompetent and untidy and in part III I share evidence of students of Olympiodorus who have been accused of incompetency, probably unjustly. They had taken down perfectly coherent texts but made some mistakes, which might perhaps be attributed to Olympiodorus.

Another scholar, Werner Jaeger, shared a different opinion in *Aristoteles: Grundlegung einer Geschichte seiner Entwicklung*, published in 1923.[9] He argued that some of Aristotle's works originated from students' extensive notes, which covered some of the philosopher's lectures. Furthermore, Jaeger remarked that parts of the incomplete *Metaphysics* failed to establish order in its many different sections, and thus had the form of notes compiled by Pasicles, a nephew of Aristotle's disciple Eudemus of Rhodes. However, Jaeger's somewhat presumptive hypotheses are in part no longer accepted, as he assumed that the school's teaching routine was based on tradition, with Aristotle delivering philosophical lectures to his students in the morning and in the afternoon delivering lectures to a larger crowd on other topics, such as rhetoric or literature.[10]

In 1966 Ingemar Düring, examining the relation of Aristotle's written works to his oral teaching in the Lyceum, became the main proponent of the view that Aristotle had jotted down personal notes

---

8. See Ross 1923, 14–15.
9. The book was translated into English; see Jaeger 1948.
10. Centuries later, Epictetus would also separate teaching into two portions in different parts of the day.

to support his teaching. Again, this was seen as the reason for their rough style.[11] More recently some scholars agreed on the fact that these lecture-manuscripts are a unique record of Aristotle's activity as a teacher. However, they did not linger on this issue and concluded that the interpretation surrounding these materials was rather uncertain. They also did not express a firm view on the identity of the author of these notes (Aristotle or other compilers).[12] Jonathan Barnes, however, argued that the view that the philosopher had redacted those notes had lost appeal because it rested on the false supposition that Aristotle lectured like a modern professor.[13] Abrupt transitions and obscure connections between different ideas, lack of ornamentation, uncertain grammar and syntax, and the presence of doublets suggested that, rather than being lecture notes that Aristotle jotted down, these works were informally compiled texts.

As can be seen from the examples above, research on Aristotle's texts has not reached any consistent conclusions. More recently though, Adam Beresford investigated the nature and origin of the *Nicomachean* and *Eudemian Ethics*, which treat the subject of character.[14] He suggested that they consisted of notes taken down at lectures. They had not, he argues, been redacted personally by Aristotle and did not represent notes that Aristotle had taken down himself, for example as preparation for teaching. Instead, they had been jotted down *by different listeners*, members of Aristotle's audience who were present at his lectures, possibly students. Beresford also argued that the full names of these works must have been combined with a term that we have already encountered: *hypomnemata*, that is, notes. In both sets of ethical texts, the central parts were identical, but the rest diverged, even though the arguments were basically the same. Beresford supposed that Aristotle continued to lecture on the same subjects and texts periodically over the years, so that members of the audience took down notes at different times. This scholar also pointed out that the title of the *Eudemian Ethics* suggested that Eudemus of Rhodes, a student of Aristotle, was involved in redacting the notes. Moreover, Theophrastus was also somewhat involved in the *Nichomachean Ethics* through Nicomachus, Aristotle's son,

---

11. Düring 1966.
12. See Guthrie 1981, 50: "lectures to his advanced pupils or perhaps notes taken by a pupil." Shields (2014, 25) concludes with some uncertainty that they are drafts.
13. Barnes 1995.
14. Beresford 2020.

who was his student and probably had taken down notes at the lectures and had organized them.

The evidence concerning notes taken down by students is very suggestive. A lost work, the *Protrepticus*, in particular provides clues.[15] Young Aristotle is presumed the author, while he was still a member of the Academy. Since the work was not copied in the Middle Ages, it has survived only in fragments, most of which are found in the third-century works of the philosopher Iamblichus of Chalcis.[16] This is why not all scholars accept its attribution to Aristotle. D. S. Hutchinson and Monte Ransome Johnson have devoted many years to producing a reconstruction of the work with a translation and commentary.[17] The *Protrepticus* belonged to the hortatory genre and addressed young people, inciting them to study philosophy. Incidentally, we can imagine that fathers were also involved, since at later times philosophers like Musonius and Epictetus tried to win them over. In all ages, fathers were fundamental in their sons' choices.

The *Protrepticus*'s beginning is not preserved, and the rest of the text is replete with lacunae. Though it is unclear where the dialogue took place, it appears to include three interlocuters addressing an audience of young students. Iamblichus intervened intermittently in the work trying to eliminate dialogic parts, converting questions into assertions, and combining various phrases, sometimes with little success. This is not very surprising, as we will see in later sections that compilers of notes recorded at philosophers' lectures eliminated most dialogues because they valued only the philosophers' *ipsissima verba*. Arrian did this when he took down Epictetus's *Discourses*, as did the notetakers recording Didymus's and Olympiodorus's lectures.

In contrast to the above scholarly attention to Aristotle, later scholars in antiquity did attempt to explain Aristotle's lack of clarity, including Galen, writing centuries after Aristotle. He referred to the discrepancies and resulting obscurity in Aristotle's speeches generally and not specifically to those that reproduced live conversation. In the first chapter of *On Fallacies*, Galen mentioned the imperfect shape and obscurity of Aristotle's works, which he attributed to the fact that the philosopher delivered his lectures with excessive velocity. "The philosopher Aristotle usually spoke with such velocity and expressed many of his points

---

15. On different kinds of protreptic literature, see Markovich 2022.
16. Teubner edition 1888.
17. See Hutchinson and Johnson 2005, 2014.

as it were by stenographic signs."[18] Such scenarios might sometimes take place as philosophers lectured. As a comparison, the sixth-century example of Olympiodorus reveals that his students were sometimes unable to take down notes because of the speed with which he spoke, an indication that some philosophers were more rapid thinkers than patient teachers.[19] Apparently, Aristotle was one of them, and as a result, Galen tried to find a cause for such rapidity.

Of course, this was Galen's point of view. In the second century he knew of stenography, even though he did not dictate to stenographers very often. At the time of Aristotle, stenography was not known in Greece, but still the comparison renders efficaciously the thumping of the philosopher's words. What were the reasons for Aristotle's obscurity? Why did he speak with such speed, even to the point of making his works obscure? Mansfeld pondered the question with surprise, considering the philosopher's general concern for clarity, but did not refer to speeches that exist in the form of live texts.[20] In his published works Aristotle strove for a clear style that used ordinary verbs and nouns, so his obscurity is puzzling. Of course, to compare Aristotle's speaking habits with his writing style is unfair. His speaking style apparently made it difficult for people to follow him—that is, unless they already knew the text he was discussing.

Mansfeld found two possible reasons for the philosopher's approach. First, perhaps the philosopher wrote for an inner circle and did not need to be fully accessible, so he could instead afford to be somewhat unintelligible in his language. Second, it is possible that Aristotle used old-fashioned terminology and did not care that it was difficult to comprehend. Neither explanation, however, is fully plausible, and we have tried to explain the difficulties in Aristotle's style by considering some speeches as live texts. Beresford put in relief another peculiar point in the texts of Aristotle's lectures that exist in the form of notes.[21] The philosopher alluded to or quoted from Homer very often, but mistakes abound, even in passages that were well known. So not only did the philosopher mangle the Homeric text, but he also attributed passages to the wrong speakers. Did his notetakers commit these mistakes, or was the philosopher himself responsible? Scholars have

---

18. *De Captionibus* 1.20.
19. *Life of Proclus* 9.
20. Mansfeld 1994, 24–26, 148–77 on teachers and pupils.
21. Beresford 2020, xiii.

been quick to absolve Aristotle, but both scenarios are possible. Over the centuries the Homeric text acquired imprecisions and errors when it was quoted by memory, and we should take this into account as we evaluate the later commentary of Olympiodorus's *Alcibiades* in light of its considerable errors of attribution. There too, scholars have quickly pardoned Olympiodorus, saying that it was impossible for him to have committed such blunders and that a student certainly must be guilty. Perhaps, however, they did not consider the informality of the delivery. Olympiodorus did not check his sources. He did not care for that and neither did his students.

What do we know of the students of Aristotle? One point that is important to emphasize is that often scholars have imagined scribes as recorders of notes, but no evidence suggests that except for the high-quality manuscripts.[22] Aristotle lectured to young men of various ages, beginners and advanced students, as was customary in schools in antiquity. The pupils studied various subjects and apparently were divided into two categories. Aristotle addressed mainly the most capable, who were provided with *phronesis* (understanding, prudence) and possessed maturity of mind.[23] He described others who were less prepared and immature, saying they might be knowledgeable and expert in mathematics and geometry but lacked *phronesis*, which came with experience.[24] Adopting a metaphor that would have resonance throughout antiquity, Aristotle said, "The soil must have been previously tilled to foster the seeds and the mind of the pupil must have been prepared."[25] No argument would be effective to persuade the immature pupils.

Diogenes Laertius said that about two hundred students attended Theophrastus's lectures, but then he showed that not everything was straightforward; there were difficulties and some resistance when it came to assembling students (presumably the older ones). In a letter to Phanias the Peripatetic, he spoke of a place where they were gathered.[26] At the time of Aristotle and Theophrastus, students did not often listen

---

22. See Beresford 2020, xliv.
23. *Nic. Eth.* 9. 1179b 7–10.
24. *Nic. Eth.* 1.3.5–7, 6.8.5–8; 10.9.6.
25. On popular morality, see Morgan 2007. On the importance of nature, cf. Cribiore 2007b, 129–34. On the mind as soil to be cultivated, see Plutarch, *Mor. On the Education of Children* 2d–e.
26. Diogenes Laertius V 37. Dorandi (2013) on the strength of the manuscripts reads *deikterion* (a place where people showed up) instead of *dikasterion*. Was Theophrastus editing his lectures? I think it is likely that he was working on lectures previously given.

to original lectures. It seems that the philosopher probably revised and edited other lectures, heightening the confusion. Theophrastus remarked: "It will not be easy to set up not only a large public lecture but also a limited circle as one wished. The lecturers engage in reading a text but they are correcting it at the same time. To give a lecture randomly[27] and without care is not allowed any more by the youth." Students in antiquity usually appear passive. In this remarkable passage, though, students appear to dictate the format and content of lectures. It is a *unicum* in education that shows older students reacting to what they were offered and refusing to be fed old works that they already knew in better forms. Far from being passive, the students had some authority and shunned gatherings they did not consider worthy of the original philosophers. They were exasperated and rebellious, and they objected to lectures that were full of mistakes and delivered carelessly. Students like Theaetetus had to take down those lectures to form their own library, and these lectures' lack of consistency impaired their work.[28]

Different versions of philosophical works were in circulation, making it very difficult to identify the original of each. This phenomenon would later become common in the Roman period.[29] Aristotle's texts suffered from this treatment. His lectures, including the *Metaphysics*, became a subject of research and "improvements." In particular, scholarly attention has focused on Book K, which is an ensemble of two parts (a doublet) and is a remnant of a longer version, where careful consideration reveals an evolution from one part to another. Pierre Aubenque argues that Book K is not entirely authentic, remarking on how valuable genetic criticism can be in identifying and solving these questions.[30] Students objected to the imperfect versions in circulation and demanded clarity.

Some of the texts that persisted through tradition presented the confusion that Theophrastus discussed, to which the students also objected. If we return to that passage, we see that even when texts were not delivered at full speed, the language and the different layers of the content created a confusion that made these lectures less appealing

---

27. One of the meanings of *anaballo* is to "throw up," and I wonder if it can be applied here to a lecture that is given uncritically and unprofessionally. To vomit speeches will be considered later a characteristic of sophists.
28. On making annotations of a lecture of Socrates, see p. 29 on Theaetetus. Theaetetus's (Plato, *Theaetetus* 143a) difficulties were different from those of Theophrastus's students.
29. Décarie 1983.
30. Aubenque 1983.

and less accessible. Furthermore, another reason for the students' dissatisfaction, as remarked on by Theophrastus, was the impossibility of capturing Aristotle's *ipsissima verba* and making satisfactory notes.

Aristotle's third-longest work, the *Problems*, requires additional consideration. The text consisted of thirty-eight books and more than nine hundred chapters. Each chapter starts with a question, which is followed by an answer (or answers), according to a very popular educational process. Throughout, it is easy to visualize a master asking questions of a student sitting or standing in front of him.[31] It is likely, in fact, that some school papyri or ostraca consisting of simple lines of text or a list of words originally represented answers to such questions.[32] The *Erotapokriseis* (as they were called) are a small body of literature, studied only to a limited extent, that became widespread in late antiquity and in the Byzantine period, mostly in Christian literature.[33] The *Problemata* continued to be published in the eighteenth and nineteenth centuries. They served to organize notions like grammar, medicine, health, wine, shrubs and vegetables, fruits, or winds. Scholars have noticed a similarity between question-and-answer texts and dialogues. These *Problemata* could also be known as *aporiai*, *zetemata*, and *luseis* (that is, answers).[34] They were probably composed according to the dictates of a genre, but only later on. *Problemata* are found in the works of several philosophers, such as the Stoics, Cynics, and others. In the second century the philosopher Epictetus mentions *Problemata* in connection with literary education in the class of the grammarian. The questions sound elementary and relentless, but their association with lower education is clear. For example,

> When asked: "who was the father of Hector?" He replied "Priam." "Who were his brothers?" "Alexander and Deïphobus." "And who was their mother?" "Hecuba." "This *historia* came down to me." "From whom?" "From Homer." (*Diss.* 2.19.7)

Epictetus placed these *Problemata* early on in education, and they appear mechanical and uninteresting. However, the genre had a technical and intellectual component beyond practice and indoctrination.

---

31. See, e.g., the Douris cup from the Staatliche Museum in Berlin. See figures 1–2 in Cribiore 2001b, 29.
32. Cribiore 1996, some exercises, nos. 98–128.
33. Papadoiannakis 2006, with bibliography in note 1. Similar collections were attributed to Democritus, Theophrastus, and Chrysippus. See also Volgers and Zamagni 2004.
34. See Jacob 2004, 25–54, who mentions various sources.

It stood between writing and orality, although writing was its only expression outside of school. In the collection transmitted under Aristotle's name, there are clusters that for several reasons (but mostly because of style) appear Aristotelian. In other clusters, the text seems to have been manipulated, with additions appearing to have been made according to the process that Theophrastus noted above. We do not know how they were written down in Aristotle's time. The structure was open; the genre was permeable and could be used by others since it allowed for elaborations. In this way the texts of Hippocrates, for instance, were pillaged. The *Problems* were not designed for publication as a treatise but instead derived from lectures, class discussions, or notes.[35] They were not meant to generate new certain knowledge but were exercises for the intellect. A search for the text's history would not produce many results, and there was no conversation between texts. I believe that C. F. Jacob is right in supposing that the collection originated from the notes of Aristotle (44–45), to which notes of his disciples were added.[36]

Carlo Natali has argued that Aristotle might have addressed some of these questions to students.[37] In Section XVIII, which was titled "Philology" and considered literature or letters, at 1.916b1–3 the question is "Why is it that some people when they begin to read are overtaken by sleep, even if they do not want to, while others who want to sleep are kept awake when they take up a book?" The scientific answer that follows this first question points to "an intellect that was moved but did not think with concentration," so that for this reader reading was a light task that did not leave lasting impact. The answer to the second question mentions those "who concentrate on something in the intellect," with the result being that reading keeps them awake because it becomes part of their thinking. Another of these *Problemata* regards why "contentious arguments are suitable for exercise."[38] The answer is that "they involved frequent victories and defeat. Victorious people enjoy them and so are induced to compete again." There are more questions beyond Book XVIII and those commented on by Natali, many of which imply a pedagogical process and strong didacticism. Questions concern verbosity or the superiority of a philosopher as compared with an orator. One asks, "Why do we enjoy hearing what is neither very old

---

35. Blair 1999, 175–76.
36. Jacob 2004, 44–45.
37. Natali 2013, 98–99.
38. Aristotle, *Pr.* XVIII 2.

nor quite new?" Of course, questions that addressed students would have been spread out everywhere when ethical concepts such as justice or morality were explained.

Finally, it is important to examine the texts of the *Problemata* themselves in an attempt to evaluate the gravity of their errors and imperfections. The accumulation of material, the lack of order, and the plurality of hands have caused scholars to denounce the form of these texts; my aim is to determine how easily those texts could have been altered. Could they map onto those described by Theophrastus, of which students did not have a great opinion? In scholars' estimation the actual *Problemata* date to between the third century BCE and the sixth century CE. We have said that Aristotle authored a number of them; at the beginning he probably ordered the collection, which then diverged from his hand. The collection grew, but there is no discernable organization of the books and their various chapters, which meander to different topics. Virtually every chapter starts with a question (Why?) and is followed by an answer, in the tradition of *Erotapokriseis*.

The most common mistake found in such a large collection consists of the presence of identical chapters that recur in various parts. They are repeated randomly, for no apparent reason. So, for example, "Why will purslane and salt stop bleeding gums? It is because purslane contains some moisture."[39] At times a problem is repeated but with some variations. Sometimes words are missing, impairing the general understanding with the result that the editor has to substitute another.[40] The subject of a question might also be unclear: "Why are people less drunk when they drink from large cups? Indeed, the cause is the same, the downward pressure of the surface heat." Here the obscurity is due to a conflation of two different chapters.[41] At XXV 14, some editors presume that some piece of the text is missing because the line contradicts the previous chapter: "Why does air not travel upward? For if the winds occur when the air is moved by heat and fire by its nature travels upward, the wind too should go upwards since that which sets in motion runs upward and that which is moved runs upwards . . ." My survey of the mistakes in the *Problems* reveals that they are usually unobtrusive and can be forgiven. Some of these mistakes could have derived from random notes.

---

39. *Pr.* VII 9. Purslane is an edible succulent with small flowers; cf. I 38.
40. *Pr.* X 35.
41. *Pr.* III 25a. Completely obscure is XXV 8, a long chapter.

After Aristotle

The farther a student progressed on his educational path, the more specialized and valuable his notebook would become. It would circulate and could be used by others.[42] The cases I consider below also show that notes allowed philosophers-in-training to compile their own publications. Yet much discernment is necessary in order to identify notes properly.

Alexander of Aphrodisias

Alexander of Aphrodisias is an important figure on whom to focus our attention, not as a philosopher who lectured in class to students but as a writer of treatises and commentaries, some of which were later compiled under titles such as "school discussions." Alexander lived between the second and third centuries and was appointed as a public teacher of Aristotelian philosophy in Athens; his surviving writing reveals what kind of school he directed. The existence of a school is sometimes considered a given, for example by Brad Inwood.[43] Questions to ask are: Did Alexander have a school where exegesis of texts was practiced as a rule, as has been claimed? Do we know if his students took down notes of his lectures? Can we regard his works, especially his minor ones, as notes? Robert Sharples, who devoted much attention to Alexander, was doubtful.[44] He remarked that some of Alexander's writings—especially those that he judged not particularly accomplished and called "inept"—might point to students' exercises, even though the light that they throw on this question is "dimmer and more fitful . . . than we might wish."

Gregory Snyder strongly defended the idea that exegesis of texts was practiced in the school of Alexander. He argued "that Alexander's commentaries show definite signs of classroom origin and that they are probably based on Alexander's lecture notes."[45] Snyder's analysis of Alexander's treatises and commentaries is in my view superficial. His observations about some pedantic features in the prose, the fact that Alexander sometimes poses problems and suggests different ways of solving them, and his sporadic use of the plural personal pronoun (we)

---

42. I will consider here notes that students made spontaneously, taking down their teachers' words, and not texts that were dictated.
43. Inwood 2014, e.g., 109.
44. See especially Sharples 2016.
45. Snyder 2000, 66–92 at 91.

do not strictly demonstrate that these are classroom notes. There is a big difference between some works of Aristotle that show inconsistences and traces of school activity, as well as the writings of Platonists and Aristotelians of late antiquity like Olympiodorus, and the meager traces of teaching in Alexander's works, which can be otherwise interpreted. One of the differences between Alexander's commentaries (even the minor ones) and the later ones, addressed in detail in part III, is the usual lack of an introduction and the fact that they are not divided into a section for general discussion, followed by an examination of various points. It is possible that some of Alexander's minor works reveal some connection with education, but they do not do so directly. In addition, Snyder presented a view of classroom activity that is redolent of teaching in the modern world. Thus he suggested that students bring to class several books to be interpreted and that the different readings of Alexander derived from those and not from his knowledge of different views and collation of manuscripts. Altogether, it is difficult to dismiss the views of Pierluigi Donini that Alexander's works were not directly connected to formal education and pedagogic activity; instead, this scholar suggests, it is more likely that these works may have addressed educated people in general.[46] In light of these considerations, I exclude Alexander's writings among the texts that reveal students' use of their teachers' lectures.

As previously mentioned, it is unclear whether students employed their notes afterward to compile new works when they were preparing to become philosophers themselves. Were the comprehensive notes that Olympiodorus's disciples drew up of fundamental relevance to their future profession? It is indicative that the notes that Olympiodorus and Philoponus themselves recorded when editing Ammonius's lectures formed the base of their subsequent scholarly activity. Below are examples of students and listeners who recorded lectures and demonstrations (in the case of Galen) at the start of their professional careers, which corroborates the circumstances of note-taking, even though their notes are not extant.

In philosophical schools, notes served as receptacles for thoughts, threads for recollection, material to peruse and study, and starting points for productive activity. Most importantly, some philosophers' authoritative texts were preserved through the work of students who

---

46. Donini 1994.

jotted down their teachers' lectures. I will start from what the literary evidence suggests about young men writing notes; though many details of this evidence might be fictional, they are still indicative of overall scholarly habit.

In the *Hermotimus*, Lucian presents the titular character as a philosopher's very diligent student who not only bent over books but also took notes at lectures (2).[47] For about twenty years Hermotimus had followed the same life, "writing notes (*hypomnemata*) at the lectures, pale and wasted in body with thoughts and studying." This dialogue is replete with references to books written by philosophers "by the hundreds and thousands" (56), yet this student could not dispense with writing down his teacher's lessons. His teacher's words, in fact, "like Zeus's golden rope in Homer," were fundamental in raising him up to a world of knowledge (3). The playful Lucian presents here a stereotyped image of the "good student." Of course, this is an ironic account. Lucian does not regard Hermotimus's diligence as an admirable personality trait. This kind of mocking reference reminds one of Lucian's portrayal of philosophers' arrogant and disputable behavior, which he attacks unremittingly.

Another text, Philostratus's *Life of Apollonius of Tyana*, confirms the strong inclination of a student to record his teacher's words. Loyalty and allegiance to one's mentor were paramount among the qualities required for a student of philosophy. While traveling in Assyria, Apollonius of Tyana acquired a disciple as devoted as Hermotimus, one Damis of Nineveh, who looked at him as a superhumanly wise being.[48] In exchange for becoming Apollonius's follower, Damis offered Apollonius his superior knowledge of not only the geographical surroundings but also the place's various languages. Apollonius replied that he himself knew all human idioms. The mention of languages reveals the imperfection of Damis's linguistic skills; educated among the barbarians, Damis lacked the ability to express himself suitably. This passage confirms that the styles of teachers' discourses and notes differed sharply. Damis was only capable enough to record what he saw and heard, including conversations with his teacher (*synousia*), by taking notes of everything (*hypomnemata*). He noted things down in his scrapbook, which Philostratus somewhat irreverently calls ἐκφάτνισμα (scraps from the manger),

---

47. Reading texts by other philosophers continued to be important. See Del Corso 2005, 31–49.
48. Philostratus *VA* 19; Jones 2001.

because Damis, determined not to let anything escape him, had the habit of jotting down every infinitesimal and negligible bit of information regarding Apollonius. Notebooks could draw criticism because of the varied and abbreviated material they included. A malignant fellow compared the trifles Damis had collected to the crumbs that fell from a table during a feast that were fitting for dogs to consume, but Damis was not at all discouraged. In this account as well as the previous, irony is palpable: Damis's obtuse diligence silently condemns him.

The information concerning the behavior of students of existing philosophers is sketchy and may appear as a conglomeration of anecdotes and various references, but it will be useful in light of the sections that follow in this book. Galen mentioned that the works of Carneades, an academic-skeptic philosopher of the third century BCE, were handed down to posterity through the notes that his pupils "treasured up" in their notebooks.[49] In the Roman Empire, individual teachers with small groups of adherents supplanted larger rhetorical and philosophical schools, albeit with some exceptions. When texts were unavailable, recording current and popular teachers' lectures and commentaries became indispensable. Porphyry, in the *Life of Plotinus*, says that there was not a ready and accessible distribution of philosophical works because their recipients were scrutinized and chosen with care, with many excluded (4). Moreover, as we will see, some philosophers chose not to write for various reasons and only to lecture and lead conversations in class.

In his *Life of Pythagoras* the third-century philosopher Iamblichus describes how the philosopher's school functioned.[50] He states that the members of the school did not employ common, ordinary words that any reader could superficially understand, instead using secret devices and symbols. This behavior made what they said difficult for the uninitiated to follow. Iamblichus distinguishes between oral lectures, course notes (which he calls *hypomnematismoi* and *hyposemeioseis*), and the books subsequently produced and published (*syggrammata* and *ekdoseis*). Students would follow oral lectures and record the same course notes that the students of Olympiodorus would take down centuries later. They then developed from these notes texts that could be disseminated and,

---

49. Galen, *de optima doctrina* 2.5 Barigazzi = 1.45 Kühn. I owe this information and that regarding Albinus to Stephen Kidd.
50. Iamblicus, *De vita Pythagorica* 23.104; Deubner 1937. Cf. the translation in 1989 by Clark. On texts attributed to Pythagoras, see Macris et al. 2021.

according to Iamblichus, transmitted to us. Iamblichus may well have attributed characteristics that were present in his time to a sixth-fifth century BCE school. From what he says, note-taking appears as a quasi-formal and obligatory activity completed during the lecture or after it. In some schools of philosophy, only students (rather than their teachers) were engaged in writing.

We know only a few details about the Neoplatonic philosopher (and later the teacher of Galen) Albinus of Smyrna, who claimed that Aristotle's logic was already present in Plato. At the age of twenty, after the death of his father, Galen went to Smyrna to hear the lectures of a doctor as well as Albinus. The latter apparently wrote in his turn eleven books of notes from the philosopher Gaius's lectures: *Sketch of Platonic Doctrines* and *Introduction to Plato's Dialogues*. These works are lost, like most of Albinus's production, and the titles are only known from the contents listed in manuscripts, but they represent one more testimony of the practice of taking notes from oral lectures.[51]

Notes were necessary because books did not circulate widely. The third-century critic, philosopher, and rhetorician Cassius Longinus pointed to a related problem: the fact that it was not easy to find scribes to copy texts.[52] He had asked his scribe to interrupt the copying of other books assigned to him and devote all his attention to Plotinus's writings. When he looked at the texts, however, he was not satisfied and had reservations about the copies, which, in his view, were full of mistakes. The errors were not due to the scribe's negligence; Longinus apparently did not know of the trouble that Plotinus encountered in writing. Plotinus's follower Amelius, in fact, had not corrected his master's written voice. Yet there were more issues standing in the way of students reading philosophers' published texts. In a letter by Longinus, as reported by Porphyry (20), Longinus remembers the outstanding philosophers he encountered in his youth:

> When I was an adolescent there were a few outstanding professors of philosophy. I had the opportunity to hear them because, from when I was a child, I visited many places with my parents as I encountered numerous people and cities and followed the lectures of those who were still alive. Now some of them strove to set out

---

51. Parisinus Graecus 1962, 146v. In Smyrna Galen had followed the lectures of Albinus; see *De libris propriis* I.2; Boudon-Millot 2007, 140.

52. Porphyry, *Life of Plotinus* 19. A new edition and translation appeared in Gerson 2018; see also Richard Goulet 1982 and Edwards 2000.

their opinions in writing to allow posterity to get a measure of benefit from them; others thought that all they needed to do was to guide their students to an understanding of their doctrine.

Philosophers in the second category who chose not to write may have possessed less interest in personal glory, but as good educators they kept in mind their students' ability to comprehend and retain knowledge. Longinus added that, among the philosophers who were engaged in writing, some only adjusted others' works or developed small points from them. What students did was not much different. Longinus, in any case, was not a philosopher, according to Plotinus, who called him a "philologist" when he read one of his works.[53] Among the philosophers he listed who did not write was Musonius Rufus, the teacher of Epictetus, who in his turn did not write. Longinus also mentioned several philosophers who belonged to both categories; among these was Plotinus, who had written many treatises.[54] Yet, as we will see, Plotinus abstained from writing for ten years at the beginning of his career. The preferable solution for a student interested in philosophy was to follow lectures. Placing oral lectures firmly in memory was not easy, though, and note-taking was needed. The student of a philosopher who never produced a book or wrote a treatise had only his memory of an event at his disposal.[55] Eunapius pointed to the difference between Alypius and Iamblichus.[56] Students of the former, unsatisfied with the fact that Alypius confined his teaching to informal conversations and did not produce a written text, ran away from his classes and enthusiastically attended Iamblichus's rich lectures. With Alypius, notes were a necessity, but classes with Iamblichus were more satisfying.

The close relation between a student and his teacher of philosophy, which will be discussed in parts II and III, manifested itself in the young man's desire not to miss a syllable from the latter's teaching. A matter of great interest is the intercourse of Proclus with the old philosopher Plutarch in the fifth century, as described by the philosopher Marinus, who wrote a life of Proclus in prose and epic verse.[57] The eminent

---

53. Porphyry, *Plot.* 14.
54. The following account of Plotinus's teaching is taken from his *Life*, compiled by his student Porphyry.
55. See the list of the philosophers in both categories in Goulet-Cazé 1982.
56. Eunapius, *VS* 460.
57. Marinus succeeded Proclus and taught the philosopher Isidorus, whom Damascius immortalized in his *Life*. See Edwards 2000, 55–115.

philosopher Syrianus took Proclus to visit Plutarch, his predecessor as head of the school in Athens. Proclus was barely twenty years old but manifested such determination and desire for philosophy that Plutarch made him part of his study circle, which was reading Aristotle and Plato. Even though Plutarch was extremely old, he found himself very much taken by the young man and exhorted him to take notes, recording what was said in the group. Of course, this episode is idealized and cannot be taken at face value, but to my knowledge this is the only instance in which a teacher recognized openly the value of notes and persuaded his ward to take the initiative. It is quite possible that Didymus and Olympiodorus did likewise. Plutarch also suggested that a new work could emerge from Proclus's eager participation and that his notes could eventually form a treatise on the *Phaedo* that Proclus could publish under his name.[58] We may suspect that in other instances a teacher might have intervened by suggesting a very useful exercise, but for that we lack evidence.

In light of what we will consider in part III, it is important to realize not only that several students might take notes at the same time but also that a lecture could be repeated with some variations. Photius reported that the student Theosebius took down a single text several times.[59] Theosebius, a very private and honorable man and philosopher, was a contemporary of Olympiodorus and the best scholar on Epictetus of the time.[60] He twice recorded the philosopher Hierocles's lectures on the *Gorgias* with confusing results, since a comparison of the versions showed notable discrepancies. But was Theosebius entirely to blame for the details surrounding the fundamental exegesis and its inconsistencies? As I have noted, tradition preferred to blame the student, but it is possible that Hierocles had actually delivered different versions of the lecture at different times.

The School of Plotinus

A comprehensive account of the writing activities of Plotinus is provided by his disciple Porphyry of Tyre. Porphyry wrote extensively about his master's life and was particularly enthusiastic about Plotinus's

---

58. Marinus, *Proclus or on Happiness* 12. Translation by Edwards 2000, 55–119. The treatise on the *Phaedo* is lost.
59. Photius, *Bibl.* 338b 35–36b.
60. See Watts 2006, 56–57; Damascius, *Vit.Is.* 45b.

philosophy, conversations in class, and his charisma, attractive physical aspect, and sweet and calm disposition. Plotinus founded Neoplatonism, which dominated the Platonic school in late antiquity. Porphyry meant to defend him from his critics and from Iamblichus in particular; he presented Plotinus as an exponent of the true philosophy. Porphyry's words were "une véritable machine de guerre," in the opinion of Saffrey.[61] In his youth Plotinus had gone to Alexandria but was very disappointed by the lectures of the philosophers there, until he became a disciple of Ammonius.[62] After attending Ammonius's conversations and lectures for eleven years, he moved to Rome, where his school became popular, even including some women. Plotinus produced many works after refraining from writing for ten years.[63] Why this refusal, since apparently people had urged him to do so? Ammonius had objected to writing too, so perhaps this was one of the reasons behind the temporary decision of Plotinus; perhaps Plato's negative attitude toward writing may have also been influential.[64]

In addition, we learn that Plotinus had one more reason to deliver his lectures only orally. Porphyry attributed his difficulty with letters, syllables, and spelling to the fact that he did not see clearly: that is, he was farsighted.[65] It appears, however, that his visual issues derived more specifically from another cause or were at least compounded by it, namely a dysgraphia, a disturbance in handwriting that is camouflaged here as a personal dislike for calligraphic letters. It seems clear to us today that Plotinus's difficulties derived from a learning disability, which of course did not affect his brilliant thoughts.[66] This impairment seemingly afflicted him all of his life, and the books that he "wrote" likely originated from students' note-taking or his dictation to scribes.

---

61. Cf. Saffrey 1982, 55.
62. Cf. Blank 2010.
63. Cf. Ammonius in the fourth to fifth centuries; see part III.
64. Plato, *Phaedrus* 274c–277a. See also the controversial seventh letter.
65. Porphyry (14) writes that Plotinus was interested in optics. See his short treatise *On Seeing or on How It Is That Distant Things Appear Small*, in Gerson 2018, 202–5.
66. Cf. Edwards 2000, 23n109. To complete what we learn from the *Life* in chapter 8, chapter 13 adds that Plotinus transposed syllables. This is further evidence of trouble with reading and writing that usually manifests itself at an early age. From Plotinus's abstention from writing in a book by hand, it seems that he wrote in cursive, so that the text's clarity was even more compromised. Besides the fact that this impairment was not commented on in antiquity, I found it basically impossible to encounter examples of that in school exercises, unless very coarse handwriting in conjunction with an exercise at a high level might be an example of dysgraphia.

Plotinus's students Amelius, Eustochius, and Porphyry wrote down Plotinus's lectures that then formed the *Enneads*.[67] Eustochius was a physician and Plotinus's friend. He started studying philosophy with Plotinus later than the others but still became a good philosopher, and he even assisted Plotinus while he was dying and Amelius and Porphyry were away. Eustochius is also credited with having completed his own edition of the *Enneads*. Porphyry divides the followers of Plotinus into two groups: the *zelotai* and the *akroatai* (7.1). The first, which included Amelius and Porphyry, were those who cultivated philosophy, and the second were those who occasionally listened to Plotinus's lectures. In the first group, Porphyry mentions a variety of personages who were passionate about philosophy and had embraced professional or literate careers. Marie-Odile Goulet-Cazé excludes from the first group regular students of Plotinus who were also young, but age is a relative concept.[68] Students like Eustochius, when he was a beginner and later progressed, must have belonged to the first category, as Porphyry in the encomium of his master mentions only those eminent figures to increase the impression that Plotinus's classes were very well attended; in reality, naturally less prominent students must also have been part of these classes. Thus the references to Epictetus and Proclus do not confirm Goulet-Cazé's argument.[69] Marinus (*Proclus* 38) only points to the obvious difference between the two groups. From Epictetus, we learn that he had not only regular students who followed him and people who occasionally came to hear him speak when they were in Epirus, but also "young" students who naturally were *zelotai*.

Amelius seems to be the most fervent and passionate notetaker of antiquity. He started to follow Plotinus three years after he came to Rome and remained with him for twenty-four years. Previously, while a student of the Syrian philosopher Eumenius, Amelius had put together some hundred books taken from lectures.[70] He surpassed everyone else in the ability to work hard (*philoponia*), the trait typical of a good student. Amelius continued to take notes and produced about a

---

67. For text and translation, see Gerson 2018, the definitive edition of the text superseding the minor edition of Henry and Schwyzer.
68. Goulet-Cazé 1982, 232–37. This scholar brings the practice of Proclus and Epictetus in support of her argument.
69. Epictetus, *Diss.* 2.19.7.
70. Porphyry 3.2021. Edwards (2000, 8n49) suggests that the fragments of Numenius came from a work that Amelius had communicated to Eusebius at the beginning of the fourth century, *Praeparatio evangelica* 11.

hundred of them from Plotinus's lectures. Porphyry, who was always very competitive, appeared not to value these very much (4). Unfortunately, Amelius's *scholia* have not been preserved. They would have given us a good idea of how Plotinus conducted his classes and how his students were able to follow him,[71] as well as an opportunity to compare them with Olympiodorus's students.

The abundance of Amelius's notes makes one suspect that he was recording everything in a kind of *apo phones* commentary, perhaps not unlike what the students of Olympiodorus did and stenographers would have done. One can perceive a definite rivalry between him and Porphyry, who cited Longinus's words that Amelius in his work "is prolix in his treatment and in his rambling exposition."[72] Amelius was a student of Plotinus for eighteen years before Porphyry arrived from Greece at the age of thirty. At that point, Amelius had not written anything besides his notes, yet he must have appeared to Porphyry a formidable rival for Plotinus's favor. The two philosophers wrote works in competition with each other, but in the end, Porphyry prevailed and published Plotinus's treatises that their master entrusted to him (18). An interesting detail that Porphyry recounts regards Plotinus's classes before he arrived in Rome (3). "Now Plotinus's classes, since he urged those who were present to ask questions, were full of disorder (*ataxia*) and a great deal of nonsense (*phluaria*), as Amelius informed me." Porphyry might have attributed the information to Amelius, but one must note that Porphyry had an interest in denigrating his rival, thus implying that under his own guidance the situation had improved radically. Questions were of great importance in a philosopher's class, as we will see. It appears that Porphyry did not appreciate this pedagogy and preferred orderly lectures that a philosopher delivered without interruptions. When several students participated, asked for concepts to be repeated, suggested that the educator return to previous points, required clarifications from a teacher or other classmates, and devoted themselves to the intense, furious activity of note-taking, the pace of a class slowed down and even the authority of teaching could be challenged. We will have to keep in mind this scenario in part III where we analyze some students' actual notes—perhaps this was a silent and disciplined spectacle of recording information in class, but the background of note-taking may have been clamorous to a degree.

---

71. Goulet-Cazé 1982, 270–71.
72. Porphyry 21.

We lack a clear picture of whether students always followed the same routine in taking notes or tailored them according to their learning needs. In medieval and early modern classrooms, notes were taken during lectures. As in antiquity, they existed within pedagogic methods based on the presence of more or less formal lectures. Unlike in antiquity, from which only a few notebooks are extant, lecture notebooks from the eighteenth century proliferate and survive in collections, particularly in Europe. They were circulated and provided the basis for some illegitimately printed books.[73] In early modern times, students in German universities tried to capture every single word of a professor using a technique called *Schreibechor*, that is, a "writing chorus."[74] In the nineteenth century, students recorded all their teachers' words during university classes by hand.[75] Nearly two millennia earlier, taking notes was already a common practice in education in the imperial period and late antiquity. We have seen that in teaching rhetoric, medicine, and philosophy, students found it necessary to record their educators' voices. This practice may have been a regular part of schooling, a method that did not require much discussion because it was implied in teaching and learning. Teachers of philosophy in the Aristotelian and Platonist schools lectured from their own notes, whether written down or memorized. Using an expression of Matthew Eddy, notebooks were "paper tools, that is, productive tools for work on paper."[76] We have seen above some manifestations of this phenomenon when notebooks (in antiquity, of course, on papyrus or tablet) not only functioned as information management but became the basis of later publications.

As we have seen in the preceding typology, notes were fundamental in organizing a text as the author recorded thoughts that might otherwise escape, which solidified notes as part of the fabric of a narrative, sometimes indistinguishable from the core text. Also, notes were strictly tied to the power of memory—comprehensive books such as those of Gellius or Pamphila contained anecdotes and notes put together with some sophistication to form collections of literary history. Individuals could also put notes together less systematically, as when preparing a list of

---

73. See Blair 2008, 39.
74. See Eddy 2016, 86.
75. Souilhé (1948, xvii) noted that students in European universities always took down their class *ad verbum*. This corresponds to my personal experience in Italy in the 1970s. Those who were more proficient could disseminate and "sell" their notes (called in Italian *dispense*) to others, and teachers were very aware of those deals. Quintilian comes to mind.
76. On the usefulness of collections see te Heesen and Spary 2001.

items to organize travel or in the hope of retaining the details and facts of a trip, perhaps with an eye toward forming a narrative of some kind.

The many types of notes that we have analyzed from antiquity clearly illustrate that the force of notes is due to their polymorphism and derivation from testimonia. It is also evident that actual examples of notes and even notetakers are rare in the classical period and late antiquity, as compared to a higher frequency in the sixteenth century and beyond.[77] However, much can be learned and understood from the notes and notetakers that we have uncovered, from their travel experiences to oratorical studies to the details hidden in the margins. In the ancient world notes were an integral part of the routine in higher education; today they help elucidate the role of students in philosophy, a role that diminishes and is actively extinguished in later centuries.[78] As a result, we are able and perhaps privileged to examine veritable literary phenomena and truly understand how notes lie at the crossroads of the history of the book and reception of written works.

---

77. Arnould and Poulouin 2008.
78. Blair 2008, 41. Cf. also 42–43 where notes are called *reportationes*.

CHAPTER 4

Notae of Stenographers

A thorough survey of note-taking would not be complete without considering the *notae* of stenographers who recorded texts *viva voce*. They were present when lectures and speeches were delivered and took them down as delivered. They listened to the words of speakers, and we will see that they tried to reproduce them with accuracy without taking much initiative. In this sense stenographers were similar to students as they listened to the voice of lecturers and preachers. Unlike students, however, they needed special training in order to learn tachygraphic signs. They also differed from students because they were professionals, and they (or their owners, if they were slaves) were compensated for their work. It is important to review their position for two reasons. On the one hand, a central question in two educational texts we will be examining in detail, from Epictetus and Didymus the Blind, concerns the eventual presence of stenographers in their classes. On the other hand, so far only the technical parts of stenographers' work have been studied. Other aspects, such as how actively stenographers participated in the classroom, how they operated when recording lectures and sermons, and whether they modified texts, have been overlooked in scholarly literature. In this chapter I seek to answer these questions by analyzing the quality of their notes, who they were, what their competencies were, and what social and educational standing they held.

Winged Words: Stenographers at Work

> Words are by nature winged. On this account they need symbols—that when they are in flight the writer may attain their speed.
>
> —Basil, *Letter* 333 (Loeb translation 1934)

In a letter to a new stenographer, Basil of Caesarea admonished him to take care to form his characters well and to punctuate the text correctly.[1] Like other fathers of the church, Basil availed himself of the service of stenographers when dictating letters and treatises and for recording sermons.[2] While in the Roman world stenographers had been employed since the Republic, they were not equally popular in the Greek world until late antiquity.

The literary evidence from a previous period provides some information, as itinerant sophists sometimes employed stenographers to record extemporaneous speeches. In the *Life of Apollonius of Tyana* (1.18), Apollonius departs from Antioch with two attendants from his father's house. One was a stenographer and the other a calligrapher, a scribe who was supposed to turn the stenographer's notes into a fair copy. Philostratus also mentions stenographers in connection with the munificent Herodes Atticus, who gave the sophist Alexander rich gifts: "ten pack-animals, ten horses, ten cup-bearers, ten shorthand writers, twenty talents of gold, a great quantity of silver, and two lisping children from the deme Collytus, since he was told that Alexander liked to hear children's voices."[3] However, the veracity of this striking passage is doubtful, because sources for Philostratus's sophists are mostly oral.[4] Lucian also alludes to shorthand writers recording a speech "so that

---

1. He is of course building on a common Homeric metaphor.
2. *Ep.* 333.1. Terms used for stenographers are *exceptores* and *actuarii*. In Greek, *notarioi* and *exceptores* occur in the papyri sporadically in the second and third centuries, though the evidence increases a great deal in late antiquity. Cf. Teitler 1985, 29-31. On the evidence of papyri, inscriptions, and the literary sources, see Boge 1974, 73-102.
3. Philostratus, *VS* 574. Alexander was traveling and the tachygraphers had to record his performances. Cf. Heath 2004, 259-65.
4. Swain 1991, 163.

nothing would be lost," but the attribution to him of the work containing this statement is dubious.⁵

Shorthand is a system of accelerated writing used to transcribe the spoken word, a technique that has been used across past centuries and in different cultures.⁶ In contrast to abbreviations, in which some or even most of the letters of a word are omitted,⁷ shorthand uses signs to reproduce the whole text, that is, strokes of the pen and symbols instead of letters. The system was invented during the last decades of the Roman Republic or the early years of the empire.⁸ Modern terminology used for such fast writing includes *Schnellschrift*, *Tachygraphie*, and *Kurzschrift* in German, and tachygraphy, shorthand, and stenography in English. In the second century stenographers' services were in sporadic demand. Galen was thought to frequently use stenographers in his practice,⁹ but more recent research found that he did not utilize the technique often, perhaps because it did not give him any personal advantage.¹⁰ Yet friends and acquaintances unable to attend some of his medical demonstrations would send their own tachygraphers to take notes, and sometimes after giving a demonstration he would need to repeat his text for them.¹¹ On one occasion, after Galen had addressed an issue, his friend Theuthras asked him to repeat the lecture to a slave whom he would send to copy it down.¹² Another friend, the consul Boethus, sent him some stenographers to whom he could dictate the text of a lecture.¹³ In these cases, unusual situations forced the doctor to repeat what he had just said, but only in the last circumstance did he dictate merely a summary to the tachygraphers.

---

5. Lucian or Ps. Lucian, *Demosthenes* 44. Scholars have criticized Libanius for apparent contradictions in his attitude versus stenography, but as usual one has to take into account that his statements were different in his orations and in epistolary communications, as the conventions of the epistolary genre prevented him from revealing any highly negative feelings. See Teitler 1985, 198; A. Jones 1973, 572–73; Cribiore 2013, 124–26 passim.

6. Cf. Samuel Pepys, who composed his seventeenth-century diaries in many books in one of the standard forms of stenography of the time. People labored to decipher and transcribe the diaries until the key to the stenography system used was apparently found in Pepys's library.

7. Cf. chapter 6 regarding Epictetus and Arrian.

8. On the Tironian notes, see Ganz 1990.

9. Mansfeld 1994, 24n36.

10. Boudon-Millot 2007, xcii–xciii.

11. Galen, *De libris* 1.12.

12. Galen, *On Bloodletting against the Erasistrateans in Rome* 1 (Kühn xi, 194, 16–195).

13. Galen, *De praecognitione* 5.20–21.

It was in late antiquity that stenographers became numerous and indispensable in producing records of church conferences and in preserving homilies.[14] In fifth-century Arles they even acquired their own saint and a martyr, Saint Genesius.[15] The increasing popularity of stenographers in late antiquity is best explained by the common habits of writing and dictation.[16] In late antiquity, when dictation was usually preferred to personal writing, it is referenced in the surviving literature as *dictare*, or "to dictate." Yet *dictare* could also mean "to say aloud and to dictate something to someone" or even "to compose something, while saying it aloud at the same time,"[17] reinforcing the power of scribes and stenographers.[18] The papyri also indicate that in late antiquity, professional hands were preferred, as letters became more elaborate and full of rhetorical expressions.[19] We may imagine that at that time, the cacophony of voices dictating texts and letters, engaging in debates, and preaching in church became staggering.

A text taken down by a stenographer would then need to be transcribed into Greek or Latin for Christian figures like Basil of Caesarea and Jerome who often used stenographers.[20] In his work *On the Trinity*, Saint Augustine appears to use the verb *conscribere* to refer to this process when mentioning that he gave a sermon in church that was then written down,[21] while in *Ep.* 223, Basil uses the term *metagrapsai*. Though it is easy to assume that a different scribe would "translate" the text and rewrite it in elegant handwriting, the ability to read

---

14. The excellent comprehensive works of Teitler are informative and irreplaceable but mostly technical. See Teitler 1985; 1990, 3–15; 2007, 518–45.

15. Genesius refused to write down the names of some Christians. Cavallin 1945; Ronchey 2000.

16. See the rhetor Julius Victor, *Ars rhetorica* 27. Cf. Pliny, *Ep.* 9.36 and Cicero, *Ad. Fam.* 16.10. Dio, however, in *Or.* 18.18 advises a young man to dictate. In the fourth century Eunapius praised handwriting, but he was isolated (*VS* 502, 551).

17. Arns (1953, 37–40), on the practice of Jerome, rightly considers *scribo* as a reference to a text being written by a secretary. Jerome listed the whole possible gamut of literary activities: *hoc ipsum quod loquor, quod dicto, quod scribo, quod emendo, quod relego* ("what I say, what I dictate, what I write, what I emend, and what I reread"). *Gal.* 3, 6, 10; *PL* 26. 433.

18. Augustine preferred to dictate even his marginal notes; *Retract.* II.58. See Cameron 2011, 490. Possidius reports that he wrote only one brief, sixteen-page text in his own hand; the rest of his vast production was written by scribes.

19. See Bagnall and Cribiore 2006, 15–19.

20. For Basil see *Epp.* 134, 135, 223. For Jerome, see *Preface to the Comm. In Gal.* PL 26.309a. See also *Pref. Comm. In Ep. Ad Gal* 3, an amusing passage where Jerome appears to be victimized by a servant. One wonders about the reasons behind this pitiful self-portrait of Jerome. One is that Jerome was influenced by Quint. 10.319–20.

21. *On the Trinity* 15.48.

stenographic signs was actually part of a specialized education with which most people were not familiar.²² The sources point to a double process: the text was first turned into Greek or Latin characters by someone with stenographic training, and then a specialized scribe might copy it into formal handwriting. At a previous stage the stenographer may have produced a copy to later be emended by the author or constitute the *Gesta* of a conference. Specifically, Jerome has described the process using the appropriate Latin terminology: a stenographer would take down (*excipere*) the text using a pen (*stilus*) on waxed tablets. He would then "translate" it, producing *schedulae*. The author would emend it, reread it, and finally hand it over to a *librarius*, who would copy it formally. A stenographer who was supposed to read from his text during a conference would have to do so from the "translation" of his work rather than directly from tablets, a procedure that was protested during the Conference of Carthage.²³

Did educated people and scholars know tachygraphical signs? This is an important question concerning the likelihood that Arrian used stenography himself. However, the evidence from the papyri is basically nonexistent. Only a text of Plato contains some signs that were regarded as tachygraphical but are unknown and perhaps were invented by the scholar who added substantive Greek notes to the text in a fast, small, and practiced hand. This papyrus from the second century, *P.Oxy.* XV 1808, contains an excerpt from Book 8 of the *Republic*, which includes the famous passage (546 b–c) on the "Nuptial" Number.²⁴ It is uncertain whether the second writer was transcribing from another book roll or taking notes during a philosophical lecture, but the speed and apparent struggle of his note-taking renders the latter scenario more likely.²⁵ The writer also employed an abundance of abbreviations of the kind typical of commentaries. No other papyri annotated by scholars or students exhibit this feature.²⁶

---

22. Arns 1953, 62–64.
23. *Gesta GCC* 2.35; the original could have some defects. Franchina 2010, 1014.
24. McNamee 2001; McNamee and Jacovides 2003 (Plato with a new edition of the notes in the margin). Cf. also McNamee 2007, 20, and more recently, Seiler 2013.
25. One should also consider the option that the notes might be preliminary material written by someone who was giving a lecture on the *Republic*.
26. The presence of signs in two other papyri is very uncertain. An oratorical text perhaps of Andocides (*PSI* inv. 2013) shows two symbols that have been variously interpreted, with the latest editor doubting that they are tachygraphical (Conti 2013). Another papyrus from the seventh century contains some lines of a Greek text difficult to identify along with

Education and Social Position of Stenographers

Competence in shorthand depended on the flawless memorization of simple signs according to a syllabary, followed by whole words and phrases and inflectional endings.[27] School training culminated in learning the so-called *Commentary*, whose texts provided a list of over eight hundred stenographic signs that referred to Greek words.[28] Learning the whole system required years of training and commitment.[29] According to this technique, words were rendered through signs that represented each syllable, with the result that less memorization became necessary.[30]

Concerning pedagogical issues, little is known about how stenographers learned their skills and training, or what the monetary compensation of scribes was for both documentary and calligraphic texts. Two papyri from the second century, *P.Oxy.* IV 724 and *P.Oxy.* XLI 2988, mention learning stenography; both are contracts of apprenticeship.[31] The first, the more complete of the two, refers to a boy apprenticed for two years to a shorthand writer (σημειογράφος). The father paid the teacher a sum of 120 drachmas in three installments; the final one would be due at the time "when the boy would be able to write from every kind of everyday language and to read (back the symbols) faultlessly."[32] It seems, therefore, that by the second century stenographers were active in the Roman East. It is difficult to know how extensive the teaching

---

some stenography. There may not have been a relation between the Greek lines and the tachygraphical signs.

27. McNamee (2001) explains the whole system with clarity.

28. Milne and Mansfield 1934, 7–8; Menci 1992.

29. In the medieval period, the simpler method of syllabic tachygraphy was devised. See Costamagna 1990, 83–94 and note 30.

30. Only seventy-six tachygraphical papyri survive, and all of them are difficult to interpret. See Menci 2019. Most of the evidence is documentary, concerning, for example, the subscriptions of notaries, which are often followed by tachygraphical signs, and notes taken during oral presentations in legal proceedings. See, e.g., Diethart and Worp 1986.

31. Other contracts of apprenticeship to learn various skills were found in Egypt. Two Coptic ostraca of the seventh to eighth centuries bear a declaration of a priest who is promising some money to a man to teach his son to read and write. See Boud'hors 2013.

32. It has been recognized that the translation of the *ed.pr.* "when the boy writes fluently in every respect" was faulty. The expression *logou pezou* should be translated as "prose or ordinary language." In *P.Oxy.* XLI 2988. 9–10 the word and the almost identical expression "when the apprentice can take down and read from any kind of prose (or everyday language)" confirms the meaning.

in these cases was, including whether it truly covered the entire system of tachygraphy.[33]

Naphtali Lewis remarked that the sum of 120 drachmas given to the teacher was noteworthy, because in the second century that could serve to buy a small house.[34] Other scholars before Lewis tried to interpret these papyri by comparing the figures with Diocletian's *Edict of Maximum Prices*, issued in the year 303. And yet, according to the *Edict*, a teacher of stenography in the time of Diocletian would have earned much less than his counterpart in the second century.[35] It is necessary, though, to consider the evidence anew and in greater detail.[36] It would have been impossible for a teacher to make a living on this amount of money. It is instructive to compare the earnings of other professionals listed in the *Edict*. The elementary teacher earned 50 denarii; the salary of a grammarian was 200 denarii, and that of the teacher of rhetoric 250.[37] It appears, therefore, that stenographers in the fourth century earned more than elementary teachers but considerably less than both teachers of higher education and second-century teachers of stenography. This is somewhat puzzling, because stenography was more popular and more necessary in the fourth century. The only solution to this dilemma would be that in late antiquity a teacher would have more than one student and what had previously been taught through individual instruction was instead imparted in a class setting.

Two further texts (not on papyrus) refer to young people learning shorthand. One is part of the *Hermeneumata*, the bilingual school handbooks in Greek and Latin that were preserved in medieval manuscripts

---

33. These boys were probably slaves; see Cribiore 2001b, 51. Lewis (2003) remarked that one should avoid overenthusiastically imagining that, like Cicero, the owners of these slaves were anticipating another Tiro. Lewis pointed to the fact that the aim of these contracts was exclusively mercenary, so that these boys were trained in order to produce income for the owner.

34. If we break down the figure, the teacher would have earned five drachmas per month per pupil, a good salary. Considering that wheat typically cost eight drachmas per *artaba*, the teacher would have been earning 5/8 of the price of an *artaba* per month.

35. Notarius, Edict 7, 68. He would have earned 75 denarii (that is 300 drachmas) per month. As wheat then cost 1,333 drachmas per *artaba*, this later teacher would have been earning only 22.5 percent of the price of an *artaba* per pupil per month.

36. See the limited remarks in Arns 1953, 60 and Schlumberger 1972–74, 223. See also Boge 1974, 76–78. Of course, the exact status of the prices in the *Edict* is much debated.

37. Scribes earned money according to the quality and competence of their writing: a hundred lines of calligraphic writings cost twenty-five denarii; of less informal literary writing, twenty denarii; and of documentary writing, ten denarii. *Edictum Diocletiani de pretiis rerum venalium*, col. vii 39–41. In these cases, the prices depended on the amount of time employed to produce highly formal texts.

and most likely derived from third-century Gaul. One vignette presented in the text says, "I go out to the school of the arithmetic/shorthand/Greek/Latin/rhetoric teacher," a phrase that cannot suggest that stenography was part of the curriculum that led to rhetoric.[38] And yet this text is significant because it refers to a situation or even a school where stenography was taught.[39] An important question is whether stenographers (or professional scribes) obtained some literary education as part of the system of liberal studies. If they did, the circumstances must have varied drastically depending on the level of their skills and power.[40] The stenographic *Commentary* involved some familiarity with literature, but it is unclear how extensive, and evidence from the papyri is uncertain and ambiguous.[41] Many shorthand writers achieved high positions under Emperor Constantius II, and in the later fourth century, after Julian's attempt to constrain their power, they gained enviable status and large incomes when found to be necessary by emperors, as H. C. Teitler has shown.[42] In these roles their tasks went far beyond taking down dictation, and some even enjoyed an emperor's confidence and became trusted advisers.

At the end of this excursus and in light of the following chapters, it is essential to vindicate the credibility and precision of stenographers, who were often accused of imprecision and omissions in their work. I have recently surveyed the available evidence, concluding that they did not inflate their work; in fact, they recorded the proceedings of Christological conferences rather accurately.[43] Stenographers were indispensable in reproducing those documents, and their texts were then "translated" to produce the official versions of the conference, the *Gesta*. These were tinged by extreme polemic, and their language was fundamentally oral. It seems, however, that stenographers were rather innocent and often simply caught in the crossfire. Diminished and insulted, they appear to have done their work as well as they could.

---

38. See C18, that is, *Hermeneumata Celtis* 18. Dickey 2015, 2:170.
39. Stenography was not taught in villages. See *Ep.* 157 of Gregory of Nazianzus: his nephews had to leave their town and go to the city of Tyana to learn the art.
40. A letter from Augustine shows that some stenographers only had a smattering of the art (*Ep.* 44.2 of the year 398).
41. Torallas Tovar and Worp 2006, 29–35. Though the stenographic signs are missing, there is no doubt where the list originated. Most of the entries belong to the stock of basic words, with the addition of some poetical and technical terms (for example, medical terminology) and words from lexicographical sources such as Hesychius.
42. Teitler 1985, 34–37; 68–72 passim.
43. Cribiore 2021.

Likewise, my analysis has shown that transcripts of sermons, which were imperfect pieces of rhetoric, can be trusted to have recorded what was delivered verbally. The evidence is admittedly incomplete, but I argue that stenographers appear unjustly accused of transforming texts and of partiality. Most of the extant sermons do not seem to have been edited, but rather represent the versions that stenographers wrote down during delivery (including preachers' informal admonitions and requests for silence). When two texts of a sermon appear in the manuscripts, one shorter and one more extensive but differing from the other in only a few points, it is possible to identify the latter as the version taken down by a stenographer. These stenographers seem to have completed their transcriptions somewhat unthinkingly, without abbreviating certain parts or taking personal initiative. Stenographers did not edit preachers' texts but instead took them down mechanically, reproducing all the numerous repetitions.

In part III we will discover that Didymus's commentaries on Psalms and Ecclesiastes, though usually considered taken down by stenographers, were actually recorded by students. My analysis of the lectures reveals that someone shortened the students' questions and included mistakes of every kind that marred Didymus's lectures, artifacts that are atypical of stenographers.

PART II

The Voice of Epictetus

Come, have you not received faculties that enable you to bear whatever happens? Have you not received magnanimity? Have you not received courage? Have you not received endurance? And why should I care any longer for anything that may happen if I am magnanimous? What will upset me or disturb me or seem grievous? Shall I fail to use my faculty to that end for which I have received it but groan instead and lament over events as they occur? "Yes, but my nose is running." Why do you have hands, slave? Is it not that you may wipe your nose? Is it reasonable then that there should be running noses in the world? And how much better would it be for you to wipe your nose than to find fault? Or what do you think that Heracles would have amounted to if there would not have been a lion like the one he encountered and a hydra, and a stag and a boar and wicked and brutal men whom he drove out and cleared away?

—*Diss*. 1.6.28–33

Remember that it is not only desire for office and wealth that makes one low and subservient to others but also desire for peace, leisure, travel, and scholarship . . . For just as salutations and office holding are among things that are external

> and without a moral purpose, so also is a book. Why do you want to read? Tell me. If you turn to reading only for amusement or to learn something, you are indifferent and lazy. But if you engage yourself with proper reading what else is this but a happy life?
>
> —*Diss.* 4.4.4

The Stoic philosopher and educator Epictetus flourished at the end of the first century and the beginning of the second, until around 110 CE.[1] He was born around 50 or 60 in Hierapolis (Phrygia) and became the slave of Epaphroditus, secretary of Nero. He never married and never had a family. On leaving Rome he established a school of philosophy in Nicopolis in Epirus and produced eight volumes of his *Discourses* (*diatribai*, lectures), of which only four survive. In addition, a synthetic *Handbook* (*Encheiridion*) has been transmitted. My account of the school of Epictetus is focused on the *Discourses* but also takes into account at least some of the *Encheiridion*, due to its vast popularity across the centuries. When he was a student, the future provincial governor and historian Lucius Flavius Arrianus (Arrian) of Nicomedia assembled the *Encheiridion* as a compendium of Epictetus's philosophy, drawing on his teaching but at the same time introducing some modifications. It is useful to have *le tout Epictetus*, whose force becomes somewhat attenuated in the larger oeuvre amid a host of issues. At the same time, a slow perusal of the *Encheiridion* is necessary, even if in that text the philosopher appears almost to suffocate under the weight of his sayings. Two examples of his teaching philosophy are in the epigraphs above.

As indicated in the excerpts, Epictetus often insists that enduring difficulties is imperative and that men have both physical and moral faculties to withstand adversity. The argument was popular in later Stoicism, but here, Epictetus adapts it to his educational principles. He berates his whining students, whom he calls "slaves," claiming that they are passive and deaf to the message of philosophy. Human beings possess reason with which they make choices and act.

Ethics, moral philosophy, needs to structure a person's life. This, rather than knowledge per se, was the aim of Epictetus's philosophical training. The first two extant books of notes show that his teaching,

---

1. According to an anecdote his master had tortured him and as a result he became crippled. Celsus, Origen, Gregory of Nazianzus, and his brother Caesarius reported the story in some detail. The historicity of these events cannot be ascertained. Cf. Souilhé 1948, iv note 3.

at least at the beginning, was intended to form his students without providing or increasing a knowledge of literature and philosophy. The highest aim and goal to achieve was *eudaimonia*—happiness, specifically the happiness of a life well lived.[2] Epictetus notes that human virtue is a condition of the mind and declares that students who left home only to read more books in his school should return home (1.4.22). Externals (sometimes called "indifferents") are outside one's power, and renouncing externals means to practice removing sorrow, disappointment, and fear of death from one's life. Progress meant turning one's attention to moral character, but real progress needed to be distinguished from delusive progress. The Stoic philosopher should not complain about what happens but find his happiness in the thought of having done the best.

Before entering Epictetus's classes, it may be good to see how he devised three areas of studies in which people who aimed at being good had to be trained (*Diss.* 3.2.1-2). These topoi concerned desire, duty, and judgment:

> The first has to do with desires and hate, so that he does obtain what he desires but never falls into what he avoids. The second concerns choice and refusal and generally with duty, so that he may act with order and good reason and not carelessly. The third is about avoidance of error and rashness in judgement.

The *Discourses* of Epictetus have often been referred to as *diatribai*, sermons of a type associated with Cynic philosophy. This term, however, should be understood to refer mostly to Epictetus's style of teaching, even if observations on Cynic philosophy are sometimes present. We should keep in mind that the extant *Discourses* in their current form transmit only a part of Epictetus's message, as four books have been lost. Thus it is possible that the most technical and theoretical details of the philosopher's teaching are missing. Though his philosophical background is not simple to define, Epictetus inherited the main lines of his thoughts on ethical theory from the Stoic tradition.[3] His distinction between things "up to us" and "things not up to us" refers to exercising choice, *prohairesis*. However, there are very few remains of the

---

2. See Cooper 2012, 150-58; Gill 2022, 15-52 on the issue that learning and practicing virtue will be conducive to happiness. Following nature as a guide will bring *eudaimonia*.

3. Diogenes Laertius (*Lives of the Philosophers*) who lived in the first half of the third century is a major source for philosophy including the Stoics. On Stoicism, see Cooper 2012, 150-51. Dobbin 1998, xiv-xix. Cf. in part III Olympiodorus's statement that he had become a Stoic in his soul.

doctrines of the Stoics (e.g., Zeno) from the fourth and third centuries BCE. Therefore we do not have direct knowledge of their teaching and depend on writers of the imperial period, notably Seneca, Epictetus, and Marcus Aurelius, who reflect indirectly the doctrines of the earlier Stoics. Prior to their writings, there are only literary and nontechnical philosophical testimonies, paraphrases, and quotations.[4]

Epictetus was neither the founder of a school of thought nor a significant innovator, yet he attained formidable status as a thinker both in antiquity and in modernity. Adolf Bonhöffer strongly upheld the idea of Epictetus's orthodoxy, but recently scholars have recognized in him certain innovations.[5] Anthony Long, who read and wrote about the philosopher with deep understanding, said on this topic, "In times of stress, as modern Epictetans have attested, his recommendations make their presence felt."[6] Epictetus has been one of the most widely read philosophers across the centuries,[7] and two major reasons for his popularity must have been the efficiency of his communication and the fact that his message was mostly accessible, even if difficult to digest. In the turbulent times in which we are now living, nonspecialists find comfort in his maxims, which can teach them how to cope with difficulties. However, Epictetus was not only a philosopher but also a formidable educator in close contact with many aspects of life.

Epictetus was a deeply admired figure. There are several examples describing how people from other countries sought his help to not only defend themselves from sorrows but also allow themselves to feel some joy after sorrow had been endured and conquered.[8] A particular episode describes an official visiting Epictetus, talking about his family, and declaring that for him his children are a source of great anxiety rather than pleasure. In this tense conversation, the interlocutor exhibits authentic anguish and concerns, and he reveals that when his little daughter was extremely sick, he could not bear to stay by her side but deserted her and returned only when he was told that she had recovered. While the man argues that his behavior had been natural and logical for a father, Epictetus instead explains how unnatural and irrational

---

4. See Cooper 2012, 148–51.
5. Bonhöffer 1890. On the originality of the Stoic treatises and the school, see Gill 2003, 38–40. On the doctrinal orthodoxy in Seneca, Epictetus, and Marcus Aurelius, see Gill 2003, 44–50.
6. Long 2002, 1.
7. Brooke 2012. Scaltsas and Mason 2007, 1–3.
8. *Diss.* 1.11; see the commentary of Dobbin 1998, 131–36.

his behavior had been. Employing an example more typical of Socrates, Epictetus compares the official to someone in Rome who, too nervous to follow his favorite horse as it competed in a race, covered his head and refused to watch. When people informed this man that the horse had unexpectedly won, he fainted and had to be revived.[9] At the end of the passage, Epictetus describes a possibility that the little girl's father might be suited to become a student.

Epictetus was a practical thinker who rarely tried to solve issues only theoretically. His capacity to identify with those who consulted him made his interventions efficacious. When we read him, we still perceive the charm and power of his message but are also made aware that people in antiquity, as now, could receive his message at two different levels. On one hand, Epictetus deals with a range of practical issues, such as loss of property, sexuality, table manners, and family interactions. On the other, Epictetus discusses ethics, theology, and freedom. On both, though, he exhibits striking authenticity when he analyzes the mind's strengths and limitations, as well as those educational practices that can make young men grow into strong human beings.

Passionate, intense, and determined, Epictetus sought to reach people deeply and convince them of the necessity of demanding the best from themselves. He aimed to make his audience understand what is important in life, urging them to pursue it. Everything else, he argued, is superfluous. Sorrows, envy, and fear of death are not supposed to leave their marks on one's psyche; rather, the functions of a human being are to reason and to become a citizen of the world. Some of Epictetus's pronouncements have been described as "repellent," promoting distance from family, children, and wives, so that one would not feel bereft in the face of adversity.[10] The rationale behind these pronouncements is indicative of Epictetus's style—informed by rhetoric and diatribe with the determination to follow an argument to its very core.[11] Alternatively, emotional statements like these need to be considered in context, and the background context available to us is limited. Self-deprecation is key to understanding some of Epictetus's statements. He declared that his students had to forgive an old man and that people laughed at his style of speaking.

---

9. *Diss.* 1.11.27.
10. Long (2002, 3) declared that he was deeply disturbed by certain passages.
11. For the argument that Epictetus's style does not have much in common with diatribe, see Jocelyn 1982. The same definition, however, is maintained by Wehner 2000.

Life offered occasions for enjoyment, delusions, and laughter, and even there a philosopher might offer help: protecting men from disappointments and excessive expectations was one of Epictetus's main objectives. In some passages his attention was focused on shows and banquets, creating a protective cage for the participants. At the public shows, people needed to defend themselves from frustration, "to wish only for that to happen which does happen."[12] In other words, the prudent man could afford a limited degree of participation free from pangs of anxiety. Epictetus also advised that shouting, laughing, and rowdy behavior after the show should be avoided. This suggests that he participated in spectacles and everyday life, but with a critical eye and a desire to help.

Guests at banquets had to respect some rules of behavior. Epictetus's observant eyes followed the guest who was disappointed by being assigned a less honored place at the table or even by the lack of an invitation. This man needed to consider that there was a price for the invitation: praise for and personal attention to the host. In addition, the guest who tried to grab a plate needed to learn to observe proper table manners, wait for his turn when the plate was in front of him, and not try to detain it when it moved away.[13] Thus patience and detachment without gluttony were to be observed (with regard to food and desire), and stretching the hand with impatience to receive one's portion needed to be an exercise in politeness. In this vein, Epictetus provides us with courteous vignettes of civility, illustrating his attention to the details of human conduct. In his writing he challenges a world where being preeminent was of fundamental importance, and the norm was to prevail over others, be admired, and raise one's voice.

Epictetus often reacted strongly to those whose pride extended to their physical aspects, their sharp minds, and their arrogant characters. Yet sometimes his virtue of toleration extended to the acceptance of some such qualities. For example, a philosopher who remarked on people's bad comportment at a banquet was not supposed to reproach them directly and tell them how they should behave but should instead inspire them through his own good example.[14] It is clear, though, that

---

12. *Ench.* 33.10.
13. *Ench.* 25 and 15.
14. *Ench.* 46.

the banquet should be understood metaphorically, and in fact, his behavior will "make him worthy of the banquet of the gods."

Many actions of Epictetus were inspired by restraint and control. He always applied the term "philosopher" to himself with great reticence. Like Socrates he sought to avoid ostentation. A philosopher needed to refrain from expounding on his philosophical principles among people who were discussing them, lest he look like an amateur and spew out something that was not completely digested. From Epictetus, it appears that some philosophers gave themselves grand airs, and that the profession was looked on as desirable.[15] A lecture by an influential philosopher could inspire in people the desire to become philosophers themselves. "Do you have a natural talent for that?" asked Epictetus, suggesting that a philosopher was born a philosopher. Just as a wrestler needed strong arms and thighs, a philosopher had to have a strong predisposition for the job, to work hard, to not give way to impulse and irritation, and to be ready to get the worst of everything in honor, in office, or in court. At the price of these things, however, the philosopher had tranquility, freedom, and peace.

In a rare moment of disclosure, we see Epictetus confronting his vocation as a philosopher after telling the story of an athlete who had chosen to die rather than cutting off his genitals, which would have prevented his demise (1.2.25-29). And yet Epictetus remarks that another would have chosen to have his neck cut off if he could have lived without his neck. At this, someone interjects, "Come, Epictetus, shave off your beard." "I reply: if I am a philosopher, I will not shave it off."[16] "But I will cut off your neck." "If that will do you any good, then do so!" In a chapter centered on being clean and presenting oneself with dignity, Epictetus remarks on young prospective philosophers' lack of care for their bodies (4.11.28). They come to him like pigs that enjoy rolling in mud: they stink and are dirty. There is a flash of humor: the image of one young man with his moustache reaching down to his knees.[17]

The great reputation Epictetus had in his time was also due to his unique character and personality that easily attracted the attention of his contemporaries. The image and references that Lucian left of him

---

15. *Ench.* 29.
16. Long beards suited philosophers; see *Disc.* 1.6.10 and below. Cf. *Disc.* 3.22.9-11: long hairs and a disheveled aspect typical of Cynic philosophers.
17. The traditional image was that of philosophers with long hair, cf. Libanius, *Decl.* 33.12. However, Aristophanes in *Clouds* 14 considers long unkept hair as a sign of luxury.

are full of deference.[18] There is no way of knowing whether Lucian had known Epictetus personally, and it is possible that the satirist's image of the "lamp of Epictetus" may have acquired a life of its own. In one of his diatribes, *The Ignorant Book Collector*, Lucian mentions an "earthenware lamp of Epictetus." Here, someone who wanted to acquire the wisdom of the Stoic philosopher was forced to spend a fortune to purchase this prodigious lamp in order to read by its light.[19] Lucian probably here was referring to an anecdote mentioned by Epictetus in which, to replace a costly iron lamp that had been stolen, he planned to buy one of earthenware.[20] Lucian presents the philosopher a bit ironically and with some indulgence as "a marvelous old man." The intimate scene of reading at night communicates an impression of the philosopher that contributed to his popularity in spite of his contradictions and what Arrian calls "the frankness of his speech."

In chapter 5 I concentrate on Epictetus as a teacher, while in chapter 6 I cover his attitude toward grammatical studies, books, rhetoric, and the Second Sophistic. These are issues that previous scholarship and commentaries on Epictetus have neglected or overlooked.[21] Like many philosophers before and after him, Epictetus apparently did not leave anything in writing.[22] His student Arrian declared that he had taken notes in his classes and that the text of the *Discourses* basically consisted of these notes.

---

18. Epictetus is mentioned in *Demonax* 3 and 55; *The Death of Peregrinus* 18; and *Alexander* 2, alongside Arrian.

19. Lucian, *Ind.* 13.

20. See *Diss.* 1.18.15–16; cf. also 1.29.21. The lesson was that we should not despise and blame wrongdoers but instead pity them, because they had less than us and made a wrong judgment; see Dobbin 1998, 171.

21. For the cultural historian there is much food for thought to be found in the *Discourses*. We know a great deal about how schools of grammar and rhetoric operated, including details both general and more personal regarding teachers and students. We are more in the dark about schools of philosophy. On students of philosophy, see Trapp 2007, 18–23.

22. Snyder (2000, 22) maintained that Epictetus might have written something for his classes but did not produce a treatise. On the writings of Socrates see *Diss.* 2.1.

Chapter 5

Epictetus as an Educator and a Man

Recording Epictetus's *Discourses*

For a long time, scholars have maintained that Arrian of Nicomedia, the historian of Alexander, had taken down the text of Epictetus's *Discourses* as class notes. Arrian was at that point a young man just out of school, having attended the classes of a grammarian and a rhetor. Probably in the period between 117 and 120, he took the classes of the philosopher in Nicopolis (Epirus). It appears that his relationship with the philosopher was close, but it is far from certain whether Epictetus left an impact on him that lasted beyond his school years.[1] The question of whether he remained faithful to Stoicism should remain open. Arrian then embarked on a senatorial career, engaged in politics and administration for many years, and later retired and devoted himself to historical writing. His prose shows no philosophical influence or historical moralizing, but he followed his historical sources with diligence, using a style that nowadays is regarded as quite rhetorical.[2]

---

1. Brunt (1977) based his analysis on Arrian's assessment of Alexander.
2. Leon-Ruiz 2021. Arrian wrote about the campaigns of Alexander the Great, calling the work *Anabasis*, presumably to recall the *Anabasis* of Xenophon. He was interested only in militaristic aspects.

His somewhat cold and unimaginative prose is very different from the extant text of Epictetus.

The traditional theory of the text of Epictetus being taken down by Arrian has been challenged and the question even regarded as impossible to resolve. I shall argue in favor of the traditional opinion, with some modifications. In the sections that follow, as I present the opinions of various scholars concerning the basis of this text, I also confute their theories and argue that Arrian took notes in class. My rationale takes into account the discussion of stenography given earlier, the evidence of papyrology, and further, the characteristics of Epictetus's text that prove that it consisted originally of notes drawn by Arrian. Altogether, this evidence implicates Arrian's traditional and spontaneous intervention in the text.

Arrian's letter to one Lucius Gellius, which prefaces the *Discourses* in the manuscripts, reveals his loyalty to his master and enthusiasm for his message.[3] Arrian says that when Epictetus was teaching, he took down the oral text "word for word, as best as I could." Though not ready for an audience and far from being a finished text, these notes started to circulate without Arrian's knowledge.

> Neither did I compose these discourses of Epictetus in the way in which one might compose such things; nor did I make them known to the public, as I declare that I did not compose them. However, I attempted to write down whatever I heard him say as best as I could, word for word, as notes for myself to remember in the future his thoughts and his frankness of speech (*parrhesia*). All these, as you might expect, are like a spontaneous conversation among people and not as one would compose for those who chanced upon them later. Now, since they were like that, I do not know how they fell into the hands of others without either my consent or knowledge. I am not much concerned if I shall appear incompetent in writing, and it should not concern Epictetus at all if anyone shall scorn his words; for when he uttered them, it was clear that he had no other purpose than to inspire the minds of his hearers to the best things. If, indeed, his words should accomplish this, they will surely have, I think, the same effect which the

---

3. On the identity of Gellius, see Bowersock 1967; Stadter 1980, 28, 198n88 with more bibliography. Gellius belonged to a family of Corinthian philanthropists who dedicated a statue to Arrian.

words of philosophers ought to have. Otherwise, let those who encounter them know that, when Epictetus delivered them, the hearer must have felt exactly as Epictetus wished him to feel. But if the words don't accomplish this by themselves perhaps it is my fault or perhaps things have to be like that. Farewell.

Arrian makes some notable disclaimers here. First, he states that he did not compose the work himself but rather recorded the voice of the philosopher. Second, he recognizes that Epictetus's vivid and impetuous prose was different from the writing style that Arrian had practiced in school, to the point that he feared being regarded as incompetent. Sometimes one wonders if Arrian really did a service to his teacher by putting in relief his *parrhesia*.[4] Arrian paid attention to the fleeting moods of Epictetus, his authoritative presence in class, and his occasionally amusing performances. He reported on the harsh "therapy" to which Epictetus subjected his pupils, their tacit and sheepish resistance, and their acute nostalgia for home. Epictetus practiced "frankness of speech" in dealing with his students, something that at times seems surprising. Arrian then confesses that he had lost track of his notes, which had fallen into the hands of unknown persons.

The questions of how Arrian was able to take down the text of the philosopher and of whether he left it intact or altered it have been debated extensively, but with no solution so far. Scholars have even claimed that the issue cannot be resolved satisfactorily. Recent work on the philosopher has mentioned the matter once again, with the result that it may be useful to recapitulate the various stages of the discussion before offering some new observations.[5] In the past, several scholars have discussed whether stenography was a sine qua non for the redaction of these notes. The idea that Arrian himself recorded the voice of Epictetus by using stenography himself is illogical, as noted in the section about stenographers, because neither educated people nor scholars practiced stenography personally at that time, when it had only recently been adopted among the Greeks. In 1905 Karl Hartmann contributed to disseminating the mistaken view that it was surely stenographers who had taken down Epictetus's words, because Arrian would not have been able to reproduce the rapidly spoken words of Epictetus. In 1926

---

4. We will see that the term *parrhesia* is the same that had appeared in the work of Philodemus by that name in the first century BCE.

5. Dobbin 1998.

W. A. Oldfather embraced Hartmann's views.[6] His observations, however, can be disproved. Since Oldfather's translations and his introduction are still used extensively, it is worthwhile to discuss his views a bit further. He argued that the difference in style between the Epictetus's text and the rest of Arrian's works is so remarkable that "one is clearly dealing with another personality."[7] Oldfather also pointed to the fact that Arrian always wrote in Attic, while Epictetus's works are in Koine. In Arrian's time, however, Koine (the common usage of Greek) was not only the language of the papyri, inscriptions, the Gospels, and lower strata of society, but was also used by educated people. In school, for example, students learned to use Attic when writing but functioned in Koine in their everyday life interactions.[8] Copying down Epictetus's words in Koine would have been easy for Arrian, whose public life would largely have been conducted in Koine.

The scholar Theo Wirth was alone, in 1967, in insisting on the literary aspects of the *Discourses*, claiming that Arrian had composed them in the tradition of Xenophon in order to offer an idealized portrait of his master.[9] This theory still finds some followers when the issue is approached superficially. Even before Wirth, in 1903, Théodore Colardeau, a fine and sensitive reader, amusedly remarked that it was fortunate for us and Epictetus that Arrian did not follow Plato or Xenophon.[10] Colardeau went so far as to affirm that if Epictetus himself had composed the *Discourses*, he would have given us a different image of his philosophy, one certainly more complete and correct but less extemporaneous and natural. In 1996 Ilsetraut Hadot also rejected Wirth's interpretation that because the *Discourses* are not set precisely in time, in terms of the locality where the teaching took place, or in the identification of the interlocutors, they should be seen as fiction and a literary production. To the contrary, she argued that these characteristics were a mark of authenticity.[11] A. A. Long later remarked that when the *Discourses* started to circulate, Epictetus had already attained

---

6. Oldfather 1926.
7. Oldfather 1926, xiii. We are indeed dealing with another personality.
8. Among its characteristics are the disappearance of the dual, different use of prepositions and conjunctions and a more frequent usage of the subjunctive. In writing people could choose to adopt Attic or a more purified Koine. Swain (1996, 19 and passim) discusses the situation. He also brings the example of Galen, who chose purism but not Atticism. Medical and technical writing employed Koine. On diglossia, see Kim 2017.
9. Wirth 1967, 197–216. He briefly discusses stenography on 150–51.
10. Colardeau 1903/2004, 33–34. Both Plato and Xenophon would have redone the text.
11. See Wirth 1967, 209, 186; I. Hadot 1996, 54.

a notable reputation, and any attempt by Arrian to make significant interventions in the philosopher's text would have been unmasked.[12]

A good point of comparison for Epictetus's text is the extant work of the Stoic philosopher Musonius Rufus, who lived in Rome and was exiled several times because of his Stoic beliefs.[13] Musonius was apparently an influential teacher and counted among his students Epictetus, Marcus Aurelius, and Dio Chrysostom. He did not write anything, like Socrates and Epictetus. It is thus difficult to fairly assess his practice of philosophy in action because his work has been preserved only to a limited extent. In the fifth century, Stobaeus (books 2, 3 and 4) transmitted twenty-one summaries of his lectures that an unknown pupil named Lucius put together. There are also fragments from sayings and anecdotes in writers such as Marcus Aurelius and Epictetus. Lucius apparently had recorded the lectures in the form of notes. Lucius or someone else subsequently edited the notes, adapting them into a conventionalized text that does not shed much light on Musonius's actual doctrine and method of teaching.[14] The form and tone of these remnants are completely different from those of Epictetus.

In the polemic regarding the origin of Epictetus's *Discourses,* two scholars particularly deserve to be mentioned. In 1998 Robert F. Dobbin[15] reopened the question of the authorship of the *Discourses* by arguing that Epictetus himself had composed and written them down. Yet Dobbin could not explain why sometimes the third personal pronoun "he" (that is, Epictetus) is used. Dobbin reclaimed the perspective of a 1933 book by H. W. F. Stellwag, who had maintained that Epictetus was the direct author and had himself written a work consisting of notes for his courses that he emended years later.[16] This scholar considered the letter to Gellius inauthentic and supposed that it had been mistakenly inserted later by an editor. This of course is an attractive thesis, because it allows for Epictetus's voice to be considered completely genuine and unfiltered, but no convincing evidence was brought in its support.

Thus we should consider other reasons to argue that Arrian recorded the voice of his master. As noted above, it is extremely unlikely that

---

12. Long 2002, 41. This conclusion has only a limited weight.
13. Cf. Hense 1905. Cf. also Dio *Or.* 7. Dio had studied with Musonius. The philosopher was born around 30 CE and his family was of equestrian rank.
14. See Gill 2000, 601–3.
15. Dobbin 1998, xx–xxii.
16. Stellwag 1933, 7–16. Stellwag's assessment had fallen into oblivion and for good reason: it is only wishful thinking.

Arrian used stenographers himself or trusted the work of any stenographers hypothetically present in Epictetus's class. The pace of delivery was not a great obstacle—keeping up with the pace of speech while recording a text by hand *ad verbum* is a function not only of a notetaker's speed but also of the speaker's pace of delivery. Arrian, then, need not have struggled to keep up with his teacher's pace because of the way in which Epictetus conducted his classes. Scholars have considered the meanings of the term *epanagignoskein* as used by the philosopher. This rather rare term is employed in the context of reading, with reference to grammarians, rhetors, or philosophers.[17] It is used for situations in which the reading of a text is accompanied by explanations and discussions. Epictetus conducted his readings by going through a text and interpreting its meaning in a leisurely way that allowed his pupils to understand and assimilate the content, and that could have permitted Arrian to jot down notes.[18] We will see in part III that the philosopher Philoponus needed to go slowly through his class to ascertain that his students were following.

There was a great difference between the teaching practice of philosophers and rhetors. Accomplished rhetors who delivered a text usually needed an uninterrupted flow of words and expressions in order to emphasize their elegant skill; for philosophers there was no such need. For example, an educator from fifth-century Alexandria, Olympiodorus, who worked in the alchemical tradition and is to be distinguished from the Olympiodorus whom we will consider in part III, was an accomplished rhetor (*dynatos legein*). An anecdote in the *Life of Proclus* by Marinus of Neapolis concerning him shows the challenge that a rhetor could pose.[19] Proclus had trouble following the *ipsissima verba* of Olympiodorus, even though he was a very advanced student. He had to entrust his teacher's words to his formidable memory:

> Olympiodorus was a polished speaker, and few of his listeners were able to follow him on account of his cleverness and volubility. Proclus, however, when he left the seminar after hearing him, recited the entire proceedings in the very same words to his companions, a long text.[20]

---

17. Snyder (2000, 23–28) renders the meaning as "authoritative readings." See Del Corso (2005, 31–49) on reading in the class of a philosopher.
18. His style of teaching is reminiscent in many places of that of Socrates and Plato.
19. In the fifth century Marinus was a student of Proclus and then became his successor.
20. *Life of Proclus* 9. I have adapted the translation of Edwards 2000, 70.

Proclus recorded words by memorizing them, because Olympiodorus's pace of delivery did not allow him to write them down at that moment. Olympiodorus, who knew rhetoric well, fully used this skill. His rapidity and fluency were such that he seemed inaccessible, but Proclus managed to make sense of him even though he could not write notes.

Abbreviations

Arrian was an educated writer and a scholar, and his success in keeping up with Epictetus's flow without much difficulty might also be attributed to his utilization of abbreviations. It is not surprising that the modern scholars who engaged with various theories with regard to the origin of the *Discourses* did not take into account this practice, as the world of the papyri does not often intersect with that of literary texts. Abbreviations effectively illustrate this point. Little attention has thus far been paid to this practice or the advantages it offered a writer. But which kinds of people used abbreviations while penning literary and subliterary texts?[21] Texts by classical authors naturally do not contain those informal abbreviations visible in working copies of *hypomnemata* (commentaries) and in marginalia. In the interest of speed, the desire to economize, and the advantage of using less writing material for a working copy, writers found it insufferable to constantly repeat certain words. Therefore they abbreviated them in various ways, whether by suspension or by using certain symbols. In 1902 F. G. W. Foat (136) admired the fact that Greek writers "relied on the perspicacity of the reader's intelligence abbreviating so much." This is not the venue for considering papyri in great detail. Numerous abbreviations are visible in a papyrus written by Philodemus of Gadara, *P.Herc.* 152/157, with corrections and abbreviations by the author.[22] Abbreviations also appear in commentaries.[23] The writers who employed abbreviations frequently and used them in ὑπομνήματα were educated persons and aimed for speed and convenience. Thus Arrian must have been familiar with this

---

21. Documentary scribes often used abbreviations of the same kind that appear in literary and semiliterary texts, but here I will refer only to the latter. These are visible in texts from the first century BCE.
22. Essler 2017.
23. Commentaries like *P.Lond.Lit.*176 = *P.Oxy.*VIII 1086: this is a long commentary on *Iliad* 2.751-827. See also an ostracon *O.Bodl.* I 46 on the *Clouds* of Aristophanes 974-75. Haslam 1994, 44-45; *GMAW* plate 58. See *P.Lond.Lit.* 138 and *P.Oxy.* LXXVI 5093. Abbreviations are also frequent in inscriptions.

system of abbreviations, which was commonly accepted and could have been used when jotting down notes and writing commentaries to texts.

The Letter to Gellius Again

Were Arrian's words a rhetorical pronouncement? Or did he respond to an actual situation? We should return now to the letter to Gellius in order to look at it from another point of view. So far, scholars have regarded the letter with suspicion, as a product of rhetorical posture, with the result that its value as a witness has been impaired. In order to fairly evaluate this prefatory epistle, however, we should consider it not in isolation but in the light of other, similar prefaces that survive from antiquity. The authors who, like Arrian, denounced the practice of disseminating texts against their will were responding to an actual need to protect their work. The routes of distribution of texts were uncontrolled. In a recent article on the dissemination of drafts, I collected more examples of introductory prefaces in which a number of authors made some declarations concerning the genesis of their work.[24] As in the case of Arrian, their texts started to circulate among the public prematurely, without their authors' awareness. They, therefore, had been unable to revise them. The mathematician Apollonius of Perga, Archimedes, Galen, Augustine, Tertullian, and Sulpicius Severus found themselves in similar situations.[25]

Galen, on several occasions, denounced the fact that his work had leaked to the public before it was ready to be disseminated, with the result that he had been prevented from editing the work. The texts that were circulating were incomplete, abridged, and incorrect. Other authors became aware that their work had disappeared. Diodorus Siculus, in the first century BCE, and the Christian Tertullian in the third century, and Augustine and Sulpicius Severus in the fourth and fifth centuries were outraged and spoke openly about thieves. In most cases, as for Augustine, the thieves were people the authors knew in their immediate circles.

These works were drafts or incomplete texts that, like Arrian's, had fallen into the hands of other people. The authors who denounced the

---

24. Cribiore 2019, 281–84.
25. Galen, *De libris* ix 1.2, XIV 16. 12–14 and I 12–13; Boudon-Millot 2007; Tertullian, *Ad Marc.* 1.1; Sulpicius Severus, *Ep.* 3; Augustine, *Retract.* 2.1 (39); *Epist. of James* 2.32 (58). See also Archimedes, *De lineis spiralibus*.

practice of disseminating texts against their will were responding to an actual need to protect their work, as they could not exercise any control over their property. In a world where no law existed to protect literary property, some action was necessary. Their prefaces are a mark of anxiety dictated by their wish to defend the proper identity of their work, making sure that nobody would introduce extraneous material. These are all authorial declarations. The phenomenon Arrian laments, that his notes had disappeared and that some men facilitated their circulation, was a familiar one in a world where drafts and notes did not go through a formal publication process. Arrian's letter to Gellius is not a rhetorical construction that should be regarded with suspicion, but in fact corresponds to a well-known situation faced by other authors who were trying to protect the legitimacy of their writing.[26]

Several important questions remain. Were the prefaces that we have examined along with the letter to Gellius rhetorical pronouncements? In which way are they different from other literary prefaces?[27] Prefaces appear rarely in literature but are found sometimes in prose and poetic works and were written after a work was completed. They presented a work in some of its literary features and asked politely for a reader's understanding and toleration of eventual errors.[28] In historical works, they also defended the veracity of their accounts. In the imperial period prefaces became fashionable in Latin literature even if they were always somewhat superfluous. These prefaces differ drastically from the letter to Gellius. They do not reveal the authorial anxiety of their writers to protect their work. Arrian's letter to Gellius, however, does show these features. I argue not only that it is authentic but also that its claim that Arrian is the author of the notes he recorded from Epictetus's classes is realistic.

Before trying to summarize my arguments in favor of the traditional explanation that Arrian recorded Epictetus's voice, it is necessary to consider another feature of the *Discourses*: the titles of the essays.[29] From the Bodleianus on (*Bodl. Auct. T* 4.13), the various chapters of the

---

26. Galen, who was always involved in the reception of his work, was clearly preoccupied to be criticized. See Raiola 2015.
27. Cf. Cribiore 2019, 281–84.
28. See Cicero's letter to Varro, *Fam.* 9.8 254 SB, presenting his books *Academica*.
29. All the manuscripts stem from an archetype edited by H. Schenkl in 1916, the *Bodleianus Misc. Graec.* 251, which dates to the end of the eleventh or the beginning of the twelfth century. See Schenkl 1916; J. Souilhé 1948, I lxxii–lxxxiv; and Long 2002, 42, who concluded that the essays originally did not have titles.

Discourses that commence after the letter to Gellius are, in fact, prefixed by titles that are either detailed or consist of short phrases alluding to their content. Were later readers responsible for the titles?[30] Or could these titles have been introduced by Arrian when he went through his notes? The essays of Epictetus do not usually follow a single theme but meander here and there. So, for example, it is curious that the title of *Diss.* 4.4 is "To those who are eager to live in tranquility." This theme is introduced by the opening sentence of the essay, but other themes follow, such as the futility of excessive reading and writing per se, the fact that we are similar to the majority (*oi polloi*), and the need to follow the will of God. Likewise, *Diss.* 2.19 is a very rich essay, but its title alludes to only part of it. It is possible that later readers decided to provide guidance to the notes by giving them titles. These "editors" were not as familiar with Epictetus's words as Arrian was. When assigning titles to the sections they were not particularly accurate, but instead chose the obvious.

Let us now recapitulate the reasons why I argue that Arrian took down the *ipsissima verba* of his teacher as they were delivered in the Koine language and without altering them significantly, but probably omitting some parts. I have shown that Arrian neither used stenography personally to record Epictetus's voice nor relied on stenographers present in the class to do so because there was no need of that. No weight should be attributed to the fact that the historical works that he wrote later in life were in the Attic language and showed a style very different from that of the *Discourses*. Actually, these are compelling reasons why the proposition that Arrian composed them on his own as a literary work has to be repudiated. If he had done that, he would have adopted the Attic language and a different style. There are no reasons to suppose that Arrian composed the work entirely, as Xenophon had done with Socrates. A comparison with the extant work of Musonius emphasizes the fundamental difference with the *Discourses*, which are lively, spontaneous, and not well ordered. Further, there is nothing to indicate that it was Epictetus himself who wrote them. The possible objection that Arrian would have found it impossible to keep up with the pace of the lectures can be countered by supposing that Epictetus did not speak very quickly, but often stopped to address and question his students. Arrian omitted unnecessary details and could use

---

30. Schenkl 1916, lx5 identifies with some contempt a *homuncio* writing with greenish ink.

abbreviations in jotting down his notes. Moreover, a new examination of the letter to Gellius and a comparison with similar messages by other writers who denounced the leaking of their work confirms the letter's value as evidence that Arrian wrote notes that then leaked to the public.

In evaluating the question of whether Arrian as a young student jotted down notes while he was present at Epictetus's lectures, as the letter to Gellius attests, we have made notable progress. Jackson Hershbell wrote in 1989, "The controversy about Arrian's reliability as the source for Epictetus may never be settled (except by scholarly fiat) since the evidence is not conclusive."[31] I hope to have shown, however, that many important factors do point in that direction. Arrian noted down the voice of his master, whom he revered. In what follows, we will have to assess whether the *Discourses* reveal the note-taking in some detail and how the personal tastes of Arrian affected the narration. It will be significant to try to ascertain in which ways Arrian proceeded and whether he recorded Epictetus's full *parrhesia* and reported the various lectures in their entirety, including students' questions and reactions to them.

Epictetus's School: Learning Philosophy in Epirus

The text of Epictetus consists of notes taken down as he was teaching. The *Discourses* are similar in this respect to the assemblages of notes written in class that I will examine in part III. But one might ask why this chapter on Epictetus is so much more extensive and far-reaching. Is this detailed treatment and the heightened attention devoted to Epictetus disproportionate? In my opinion, the thorough examination of this text is fully justified by its nature and importance. In comparison, the lectures of Philodemus, Didymus, and Olympiodorus are not very long and require less attention. Their value rests eminently on the different ways they put in relief pedagogic methods of teaching philosophy that need to be investigated. Not only does the text of Epictetus clarify those issues but its richness and dramatic quality also validate a complex account. Nowadays the Stoics are attracting more public attention than before, but usually it is Seneca and Marcus Aurelius who are quoted and analyzed.[32] In comparison Epictetus is not as widely known, and

---

31. Hershbell 1989.
32. See, e.g., Holiday 2014; Holiday and Hanselman 2017.

the aspects of his character and teaching that I explore have been largely ignored.[33]

Did Epictetus teach in "the wrestling schools and cloistered walks," as Dio Chrysostom imagined philosophical instruction taking place, or perhaps in the countryside in total symbiosis with his pupils, as Musonius recommended?[34] Almost no information is available as to where Epictetus held his classes in Nicopolis, which lay on the main route between Rome and Athens.[35] In 2.21.19 he mentions a covered walk close to the school where students would stroll, discussing what they had learned.[36] Philosophers were often presented as strolling under porticoes. Dicaearchus contrasts their nonchalant stroll with more practical ones.[37] Epictetus very occasionally appears to advertise for the school, as when he shows visitors the advantages of a philosophical training, which is in sharp contrast with advertisement in rhetorical schools.[38] And yet, while a location in Epirus forced young men to travel from afar, its relative isolation made the place more conducive to concentration and intense philosophical studies. Epictetus, in fact, often mentioned the dangerous distractions in other localities. In an essay on social relations, which he argues must be entered with caution because of the human tendency to emulate others to one's own detriment, Epictetus says, "That is why philosophers recommend that we should even leave our native land, since old habits pull us back and do not allow us to take a new course."[39] It seems that he was not referring to his students alone but included himself among those in search of a new beginning. But why did Epictetus choose Nicopolis as the seat of his school? In Hierapolis and in Phrygia in general philosophy was strong enough that he could have remained there. He must have had more precise reasons not to teach in his native Hierapolis. He may have known people who had inspired him or invited him to come to Nicopolis. In one of his essays he represents the governor of Epirus coming to consult him, displeased that a certain comic actor he supported had

---

33. But see now A. A. Long's translation of selections in Epictetus 2018.
34. *Or.* 13.31, in the manner of Socrates; Musonius 11 Hense/Lutz, avoiding those philosophers, "spoiled and effeminate men." Cf. Hense 1905; Dio *Or.* 7.
35. On Epirus, see Dominguez 2018.
36. It is suggestive to compare the long walk that passed alongside the Kom el-Dikka classrooms of the fifth and sixth centuries.
37. Plutarch, *Mor. Old Men in Public Affairs* 796.
38. Libanius mentions very frequently his school and his need to have better enrollment; cf. Cribiore 2007a.
39. *Diss.* 3.16.11.

been booed by other people.⁴⁰ Apparently, when the citizens saw the governor's open display of partiality, they took the other side. The situation has comic overtones. The philosopher gave the novel "tyrant" a lesson in democracy that he probably did not appreciate.

Evidence for the accommodations of other educators suggests that Epictetus may have taught in his residence or in rooms that he rented for the purpose.⁴¹ His students likely leased rooms close to the school, as their counterparts did in Egypt.⁴² A letter of Seneca seems to suggest an interesting possibility.⁴³ In letter 6 Seneca contrasts students who learned in the classroom with others, as he said, who learned directly from their teacher by living together with him. Since Epictetus mentions certain particularly outstanding young men living under the same roof with him, it seems possible that he shared his accommodations with the most promising of his students.⁴⁴ Because his class probably had fewer students than that of Libanius, who offered a more popular discipline, it is less likely that Epictetus used an existing building devoted to this purpose.⁴⁵ Did his classroom resemble the configuration of the much later Kom el-Dikka rooms in Alexandria that we will encounter in part III? There students sat in a semicircle around a teacher who expounded on philosophy and stood or sat in the middle. This does not seem to be the case. In 2.13.26 Epictetus disdainfully dismisses a student by telling him to go and sit in his corner (*gonia*). In 2.21.19 the same student is described as sitting at his side. Clearly Arrian was not interested in these specifics.

It is unknown how large the student body was; some pupils seem to have stayed with him for a number of years, while others were dissatisfied and frustrated, and longed to return home. Also present were visitors of varied age and status who would remain in Nicopolis for a day or a relatively short time.⁴⁶ Most of the visitors appear to have come from Rome, which is often mentioned in discussions of imperial careers. The

---

40. "To someone who became a little too excited in the theater" (*Diss.* 3.4).
41. Libanius, *Or.*1. 15; he taught fifteen students at home. Cf. Cribiore 2007b. It is unlikely that Epictetus taught outside where passers-by could hear him as Long (2002, 43) suggests, because such a setting was appropriate only for elementary instruction.
42. Cribiore 2001b, 115–18.
43. Seneca, *Ep.*6.5–6.
44. In compiling his notes, Arrian disregarded information of this sort.
45. In his best days, when he was the "sophist of the city," Libanius had eighty students so that he occupied Antioch's town hall. There were other sophists in the city who occupied less desirable locations.
46. Brunt 1977, 20–21.

ages of the students must have ranged between fifteen and twenty-five, depending on whether they had previously attended a school of rhetoric or only the classes of a grammarian.[47] They came from prominent families and not from the middle class, as has mistakenly been supposed.[48] Two passages in the *Discourses* concern students who are rather young. In 1.26.13 Epictetus interrupts an inexperienced young man who is butchering a passage. The youth was having difficulty reading the hypothetical arguments, a task that an older student had assigned to him.[49] The philosopher rebukes the older student for laughing at the struggles of the other, saying that he had failed to prepare his classmate; yet another passage is permeated with the wistfulness of a young student yearning for home.[50] As Epictetus scornfully puts it, the young man is grieving for "a little gymnasium, a little colonnade, a group of youngsters, and that way of spending time." The student had been confronting demanding studies, while the memories of what he had left behind were still vivid. In general Epictetus did not have any sympathy for people who complained or felt dejected, and this extended to his students. To someone who apparently asked him for advice, he says that God favors people who participate in the "dance" and revel, and not those who are grumpy and dour, for the latter do not appreciate what they have, but instead whine and curse their fate.[51]

The *Discourses* sometimes allude to a number of students.[52] The philosopher derided rivalries for preeminence that arose, such as a case in which two students each claimed superiority over the other: one's father was a consul, while the other was of the rank of tribune.[53] Epictetus humorously (and acridly) compares them to racehorses who boasted about their special food and neckpieces, an appropriate comparison

---

47. Perhaps some students were even younger when they received the first notions of philosophy. John Sellars (2021, 7) reports passages from the biography of Marcus Aurelius in the *Historia Augusta* (4.1.1 and 4.2.6). Marcus supposedly had started to study philosophy at the age of twelve. On the ages of students of rhetoric, see Cribiore 2007a, 31–32, 154, 181.

48. Colardeau (1903, 92) calls them *bourgeois* who were dissatisfied that their sons did not take lucrative professions. But see Reydams-Schils 2010, 561; "the elite among the elite" attended a school of philosophy.

49. We have no knowledge otherwise of an assistant teacher in the school, but the practice of using more advanced students to teach is well known. Perhaps the younger student had difficulty reading also because he had not encountered the text before; see Gellius 13.31.

50. See Dobbin 1998, 213; *Diss.* 2.16.29.

51. *Diss.* 4.1.108–109.

52. *Diss.* 1.26.13; Dobbin 1998, 213.

53. *Diss.* 3.14.11–13.

because young students were sometimes called *poloi* (colts) in educational sources.⁵⁴ Maximus of Tyre in 14.11–17 presents the philosopher as "the man who elevates the souls of the young and guides their ambitions. He is like a horse trainer who maintains a balance."

Often, however, the scenario is less clearly defined, and the philosopher appears to have conflictual interactions with individual students. Epictetus admonishes and restrains. The students are mostly silent and stay in the background. Occasionally families or other figures make fleeting appearances. One vignette recalls Philodemus, *Peri parresias* 60: "Men who are charlatans divert many, seizing them after some stress and enchanting them with their subtle kindnesses." Philodemus refers to people from outside the school who would exploit some students' malaise in order to lure them away. Epictetus describes a similar man, real or imaginary, coming to the school to deride the profession of philosophy and challenging Epictetus's assertion that the moral good is a mandatory choice. This man is characterized as a bon vivant; he is old and wears many gold rings to signal wealth and worldly experience.⁵⁵ He shakes his head and proclaims that the whole thing is nonsense. Though *some* philosophy might be all right, one should be sure to "keep one's head." Was this man real or imaginary? The scene attracted the attention of Arrian, who put it down in his notes.

Home

Young men came from their homes with solemn demeanors and the desire to impress their teacher with their learning.⁵⁶ Epictetus was far from being captivated. At home his students would have fought with slaves, perturbed their households, and disturbed their neighbors, but now they wanted to pass themselves off as philosophers (2.21.11). This realistic depiction of youthful misbehavior and futile hopes is not dissimilar from what the papyri reveal at earlier stages of education.⁵⁷ These students' desire to demonstrate the agility of their minds may have partly derived from the fact that now they feared new obstacles and had to show their fathers at home that they had made a good choice.

---

54. See, e.g., Libanius, *Ep.* 285.1.
55. *Diss.* 1.22.18. The old man has lost his idealism and appeals to the bitter lesson of experience.
56. Cf. the beginning of this Part.
57. See *P.Oxy.* XVIII 2190; Cribiore 2001b, 121–23.

Plato in the *Gorgias* had ironically approved of young men learning philosophy.[58] "Philosophy was a pretty and charming thing" that fit them and made them people of liberal mind. Those who did not follow it were ungenerous and illiberal. And yet whereas learning a bit of this discipline at a young age was appropriate, older men had to avoid it, because they would never engage with the affairs of the city and pass on to greater things. It is not surprising, therefore, that some fathers appear to have been hostile to philosophy on the grounds that it taught unpractical notions.

In a letter to Lucilius about vegetarianism, Seneca reveals that his father hated (*oderat*) philosophy.[59] We know from Gellius (2.7) that a favorite topic of philosophers was children's obedience. This was a subject on which many expressed their thoughts and left copious quotations. Musonius Rufus also expanded on this topic.[60] When prevented by his father from studying philosophy, a student could disobey on several rational grounds. If the imposition was not right, he had no obligation to respect it. If the father did not know much about philosophy, he was obliged to instruct him. The son could show how much better he would become with the aid of that discipline. If the father remained unpersuaded, the young man said that he would obey the will of the common father of all, Zeus, who guided men to justice and honesty, a goal that could be achieved through the study of philosophy. At the end of the piece, Musonius, appearing to have exhausted his rational resources, gives up. Taking refuge in worn-out arguments, he advises the student not to irritate his father by wearing a worn philosopher's cloak or growing long hair.[61]

Epictetus's rendering of the same situation is much livelier than that of either Gellius or Musonius. Instead of a frigid and rational account, here we have an imaginary dialogue between a youth and his absent father, rendered in Epictetus's voice.[62] As he begs to learn philosophy and be rid of his ignorance, the son's words are a point-by-point response to the objections of his father. Undoubtedly Epictetus took advantage of

---

58. See the whole passage in *Gorgias* 484b–485e.
59. Seneca, *Ep.*108.22. See, however, the commentary of Summers (1910: 338) on the fact that the older Seneca appreciated philosophy for himself.
60. Lutz 1947, 101–7; 16 Hense/Lutz.
61. On long hair and beards appropriate for philosophers, see Epictetus, *Disc.* 1.2.29, 3.22.9–11; 4.11.28. Cf. Lucian, *Icar.* 5. However, in Aristophanes, *Clouds* 14 the long hair of Pheidippides is considered a sign of luxury and sophistication.
62. *Diss.*1.26.5–7; Dobbin 1998, 22.

rhetoric and his knowledge of *ethopoiia*.⁶³ The angry father claims that philosophy should not be taught as a specific discipline because life itself could instill the same notions. The frustrated young man retorts that in that case his father himself should teach him, but if he were not capable of doing so, he should allow the son to receive lessons from an expert teacher. It is true that these passages are inspired by tradition, as when in the fourth century Eunapius of Sardis reported similar difficulties that the young philosopher Aedesius had with his father.⁶⁴ He was expelled from his house, but when he told his father that philosophy taught him to love him, he was recalled. In reality, however, some fathers retorted that their sons learned futile and unpractical notions. By contrast, rhetorical studies had always aroused parental enthusiasm because they were believed to open the way to concrete, remunerative careers and prestigious positions.⁶⁵

The role of philosophers in the human world was not well defined. Pierre Hadot commented on its *atopia*, as related to Socrates.⁶⁶ Socrates was *atopos* because he did not accept life as people of his time conceived it. Lucian had battled with unworthy philosophers whom he considered charlatans, but even when philosophers were competent, they stood somewhat outside of common expectations. Epictetus was aware of this obstacle. Two further passages evoke related concepts. In one he warns a young man that in order to be able to make serious decisions he would need to join the school, even though "a student (of philosophy) is a creature that everyone mocks."⁶⁷ And in a different essay he cautions another about the common saying that "nobody derives any advantage from school." In his opinion, the problem was that young men would return home with the same judgments they had brought in, without having corrected them or replaced them with others.⁶⁸

Students would remain in touch with their families at least emotionally, but conflicts and unfulfilled expectations emerge from the *Discourses*. A section on Providence mentions the composure one should

---

63. A speech in character, one of the basic *progymnasmata*. On *ethopoiia* see Amato and Schamp 2005; Peirano 2012.
64. Eunapius, *VS* 461; the episode is idealized.
65. See Philostratus, *VS* 521; later Libanius constantly applauded parents' decisions that would allow their sons to become part of the administration. Cf. Van Hoof 2013. See Cribiore 2007a, 205–13. Cf., e.g., his letter 886 (Cribiore 2007a, no. 80).
66. See P. Hadot 1990, 492–93. The best example of the *atopos* philosopher was Socrates.
67. *Diss.* 1.11.39. The whole section 1.11 is titled "On Family Affections."
68. *Diss.* 2.21.15.

attain when confronting issues of prosperity and poverty.[69] This frequently expressed message of Epictetus elicited a dry response from one young man: "My father doesn't give me anything." In another *ethopoiia*, Epictetus gives voice to a young man who becomes distracted by disturbing thoughts during a lecture.[70] This student was troubled because he anticipated that his father and brother at home expected that "he would know everything" on his return.[71] His initial goodwill and enthusiasm for the school had been dampened by the hard work requested of him. His anxiety over an apparently imminent encounter with his relatives and his discontent with himself unleash a general gloominess in the student: he also complains that he received no supplies from home, the baths in Nicopolis were rotten, and his lodgings and the school itself were awful. His bitter voice is filtered through that of his teacher, but protests of this kind do not seem unusual when compared to the reality of ancient schooling. When young men studied away from home, supplies would be sent back and forth, but some fathers may have shown a lack of interest in their sons' needs.[72]

Diseases might strike young men away from home, and Libanius mentions that illnesses were not uncommon among his students. They would arrive in Antioch in the company of pedagogues, who were supposed to take care of them and would remain in touch with their families. When a student fell ill, his pedagogue supposedly would tend to him better than a mother and would be inconsolable if the worst happened.[73] No mention is made of pedagogues in Epictetus's school, and so perhaps the advanced ages of the students made them unnecessary.[74] In one essay a young man manifests his desire to go back home

---

69. *Diss.* 3.17. Cf. below for the harsh reaction of Epictetus. On the Stoics and providence, see Collette 2021.

70. See the many ways in which young men could disturb lectures in Plutarch, *On Listening to Lectures* by not paying attention and thinking of personal issues.

71. *Diss.* 2.21.12–14.

72. Cf. the mention of supplies for students from fathers that appears in some letters on papyrus (Cribiore 2001b, 115–18). A letter of Libanius reveals the pain of one of his students who did not receive any money from home and declared that his father had forgotten him. See Cribiore 2007a, 422; Norman 1992, 1, 376–77.

73. Cribiore 2001b, 119–20; Cribiore 2007a, 118. Of course, some rhetoric is involved. Two inscriptions from Claudiopolis in Asia Minor show that dying in a foreign land was not just a topos. The student in question, who had arrived in that city to study rhetoric, died "in alien bosoms stretching out his hands to his mother." See *SEG* 34.1259 from the first century CE.

74. But in *Diss.* 3.22.17 the Cynic philosopher is called the universal pedagogue. On edition, translation, and commentary of this discourse, see Billerbeck 1978.

because he is sick.⁷⁵ The gravity and discomfort of his disease are unknown, but Epictetus certainly treats it with nonchalance, as an excuse for the student to go back to his former life. After quickly mentioning that by doing so the student would have studied in vain, Epictetus debunks his reasons for leaving. He predicts that on returning home, the young man would stroll in the marketplace, take care of his old father and brother, increase his fortune, and occupy an office. According to Epictetus, disease and death should find one occupied in ethical concerns, "with no passions, constraints, and limitations, and free" (*apathes, akolutos, ananagkastos,* and *eleutheros*). A moving prayer follows, addressed to God, in which the philosopher describes himself as suffering disease, poverty, and a modest lifestyle without losing his smile. He expects to encounter death too, but he prays, "may death grab me as I am thinking, writing, and reading." The touching prayer is so sincere that the irony and mockery that follow seem out of place. In another of his solo dialogues, Epictetus depicts the student complaining that he needs his mother to support his neck, and that he wants to sleep in the "pretty little bed" he has at home.⁷⁶ The ironic words are of course the philosopher's and belong to those expressions that Arrian, the good student, does not fail to record.

The Responsibilities of Teaching

The *Discourses* show that lethargic young men abounded in the school, at least in Epictetus's opinion. Such students may have lost their initial enthusiasm and begun to react apathetically to instruction in philosophy.⁷⁷ We shall see that Epictetus confronted their reactions forcefully but occasionally asked himself who was ultimately responsible. "I am your teacher," he told one student who did not complete his work, "and you are educated by me and my purpose is to make you strong."⁷⁸ He declared that he had not only the will to teach but also the right kind of preparation. He was like an able craftsman with all his material ready and, unlike many other things in life, teaching and learning were within

---

75. *Diss.* 3.5; see also 3.10.11–13. Cf. also *Diss.* 3.22.62 where another young man asks the hypothetical question if, in case he would fall ill, he would be able to go to a friend and stay with him. See in 3.22.73-74 the mention of various diseases and even surgery.
76. *Diss.* 3.5.12–13. On mothers and nurses left at home, see the section on emotions.
77. Epictetus calls them "stones." See the section about emotions.
78. *Diss.* 2.19.29-34. Epictetus's unusually humble reaction suggests that he may have been very interested in this young man.

his control. "So why don't you finish the work? Tell me the reason, for it lies either in me or in you or in the nature of the thing." He does not always show the same humility (1.5.1–5). On the contrary.

Young men would leave their countries and their parents not just to hear philosophical commentaries but also to assimilate and practice certain principles, thereby becoming able to return home stronger, without passions, and ready to render service.[79] And yet, on leaving Nicopolis some of his students were less than humble and considered becoming teachers of philosophy right away and opening their own schools.[80] The information from the *Discourses* is intriguing (though, of course, filtered through Arrian) because little is known about the nonchalance with which the profession was approached.[81] Fascinated by philosophy (*psychagogein*), these young men called themselves philosophers and were identified as such by others. Epictetus's response was that youth was an obstacle to teaching; it was indispensable to be of the right age, as well as to adhere to a proper way of life, and to have God as a guide.[82] Having received the bare principles, these students intended "to vomit them back" without digesting them, unaware that at this point they "could not be eaten again."[83] With these extreme words he jeered at some of his students who had not truly assimilated philosophy. Otherwise, Epictetus proposed with his usual exasperation, it was better to play dice (*kydeuein*) and engage in customary behaviors without worthy ambitions.

One wonders how truly objective his judgment was. The example of Libanius shows that teachers would have liked to extend their pupils' attendance forever. The matter was serious enough that Epictetus even suggested that wisdom itself was not sufficient to shape would-be philosophers. Teachers of philosophy, whose calling came from God,

---

79. *Diss.* 3.21.8–10.
80. *Diss.* 3.21.1–24.
81. Libanius gives mixed messages (Cribiore 2007a, 200–201). The students he deemed ready to occupy his place had attended the school for many years. He also presented cases of young men who attended only two years but were very successful as lawyers. The sophist's most meaningful letter regarding competence in officials is F366. Symmachus's letter V. 74 plays on competence as a meaningful requirement. However, the question of competence in antiquity needs to be researched. On competence of officials, see Cribiore 2007a, 198–99, and of sophists, 202–5. Passages that judge qualification for a profession based on skills or attitude are almost nonexistent. Competence was judged according to personal and social criteria.
82. On God who was in charge of all of us, see 1.14.
83. Epictetus in his feeling of disgust may have been referring to dogs. On the theme of vomiting notions of previous education, see below the section on books.

had to be endowed with special qualities and a true vocation.[84] Among the prerequisites, the mention of the necessary qualification of "a certain kind of body" (*soma poion*) is surprising.[85] By this, Epictetus was probably alluding to the fact that a young teacher would not yet be endowed with the physical dignity that he thought mandatory for the profession. Whiteness in hair and beard were probably a sine qua non. The statue of old Chrysippus showed these characteristics and had an inspired look.[86] All of the philosophers whose portraits were studied by Paul Zanker, beginning from the third century BCE onward, are distinguished by these features.[87] The later shield portraits from Aphrodisias are also suitable *comparanda*, especially because they show a philosopher and a pupil. Two bearded portraits have been identified as Socrates and a mature philosopher, with Socrates's facial hair looking somewhat unkempt. Smith defined the tondo of the unidentified philosopher as that of "an inspired, visionary philosopher, a man of the spirit, an impassioned thinker of divine thoughts."[88] Another portrait represents a pupil of roughly the same age as those taught by Epictetus, with full cheeks, cropped hair, and a smooth chin. The contrast with the tondo of the philosopher is remarkable. Aside from hair and beard, Epictetus may have had other physical features in mind for his perfect philosopher. In a portrait of the Cynic, he mentions that this philosopher needed to show his fitness and competence not only in his thoughts but also with his bodily characteristics.[89] His message would not spread with equal force if he were sickly looking, pale, and thin. Through his physique he had to show that a simple life outside would benefit body and soul.

Authority and Emotions in Class

Stoics define emotions in two steps: a belief generates a motive, which then causes an emotional reaction. Though some scholars have mentioned Epictetus's position on emotions and his pedagogy, no one has examined the passages of the *Discourses* that show this. Thus in

---

84. See also *Diss.* 3.22: exercising the profession badly will arouse God's rage.
85. *Diss.* 3.21.18.
86. Zanker 1995, 98–102. For Chrysippus, see the section on emotions.
87. The beards could be long or closely shorn. See the portrait of a second-century BCE Stoic philosopher in Zanker 1995, 184. Cf. above Epictetus on beards.
88. Smith 1990.
89. *Diss.* 3.22.86–89.

this section I confront the harsh "therapy" to which he subjected his students.[90] Once more Arrian registered everything in his notes, even those aspects of Epictetus's teaching that are not very alluring to our mind. The more relevant question, of course, is how they might have looked to someone of his own time. In what follows I concentrate on instances in which Epictetus displays his authority over his students by exercising harsh restraint and strict control over them.[91] I will evaluate specific passages trying to understand whether Epictetus was an exception among Stoic educators. This is of course difficult to ascertain given the fact that there are only fragments surviving to inform us about the attitudes of other Stoics, though, for example, a passage of Chrysippus is illuminating.[92] Where was Epictetus's unimpassioned Stoic composure in these circumstances? And most importantly, did these outbursts of seeming anger affect him personally?

In antiquity a system of power relations in education was always defined by some form of violence. In classical Greece and in the Roman period, physical punishment was applied, sometimes brutally, to correct academic and behavioral infractions and transgressions; it was an expected part of teacher-student relationships.[93] The violence of punishment was in inverse proportion to students' ages. Teachers inflicted on young students the same harsh degree of corporal punishment that was administered by parents in the home. The occasional voices that condemned such methods remained in the realm of theory.[94] At higher levels of schooling, students were apparently treated more mildly because of their age, the discipline in order and self-control in which they had been trained, their invariably upper-class status, and occasionally the close relationship existing between families and educators.[95] At that point, moreover, families showed less interest in problems of comportment and concentrated on academic results.[96] Plutarch claimed that at higher levels of learning, teachers did not rule over students.[97] In his

---

90. On emotions in philosophers of the imperial period, see Trapp 2007, 63-97.
91. Gill (2022, 214-19) divides emotions in two groups: defective emotions (bad, sometimes called passions) and good emotions.
92. See Long 1999, 582; Gal. *PHP* IV.2. 1018.
93. Cribiore 2001b, 65-73.
94. Ps. Plutarch, *De liberis educandis* 8f; Quintilian 1.3.14 argued that the student who was treated harshly developed the fear typical of a slave.
95. Roskam 2004.
96. Cribiore 2007a, 128.
97. Plutarch is referring to the rhetorical and philosophical levels. See Plutarch, *De adulatore et amico* 73e-74a and 74d-e. On punishment and disregard for students' feelings, see

opinion, they were supposed to admonish, praise, and avoid harshness and sharp refutations.[98] They had to refrain from displays of temper and avoid inflicting pain. Teachers were like surgeons who treated the healing body part with soothing lotions.

Epictetus declared that "the school of a philosopher is a hospital," and, like Seneca, he used medical imagery related to healing.[99] He argued that students should suffer as they acquired an education because learning and struggling with the message go together. Confronting "sick" young men in need of therapy, the philosopher was not supposed to sit by their bedside reciting clever phrases or calmly using reason but should instead correct and heal them promptly. A relationship of pedagogic communication implied the transmission and receipt of a message of authority that students had to swallow, apparently with limited reactions.[100] We do not know the particularities of the space Epictetus occupied, including whether he used the imposing teaching chair traditional in higher stages of education.[101] Even if he did not, the symbolic conditions of his teaching and his oratorical manners and long monologues rendered him an authoritative figure.

On occasion, Epictetus presented himself in a humble way, as when he called himself a "layman" (*idiotes*) in greeting an Epicurean philosopher, and in general he was reticent to use the term "philosopher" for himself.[102] This is evident in the previously examined passage in which he asked whether he was personally responsible for a student's failure and called himself simply a "teacher/trainer" (*paideutes*).[103] His reticence to use the term "philosopher" was probably related to Socrates's ironic denial of knowledge and to the modesty of demeanor that he recommended to his pupils. In antiquity and even today, there was a close relationship between an educator and a learner, in which the former became a paternal figure, as sometimes appears to be the case with

---

Diogenes Laertius 6.21 where Antisthenes strikes a student who was following him in the hope to become his student.

98. In *Listening to Lectures* 46c–d he showed students laughing at and disregarding the criticism.
99. *Diss.* 3.23.30. See Nussbaum 1954. Cf. chapter 8 about Philodemus.
100. Bourdieu and Passeron 1990, 108–14.
101. See Libanius *Or.* 5 and the exercise called *chria* and also Cribiore 2007b.
102. *Diss.* 3.7.1; cf. Long 2002, 121–25. Reydams-Schils (2010, 571n7) remarks on the modesty of Musonius Rufus who in counseling a youth does not present himself as a figure of authority (16 Hense/Lutz).
103. *Diss.* 2.19.29.

Epictetus.¹⁰⁴ However, it is unquestionable that in his dealings with many of them, he projected an image of authority.¹⁰⁵

Epictetus seems to have resembled the sophist Maximus of Tyre in his treatment of students. These two teachers may not have approved of corporal punishment, but they were firm in checking young men's negative traits and promoting their positive qualities. As a philosopher/pedagogue, Maximus had to administer "pains and pleasures," that is, administer some form of coercion but also grant them some rewards.¹⁰⁶ He had to guide their ambition and help them achieve self-control. Yet an imposition of some degree of force did continue to characterize pedagogic relations at upper levels of learning.

The "therapy" Epictetus offered his students was challenging.¹⁰⁷ His message of authority was framed in intimidating language. His term of address "slave" constantly underscored his superiority.¹⁰⁸ He remarked that it was impossible to "hook" students who were "soft": they were like cheese and could not be turned toward philosophy.¹⁰⁹ At times, however, he calls these young men *malakoi* (weak) and "stones," a pedagogic term of denigration later used by Libanius that had a ring of finality.¹¹⁰ He reported that his teacher Musonius had made a distinction between dull students and those who were naturally well endowed. "If one threw a stone up in the air it would fall to the ground because of its nature."¹¹¹ Students such as these could not fly and were hopeless. "Petrification" was not only an inborn condition but could also affect an advanced student who would harden to stone when entrapped in an argument. There were two kinds of petrification, Epictetus said: one affected the intellect that had lost its flexibility, and the other made a student lose his sense of shame when he acquired "a belligerent stance" and refused to surrender to the truth.¹¹²

---

104. However, Epictetus did not regard his students as sons.
105. On loss of teachers' authority nowadays, cf. Kincheloe et al. 2013.
106. 14.11.12; Koniaris 1983, 225.
107. Gill 2000, 601. Lucian in *Demon.* 55 represents him with a reproaching attitude.
108. See *Diss.* 2.16.41-42: "Lift up your neck at last like a man escaped from slavery." It probably had some relation to his past status of slave. On moral slavery and freedom, cf. *Diss.* 4.1. Cf. Musonius on some of the terms applied to students.
109. Cf. Musonius fr. 46. See also Diogenes Laertius 6.36: a teacher asks a student to hold a fish or a cheese in order to mortify him.
110. Libanius *Or.* 4.18; Cribiore 2007a, 133-34. See also in Lucian, *Vit. Auct.* 25, the disquisition about a man turned to stone and ending up an animal.
111. See *Diss.* 3.6.9-10.
112. *Diss.* 1.5. See Dobbin 1998, 99-100.

Pedagogic rebukes might have a different tenor and need to be differentiated. Epictetus's indictment of students who liked gladiatorial combats and other spectacles in the gymnasium, along with his stern condemnation of their frequent attendance at them, is part of a traditional representation of youthful pleasures that stretches from Aristophanes to Libanius.[113] Accusations of laziness also had a conventional place in schooling.[114] *Discourses* 1.7 argues that logic needs to be studied and to have a place in the training of the good man. It has relevance and moral significance in everyday life. Failure to train in logic would have crucial repercussions on moral values and could not be regarded lightly. Toward the end of the chapter, the theoretical and important discussion descends to the level of students who apparently were not passionate about the subject. Confronting their laziness, Epictetus snaps: "Why are we still indolent, sluggish, and dull? Why do we seek excuses not to toil nor to spend sleepless nights working on our own reason?" This reproach appears bitter only at its beginning; its tone changes perceptibly when Epictetus injects a note of caustic humor in the dialogue. The student admits he has made a mistake but tries to minimize its import with a common saying: "I did not kill my father." Epictetus promptly retorts, "No, slave, for there was no father for you to kill."[115] Then softening his tone considerably, he returns to his years of training under Musonius Rufus, who had reproached him for a similar mistake in logic. Here, an acrimonious remark becomes a rare point of closeness between the educator and the educated.

However, when the philosopher's voice makes students painfully confront their imperfect nature, his "therapy" is bitter and difficult to digest (especially for us). The entire section 24 in book 2 is titled: *To One of Those Whom He Did Not Consider Worthy*.[116] The man in question appears to have consulted Epictetus many times. The philosopher derisively sets various mythological Homeric figures against his claim of being wealthy, handsome, strong, and of noble ancestry before losing

---

113. *Diss.* 3.16.4 and 14, where Epictetus remarks on the continuous going from the school to those places. Cf. Aristophanes, *Clouds* 27; cf. Libanius, *Or.* 3.12. See also Libanius, *Declamation* 33.15, where a father's reproach appears commonplace.

114. *Diss.* 1.7.30–33.

115. *Diss.* 1.7.31–32. The implication is that this was a serious mistake that could have compromised his understanding of logic. Killing one's father was traditionally considered a monstrous crime on the same plane as burning the Capitol, which is mentioned later. See Dobbin 1998, 113–18. Cf. Musonius fr. 44.

116. *Diss.* 2.24.24–29.

his patience. "This is all I have to say to you, and even this without wishing you well, because you did not excite me."[117] Horse trainers, by analogy, felt excited and stimulated when they encountered thoroughbred horses. This student was vain, handsome, well dressed, arrogant, and quite ordinary. A philosopher had to feel stimulated in order to teach with satisfaction.

The contexts of conversations in the *Discourses* are not always evident, but in 3.16 it appears that a student has been trying to leave the school. Epictetus sternly discourages him, saying that he is too weak to confront outside forces. People in society with insane desires and propensities have firm convictions that strengthen their stances and make them invincible, while the student proclaims honorable opinions and utters theoretical exhortations that do not go any further than his lips. Exposed to regular individuals (*idiotes*), he would encounter extreme situations and see what he had learned in school melt like wax. Since his opinions are faint, washed out, and soft like wax, it is mandatory for him to keep away from the sun and from outside contacts.[118] Epictetus displays no sympathy for the young man's efforts. He describes him cruelly as "babbling on" about "wretched virtue," saying that his words have no effect because they are "flabby and dead" (*atona kai nekra*). Those who could hear him "were disgusted"—these were abrasive and offensive words.

Chapter 1.6 is devoted to the gratitude men should have for Providence and for the concept that God exists and cares for nature and the universe, which was particularly important to Epictetus.[119] Toward the end of the argument he concentrates on the moral and physical faculties (magnanimity, courage, and endurance) that can help one withstand difficult predicaments. One should be able to endure anything without groaning over challenging events. This essay on the way in which God provides for the universe is serious and momentous.[120] The Stoics postulated the existence of a creator God, from whom progress in the world derived and who imposed a virtuous behavior on men. A single god caused the progress of the world and imposed the obligation to

---

117. *Diss.* 2.24.28. Oldfather translated the verb as "stimulate." Epictetus means that the student was not interesting and he did not feel inspired by him who failed to light up in him the spark.
118. *Diss.* 3.16.10–11. In 3.23.27, however, a philosopher represents the sun.
119. See the commentary of Dobbin 1998, 101–13. For another section of this essay see previously.
120. See the long comment of Dobbin 1998, 101–13.

act virtuously. The world of nature depended on Zeus, and living in agreement meant to agree with Zeus's thoughts.[121] Yet from the thought of a creator God the reader is suddenly plunged among complaining boys. These, of course, were the "slaves." One wonders if this is the actual voice of a specific student, or if Epictetus is simply belittling his class. Probably the latter is true, and the suppositious boy is a symbol for others who are young and unprepared for the discipline. Epictetus impatiently concludes, "It is so much better for you to wipe your nose than to find fault!" This is an exercise in mortification.

In another chapter the single boy is replaced by many *paidia* (children) who have so far studied in vain. Despite their readings and exercises and their being "spirited and vocal" (*gorgoi kai kataglossoi*) in the classroom, these "children" did not even begin to "enter the door of the philosopher."[122] They were incapable of making practical application of what they learned and were like sailors lost at sea. Studying Socrates and Diogenes was useless. Epictetus presents these young men whining like little children who want a cookie, longing for friends, nurses, and their mommies. They are not willing "to be weaned and to partake of more solid food." They fear they have caused sorrow to the women back home. Is Epictetus here menacing distressed students who want to leave Nicopolis? The sharp response of the philosopher appears out of bounds: "Sit rather in the house as girls do and wait for your mommy until she feeds you."[123]

Chapter 1.9 finds the philosopher frustrated as he tries to instill into his audience the concept that attaining freedom from outside forces requires one to be indifferent to externals. Here he addresses boys who do not respond to the instructions, driving him to burst out furiously, "A corpse is your teacher, and corpses are you!" Teaching and learning are dead and have produced cadavers of education. Young men do not live day by day, he complains, but are projected into the future by their concerns. "Whenever you have eaten your fill today, you whine about tomorrow, where your food will come from. Slave, if you get it, you will have it; if you don't, leave: the door stands open! Why do you grieve? What cause is there anymore for tears? Why do you start flattering?"

---

121. See Cooper 2012, 152–53.
122. See *Diss*. 2.16.20 and 34 and the whole chapter. The students become competitive when they think they know something.
123. Centuries before, when threatening a terrified student, the teacher Lampriskos had said, "I will make you more orderly than a girl." Herodas, *Mime* 3.66, a vague threat of castration.

The sharp rebuke brings the student to tears. Crushed and overpowered, the "slave" appears to have become a slavish flatterer in reality.[124]

On a very few occasions, Epictetus seems aware that he might cause offense by berating "feverish desires and inconsistent purposes." He was a mirror that could not lie but had to represent truthful likenesses. He was the doctor who ministered strong, unavoidable remedies for a disease. In one case, a man is able to withstand an accusation of being ignorant in philosophical matters but not the rebuke that he does not know himself. "What harm have I done to you?" Epictetus asks, but the interlocutor is stung by what he perceives to be an insult.[125] A chapter on "Beautifying Oneself" concerns the visit of a rhetor.[126] It is unclear whether this was a one-time encounter, or if the man intended to stay for a while in the school. Everything about this visitor showed extreme personal care: his clothes, a fanciful coiffure, the removal of hair from his body. Epictetus tries to convince him that if he wants to be beautiful, he needs to achieve spiritual beauty and human perfection. He presents himself in philosophical garb, with white hair and a rough coat, and tells him he is not going to treat him "cruelly" (*omos*) since the man has come to him as to a philosopher.[127] Epictetus manifests some concern that he might offend the man by telling him his criticisms right away, and yet he recognizes that sincerity is in order because a visit to a philosopher must bring some profit.[128] These passages appear to address two interlocutors older than the other students, perhaps visitors.

In an otherwise still valuable book, Théodore Colardeau presented a peculiar, idyllic, and romantic vision of the rapport Epictetus had with his students: the philosopher would take them by the hand, avoid discouraging them, and lead them where he wanted with wisdom and gentleness (*un sentiment assez délicat*). According to this scholar, Epictetus showed patience and thus imitated a virtue of Socrates.[129] The examples I have shown, however, tell a different story, even though the

---

124. Epictetus says in *Diss.* 3.23.29, "(Musonius) Rufus used to say: If you have nothing better to do than praise me, I am speaking to no effect."
125. *Diss.* 2.14.20–22.
126. *Diss.* 3.1.
127. *Diss.* 3.1.24. The term shows his awareness that his behavior with his audience might be excessive at times.
128. In spite of showing initial concerns, however, Epictetus regaled the rhetor with plenty of admonitions telling him that he had to be different from a woman and an effeminate homosexual (*kinaidos*).
129. Colardeau 1903/2004, 79.

philosopher's strict teaching mode might not have been the norm and might have been directed only at the more mediocre students.

The harsh therapy Epictetus offered his students is not directly reflected in our limited knowledge of other Stoic teachers; it seems unique in its concrete manifestations at the beginning of the philosophical instruction. Setaioli remarked that the writings of Seneca were instruments of education, but none of those that are extant addresses someone starting on the path of Stoic knowledge. Seneca's addressees were already progressing toward virtue. Through pervasive medical imagery, Seneca shows the obligation to intervene when someone is in need of healing and moral improvement.[130] The therapeutic process at this first stage could not depend entirely on reason but had to adopt disciplinary and aggressive measures.[131] Musonius had aimed at educating the young by Stoic principles, but his message, as we have received it, may have been made more palatable by his pupil Lucius, who presented summaries of his discourses. We know little about the philosopher's direct interactions with the young men under his tutelage. Interestingly, however, Epictetus suggests that in class Rufus was very intuitive about the backgrounds of his students and vividly evoked their own private faults as if he had been informed by another source.[132] As I mentioned earlier, Paul Zanker brought attention to a remarkable earlier portrait of the Stoic Chrysippus in discussion with an interlocutor.[133] Emotions do not seem to affect the philosopher's intellect.

Epictetus, however, displayed an apparent lack of empathy for those of his students who struggled with his message; still, the popular view of his philosophy as advocating complete emotional repression is not correct. The Stoics recognized that feelings of irritation, disappointment, dislike, or hatred can occur, but they are prerational feelings, something similar to *propatheia*, a premonitory reaction as in Plutarch and in some Christian writers.[134] The ideal Stoic, exhibiting a life free from disturbing emotions, sometimes described as "malfunctions of

---

130. Setaioli 2013.
131. *Stoicorum veterorum fragmenta* III 389.
132. *Diss.* 3.23.29.
133. Zanker 1995, 97–102, 134–35. Cf. Sorabji (2000, 8), who thought that the statue portrayed Chrysippus in the act of teaching. The statue probably dates to the period after the philosopher's death and represents him as a frail old man concentrating on his thoughts and absorbed in argumentation and judgment.
134. Plutarch *"Advice about Keeping Well"* e.g. *128 B 7. Propatheia* then is an initial reaction, present in Christian writers such as Didymus the Blind, *Comm. In Psalmos* 35–39, which we will consider in chapter 9.

reason," did not exist.[135] Epictetus, in any case, did not expand on a theory of the emotions as systematically as other Stoics did.[136] Stoicism offered a way to cope with emotions and reach tranquility of mind that distinguished between an emotional outburst at a specific event (of the kind Epictetus might have occasionally suffered) and a continuous feeling of anger (which was alien to him). People may have become accustomed to feeling irritated or upset under certain circumstances, but that feeling was not anger, in the sense of a movement of the soul that convinces them that there are good reasons to be disgruntled and act with anger. As a Stoic thinker, Epictetus could only share in other people's adversities and troubles from afar, without being touched by them personally. His participation was minimal. He could express words of sympathy when confronting others in distress without becoming moved inside and experiencing distress himself. "I cannot be insensitive like a statue," he declares, "but should maintain my relations, both those natural and those acquired."[137] Emotions are actions, and people are as responsible for them as they are for other actions.[138] Negative emotions, such as passions of various kinds, should not involve sudden irrational forces overcoming one. Emotions must be under people's control, and when they arise powerfully, it is because one has judged a situation wrongly.[139]

Was this a traditional pedagogic method, or had Epictetus devised and tested it himself? Of course, there is no direct testimony of earlier Stoic thinkers. As a Stoic educator, Epictetus did not have an attitude of indifference and did not wait passively for his students to improve. The goal (*telos*) of a stay in Nicopolis was to achieve knowledge concerning previous thinkers, and especially the application of principles to practical concerns, a whole way of life. Epictetus wanted to eradicate false ethical beliefs in his students and change the whole person.[140] He would follow a student for a while, but ultimately the young man was supposed to progress by himself, monitoring his own improvements

---

135. On Stoic psychology see Long 1999, esp. 83.
136. Several scholars discussed emotions in the Stoics. Among them, see Nussbaum 2004, 183–99; Gill 2005; Graver 2007.
137. *Diss.* 3.2.4. For a discussion of the philosopher's attitude toward emotions, see Long 2002, 231–58.
138. Graver 2013.
139. In the *Discourses* he also displayed positive emotions such as cheerfulness, enthusiasm, love for families, and a sense of humor.
140. Gill 2000, 607.

as he went through life. At times he would have to contain his expectations; when school was left behind, its principles stayed back too: "No one takes them with him when he reaches home. War then immediately breaks out with slaves and neighbors."[141]

Seneca's distinction between true anger and a preliminary to anger is helpful in attempting to evaluate the meaning of Epictetus's aggressive approach to his students.[142] According to it, anger has two components: an initial refusal to be wronged and a desire to take revenge. Neither is present in Epictetus. What we see here is the preliminary to the emotion, an involuntary impulse caused by judgment that something or a behavior is inappropriate; Seneca calls it "biting," *morsus*.[143] An emotional reaction is caused by the initial judgment, which then causes a supposedly angry outcome.[144] It is also essential to keep two things in mind. First, it is possible that the existence of more concrete attestations of emotional outbursts in philosophers' classes would make Epictetus's way of dealing with students appear more ordinary and less extreme. Second, there is no way of knowing whether the therapeutic approach Epictetus adopted affected him personally, and if so in what measure. Did he really lose his composure? Were his reactions due to the misuse of reason and the failure to interpret situations correctly? Are we witnessing passions and a real desire to hurt and mortify hopeless students? The intensity of his rapport with some students and his rage at failing them might only have been external manifestations of his desire to affect them deeply. In trying to stimulate them, in shaking them to provoke a spark in them that was not there, he was reacting to their conditions in urgent need of healing. Without a prompt and decisive intervention, those students would have been lost to philosophy. The doctor of the soul needed to cut and burn, not to restrict himself to medications and advice.

---

141. See *Diss.* 3.20.18.
142. Cf. Graver 2013, 270–71.
143. *De ira* 2.11.4.
144. Cf. Gill 2022, 211–46, a whole section on Stoics and emotions.

Chapter 6

Epictetus and the World of Culture

A Rhetorical Wizard: Epictetus and the Second Sophistic

Epictetus's negative views of rhetoric and the cultural baggage that the young men attending his school brought with them have always been evident, but his own assimilation of that culture has been less obvious and never properly studied. It is possible that if we were able to disclose to him the rhetorical characteristics of his prose and the ways in which he had absorbed the literary culture that surrounded him, he would still sneer. The spontaneous notes of Arrian, however, reveal what is behind his apparent contempt. Many of Epictetus's students came to his school after learning rhetoric.[1] They had practiced the technique of declamation, attended the speeches of sophists, and participated in the general frenzy at such performances. Their skills in writing and speaking had improved, but they had come to Nicopolis for a different type of education, one focused on content and not form. Defining himself in contrast to the rhetoric of his time was crucial for Epictetus, who wanted to leave an enduring, life-giving impression on his students. In one essay he refers to two different types of teachers, a sophist and a

---

1. As an example of a school of rhetoric in the fourth century, see the school of Libanius in Antioch, in Cribiore 2007a.

philosopher: "A teacher who will teach him [the student] how to live? No, fool, one who will teach him how to speak well. That is what he admires you for. Listen to him, what does he say? 'This person writes with the greatest art, more elegantly than Dio.'"[2]

The comparison was well taken. In this essay Epictetus refers to Dio as a champion of rhetoric with a huge following.[3] He may not have known that, during his exile, Dio claimed that people considered him a philosopher, not a rhetor, and asked him to talk about good, evil, and the duties of man.[4] Or perhaps Epictetus was not interested in this side of the writer.

The rivalry between rhetoric and philosophy goes back at least as far as Plato, who knew rhetoric and took advantage of it but presented it as the manipulative art of persuasion. Education was at the center of this polemic.[5] In the classical period, as in the second century CE, sophists and philosophers each claimed that they knew how to create the best citizen. The art of persuasion was regarded as a skill that could provide pleasure and assure success in society but could not impart real knowledge. By contrast, philosophy allowed its devotees to reach insight, acquire knowledge of reality, and gain inner peace, thereby transforming their lives. In general, many writers of the Roman Empire upheld the superiority of philosophy over rhetoric but continued to cultivate the latter, which appeared to have gained the upper hand in society. We shall see that Epictetus scorned literary form to a point, attributing relative importance to books containing past doctrines. He was adamant in his hatred of rhetoric's flamboyant manifestations, *epideiktikos*. He cited Socrates, who in *Apology* 17c had said that at his age he could not present himself to his audience fashioning discourses like a young man.[6] Epictetus considered rhetoric "an elegant little art of choosing little words,[7] joining them together and reading or reciting them to

---

2. *Diss.* 3.23.17. It is generally recognized that Dio Chrysostom is mentioned here. See below about the same speech. He studied with Musonius Rufus together with other philosophers mentioned by Fronto, *Letters to Verus* 1.1 (Naber 113, *Vat.* 1–8). See Van den Hout 1999, 135, 19. Fronto had an aversion for Epictetus.

3. See 3.23.19.

4. See Dio *Or.* 13.10–12. It is unsure if at the time this essay of Epictetus was written Dio had already started to circulate his idealized interpretation of his exile. See Desideri 1978, 91–97.

5. Cf. Cribiore 2020b.

6. *Diss.* 3.23.25–26.

7. Here as elsewhere diminutives reduce the meaning of a word, adding an accent of contempt.

a public and saying in the middle of the reading 'by God, there are not many people who can understand this.'"[8] Yet, apparently, rhetoric was not all negative. It had one redeeming quality that Epictetus advised his students to imitate: the use of incessant practice to improve performance, that is, hard work.[9] The rhetor was not content merely to work on and memorize his speech, but he went further, continuing to prepare because he aimed at perfection and feared his audience. Through his constant training he became better than others, and young aspiring philosophers could improve their understanding by persistent application. Of course, Epictetus did not approve of the reason for the relentless practice of the success-seeking rhetor and painted a pathetic vignette: "If he is praised, he leaves all puffed up, but if he is laughed to scorn his inflated little conceit sinks down deflated."[10] One of the reasons for his aversion was that sophists solicited an audience and advertised their art. A philosopher did not need to invite listeners.[11] He was not looking for applause or acclamations. Addressing the main interlocutor of this essay, Epictetus says, "Do you need to set up a thousand chairs, to invite auditors, and be dressed in an elegant robe or gown and on a podium describe the death of Achilles? I beg you by the gods, stop dishonoring such famous names and deeds as much as you can." We shall see that Epictetus's attitude toward mythology was complex. Here he objects to its empty overuse by rhetors.

The feverish atmosphere accompanying sophistic performances had started to contaminate the delivery of philosophical discourse.[12] Gellius reports the indignant comments of Musonius, who condemned applause, trite comments, loud shouts, unrestrained praise, and gesticulations at a philosopher's lecture.[13] Those who were enchanted by the rhythm of the words were not captured by their moral content,

---

8. *Diss.* 3.23.26. I prefer to adopt the traditional reading of Souilhé (1948) rather than that of Dobbin (2008, 172), who eliminates *eipein* and introduces with *tina* the comment of someone in the audience. *Eipein* together with "reading" shows different kinds of performance, and the arrogant comment of the speaker shows the vanity of the profession.

9. *Diss.* 2.16.4–10. In looking at Philostratus's *Vitae* the hard work of sophists is evident in spite of extempore performances.

10. *Diss.* 2.16.10.

11. 3.23.27–29 and 35. Likewise Epictetus abhorred that doctors advertised for patients as they did in Rome at that time. It appears that invitations to lectures were done later in the fourth century; see Libanius *Or.* 3.10, who sent his slave to make the calls. His presentation of one of these sophistic performances evokes Lucian's *Professor of Rhetoric*.

12. Brunt 1994, 25–52, on Philostratus.

13. Gellius, *Noctes Atticae* 5.1. On Musonius, see for the Greek text Lutz 1947. See also Lutz and Reydam-Schils 2020; Gill 2000, 601–3.

according to him, but were hearing the presentation as if it were a flute player's recital. A listener at a philosophical address could not help but have a gamut of powerful feelings. The greatest admiration should not rouse applause and words of praise; silence was the best response. Plutarch also testifies that in his time all lectures had become rowdy spectacles. He contrasts the performance of a philosopher with panegyrics "on vomiting or fever or even a kitchen pot" (44f). His essay *On Listening to Lectures* is an educational work poised between rhetoric and philosophy.[14] Silence, remarks Plutarch, is a safe adornment for the young man, who in listening should not get overexcited (39c). A harmonious style that resembles singing gives way only to pleasure and entertainment; it needs to be stripped from the lecture so that its content can be revealed, and so that the hearer realizes he has not come to a theater or a music hall. When a philosopher speaks inside a hall, the clamor and shouting is such that people outside cannot understand who is being applauded—a flute player, perhaps, or a dancer? (46c). Plutarch concludes that one must acquire a philosophical mind, not a mind that is sophistic or an attitude that concentrates on mere information (48d).

Here I focus on Epictetus's use of rhetoric and on what he seems to owe to the prevailing practices of his time. In his writings we need to consider closely the dialogic parts, his solo performances, his use of the argumentative technique of antithesis (very popular in the so-called Third Sophistic), and his reliance on speeches of impersonation. In other words, when reading the *Discourses*, we need to think more directly about whose voices we are "hearing."

Arrian, who at times struggled with keeping pace and with transitions from one thought to the next, is present behind the whole text.[15] Epictetus's voice is one of restraining, teaching, advising, and reprimanding. He is the authority that nobody challenges, even if the outside world sometimes attempts to confront him. Arrian's presentation gives us a much richer sense of the classroom than we have with Musonius, where dialogue appears only to a very limited degree. The texts of Musonius were compiled by a student who only cared for the voice of the philosopher.[16] As a consequence, questions are sprinkled very sparingly throughout Musonius's conversations, which are mostly monologues.

---

14. Xenophontos 2013, 2016. For a full bibliography on Plutarch, see note 1 of Roskam 2004.
15. See, e.g., 2.20.27–28. See also 1.23 with Dobbin's comments.
16. Lutz 1947, 11–13.

Essays 9 and 16 each start with a question that appears to be an excuse for a single discussion. Text 5 seems to be a dialogue: Musonius asks questions, but short answers are given in indirect discourse and are not fundamental to the development of the conversation.[17]

The *Discourses* of Epictetus display more variety, vividness, and spontaneity than those of Musonius. It has been observed that he "engaged his interlocutor in brilliantly challenging dialogues."[18] In a useful publication, Barbara Wehner studied the dialogic structure of the *Discourses* in connection with the genre of diatribe, but her excessive distinctions among dialogues do not offer many general conclusions.[19] On close inspection, it seems that the text of Epictetus does not actually include many dialogues that show real interactions between himself and an interlocutor or a student.[20] There are, of course, exceptions. A full dialogue is present, for instance, in *Diss.* 4.6, with both participants discussing their respective positions. This piece is unusual because in it the interlocutor, who does not want to be pitied by others, exposes his point of view at length. He has invested much effort: listening to philosophers, learning geometry and syllogisms, and reading, writing, and reflecting on arguments, all however without paying attention to important values. Epictetus's sharp final rebuke is the result of his full understanding of the situation of his interlocutor.[21] In *Diss.* 3.23 Epictetus himself utters most of the exchange, but in some dialogic parts the protagonist, a sophist in search of praise, manifests his worry that his audience was limited. Interestingly, many voices can be heard here. In 3.23.10–11, after Epictetus remarks that the orator was dejected one day because his audience did not applaud, the dialogue that follows seems to be uttered by another person, who responds to the sophist's questions by reassuring him how marvelous his performance was. Do we see here a sign that Arrian was confused in reporting the event? Perhaps the same person (or maybe the sophist himself, asking questions and responding internally) later intervenes to remark that the

---

17. Consider the one-line fictional and theatrical dialogues at the end of the work.
18. Long 2006, 207. On dialogue in antiquity, see Andrieu 1954; Goldhill 2008; Müller 2021; Müller and Föllinger 2013.
19. Wehner 2000. The discussion of the many parts of a dialogue (e.g., opening, address, prayer, declamatory part, etc.) does not let one perceive the overall function of the dialogic mode of presentation.
20. Colardeau (1903, 282–85) noticed that and related it mostly to Plato and the Attic orators. For a narratological view of dialogues, see Finkelberg 2019.
21. A similar subject in 3.2.

audience had been huge, bigger than that of Dio, "five hundred, nonsense, it was a thousand at least." We also encounter one-line exchanges between the interlocutor and members of his audience who praise his rhetorical performance and point to the large number of spectators. These, too, are false dialogues in which the philosopher performs as a kind of ventriloquist. The notes of Arrian must be responsible. In a different section, words of admonition that a student might repeat to himself are uttered by Epictetus.[22] He does not address the young man directly but becomes an external voice. Generally, questions abound in the *Discourses*, often in rapid escalation, but although they may appear ambiguous at first sight, it is the philosopher himself who responds to them. In 1.12.18–23 the "dialogues" are along these lines: "Is someone dissatisfied with his parents? Let him be a bad son and complain. Is someone dissatisfied with his children? Let him be a bad father." This is a "dialogue" consisting of only one voice, that of Epictetus, although the responses have sometimes been represented visually as if they were uttered by a different person.[23]

We may wonder why the *Discourses* contains so many instances of Epictetus giving solo performances in which Stoic philosophy rings true. This is one reason why we should not treat the *Discourses* as a complete work, to which its author had given the final touches. Rather, these are the notes Arrian made as he was listening to the philosopher's message. He may have chosen to omit real dialogues containing the contributions of students that, in his opinion, did not deserve to be immortalized.[24] Moreover, although Arrian was able to record the *Discourses* as they exist now, he would have needed some short-cuts in doing so, and the omission of unnecessary details would help him. Ignoring the objections and requests for explanation of students would have allowed him to keep up the pace of the narrative and to avoid becoming mired in minutiae. The formula *phesi* (he says) appears in dialogues that are conducted mainly in Epictetus's persona. These are not completely soliloquies, however, and the presence of an interlocutor is at least signaled. Was Arrian behind all that?[25]

---

22. *Diss.* 3.1.36–37.
23. Long (2002, 235) prints them as true dialogues while Dobbin prints them as a continuous discussion.
24. He probably knew those young men up close and could evaluate their performance.
25. Yet we should not completely discard another hypothesis. It is unclear how much active participation was required from students in philosophical classes in general, and in that of Epictetus specifically. The assumption that much discussion went on is far from certain

Evaluations of Epictetus's supposed writing style were negative for many years following the trenchant judgment of Fronto, who maintained that neither the philosopher's rough and vulgar style nor his life and social condition depended on a conscious choice but were instead the consequence of his initial life circumstances.[26] Views have changed, and some recent scholars have remarked that Epictetus was a master rhetorician, a rhetorical wizard. If, as I have argued, we have not a polished text written by Epictetus but Arrian's record of his oral teaching, this character is all the more marked. Rhetoric was certainly part of the education he received, even though he scorned the fanfare, display of vanity, acclamations, and large boisterous crowds of the rhetorical *epideixeis* of his time, in which the ludic elements appeared to be the goal.[27] At a time when the Second Sophistic was raging, Epictetus cherished different kinds of performances: those that were intense, introspective, and that had as their goal to change lives.[28]

Scholarly attention has so far focused only on Epictetus's debts to Socrates and Plato, particularly the *Gorgias*.[29] A. A. Long has brought attention to three styles that the philosopher himself mentioned: *protreptic*, *elenctic*, and *didactic* (3.23.33). The exhortative and the didactic style permeate all the *Discourses*, but I have found that the *elenctic* style, which has a question-and-answer format typical of Socratic discourses, appears less frequently, because Epictetus's "dialogues" often do not consist of two voices. Among the other predecessors who might have had some influence on Epictetus were Zeno the Stoic and Diogenes the Cynic. I suggest that the *Discourses* echo some characteristics of speeches that were fashionable at the time. Epictetus refused the whole package of epideictic rhetoric, and especially the noise that came with it, but certain rhetorical features influenced him to some extent when he used antithetical arguments and speeches of impersonation. These

---

and stems mostly from what we know of education in modern universities in Europe and North America, where student-teacher interaction is highly valued.

26. Long (2002, 49–50, 52–57) does not expand much on the subject. Costa (2008, 106) claimed that there was no rhetoric in the *Discourses, but he is isolated in this respect. Of course, the lectures show an oral style, and the text was not edited. In Diss.* 2.23.1 Epictetus expresses his appreciation for an attractive style and appropriate language.

27. Bowersock (1969) argued that the remaining texts were rhetorical showpieces on fictional or traditional themes. See Puech 2002.

28. On the status of sophists and on their life day by day, especially in the second century, see Favreau-Linder et al. 2022.

29. On the influence of Socrates, Plato, Aristotle, and the early Stoics, see Jagu 1946; Wehner 2000, 9–13.

were typical of the declamations that his students had grown to appreciate. From the elementary to the rhetorical levels, ancient education was structured in tightly connected links, each one joined to the previous and following stages.[30] It is not surprising that an education in philosophy would maintain the same structure by encapsulating some elements connecting it to previous levels.

Epictetus used rhetoric to persuade, and in so doing he observed some principles that would make his discourse more effective. In his time, rhetoric had become a mandatory feature in higher education,[31] and Epictetus and many of his students had been exposed to the belief that studying it would better one's social, economic, and political position. Epictetus did not observe and organize rhetorical features rigidly but managed to maintain the spontaneity of his communications. His main preoccupation was to ensure his audience's attention. The audience had to not only assimilate information but also react to it, so arousing emotions was fundamental. In the second century, Hermogenes of Tarsus codified a body of theory addressing different kinds of disputes that speakers would have to confront. The rhetorical system he constructed remained unsurpassed in the ancient world. Alternative strategies consisting of an antithetical argument followed by an objection were typical of forensic speeches. Hermogenes called these "antithesis" (contraposition) and considered the technique useful for introducing arguments for the opposition (called "answers") that could then be refuted.[32] Dio Chrysostom used antithesis/answer several times.[33] The format functioned very well in declamations, giving them a fluid structure that could easily be imitated. This is how the later extant declamations of Libanius are organized, for example, showing that the structure had become part of the normal fabric of speeches.[34]

---

30. Cribiore 2001b.
31. Cf. Lendon 2022.
32. See Heath 1995, 252. On declamations adopting this technique, see Russell 1996; Martin 1974, 124–25, 294.
33. Antithesis and answer appear, e.g., in Dio *Or.* 33.19: "Didn't Odysseus come from a small rugged island that only pastured goats? Yes, but he was able through his counsel to take a city like Troy." *Or.* 11.15 with antithesis and answer: people object that Homer who was a beggar told truthful stories, but beggars of the present time tell nothing but lies; 11.18: what prevented Homer who said untruths about the gods from speaking the same way about men? He did indeed make use of all possible falsehood; see also 10.7 and 10.13.
34. Libanius, *Declamations*, e.g., 26 and 27. Most speeches of Libanius show this feature, e.g., *Or.* 9, 19, 21, 25, 27, 34, 36.

However, the antithesis and objection in *Discourses* 2.1.32 is important to consider—"But Did Not Socrates Write, and Who Did More Than He and How"? "Since there was not always someone available to test his judgment or to be tested by him in turn, sometimes he would test and examine himself."³⁵ In a passage from his essay *On Freedom*, Epictetus examines the condition of caged birds that would do anything to escape and would even starve to death in order to gain freedom. Antithesis: "What is wrong with you here in your cage?" Objection: "I was born to fly wherever I like; to live in the open air, to sing whenever I want" (4.1.28). Or again, in another passage that exhorts listeners not to share personal information with others, the antithesis is: "Did I invite your confidences, did you open up to me only to hear mine?" The answer considers two people, one with an intact jar and another with one that has a hole. The first would not entrust wine to the second.³⁶ These and other similar instances in Epictetus could be regarded as a spontaneous feature of his speech that he had assimilated through an education in rhetoric.³⁷

Speeches of impersonation (*ethopoiiai*) were parts of *progymnasmata*, preliminary exercises in rhetoric.³⁸ They are very numerous in the *Discourses*, and it is peculiar that they have gone so long unnoticed. Rather than choosing examples here and there, in what follows I survey a very long and beautiful essay on Cynicism in order to put into relief the many speeches of impersonation contained therein.³⁹ This essay abounds in rhetorical questions, examples of *epanaphora* (repetitions at the beginning of a clause or sentence),⁴⁰ and *diaphoresis* (pretended doubt). Many metaphors and similes come straight from the rhetor's handbook; topics include medicine, athletic practices, family, and nature. The first few lines refer to a young man inquiring about the profession of a Cynic philosopher. This individual could have been an acquaintance, but I am inclined to see him as idealistic pupil whom Epictetus treats with

---

35. See note in Oldfather 1926.
36. *To Those Who Lightly Share Personal Information* (4.13.11–13).
37. See, e.g., *Diss.* 3.3.2; 4.1.108.
38. On *progymnasmata* in general, see Webb 2001. On the teaching of *progymnasmata* in rhetorical schools, see Pernot 1993, 56–66. See also Cribiore 2001b, 220–30. *Progymnasmata* could be used as models for students to recite them or to verify that their written samples conformed to those. See Theon of Alexandria 70–72; Patillon and Bolognesi 1997, 15, 17. Individual *progymnasmata*, especially encomium and invective, might be part of declamations; cf. Libanius 25–27.
39. *Diss.* 3.22.
40. See 3.22.13 and 31.

disdain.[41] This young man reappears very briefly at various points, but the dominant voice is that of Epictetus. Sections 2–8 constitute a proem for the whole discourse, in which the philosopher says that he will respond "at leisure" and that the help of God is essential when embarking on such a profession. In Sections 9–11 Epictetus performs a speech of impersonation (*ethopoiia*) in the voice of this man or young man who is inclined to the Cynic way of life:

> Already I wear a little worn coat and I will wear it then;[42] I sleep right now on the ground and I will do so then; I will take a little satchel and a staff; I will wander, beg, and insult the people crossing my path. And if I see a man who shaves his body hair, I will abuse him and will do the same to one with an elaborate coiffure or one who is strolling in purple garments.[43]

Epictetus may have used a farcical tone in class, insisting on the use of diminutives unrelated to the "size" of his students but intended to belittle their claims. Solo voices like this may have aroused some hilarity, but the protagonist probably would have felt mortified. The presentation of Cynicism implicit in the philosopher's initial mocking words clashes sharply with the rest of this long discourse. After some exhortations, Sections 12–13 continue into a sort of narration (*katastasis*) that shows what kind of a philosopher the Cynic is: a citizen of the world, "the common educator, the pedagogue." In Sections 19–22 Epictetus exhorts the student to purify his soul, and the latter gives voice to his future program in another *ethopoiia*:

> Now my matter is my mind, like wood to a carpenter and leather to a cobbler, and my proper work consists of using my perceptions. My miserable body is nothing to me and its limbs are nothing. And death too, either of the whole body or a part, can come when it likes. Exile? Where can they banish me? Nowhere outside the world. Wherever I go, there will be the sun, the moon, the stars, the dreams, the presages, and conversation with the gods.

---

41. Dobbin 2008, 157–68. In section 10 Dobbin failed to translate the diminutives that indicate the contempt of Epictetus. In the final part, 3.22.108, the interlocutor is dismissed and compared to a woman, Andromache, who should not mix in men's affairs.

42. The young man shows how well the new profession will fit him.

43. Some elements of this description at *Diss.* 4.8.34; cf. also 3.12.9. Cf. Lucian, *Vit. Auct.* 9.

The words are too poetic and refined to actually belong to the student. It is Epictetus who breathes life into them.

In another speech in character, the Cynic shows that he has nothing—no resources, no wife, no children, only the earth and the sky and an old cloak—and yet he has a happy countenance.[44] The *Discourse* on the Cynic continues with another short description/narration in which he is called a messenger of Zeus, with a very long *ethopoiia* in his own voice. This expands on a few words of Socrates in Plato's *Cleitophon*.[45] Epictetus is aware that this is a grave and formal speech "on the tragic stage." The Cynic philosopher reproaches men at length, exhorting them to search for peace and happiness and citing myth. He exhorts Agamemnon, and his words intersect with those of the Greek warrior in a complicated dialogue within the *ethopoiia*. Epictetus, who cites only two Homeric verses, further lends his own words to Agamemnon by attempting to console him. The voice of the Cynic reappears from 22.47 to 49 with another speech of impersonation, in which he again reveals his detachment from worldly things and his utter contentment. "Here you have the real words of the Cynic, his character and way of life" (50), comments Epictetus. He then impersonates Diogenes, who manifests his contempt for those men hurrying to see the "damned" games (58). The rest of the essay is taken up by a lengthy description of the life of the Cynic and an enumeration of all his physical and moral qualities.[46] It is evident that Epictetus does not touch on the most controversial aspects of the Cynic, "nothing about masturbation and the belly, more on healthy living and natural charm," showing that his portrait is anachronistic.[47] The Stoics needed to justify the Cynics' opposition to civic responsibilities, marriage, and begetting children, though they approved of virtues. Epictetus considers the Cynic's mission a religious one and idealizes him.[48]

In this essay, as in others, Epictetus uses *ethopoiia* very frequently, conferring on his discourse a vividness that his students would have experienced in class. Arrian was able to transmit the excitement in his notes. Epictetus condemned the emptiness and verbal games of sophistic performances but made use of some rhetorical features to enliven

---

44. *Diss.* 3.22.45–49.
45. *Diss.* 3.22.26–30; *Cleitophon* 407a.
46. *Diss.* 3.22.62–109.
47. Schofield 2007, 84–85.
48. On the Stoic idealization of the Cynics, see Allen 2020, 67–99. See also Goulet-Cazé 2017.

his teaching. It was not only *l'air du temps* that influenced him. Many of his students would have been exposed to the technique of argument practiced in the schools, and he fortified his instruction with certain educational aspects of proven value. By adopting some features of the rhetorical art and of declamations, the philosopher could make his message less threatening and more irresistible. Although contemporary critics have confined Epictetus to his readings of Plato and Stoic philosophers, he was not deaf to other voices. Rather, like all exceptional educators, he had access to resources that could make his messages more familiar to his audience and thus more effective.

The Voice and the Written Word: Books and Philosophy

In a letter, Seneca assures Lucilius that he will send him certain books but adds the disclaimer that in philosophy, intimate contact with one's master is much more useful than the written word. Seneca adds that the greatest students of philosophers had become such by living under the same roof as the philosopher.[49] Dominant themes in the *Discourses* are the contrasts between books and the *viva vox* of a teacher and between reading a text passively and interpreting it by putting it into practice. In large part, these are contrasts between traditional liberal studies and the learning of philosophy.[50] The learning techniques and content that students had assimilated for many years would not disappear the instant the students arrived in another environment but would leave important traces. Epictetus's work allows a glimpse at the transition from literary and rhetorical studies to philosophy. Any young man who left his hometown to join the philosopher would have brought with him a baggage of long-held notions and working methods that would be difficult to shed. By paying attention to these, we can understand and justify many of Epictetus's assertions.

As a young student, Arrian must have been very aware of the issues raised by the education of the grammarian, the attempt of Epictetus to dismantle those notions, and the difficult position of some students. An aspiring philosopher had spent previous years reading books with an attention to minute details and relying on the help of a teacher who

---

49. See *Ep.* 6.
50. Cf. Marcus Aurelius *Meditations* I 17.4.8; II 2–3; III 14. For him books were useless, and one was not supposed to go back to review readings.

would have guided him through the meanderings of *historiai*.[51] These consisted of all the contextual and historical points that might enrich the meaning of a text by providing glossographical notes and details on history, geography, and myth. These fragmented pieces of knowledge could swell up ad infinitum in a proliferation of exegesis of a text. Epictetus needed to challenge, and eventually eradicate, what had become for his students an accepted *forma mentis*. He employed the same term as grammarians (*historia*) to describe a method he considered pernicious.[52] The same static system was also used when studying rhetoric. Students needed to accept past myths and historical events and develop and enrich various aspects that depended strictly on the canonical forms.[53] A deferential attitude toward books was the norm in conventional liberal studies. The written word and real-life experiences lay at opposite poles. "It is enough for us to learn what is written on a subject and be able to explain it before someone else," Epictetus wrote, aptly describing the previous educational process that he rejected.[54] At the various stages of a liberal education, "to read, write and attend classes on a subject" without asking many questions was the rule, but in Nicopolis students were expected to go further and be responsible for their own educations. "Enter, young man, into your own . . . yours are these possessions, yours are these books, yours these discourses," Epictetus would announce to newcomers, but these books were supposed to be no more than points of departure for philosophical discourse.[55] Generations of educated people had learned to cry over the fates of Priam and Oedipus, but philosophy looked at their misfortunes as "externals" (*ta ektos*): "For what else are tragedies but the portrayal in tragic verse of the ordeals of people who have come to value externals?"[56] Priam and Oedipus "were guilty" of having indulged in lamenting their cruel fates rather than accepting them with equanimity. Students of philosophy, who had to learn to overcome sorrows and disappointment, would have

---

51. See what the grammarian Dionysius Thrax declared around 100 BCE in *Grammatici Graeci* 1.1, p. 5, 1–5. From the same century see Asklepiades of Myrlea, Sextus *Math*. 1.91-94 and 252–53. Cf. Cribiore 2001b, 185–86.

52. 2.21.10. The passage is misinterpreted by Oldfather (1926, 377), who translates it as "history of philosophy." Dobbin (2008, 134) is also misguided translating "memorizing its doctrines." In 2.19.7 Epictetus mimics a grammarian who is asking minute questions such as who Hector's father was and so on.

53. Only in the exercise of refutation was there room for some creativity.

54. *Diss*. 4.4.14.

55. *Diss*. 2.17.30.

56. *Diss*. 1.4.25–26; see Snyder 2000, 30–38; *Diss*. 2.19.

to either keep away from those books or learn to interpret them in the right way. It was useless to depend strictly on a text without relating the misfortunes described therein to one's own experience. In two letters, Seneca too clarified that total symbiosis and acceptance were inconsequential and dangerous.[57]

A philosopher was expected to dismantle the authoritative message that education had from its earliest stages inculcated into young men. At its core was imitation of content and form. From the start, Epictetus had to confront and combat his students' attempts to appropriate ready-made cultural products. In one vignette, two young men praise each other for how they read and write: "You have a great gift for writing in the style of Xenophon," says one, "And you for that of Plato," "And you for that of Antisthenes."[58] Rhetorical schools trained students in stylistic exercises. Epictetus objected that this type of exercise did not touch the heart and the mind, because one's feelings would remain unchanged, and no inner improvement would occur. His antipathy for writing and books is clear in cases when texts are read passively. Of course, Socrates in the *Phaedrus* had maintained that the written word was inferior to spoken communications, and that books were mere reminders of philosophical teaching.[59] At worst, they could make people passive and inert. Metaphors that would become standard educational jargon were that teaching was sowing seeds and planting them in suitable ground. Writing could also be compared to painting, in that the characters resembled human beings but remained silent and unable to answer questions (275d). In his conception of books, Epictetus seems to echo a passage from the *Protagoras*, in which books appear inert and unable to answer or to be interrogated. "And if one questions even a small point . . . just as brazen vessels they go ringing on after they have been struck and continue to sound until someone puts his hand upon them."[60] Some philosophers continued to regard writing with suspicion. In the fifth century CE, Proclus refused to write a commentary, even though he had wanted to, because he had been categorically forbidden from doing so by certain visions: his own master had restrained him from writing with threats.[61]

---

57. Seneca *Ep.* 33 and 88; Nussbaum 1994, 346–47.
58. *Diss.* 2.17.35–36.
59. Plato, *Phr.* 274b–277a.
60. *Diss.* 4.4; Plato, *Protagoras* 329a.
61. Edwards 2000, 99. His students devised a stratagem employing notes. Cf. in part III some Neoplatonic commentators' reluctance to write.

Stoic teaching developed these concepts and focused on the contrast between the reception of the written word and the active use of it for one's benefit. Written texts were inferior to personal communications, and like other later Stoics, Epictetus focused on ethics in action.[62] It is uncertain whether Epictetus followed Musonius in his ambiguous conception of books. Snyder claimed that Musonius must have dealt with technical material in class, but no allusions to him doing so have surfaced.[63] Only once does the philosopher mention books, but these are texts of medicine, music, and cookery.[64] It seems so peculiar that he did not allude to Stoic texts that one is tempted to surmise that he did discuss them with his students even if he did not use books actively in class. In an essay on acquiring virtue, Musonius dismissed theory in favor of practice. This may be a sign that he mostly valued his direct message and his students' practical application of it.[65] A question that we will have to try to answer in what follows is to what extent Epictetus relied on books.

The students and visitors arrived at Nicopolis proud of their cultural baggage and of the books they had read. They looked forward to reading more books. They came from an upper-class society that apparently read avidly, and they showed disappointment when there was no time for that (4.4.2). Books dominated the cultural landscape of the elite. The message young men received on arrival was that if their sole passion was reading books, they should turn around and go back immediately, because they had left home for nothing (1.4.22). They counted how many lines they read or wrote, but even a thousand were useless without moral thinking (4.4.8 and 18). At a previous stage of education, when they were in school and had time available, they would have dutifully devoted themselves to reading and writing as preparation for life (4.4.11). Now they were expected to show what they had learned from that training by becoming engaged in moral improvement, using books as guides for growth and self-control.[66] Even though Epictetus

---

62. Reydams-Schils (2010, 565) surmised that they avoided theory in the attempt to move beyond the controversies of their predecessors. On Socrates's cultivation of ethics, see Aristotle, *Metaphysics* 978b2. Wolfsdorf (2020) considers ethics before Socrates. On ethics in the Stoics, see also Sellars 2014, 107–34. On ethics before Epictetus in the early Roman period, see Inwood 2014. See also Coope and Sattler 2021.

63. Snyder 2000, 18–19.

64. Musonius 18A Hense/Lutz.

65. 5 Hense/Lutz. In 6 Hense/Lutz he urged students to practice what they learned from him in order to train their souls.

66. *Diss.* 4.4.15–18 with a list of books to be used for better reading.

often commented on the unreliability of books and on what exercises were actually useful to moral life, he was not an anti-intellectual who had reduced philosophy to a narrow moralism.[67] He denounced books as instruments of a culture that was based on notions and information per se. Culture was not intrinsically superior to possessions and material goods, and could not be an instrument of freedom unless it was used in a specific way.

The reasons why Epictetus objected to immersion in books were manifold. He denounced the notion that books were capable in themselves of bringing satisfaction. Books, along with the information they conveyed, were approached as silent fragments of knowledge. They did not reverberate through people's lives. People tended to gorge themselves on books when they were not ready to absorb their content, with the result that their effect was not only insignificant but actually detrimental. Like Socrates's brazen vessels, books were unresponsive and silent when they were approached passively. They did not have a voice. They also had no ready connection to life. Plato had said that knowledge was the food of the soul, and two passages in the *Discourses* equate food and books.[68] One, in which the term "to vomit" is employed three times, shows the disgust Epictetus felt for those who aimlessly filled themselves with books (3.21.1–6). While an athlete in training could show off his muscular shoulders as proof of his hard work, those who crammed their minds with books had little to show, could not digest them, and should take care not to vomit their knowledge. In another essay Epictetus points to people who bought whole treatises and proceeded to eat them up: "they vomit or have indigestion and after that come colic, discharges, and fevers" (1.26.16). Undigested books were dangerous and could seriously damage the reader who indulged in them. Seneca too used the analogy of a proper assimilation of knowledge not to risk vomiting it back up (*Ep.* 2.2–4). Books had to be read slowly, without approaching too many of them. The comparison of food to culture was also used outside of philosophy. Sophists such as Philostratus, Aristides, and Libanius used the term "to vomit" for those rhetors who practiced extempore rhetoric without much preparation, only to dazzle their audience.[69] These speakers would vomit a flood of

---

67. Bénatouïl 2009, 52–53.
68. Plato, *Prt.* 313c.
69. On vomiting words, see Philostratus, *VS* 491 on the eloquence of Favorinus who was like an immature youth; Eunapius, *VS* 488 reporting the words of Prohaeresius about

words, and their half-digested speeches would intoxicate those who valued pleasurable performances. The terminology used at various stages of education was similar or even identical, though the meaning varied somewhat.

Scholars have mentioned texts that might have been present in Epictetus's class, but his references to them are very cursory and inconclusive.[70] They usually consist of little more than names of philosophers he knew, Stoics or not, but it is unclear how and to what extent he used these texts. He scatters their names in his essays, usually without including his students (even the more advanced ones) in the discussion of their doctrine. A suggestion that Epictetus might have used several books in class and shaped his lessons around them was based on the large number of texts ascribed in general to certain philosophers like Chrysippus, Zeno, or Cleanthes,[71] but this hypothesis cannot be sustained in the *Discourses*. On the one hand, Epictetus remarks that education (theory, *theoremata*) in the past had dwelled on these matters unceasingly with no change.[72] On the other, it seems that his teaching was rather individualized and that he catered to the needs of his students (3.12.8).[73] Some form of a curriculum must have existed in Epictetus's school, but we would know more details if Arrian had taken notes during all the lectures and if those four missing books had been transmitted.

In principle, we should not be averse to believing that students owned books and took them to class, even if some scholars resist the idea.[74] Some who were assiduous readers may have brought them from home. In one case there is a reference to buying books, and in another

---

Aristides on speeches not elaborated. On Aristides himself who refused to declaim extempore, see Philostratus 583. In Libanius, see *Decl.* 27.6-11. Cf. the derisive terminology of Eunapius, *VS* 454 about Philostratus who "spat out" the *Lives*.

70. Snyder 2000, 20-21; Del Corso 2005, 37-38. However, Snyder (2000, 86-98) considers it very likely that books existed in the classes of philosophers.

71. Del Corso 2005, 43-45.

72. *Diss.* 2.23.43-47. He made the same observation regarding rhetoric. Judging from this, he seemed in favor of some change.

73. In general, information and even mention of the existence of a curriculum by educators at other levels is rather scanty with the exception of Quintilian. In *Or.* 34.15 Libanius inveighed against a pedagogue who had criticized him for debating on Homer and Demosthenes without end. The resentful response of the sophist was that the fault was with the curriculum. See Cribiore 2007a, 147-55.

74. Snyder (2000, 24) maintains that it is very unlikely because local bookstores in Nicopolis would not provide texts.

a student proud of his ability to expound on books is sarcastically invited to write his own, which Epictetus predicts will ultimately cost the paltry sum of only five denarii (1.4.16).[75] Thus the low cost of books for upper-class students somewhat contributed to diminishing their value. The presence of the school in Nicopolis may have stimulated copyists to produce some cheap texts. The same student's invitation to the teacher to witness how well he could read a book presupposes that the text was physically in front of him. At the same time much is uncertain, as I have argued about Alexander of Aphrodisias.[76] Certainly in later times, Libanius's students would go to school with a quantity of heavy books that could double as weapons in fights, and in sixth-century Alexandria the students of Olympiodorus must have had a text of Plato with them in class.

In Nicopolis writing suffered the same fate as reading. Most often this activity is mentioned together with reading books and receives only the conditional approval of Epictetus. A would-be philosopher "had to devote himself to learning, had to converse with himself, write about that, read, listen, and get ready."[77] There are some instances suggesting that much writing took place. One discontented student, for example, considered it "worthless to have listened to so many lectures and written so much" (2.6.23).[78] Most of the time, however, students were discouraged from excessive writing. It was a school activity that those coming from previous levels of education did automatically, as they had been taught. Epictetus derisively presents a vignette, in 2.17.35, in which polite students praise each other's reading and writing in various styles. He felt that those rhetorical exercises were pointless and did not help them grow and mature. "Write a book," he told one of them; "it will cost nothing and will be worth nothing" (1.4.15).

One essay contains some information on writing that was not rhetorical (2.1). In it a relatively advanced student bemoans the lack of any improvement from his reading and writing.[79] The student had practiced with arguments and syllogisms but had not done those

---

75. The sum was little for an upper-class individual, but for a poor man it was a week's wages. I owe this information to Roger Bagnall.

76. See part I.

77. See *Diss.* 4.4.30 and 3.5.11.

78. Of course, the young man's mood may have influenced his statement. In *Diss.* 4.5.8 the mention of writing a thousand lines is hypothetical but still indicative of its presence in class.

79. *Diss.* 2.1. 29–40. See Del Corso 2005, 46–49.

exercises that could free him from passions, desire, and fear. As usual with Epictetus, reading and writing were meant to lead to introspection and meditation, and in this the student had failed. He had written something, read it aloud, and now was wondering why Epictetus did not appreciate his *periodia*, "little convoluted writings," and told him to get rid of them.[80] And yet Socrates had done a lot of writing, the student objects. Epictetus assents, leaving scholars perplexed and questioning Diogenes Laertius's statement (1.16) that in antiquity some believed that Socrates had written nothing. Epictetus's indulgence in writing was perhaps similar to that of Socrates: not philosophical treatises, but instead informal writing, preparations, and annotations.[81] It is likely that students had to take notes while attending classes. Epictetus's voice would have reverberated through the class and ended up in notebooks.

Resistance

"Epictetus is a frustrating author—at least for an historian of logic," wrote Jonathan Barnes. "Like the Lord whose oracle is at Delphi, he neither states nor hides."[82] Epictetus had undoubtedly been instructed in logic by Musonius, but his attitude toward the discipline was ambivalent. While he does not engage directly with logic in the parts of the *Discourses* that have been transmitted, at times he discusses the necessity of learning it in order to be able to enter into complex arguments. At other times, however, he discourages students from devoting too much time and effort to it.[83] From *Diss*. 1.26.13 it appears that logic was a standard part of instruction but was taught at a secondary level at an unknown level of intensity. Epictetus says that an understanding of logic allows one to enter complex arguments, master puzzles, and study syllogisms and paradoxes. Formal and sophisticated training in logic, however, was complex and would require a long time, and therefore doubts arose about its real value. Both Seneca and Epictetus were ambivalent about promoting a strong interest in logic in others.[84] The danger for the student who developed logical sophistication was that

---

80. Another diminutive to indicate disdain.
81. The fact that the student does not mention Epictetus as a writer may indicate that he felt that his teacher wrote less than Socrates.
82. Barnes 1997, 126. His full consideration of logic in Epictetus is on 24–99. On logic, see Dobbin 1998, 113–14; Sellars 2014, 75–80.
83. *Diss*. 1.7, 1.8, 1.11.39–40, 1.17.4–12, 2.14, 2.13.21, 2.25, 2.23.41.
84. See Nussbaum 1994, 148–51.

he might then overlook other, more significant, aspects of philosophy. These studies were seductive and threatened to become an end in themselves. Young men felt excited to practice logic, thinking that it conferred on them real power and control over others. We have seen that Epictetus condemned books when they were read superficially for the purpose of extracting content and without inducing further reflection. Knowledge of logic made young men arrogant and developed in them a false sense of confidence.

The influential philosopher of the Early Stoa mentioned most often by Epictetus is Chrysippus, the greatest of the Stoic logicians. He had written on hypotheses and hypothetical arguments, and to judge from the catalog of his works, his breadth of interests was vast.[85] The reasons behind Epictetus's caution and restraint in considering Chrysippus's work are twofold.[86] On the one hand, he never granted him as high a status as philosophers like Plato; he suggested that Chrysippus had not fully shown how to proceed toward virtue and true happiness. On the other, his works were perused and closely commented on, and students considered them authoritative texts, accepted them for what they were, and memorized them. The simple knowledge of many of his works and the capability of "reading Chrysippus by oneself" did not create progress in the sense of an improvement in virtue (1.4.5–16). Analyzing syllogisms as in Chrysippus could not prevent one from being unhappy (2.23.44). The fact that Chrysippus was notoriously obscure fed into the satisfaction and vanity of those who could understand the meaning of his words, but the benefit stopped there.[87] Students felt that they earned some merit for deciphering his texts and simply doing grammatical work. Exhibiting knowledge of Chrysippus and other philosophers at banquets drew admiration, which could become an end in itself (2.19.5–10).

The strong roots of past education may have seemed impossible to eradicate. Their previous studies had given young men the conviction that applying the rules automatically produced success. It was a comforting thought that application (*ponos*) could not fail. Confronting students who read passively, without forming their own judgment,

---

85. Barnes 1997, 85–98; of these some fragments survive. Diogenes Laertius 7.189–202; Dorandi 2007. Unfortunately, his work is mostly lost.
86. See Reydams-Schils 2011a, 298–310.
87. See the whole passage in *Diss.* 1. 4.7–18 with commentary in Dobbin 1998; 1.17.13–18, Dobbin 1998, 166–67.

Epictetus sarcastically said that they would end up speaking of "Helen, and Priam and the island of Calypso," that is, of the kind of fiction they had studied under the grammarian and not out of their own knowledge. He was aware that if he admired the *translation* of Chrysippus, he would be a grammarian instead of a philosopher, "with the difference that instead of Homer I would interpret Chrysippus."[88] He was infuriated with a young man who was determined to explain *ta Chrysippeia* using the same attention to detail and who insisted on showing him his commentaries (*scholia*).[89] Commentaries dominated the cultural landscape not so much because of a spontaneous taste for erudition, but because of the influence of educational methods and because students had trouble understanding the orginal texts.[90]

Epictetus and Literature

We have seen that Epictetus denounced books as instruments of a culture that, he argued, was based on notions and information per se and from which his students extrapolated trivialities. Culture was the aim of traditional education, and his students arrived in Nicopolis expecting to read and embrace further written texts and to treat philosophy as literature. They would instead have to learn from Epictetus's *viva vox* and accept that books might be useful only when they were approached to guide ethical choices and behaviors, and that they did not have any intrinsic value.

In the modern world, learning skills relies on preceding activities; the ability to write an accomplished essay comes after years of practicing on various texts. More surprisingly, as I have said elsewhere, ancient education revolved around the same limited group of texts: revisiting them, deepening their content, and considering them from different points of view. When a beginner noted down a passage of Homer, he would pay attention to correctly copying, responding to dictation, or writing it from memory. The same passage (or a similar one) would be meticulously analyzed into all its constituent parts at the grammarian's lessons. But Homer's verse and mythology also found much traction with rhetors. Exercises of *progymnasmata*, from fables to descriptions, could revolve around the *Iliad* or the *Odyssey*. An exercise that involved some creative

---

88. *Ench.* 49.
89. *Diss.* 3.21.7.
90. Bénatouïl 2009, 142. See part III.

thinking was "refutation" (*anaskeue*), in which a myth was contested to show that it was illogical and improbable.[91] Thus in the myth of Daphne it could be objected, for example, that Apollo, being a god, was a fast runner and should have been able to immediately catch the nymph, who was much slower.[92] Dio wrote *Oration* 11, *The Trojan Discourse*, by using *anaskeue* to show that despite the reverence that had surrounded Homer for centuries, his *Iliad* and *Odyssey* could be disputed. His most controversial point was that Troy had not been taken. With agility of mind and great attention to detail, the student of rhetoric would dissect a narrative, cut out some parts, and reassemble the whole again. Epictetus fought a continuous battle against the education his students had acquired at previous levels. The dangerous sentiments derived from that education encouraged an excessive attention to individual words. Books were fragmented into terms and expressions, and a point-by-point analysis of them would impede a proper understanding of content and issues. Jumping from word to word and lingering on the meaning and signification of individual units would impede the proper integration of a thought. The irritation and disappointment of the philosopher is palpable in his use of a number of diminutives to convey his disdain. There exist to my knowledge no specific linguistic studies on diminutives in Roman times, but in the *Discourses* it is evident that they do not hint at actual size, as they do in other cases.[93] Epictetus argues with some contempt that the explanation of "little words" (*lexeidia*) should not take place in the school of a philosopher.[94] Proud students cared to demonstrate what they had done with "little words," which then would become part of "little periods" (*periodia*), but he asked them to destroy that useless work (2.1.31-33). Philosophy did not consist of reciting "little words" and "proclaiming little principles" (*theorematia*). The grammarian and the sophist had taken care of that. As usual Epictetus found an ally in Socrates, who would have sent someone in love with elegant speech to the sophists Protagoras and Hippias.[95]

---

91. See Aphthonios, *Progymnasmata*, ed. H. Rabe, 1926, Leipzig.
92. Patillon (2008, 121-24) on Aphthonios. Cf. ps.-Hermogenes 190-91 on *anaskeue* (refutation).
93. In the papyri diminutives refer to size and age. In the Archive of Apollonius (139-63), Heraidous, the strategos's daughter, is called "little" not only because she was young but also to distinguish her from another older Heraidous. See Bagnall and Cribiore 2006.
94. *Diss.* 3.21.6-8. Cf. his identical dislike for *logaria*, a diminutive of "words," in 2.18.26.
95. 3.5.15-17. See Plato's *Protagoras* where young Hippocrates visits a group of sophists including Protagoras; and *Theatetus* 151b, sending people who cannot benefit from his

Another term Epictetus charged with a negative connotation is *onoma*. Its meaning is similar to *lexeidion* (word) but at times can expand to include "expressions." While Epictetus condemns his students' attention to *lexeidia*, a term that evoked pedantic work without any reference to harmony or elegance, *onomata* is more associated with expressions that are arranged ornamentally, as in the sophistic art. Though only once is the term used to refer directly to the performance of a sophist who knows "the elegant art of choosing expressions and arranging them,"[96] as a rule the reference to sophistry is always implied.[97] The diminutives of disparagement (*onomatia*) show Epictetus's disdain for an art that he considered mere noise and the arrangement of empty names, like hairdressers prettifying hair.[98] Can we try to imagine Epictetus spewing diminutives that conveyed his disgust and showing his repugnance on his face? The scene in class must have been less than edifying, with some students manifesting an amused interest. And Arrian? He reported all this with a straight face.[99]

From literary education Epictetus borrows two other terms, *melete* and *askesis*. We should verify whether they maintained the same meaning they held in the classes of the grammarian and the rhetor, or if their sense changed significantly.[100] The dilemma of ancient educators had always been to reconcile natural talents with training and practice. Needing to remedy a concept of education that was based solely on inherited qualities, sophists in fifth-century BCE Athens created a trinity: nature, teaching, and practice.[101] Rhetoric embraced the concepts of both *askesis* and *melete*. Training and practice were at the base of the creation and delivery of discourses. Rhetorical studies led a student

---

teaching to others, like Prodicus. The comparison with people wanting to buy humble vegetables shows Plato's scorn for this type of work.

96. *Diss.* 3.23.25–26. Another reference to Socrates in Plato, *Apology* 17c.

97. *Diss.* 2.23.2 and 14.

98. *Diss.* 2.23.14 and 3.23.26.

99. We can bet that if he had composed the *Discourses* artistically in the manner of Xenophon, as Wirth argued, provoking language like this would have been avoided. In one instance the use of *onomata* appears slightly different because it refers to work done in the class of the philosopher (2.14.14). Epictetus urges an interlocutor to do some work to deepen the meaning of "expressions." The man is outraged by the implication that he did not know his *onomata*, but Epictetus replies disparagingly that he knows them as well as illiterates know written speech.

100. In one essay, moreover, he mentions some "preliminary training" (*progymnazo*) that an expert student was supposed to impart to a younger one (1.26.13); the older pupil had set a difficult passage to read and hints at a connection with logic. On some suggestions about the content of these *progymnasmata*, see Del Corso 2005, 45; Snyder 2000, 25.

101. See Diels 1952, 264. Cf. Plato, *Protagoras*; cf. Cribiore 2007a, 129–34.

from preliminary exercises to a finished oration, which was called *melete*.[102] Plato had considered unremitting practice typical of rhetoric, and Aristides and Lucian had followed.[103] In Plutarch, however, *askesis* sometimes acquired the parallel meaning of "practice in virtue," and in Lucian's *Hermotimus* it referred to "training" in a philosophical school.[104] Did the interpretations of *melete* and *meletao* evolve notably when the terms were used by a philosopher?

Thomas Bénatouïl attributed to *melete* the meaning "meditation," that is, an introspective and somewhat static activity.[105] Calling *melete* "meditation" does not fully convey the active and repetitive connotation of the practice denoted by this term, which was necessary to achieve success. Epictetus maintained the traditional meaning, even if he adapted it to new circumstances. When young men had just arrived at the school, Epictetus declared that his goal was to make them happy, free, and in everything contemplative of God, and explained that learning and "practice" were paramount in attaining these states (2.19.29).[106] Not every student followed; some refused to practice the tasks they were assigned and asked to change them.[107] Epictetus would repeat to them over and over that they needed to practice and have ready at hand concepts that would help them (2.1.29). *Discourses* 2.16 shows that he knew and used both senses of the word applied by sophists and philosophers. The *melete* (exercise) of an orator consisted of composing, memorizing, and pronouncing a speech. The practice he wanted his students to do, however, was one of moral purpose (*meletao, askeo*).[108] Too often, he found his pupils worthless, cowardly, lazy, and unwilling to practice because they had not been exposed to such expectations before. "If we were afraid not of death or exile but of fear itself, then we would practice how not to encounter those things we believe to be bad" (2.16.18-19). In an important passage Epictetus clarifies how practice

---

102. Cribiore 2007a, 150, 153.
103. Plato, e.g., *Alc.* 20b; *Grg.* 509e; *Prt.* 323d with *askesis, epimeleia* (application), and *didache* (teaching). Lucian, e.g., *Apology* 15.4. Aristides mentions the noun and the verb very frequently in all his works.
104. Plutarch, *Lycurgus and Numa* 4.4; Lucian, *Hermot.* 7.12, referring to those who complete their training. See also *Nigr.* 27.6, practice of *arete*.
105. Bénatouïl 2009, 148.
106. Cf. *Diss.* 2.9.13: the philosophers say that learning is not enough but practice (*melete*) and training (*askesis*) need to be added.
107. *Diss.* 1.29.39-43. The comparison of the athlete is again used.
108. Cf. 2.2.38: "Let others practice lawsuits, or problems, or syllogisms"; they were supposed to practice how to die. *Melete* could embrace many activities.

must be applied in order to free a person from those things that were not indispensable. *Melete* was supposed to occupy a would-be philosopher from morning to evening. One would start by detaching oneself from less valuable material things, such as a pot, and would proceed to larger ones like a tunic, a puppy, and an old horse. The practice then expanded to one's body, children, and wife.[109] This was a daily training, and it was fundamental to practice slowly and in stages.[110] In another passage, Epictetus says that one should practice on small things such as a headache or an earache; some groaning was permissible, but not groaning internally.[111] Training and practice (*melete* and *askesis*) differed for each person according to his needs and weaknesses (3.12.7–12). One person would need to fight an inclination to pleasures, another laziness, and the avoidance of hard work,[112] and yet another an irritable temper or a tendency to indulge in wine, pretty girls, or cakes. Training was the cure. *Meletao* meant to practice over and over, all day long, to achieve moral purpose. Students of Epictetus were expected to struggle against desiring what was not given, to make use of what was given, and to accept it when something was taken away.[113] At previous educational levels, *melete* had concerned grammatical points and forms, and applying the rules of rhetorical style. And yet the evocation of the gymnasium or of the work of an athlete, with a division of exercises according to difficulty, reveals that the old concept of mental gymnastics was still there.[114]

"Impressions"

Epictetus often reproves his students for glibly discussing ideas in class but failing in their practical application, thereby finding themselves in the midst of avoidable terrifying moments. A scene that Epictetus presents to his students in order to relieve them from fear has touches of humor (2.16.22). Epictetus puts himself at the center of the picture,

---

109. *Diss.* 4.1.111. Externals had to be eliminated and things should be mentally discarded.
110. In *Diss.* 4.6.16 there is the same combination of *melete* and *gymnazein*.
111. *Diss.* 1.18.18–19. Groaning within oneself and lamenting the unfairness of a situation were much worse than venting some pain outside.
112. *Ponos* and *philoponia* were precious words in education. Epictetus does not use them frequently and criticizes those who stay up all night reading and writing (4.4.40–41). He is not impressed by the *philoponos* because he does not know his motivation. In two instances, *ponos* refers to learning and the hard work required in Nicopolis (1.20.13 and 2.21.14).
113. *Diss.* 2.16.27–28.
114. Comparisons with athletes are numerous, e.g., 3.22.51–52; 3.25.2–5; 4.4.30.

and for a moment it seems that he will be lost to his terrors. He is on a boat gazing into the deep and looking around at the vast expanse of water without seeing land. When he starts to fear that the boat might sink, he is beside himself, imagining that he will have to swallow "all that sea." Actually, he quickly adds with a sneer, three pints of water will suffice to undo him. Impressions can destroy people. In an earthquake, the same happens: he imagines that the whole city will fall on him, "even though a little stone is enough to knock my brains out."

Another shipwreck is conjured as a response to a student who, trusting theoretical thoughts, speaks somewhat arrogantly and self-assuredly on virtues and vices (2.19.15-17).[115] Did he evaluate those ideas clearly, Epictetus asks? Would he maintain those subtle distinctions between good and evil on board a ship in a storm, with the sails flapping madly? A fellow passenger asks sarcastically at that time: "What were you saying a little while ago by the gods? Is it a vice to suffer shipwreck?" Epictetus's answer is fast and definitive: wouldn't you pick up a piece of wood and crack his brain? Like Musonius and Marcus Aurelius, Epictetus believed that mistakes were due to faulty judgment, and so people could not really be blamed for them. They needed to be treated patiently, without getting irritated at their shortcomings. We have seen in the section on emotions, however, that Epictetus's patience had limits.

In his *Rhetoric*, Aristotle discusses "examples" called *paradeigmata* that could also be employed in philosophy.[116] What he calls *logoi* ("fables" or "narrations") are traditional fictional examples, either mythological or invented. These suit real situations better than narrations of authentic facts, which are more difficult to match. They are similar to comparisons, and Aristotle says that those familiar with philosophy (*philosophia*) would be able to find analogies most easily. *Paradeigmata* were useful in persuasion. Resembling actual evidence, they could be mixed in throughout or come at the end of an argument. Epictetus uses a number of historical examples that appear at the end of an essay but are also sometimes embedded within arguments. These could refer to contemporary or past history as well as to common experiences that he would bring to his pupils' attention.[117] Mythological examples also

---

115. In 3.5.17 Epictetus says that Socrates was only preoccupied to improve himself and sent those concerned with theories to sophists like Protagoras or Hippias.
116. *Rhet.* 1394a 2-18.
117. See, e.g., 1.18-32 the Pisonian conspiracy against Nero; 2.8-11 holding the chamber pot for another; 2.12-13 contemporary history; 2.19-24 Vespasian and Helvidius Priscus; 2.25 the dying athlete; and in 1.9.27-34, two personal examples.

find a place here. Martha Nussbaum identified an analogy with medical philosophy, which, in addition to having a consistent and rigorous argument, needed to appeal to imagination and memory through striking examples.[118]

Epictetus attracted his pupils and persuaded them to embrace a different *forma mentis* by appealing to their pasts and their families, friendships, and relationships, but also by referring to and closely examining literature and rhetoric, *paradeigmata*. In Nicopolis some students were disoriented, regretted leaving their past lives, missed the myths that had occupied them for so long, and lamented like "the man who wept for a maid."[119] Far from starting in a vacuum, Stoic philosophy paid much attention to past learning, forming a visible chain extending back to the past and forward into the future. Both Musonius and Epictetus believed that it was crucial to delve into their students' past experiences and sought to become deeply aware of their histories.[120] While students' experiences, passions, and beliefs might vary widely, necessitating different cures and individualized attention, their shared educational past constituted a common basis on which a philosopher had to work.

Stories of various kinds (drawn from history and myth) were the foundation of teaching and would have been worked up at previous educational levels. An understanding of *phantasiai* (impressions) is necessary to identify stories and myth within the fabric of the *Discourses*. Vivid narratives and concrete examples abound, in which the philosopher teaches his students to combat *phantasiai*. Theses needed to grab their attention and help them connect disturbing thoughts to their personal experience. In an essay concerning the uselessness of books read without a critical eye, Epictetus writes, "We have never read and never wrote in order to be able to utilize according to nature the *phantasiai* (impressions) that come to us."[121] Epictetus's principal endeavor was to help apprentices of philosophy learn "the use of impressions"

---

118. Nussbaum 1994, 35–36. On medical imagery, see part III regarding Philodemus.

119. *Diss.* 2.16.28–29. Divine law—says Epictetus—dictates not to take things that belong to others but to use what you have, and not even to desire what you do not have, and if something was taken away from you to give it up easily. The allusion is to Achilles who is not considered a real hero. A young man who complains about what he left behind is like Achilles lamenting the loss of Briseis.

120. Notice the difference from Epicurus; see Suits 2020. See part III about Philodemus and *Parrhesia*.

121. *Diss.* 4.4.14. What follows shows that he attempted something similar with Homer. See also 1.27, all devoted to impressions.

(*chresis* of *phantasiai*) by employing reason. The duty of a reasonable man was to correctly judge these disturbing thoughts and apply a remedy. As a rule, Epictetus refers to impressions that trouble the thoughts of actual individuals, a notable exception being his demonstration that the careful reading of books of poetry can allow one to scrutinize the motivations and actions of characters. The Homeric poems abounded in personal impressions that caused doom and devastation. Books examined critically helped one condemn old motivations and diminish personal apprehensions.

Worrisome impressions could cause much disarray, and an individual would have to learn to create some distance between himself and these painful thoughts.[122] Without being responsible for the thoughts, which arose by themselves, an individual would have to do the necessary work in order to free himself. Impressions regarding oneself were also called *phantasiai*; they caused people anxiety about their behavior and motivations and were disturbing (2.21.9-10). The most vivid essay concerning "impressions" and how to confront them is 2.18, which depicts the authentic struggle of an individual, the necessity of endurance, and the power of these representations that, if not vanquished, would take hold of someone and sweep him away.[123] "Impressions" were disturbing thoughts that could suddenly intrude into one's consciousness or that may always have been part of one's existence. They could be ingrained in those who suffered from depression, could come during sleep at night, or could arise when one was inebriated.[124] They could "bite," and people should fight them powerfully (3.24.108).

The images and types of "impressions" that Epictetus evokes are vivid. Sudden encounters with pretty girls or boys can plunge one into distress.[125] A violent storm can cause terror, unless one can counter it with the idea that death should not be feared (2.19.30). Epictetus also renders graphically the important concept that impressions are not factual, even when they seem to be, and therefore can be controlled and eradicated. "The soul is like a bowl of water and impressions are like a glimmer of light that strikes the water. When the water is disturbed, it seems that the light is disturbed, but it is not" (3.3.20).

---

122. Bénatouïl 2009, 97-125. See also Dobbin 1998, 73, 214-18.
123. See especially 2.18.24-32, against depression.
124. 3.2.5, students of philosophy have to become stronger in order to confront "impressions."
125. 3.2.8 and 3.25.6. Unchaste thoughts can assail the onlooker. The meeting of Paris and Helen had caused much ruin.

Distressing thoughts could also originate from practical and domestic concerns such as oil being spilled, a bowl being ruined, or a fire erupting in one's absence and consuming all one's books (4.10.26). "Using impressions" meant to work actively on them (*melete*) to try to recuperate a more objective attitude. A powerful example of dominating one's distress is given by Galen in *Peri alypesias*.[126] Among people who could not overcome their grief for losing their books, there was a grammarian who died in shock and distraught people who dressed in black (8). Incoherent thoughts and secret fears were the obstacles. Reason should guide someone through critically manipulating impressions that pose dangers to one's well-being. Epictetus uses the noun *oxytes* (sharpness) to refer to the intrinsic quality of impressions, thus conveying an idea of swiftness, sharpness, and bitterness.[127] Impressions can materialize suddenly, intrude surreptitiously, and damage the soul. How could people defend themselves? Though this is the dominant theme of Epictetus's philosophy, he does not suggest much beyond examining external impressions from up close and pausing to put them to the test before one is swept away. Sometimes he offers more pointed advice: "Wouldn't you rather introduce and set over an impression, a fair and noble one and throw out this dirty one?"—an interesting suggestion on which he does not elaborate (2.18.25).[128] An individual who wanted to combat an impression and who in general cared to have a more satisfying life, free of sorrow and envy, would need to practice strongly to achieve that. In *Encheiridion*, Epictetus uses the term *melete* in conjunction with *phantasia*: "When a rough impression comes, make a practice to say to it, 'An impression you are, not the source of the impression'" (1.5).

Myth and Philosophy

Stoic philosophers treated myths and Homeric epic in a subtle and enlightening way. Homer was *the poet* for the Greeks, and his primacy in that culture was such that cultivated individuals were sure to have some lines of his poetry on their lips. A. A. Long rightly confronted the widespread opinion that Stoic philosophers, beginning with Zeno

---

126. See Boudon-Millot and Jouanna 2010.
127. *Diss.* 2.18.24.
128. *Diss.* 2.18.25. See also 3.12.6–7. He hints more vaguely at that procedure in 1.27.4–5.

in the third century BCE, had interpreted Homer as an allegorist.[129] A truly allegorical text would be composed with the intention that readers would interpret it as such. Philosophers had not read Homer literally since before Plato, and instead considered his text a mixture of poetry and fiction. The Stoic views of Homer were complex. According to Diogenes Laertius (7.4), Zeno had written five books of *Homeric Problems* that are entirely lost but in which he displayed some interest in discussing philological points. Likewise, Chrysippus had engaged with grammatical criticism of Homer, emending the text and examining his poems literally. Epictetus could use poetic lines to make ethical points. Somewhat differently from rhetors, he did not look at texts from the outside in order to play with their components in bizarre sophistical games, but instead appropriated them fully so that he could transmit their ethical significance to others. Students, in turn, would absorb them and make them part of their thinking. Homer could therefore speak to a reader not exclusively through his poetic charm, but also in a new voice that Epictetus showed had always been part of his verses.

Epictetus quoted Homer fairly frequently, sometimes just a line or two and at other times by alluding to or paraphrasing passages. It is difficult to ascertain how deeply he knew the Homeric texts, and if he had ever been exposed to the entirety of both the *Iliad* and the *Odyssey*. Stoic philosophers cited Homeric lines to use them in ethical pronouncements, but not systematically. In general, it appears that Epictetus cited the *Iliad* more frequently than the other epic, an observation consistent with what the papyri show.[130] Mythological summaries, companions, and paraphrases were available to the educated public, and Epictetus perhaps had access to those.[131] He would have derived his knowledge of the Homeric texts from his years in school, and he may not ever have gone back to them systematically. A survey of his quotations shows that at times he referred to popular verses that circulated among the cultivated public, such as his quotation of *Iliad* 2.24–25, "that a man who was a counselor should not sleep all night."[132] These verses from the dream of Agamemnon were well known in educational contexts, cited by several sophists like Hermogenes

---

129. Long 1992. Philosophers had interpreted Homer allegorically before the Stoics. See Lamberton 1986; Lamberton and Keaney 1992.
130. Cribiore 2001b, 194–97.
131. Cameron 2004, 52–69.
132. Also see 2.61–62. Cf. Maximus of Tyre *Diss.* 15.6.32.

and Libanius, and developed by students as *gnomai* in writing.¹³³ Their appearance in the margin of a papyrus letter as a humorous exhortation not to delay sending some produce is proof that they had become a sort of proverb.¹³⁴ Occasionally, however, Epictetus used lines that seem to have been less well known and are quoted only by much later writers and philosophers.¹³⁵ A good example is his quotation of *Od.* 11.529–30, which appears only in Eustathius of Thessalonica's twelfth-century commentary to the *Odyssey*.¹³⁶ Yet the figures from literary quotations can be slightly deceiving. The papyri show in Egypt that *Odyssey* 11 was widely read, both in school and by the educated public, because it brought back key figures from the *Iliad*, in this case the fate of Achilles.

The most interesting Homeric passages that appear in the *Discourses* form attractive and compelling narratives connected to people's consciousnesses. Vivid stories and concrete examples were evoked when Epictetus taught his students to combat *phantasiai*, "impressions." Thus mythological and Homeric passages had to grab their attention and help them to connect disturbing thoughts to their personal experience. An important part of his teaching was to inspire his students to read myths and literature in exactly that way. In a passage quoted in the previous section, Epictetus writes, "Books? How and for what end . . .? We have never read and never wrote in order to be able to utilize according to nature the *phantasiai* (impressions) that come to us."¹³⁷ The examples in which he shows that careful reading of poetry books allows one to scrutinize the motivations and actions of characters are fascinating. Admiration for the conduct of a heroic figure could inspire respect and a desire to imitate him. In the first centuries of the Roman Empire, Odysseus was a favorite figure of the Homeric poems, not only in Epictetus but also in other Stoics and stoicizing authors such as Seneca, Musonius, or Dio Chrysostom, who could understand his plight because they were exiled like him.¹³⁸ The hero embodied a major theme of Stoic philosophers, that of submitting to fate and to so-called misfortunes

---

133. Hermogenes *Prog.* 4.4 and in Libanius *Prog.* 4.1.
134. *P.Flor.* II 259; the writer was not a particularly cultivated person.
135. See *Diss.* 3.22.30. These verses were quoted by Galen and only later by some philosophers. They are all from the *Iliad*, book 10.15; 91; 94–95, and 18.289.
136. *Diss.* 4.8.32, the emotional passage in which Odysseus reassures Achilles about the preeminence of his son Neoptolemus.
137. 4.4.14. What follows shows that he attempted something similar with Homer. See also 1.27, all devoted to impressions.
138. See Montiglio 2011, 66–94. Cynic philosophers also regarded Odysseus with admiration and were attracted to the hero as a beggar. See n. 43 in Montiglio.

but without bending. Virtue was schooled in adverse fate, but the philosopher had to continue to be active. In the idealization of Odysseus, misfortunes had a positive role in forming and strengthening character.

> And when Odysseus was shipwrecked and cast ashore, did his need diminish his spirit or break it? But how did he go to the maids to ask for necessities, which is the most disgraceful thing for one to ask another? "As a lion reared in the mountains." In what did he trust? Not in reputation, or money or office, but in his own might, that is, his judgement about the things which are under our control and things which are not under our control. For these are the only things that make men free.[139]

An individual who correctly interpreted the Homeric words was a bold human being who did not tremble at his human condition. Homer inspired the student of literature to consider his narratives in a novel way.

On other occasions the message of poetry was distorted. The Homeric poems abounded in personal impressions that caused doom and devastation. When examined critically, books could help one control individual apprehensions. In such cases, admiration for characters and poetry was to be put aside. Characters were scrutinized for their mistakes and follies, while Epictetus remarked on the deleterious consequences brought by miscalculations and faults. The *Iliad* appeared as a conglomeration of human errors.

> The *Iliad* is nothing but an impression and a poet's use of impressions. Paris got an impression to carry off Menelaus' wife and an impression came to Helen to follow him. Now if Menelaus had gotten the impression that to be deprived of such a wife was a gain, what would have happened? We would have lost not merely the *Iliad* but the *Odyssey* as well.[140]

The delusions of those fictional characters affected young men's minds and put their own secret concerns into relief. An abstract, general argument would not have the same force. The Homeric poems were imprinted in students' minds. These examples would capture their attention and help them connect their own disturbing thoughts and behaviors.

The short passage on the *Iliad* examined earlier continued with a commentary, forming one of the most fascinating messages of the

---

139. See *Od.* 6.130; *Diss.* 3.26.33–35; "necessities," that is, food.
140. *Diss.* 1.28.12–13. See Lamberton and Keaney 1992.

CHAPTER 6

Discourses (1.28.14–28). It is worthwhile to spend a little time on it. The dialogue is tight, and the student's attention is awakened. The conflict lies between the student's conviction that the destruction at the end of the siege of Troy was catastrophic and Epictetus's argument that wars are not the true disasters, a point he makes by pointing to the relative insignificance of human death. In wars it is not only human beings who are destroyed; there is also the "death of many oxen and many sheep and the burning and destruction of many nests of swallows and storks." The student is confused. What is a man? Should his death be on the same level as that of a stork? What is a real calamity? Epictetus returns to the Homeric narrative. Was Alexander destroyed when the Greek ships arrived in Troy and devastated the land? This was merely the destruction of storks' nests. No, he was ruined when he lost his honor, self-respect, and decency. In the same way, Achilles was not destroyed when Patroclus died, but instead when he raged and cried for a woman, forgetting he was a warrior. This is the true adversity that comes to humankind when correct judgment is destroyed. This powerful essay concludes with a consideration of some tragedies in order to show that the protagonists had become trapped by their impressions.[141] If men who follow impressions are crazy and irrational, asks Epictetus, "Are we then acting differently?" With the myth having been debunked, a traditional heroic narrative was shown to be troublesome. A different reading reveals how the Homeric poems could be enlightening and formative.

Stoic philosophy was concerned with death, destiny, and assertion of moral requirement, and not with purely intellectual reasoning. It reiterated that death was a necessity and a duty. While there was no way to combat death, the fear of it needed to be pushed away along with fearful impressions and habits. Exercising strong discipline, a Stoic needed to fight things that deterred and frightened him, like death or pain, by counterbalancing them with contrary habits. In *Discourses* 1.27, after discussing *phantasiai*, Epictetus uses the outstanding example of the warrior Sarpedon in a paraphrase of *Iliad* 12.322–28.[142]

> When death appears to be an evil, we must have ready at hand the argument that it is a duty to avoid evil things and death is necessary. For what am I to do? Where am I to escape it? Suppose that

---

141. *Diss.* 1.28.32–33: Atreus, Oedipus, Phoenix, and Hippolytus were blinded by their impressions.

142. See the commentary in Dobbin 1998, 214–18.

I am Sarpedon, the son of Zeus saying nobly: "I have come, and now I wish either to win the prize for valor myself or give another the opportunity to win it. If I cannot succeed myself in something, I will not begrudge another the chance to do something heroic." (1.27.7–8)

Epictetus comments that this example may be beyond most people, and yet it is not completely unreachable. Death cannot be escaped, and no magical charm against it can be found. Modern readers are always fond of the Homeric episode involving Sarpedon and Glaucus, but it is not the heroism and gallantry of Sarpedon's words that win them over. Sarpedon's *cri de coeur*, with his sincere and moving desire to survive and be forever young and immortal, emerges from the depths of the human soul. Epictetus was not interested in those words, which show the warrior in the momentary grip of a *phantasia*. He reported only how Sarpedon overcame a moment of weakness to become strong and aware of his destiny.

Often only one line of poetry is evoked. Epictetus mentions the examples of two blessed and happy heroes, both devoted to Zeus, who traveled everywhere and grew acquainted with many men: Heracles, a perennial hero, and Odysseus.[143] A student immediately rebuts: "But Odysseus suffered for his wife and cried sitting on a rock."[144] The Homeric passage must have impressed him because of Odysseus's manifestations of utter desperation. Epictetus promptly reacts: "But do you believe completely what Homer and his stories said?"[145] He continues to say that if Odysseus had really cried and lamented, he would not have been a good man, because he would be acting against Zeus, who cared for the happiness of everyone.[146] One should note that Epictetus alluded to the tradition of Plato and Socrates, and in another section he credits Odysseus with authentic courage.[147] If we find it difficult to truly understand the Stoic concept of happiness and its dismissal of seemingly justified mourning, we can identify with the student of this essay who, unconvinced, objected, "But my mother cries when she does

---

143. Odysseus was preferred as a hero because one could suspect in Heracles an excessive willingness to sustain labors.
144. *Od.* 5.82. "Rock" was a variant of "shore."
145. See in Dio *Or.* 11 the criticism of Odysseus.
146. *Diss.* 3.24.17. Cf. the commentary to this passage in Long 2002, 191–94.
147. *Diss.* 3.26.33–34 where Odysseus reacts with dignity after the storm, trusting his judgments.

not see me" (3.24.22). This is a plunge from Homer to philosophical interpretation and then back to reality and life.

The Theater

Two mesmerizing passages show the strong degree of attention Epictetus paid to the theater.

> Remember that you are an actor in a play, the nature of which is up to the director to decide. If he wants the play to be short, it will be short, if he wants it long it will be long. Whether he wants you to act the part of a poor, or a cripple, of a ruler or of a commoner, see to it that you portray the character convincingly, but the assignment of roles belongs to another. It is up to you to play the part assigned to you, but the choice of the role belongs to another.[148]

In this world, he assumes, everybody plays a part and is expected to fulfill his role, no matter how high or how lowly. There is no choice. God is the stage manager and dramatist. And again, in *Diss.* 1.29.41-43:

> A time will soon come when the actors (*tragoidoi*) will think that their masks and boots and robes are themselves. Man, you have these things as material and plot. Say something so we may know whether you are a tragic actor or a jester. Both of these have the other things in common. For this reason, if someone removes their boots and mask and brings them on stage as mere shades, has the tragic actor vanished or does he remain? If he has a voice, he remains.

In this passage, actors are compared with those who pursue careers in important offices, such as provincial governors. They have identified with the symbols of their power. While actor and character are distinguished in the previous scenario, such separation now vanishes, and the actor loses his individuality. What is left when they strip off the senatorial toga, Epictetus asks?[149]

---

148. Epictetus, *Encheiridion* 17. On theater see also fr. 1: the actor Polus performed Oedipus as a king and as a beggar. The good man should perform well in every costume. Maximus of Tyre *Or.* 1.2 argues that the actor should respect "the beauty of the compositions he plays and never allows himself to be stricken by speechlessness."

149. See Long 2002, 242-43. The actor's costume corresponds to life circumstances, and the voice is his true self.

Scholars have commented on Epictetus's interest in the theater.[150] Here I offer some observations in the hopes of better defining what theater meant for him. The images of men as actors in the drama of life and of a philosopher as an actor performing different roles probably originated with Cynics and Stoics.[151] These metaphors became rather popular, as shown by references in Favorinus, Lucian, and Maximus of Tyre, among others.[152] At the beginning of *Or.* 1, for example, Maximus says that actors could play different roles (Agamemnon, Achilles, Telephus, Palamedes, and others), and therefore philosophers/actors should be versatile.[153] In a number of "theatrical passages," Epictetus shows himself a master pedagogue, able to swiftly combine reality and myth. Examples could be used in interesting ways that appealed to students' familiarity with the theater. The written forms of tragedies and comedies maintained a level of prestige in the second century, even if they had to be read with a different attention and sensibility in the class of a philosopher. In *Diss.* 1.28.32-33 Epictetus shows that Achilles and Agamemnon acted foolishly, and that both did and suffered wrongs because they were following impressions. Tragedies provided further examples of random behaviors generated by sense impressions. "What is the *Atreus* of Euripides? An appearance (*to phainomenon*). The *Oedipus* of Sophocles? An appearance. The *Phoenix*? An appearance. *Hippolytus*? An appearance." Men trapped in the clutches of sense impressions were called madmen, yet they continued to act irrationally. Epictetus evokes or randomly mentions Heracles, Oedipus, Laius, Aegisthus, Eteocles, and Polyneices. In *Diss.* 2.17.19-22 he paraphrases Euripides's *Medea*, providing a commentary in which he calls her "a great spirit" on account of her clairvoyance and knowledge of herself.[154]

Epictetus's allusions to the theater did not rest on books alone, however, but depended on living performances that took place at the time. To what kinds of spectacles was he referring in the second quotation above when he mentioned masks, boots, and robes? The common assumption regarding his theatrical allusions has always been that he was

---

150. Marcus Aurelius 12.36 also used the comparison of the play of life. Death arrives even when the actor complains that he had not acted in all his five acts; see Sellars (2021, 97), who thinks that Marcus was inspired by Epictetus.
151. But cf. Plato *R.* 577a-b. More in Dobbin 1998, 231.
152. Koniaris 1983, 220-22; Favorinus *de exilio* 3; Lucian *Saturnalia* 19; Maximus of Tyre *Or.* 1.
153. Maximus *Or.* 1.1; Trapp 1997.
154. Euripides, *Medea*: the part of the text he paraphrases is roughly lines 790-810.

calling attention to classical drama, but this is only a part of the reality. The classical tragedies and comedies of the fifth century BCE continued to be represented, sometimes in abridged form. Dio in *Or.* 19.5 writes that the iambics of tragedies had been preserved but the lyric parts had fallen away. In *Or.* 11.9 he mentions a series of mythological themes interpreted by the flute or sung in the theaters, where those who offered the most emotional spectacles received prizes.[155] When Dio mentions that these actors were interpreting stories "in words or music," he alludes to tragedies interpreted by *tragoidoi*, actors who would break into songs.

Other genres, however, had developed in the Hellenistic and Roman periods: mimes and pantomimes.[156] These attracted enthusiastic crowds throughout the Roman Empire and continued to enjoy great success in late antiquity, despite the reservations of Christians such as Tatian and John Chrysostom. Pantomime actors wore beautiful masks suited to the story, which had closed mouths because the actors were silent and interpreted the drama through exaggerated gestures and dance. By contrast, Lucian considered hideous those actors of tragedies who performed wearing huge masks with gaping mouths, shoes with very high soles, and padding all over.[157] Epictetus and his students must have been very familiar with these entertainers.[158] Long's remark that the students came from well-off families that belonged to the upper echelons of society, and therefore were fond of spectacles, is not particularly relevant here, because these performances were open to all classes.[159] At that time a multitude of local festivals were still held in the empire, organized and endowed by private citizens.[160] Pantomimes apparently played a role in disseminating tragic stories at the beginning of the empire.[161] Though pantomimes were performed by masked dancers who acted out mythological subjects through movement, mimes could be staged not only in theaters but also in private houses and in

---

155. For other passages that testify to Dio's attention to the theater, see Webb 2018, 302–15.
156. See Hall and Wyles 2008. On the difference between mime and pantomime, see Wiseman 2008; Webb 2008. Quintilian 4.2.52 and 53 mentions mime as having a credible pattern of events and crude subjects. The most extensive farce and mime on papyrus is *P.Oxy.* III 413.
157. Lucian, *On the Dance* 27–30.
158. The festivals he mentions in 4.4.24–27 must have provided these spectacles.
159. Long (2002, 243) talks about "performative demands of elite Roman culture."
160. Wilson 2007.
161. Lucian, *On the Dance* 37–61 has a long list of subjects for pantomimes. Garelli (2007, 271–80) provides a list of known pantomimes that took place.

the street. Actors would perform a single role with quick reversals and a varied repertoire in which gods and heroes were presented in banal situations.[162] These were burlesque performances comparable to, but much less refined than, Lucian's four groups of very brief dialogues, the *Dialogues of the Dead, of the Courtesans, of the Gods, and of the Sea Gods*.[163] The latter of these drew inspiration from Homer, among others. As we shall see, Epictetus played on his students' familiarity with both spectacles and Homer to construct tight mini-vignettes that would not only amuse them but also show how much he despised that world of counterfeit heroes. As in the world of Lucian, traditional heroes and episodes were seen from new perspectives and with undertones of Cynic and Stoic lines of questioning.

In *Diss.* 1.22.3–8 Epictetus mentions contemporary conflicts between Jews and Syrians and Egyptians and Romans.[164] The humor of the following Homeric vignette derives from the rapid and insipid verbal exchanges of the characters. The debate between the heroes does not center on heroic issues, but on girlfriends. Agamemnon and Achilles are the protagonists of a childish drama centered around Chryseis and Briseis.

> AGAMEMNON: "If I have to return Chryseis, then I should take from *someone* the prize he has won."
> ACHILLES: "Would you then take the woman I love?"
> "Yes, the woman you love."
> "Shall I then be the only one . . . ? Am I going to be the only one to have nothing?"

The petty way in which Epictetus presents these personal hostilities in the Trojan War was also meant to trivialize the modern conflicts he mentions.[165] New comedy and issues of bourgeois life were both objects of attention.

A similar exchange takes place in *Diss.* 2.24.21–23. Here Agamemnon does not think it expedient to return Chryseis to her father, but Achilles considers the move advantageous. This disagreement makes them

---

162. G. Theocharidis 1940; Sonnino 2014. See Webb 2008, 12n19 with extensive bibliography on pantomime.
163. Cf. for example in Lucian's *Dialogues of the Gods* 21 (17) the fast lines in the opening of *Apollo and Hermes* or of 13 (8) *Hephaestus and Zeus*.
164. The reason of the conflict was the debate over whether eating pork was holy or not. The comparison with the quarrel of Agamemnon and Achilles continues in 1.22.5–8.
165. Wehner (2000, 157–75) looks at fictional dialogues with heroes of the myth and considers Agamemnon and Achilles the only figures present in dialogues.

forget the important reason for which they had come to Troy and their duty to engage in the war as warriors. Here Epictetus seems to address an actor in the little play.

> "Hey, man (*anthrope*), why did you come here? To get girls or to fight?"
> "To fight."
> "With whom, the Trojans or the Greeks?"
> "The Trojans."
> "Well, are you neglecting Hector and drawing your sword against your king? And you, most honorable man, are you neglecting your duties as king?"

The passage continues by addressing the two warriors who "engaged in a fist-fight" for the sake of "a young maid."

In another scene[166] Epictetus discusses hypothetical arguments that "are similar to a game or a drama in that they depend on certain premises."[167] This time, he embodies the persona of a dependent or servant of Agamemnon: "And again we have agreed to play the story of Agamemnon and Achilles. The one who has been appointed to play the part of Agamemnon says to me: 'Go to Achilles and drag away Briseis.' I go. He says, 'Come' and I come." A much longer debate with Agamemnon occurs within the essay on the Cynic philosopher (3.22.33).[168] Parts of it are in the same short and crude theatrical style as the lines before.

> "Poor me, the Greeks are under attack."
> "Too bad for your mind, the one thing you have neglected and been indifferent to."
> "They are going to die at the Trojans' hands."
> "And if they are not killed by the Trojans, wouldn't they die?"
> "Yes, but not all at once."

A few lines below, at 3.22. 36–37:

> "Why did you come? Was it a question of desire, avoidance, choice or refusal?"

---

166. *Diss.* 1.25.10–13.
167. Dobbin 1998, 207. Cf. 1.12.17 and 1.7.22–25. See 1.26.1: "As a student was reading the hypothetical arguments, Epictetus said: 'This also is a hypothetical law, that we must accept what follows from the hypothesis.'"
168. I covered this Cynic essay in reviewing Epictetus's attention to rhetoric.

"No, but the little wife (wifey)[169] of my brother had been taken away."

"Wasn't it a blessing in disguise to get rid of this little wench of a wife?"

"Well, should we just have let the Trojans insult us?"

"What kind of men are the Trojans? Are they wise or foolish? If they are wise, why are you fighting with them? If foolish, why do you care?"

These exchanges are frozen and unrealistic, and because of that they are humorous. The protagonists seem like foolish puppets in a world of spectacles that would also include acrobats, clowns, jugglers, and dancing bears.[170] The Homeric texts and tragedies they are intended to mimic are far in the background. There is no character development, and the issues at hand are reduced to artificial dialogues of no importance. Epictetus is the puppeteer, and he holds his marionettes tightly in his hands. They do not have any independence or ability to escape their destinies. One surmises that in addition to arousing some hilarity in class, these vignettes would also have reinforced students' perception that the literature they relished, and into which they had delved for many years, was merely fiction and therefore not so far removed from the contemporary world full of pretension and posturing. In these exchanges, are we supposed to imagine pantomimes constantly transforming themselves with eloquent gestures from one character to another, from Agamemnon to Achilles? Or are these burlesque mimes presented and read in a comic vein and intended for humor and laughter? It is not important to identify them precisely, but the world of spectacle is visibly exuding mockery and disdain.

Listening to the Philosopher: Are These Arrian's Notes?

Some scholars continue to maintain a view of the *Discourses* as a text that Arrian fully composed while trusting his memories, as Xenophon had done. Were these notes that Arrian jotted down spontaneously after hearing Epictetus's lectures, or do we have to regard this account as

---

169. A diminutive that diminished the stature of Helen. Oldfather's translation as "frail" is wrong. Agamemnon is contemptuous.
170. Webb 2008, 25–26.

a continuous literary text? Arrian tells us that they were annotations of what Epictetus delivered in class. I showed above that the letter to Gellius is an authentic document, on the basis of which we can maintain that Arrian took down notes. However, it is now time to see whether the text itself contains some indications in this respect. Here and there in what precedes, I have pointed to the fact that the text can be regarded as extemporaneous and artless; it is time to gather my observations. The titles of the various essays, which have been added later on, give some artificial uniformity to the story. Those individuals who according to Arrian had gotten hold of his notes and leaked them to the public must have understood their value. Arrian's initial annotations may have been disorderly to a degree; of this there are signs. A clean text with good handwriting and no abbreviations was a sine qua non. It is logical to assume that he took rough notes initially and later roughly edited them for himself, even if they were not thoroughly revised. He either personally copied the text from his notes or dictated them to a scribe without eliminating episodes, leaving the expressions and verbal peculiarities of the philosopher as they were in reality.

Arrian's notes thoroughly convey the ways in which he experienced Epictetus's brilliance, his intensity, his sometimes difficult rapports with others, his intransigence, and his ardent demands that his students internalize his discourse. But how did he do that? He wrote his notes without making them more palatable and presented sometimes disputable but spontaneous traits of the philosopher that would not be there in a literary and artificial account. When Epictetus spewed out his furious diminutives that showed his outrage, Arrian and his classmates must have been thoroughly entertained. And what about when the philosopher became the puppeteer of some mythological figures? His line-by-line dialogues show that he was the amused "director of the play," who surely provoked hilarity while giving some crucial lessons. Scholars have observed that the image that the philosopher projected was quite different from late antiquity, when some philosophers (Proclus, Plotinus) appeared larger than life. And yet Epictetus was indeed larger than life and captured the full attention of his student Arrian.

Arrian was able to render the atmosphere of the class eloquently by annotating the various and entertaining teaching strategies. It was important to the philosopher to disconnect his students from the academic world they had left behind and the cultural milieu to which they were habituated. In some cases, he had to dwell on myths and on Homer, putting into relief how characters were deluded, and how their expectations were wrong. He showed that these figures desired futile objects and insane relationships, and that impressions were there to ruin them. While all these lessons were conducive to serious reprimands and abrasive criticism, sometimes Epictetus tried to reach the same goal through laughter. By representing the frozen characters of the little story of Achilles and Agamemnon and others, Epictetus must have generated some relaxation that Arrian thought was essential to record in order to depict realistically his pedagogy. The humor of the Homeric vignettes derives from the rapid and insipid verbal exchanges of the characters.

Arrian was an enthusiastic disciple who aimed at preserving Epictetus's ideas and communicating their significance to others. We do not know for sure if he made some cuts in Epictetus's words while taking them down. His notes transmit more than just the content and the ethical message of the philosopher. They also give the essence of his classes, the behaviors of students, their resistance and arrogance, and, at times, Epictetus's disappointment at their lack of understanding. Students' emotions such as envy, regret, and loneliness are revealed too, sometimes with ridicule. We are exposed to Epictetus's oral style, his use of the contemporary Koine, and the vocabulary of philosophical teaching. In the four books that have been preserved, Arrian chose to transmit the conversations of Epictetus and his students rather than the philosopher's theoretical teaching, which probably took place in the afternoons when Epictetus read Stoic writers with his class. At earlier stages of education, knowledge was considered a movable object, and a teacher was simply its transmitter. In philosophy, by contrast, knowledge was fire and the teacher ignited it. Education was not conceived of as filling a vase but as a way to light a spark.[171] Arrian was deeply aware of this and was right to fear that Epictetus's words would be lost or misinterpreted, as he manifests in the letter to Gellius.

For Arrian, dialogues between Epictetus and his pupils were the most valuable part of his teaching. At the same time, we have noticed how few of these are real dialogues and that Arrian often put in Epictetus's mouth the responses of others through his solo performances. But why did he do that? This was a necessity if he cared to keep up with his master's pace. By often omitting the questions and answers

---

171. Cf. above, 2.24.28 when Epictetus declares that there was no spark between him and that student.

of his classmates, he gave his note-taking some respite. When reading the *Discourses,* some have wondered whose voices we are hearing. This is certainly the voice of Epictetus. He was the puppeteer of the class play and its director.

Returning now for a last look at the *Discourses*, one passage recounts a little story (2.17.30–33). It presents a new student, whom the philosopher welcomes to the school warmly, saying that it is the youth's destiny to adorn philosophy. The young man goes through his first level of studies "and masters it like an athlete." He then goes back to Epictetus for advice, saying: "Surely, I want to be calm and peaceful, but as a pious man, a philosopher, and a diligent student, I also want to know what my duty towards the gods is, towards parents and brothers, towards my country and strangers." When the philosopher tells him to move on to the second level, the student objects that he has done so already, but that his goal is to achieve tranquility and security forever.

Overwhelmed, Epictetus proclaims, "Man, you are a god!" We wonder about the identity of this perfect young man. Was he an ideal student, someone Epictetus conjured up as a reassuring counterpart to the average young men who disappointed him? Or perhaps was he Arrian himself?

PART III

Recording Lectures of Philosophers

In the following chapters I concentrate on extant notes taken down by students during the lectures of three different teachers of philosophy. These have been preserved and are of great significance. They provide a "window" into ancient philosophical classrooms by giving us more direct access than before. One of the fundamental subjects that chapter 7 considers is how fluid ancient education was, especially in late antiquity, when levels and materials to study did not embrace circumscribed and exclusive areas. After the second century CE, philosophical instruction became essentially exegetical. Texts had acquired a fundamental importance at the expense of discussions on current events and issues, which especially Didymus and Olympiodorus avoided completely.

The collections of notes that I examine include annotations that the first-century BCE philosopher Philodemus of Gadara wrote in Athens when he took down the lectures of his Epicurean teacher Zeno (chapter 8). When Philodemus went to Naples, he lectured in school about these notes, certainly adding some commentary. Philodemus is here the notetaker, but we don't know about the note-taking of his students. In chapter 9 I study Didymus the Blind, teaching in Alexandria in the fourth century CE, and the lectures on the Sacred Scriptures, transmitted by the Tura papyri, that he delivered to his pupils. I shall argue that some of his students wrote them down. In chapter 10 I look at philosophical lectures taken down *apo phones* by students in Alexandria in the sixth century. I consider in particular the students' annotations on Plato's *First Alcibiades*, recorded from the lectures of the philosopher Olympiodorus.

CHAPTER 7

Introduction
Ancient Commentaries

To have a proper understanding of the works discussed in chapters 8–10, it is necessary to make some preliminary observations (both grammatical and textual) on ancient commentaries, which may not be familiar to some readers. Philodemus wrote several commentaries, some of which, along with his philosophical works, use the terms *hypomnemata* and *hypomnematikon*, which will need explanation. The work *Peri Parrhesias*, which is at the center of my investigation, is not a commentary in the proper sense of the word but was a running discussion. Yet it can be considered a sort of commentary on commentary, since it reproduces Philodemus's teacher's lectures.

Didymus the Blind's commentary was essentially grammatical, even though he did not preserve all the features of grammatical works and expanded on other areas. His main purpose was to clarify the text of the Bible, but he also added some notions of elementary philosophy. Olympiodorus's commentary was philosophical, but he also devoted some attention to linguistic explanations in order to clarify the text, since at such a late date his students had some trouble understanding it. Both Didymus's and Olympiodorus's commentaries were based on lemmata, passages of varying length taken from the text they commented on. After talking about commentaries in general, I inspect marginalia, that is, notes that appear in ancient papyri in the margins and in the interlinear spaces. These notes are fragments of ancient commentaries from the Alexandrians and later scholars and sometimes preserve traces of school activity.

Grammatical Commentaries

We should first observe that grammatical commentaries were different from the textual commentaries on ancient authors. The commentaries of the grammarians had to serve the needs of students at the second level of instruction, including those young pupils who were just out of elementary education. They needed special guidance because, to quote Gellius, they were part of a "vulgus semidoctum" (half-taught crowd) and had just started to breathe the air of education.[1] In addition to tailoring his teaching to advanced students, Didymus the Blind had to address those needy young men and adjust his teaching accordingly. Quintilian appropriately said that a lecture "was not like a dinner that was insufficient for many, but it was like the sun that offered light and heat to all."[2] This eternal problem of teaching was more acute in late antiquity when, as we will see, the levels of instruction were not neatly divided as in the age of Quintilian and Plutarch. Commentaries had to respond satisfactorily to the requests of a diverse audience. In commentaries, grammarians could cover a text line by line and word by word or divide it into distinct lemmata. Their notes concentrated on punctuation, meter, and especially points of grammar, covering morphology and syntax. In the late fourth to early fifth century, the learned grammarian Servius wrote a commentary to Vergil, for which Robert Kaster has remarked on the disproportionate place of notes concerning language.[3] The traditional text that described the expertise of the grammarian is the grammatical treatise of Dionysius Thrax.[4] Grammar addressed the poets and rarely prose, and embraced prosody, explanation

---

1. Gellius, *NA* 1.7.16–17.
2. Quintilian 1.2.14.
3. Kaster 1980 and 1988, 169–97.
4. As I explained in an earlier work (Cribiore 2001b, 185–87 and note 2), the initial section of Dionysius's commentary where he defined grammar in all its aspects is considered authentic by scholarly consensus and should date to about 100 BCE. The rest of the work, however, was probably a product of late antiquity. See Wouters 1979, 1995 and Schenkeveld 1993.

of literary figures, phraseology, subject matter, etymologies, analogical regularities, and the critical study of literature.

In the class of the grammarian, a young man achieved the status of a person of culture, and in this respect an expertise in rhetoric did not bring him a substantial advantage unless he aimed at political life.[5] What he had learned in grammatical school served as a passport that allowed him to address cultured and sophisticated people in different parts of the ancient world and to be recognized by them. Quintilian described the grammarian's activity as lecturing on correct speech, explaining problematic issues, giving the background of a text, or paraphrasing poems. The "historical" side of that activity consisted of extracting historical, geographical, and mythological figures and tropes. *Scholia* to an author taken from advanced commentaries inform us about that side of literary activity. We have seen that Epictetus regarded "historiae" with distaste as the epitome of the grammatical instruction to which his new students were addicted. Learning rules upon rules and imbibing often irrelevant information was simpler than aiming to improve one's moral stature. "Histories" communicated the weight of tradition and a knowledge of the past that was fragmented into unconnected parts.

Grammatical commentaries also insisted on elucidation of unfamiliar vocabulary. Glossographical analysis was a powerful tool in the hands of the grammarian. *Scholia minora* to Homer, which appear in so many school papyri, consisted of lists of words or expressions that were given corresponding and easier terms taken from current usage.[6] They are distinguished from the *scholia vetera*, a compilation of exegetical material that went back to the Alexandrian scholars. The most elementary part of grammatical commentaries addressed the correct reading of a text. It was crucial for students to learn how to approach a literary work with understanding. Didymus the Blind in fact was acutely aware of the power of words and the insufficient preparation of his pupils. Two more points need to be elucidated. It was typical of grammatical commentaries to be very detailed at the beginning of a book and then include only sparse notes.[7] We will see that Olympiodorus observed

---

5. On the education imparted in the class of the grammarian, cf. Cribiore 2001b, 185–219 with references.

6. Cribiore 2001b, 207, 210.

7. This is a characteristic of ancient educational works. The grammarians covered the first parts of a text, something that is present in ancient scholia; cf. Cribiore 2001b, 194.

the same method. In grammatical commentaries, moreover, the personality and quirks of the compiler disappeared entirely, leaving a work with little connection to him.[8]

Textual Commentaries: *Hypomnemata*

The last decades have seen a strong interest in ancient commentaries to authoritative texts that provided access to a cultural tradition. The primary motivation for writing commentaries was the need to fully understand ancient texts that had lost their immediate appeal or intelligibility to readers and to explain language and context to students. As Eleanor Dickey has shown, traces of ancient scholarship can be found in the fifth century BCE, but this reached a peak with the Alexandrian scholars who produced commentaries on authors in the first century BCE. More interest was aroused in the imperial period.[9] The Alexandrian scholars established securely the texts of many classical authors and produced commentaries on them. These have not survived, but their influence and some fragments appear in the scholia, marginalia, and later commentaries. Aristarchus was the most conservative of them, and the standardization of the Homeric text that was a constant in education was due to his influence.[10] His commentaries were little altered after they were created, although multiple versions circulated. The Alexandrian Didymus Chalcenterus (to be distinguished from Didymus the Blind), who lived in the Augustan Age, wrote innumerable books and was a tremendous producer of commentaries. None of those was preserved in its entirety, but again fragments appear in later works and in marginalia.[11] The same is true for the commentaries of the grammarian Theon in the age of Tiberius. The fragments of Theon that have been transmitted to us have lost their linguistic content and concern almost only mythography.

Craig Gibson has argued that earlier commentaries were not necessarily any more exempt from errors than later ones.[12] Commentaries

---

8. Kaster observes that in contrast to Macrobius, Servius at times revealed a self-image. See Kaster 1988, 171; Kaster 1980.
9. Dickey 2007, 3–17. On Latin philology and commentaries, see Zetzel 2018.
10. McNamee (1981) has shown that while early papyri and annotations occasionally mention the work of other scholars, later ones recognize absolutely the authority of Aristarchus. On Aristarchus, education, and the papyri, see Cribiore 2001a.
11. See Dickey 2007, 7, 63.
12. Gibson 2002, 6–7.

could circulate independently from a text and were self-standing, but in what follows I consider those in which lemmata were explained through observations on the language and thus led to exegesis of a text. The commentaries of both Didymus and Olympiodorus maintain this format. They are not the kind of commentaries in which an author's text is discussed in its entirety (or almost), but they cite selected passages.[13]

Marginalia in Papyri: Facts from Fragments

Marginalia consist of notes written in the margins or interlinear spaces of a text. They are fragments from ancient scholarship that refer to commentaries that have mainly disappeared.[14] Not only are they of great importance because they preserve traces of those ancient commentaries that we would not know otherwise, but they also, something of great significance for this project, often represent the works of scholars, teachers, and students. The ultimate source of annotations was oral. Notes arose from the reading of commentaries, from lectures that took place in school, and from students' memoranda.

Notes written in the margins are sometimes called *scholia* and need to be distinguished from *hypomnemata*, self-standing commentaries.[15] The latter, which often are the remnants of ancient commentaries, have close connections with ancient authoritative texts, but in the former the connection is dispersed in sporadic notes and comments. Marginalia and notes on papyri are scattered on texts from the third century BCE to the seventh century CE, but until later antiquity annotation was not a frequent practice.[16] Sometimes notes may look similar to commentaries, but undoubtedly the influence of commentaries like those of Didymus and Theon are the common factor. Papyrus commentaries preserve the names of these commentators only very occasionally, because the name of a commentator is most often concealed. The eminent interest of commentaries was to transmit some of the research of predecessors. We will see that Didymus's text and the commentaries of the Neoplatonists such as Olympiodorus include several expressions that give us

---

13. Cf. in part I the observations about the commentaries of Alexander of Aphrodisias.
14. "Facts from Fragments" is the title of a great article written in 1982 by Peter Parsons.
15. See Dickey 2007, 11n25, 11–16, 18–71. Scholia were originally intended to be "notes" and were so called by Byzantine scholars.
16. McNamee 2007, 60. In considering marginalia on papyri, I refer to this book, adding my interpretations.

the flavor of teaching and oral communication. These expressions refer to parts already covered and to explanatory terms and expressions that often are responses to students' questions. In the same way, the papyrus marginalia often commence with expressions like "instead of," "that is to say," "for example," "this means," and "the sense is" and let us perceive the atmosphere of the classroom.[17]

The notes in texts before late antiquity are shorter and sparser, but later they increase in length and become considerably denser. Kathleen McNamee rightly argued that the notes do not represent personal contributions to a text, such as ideas and original suppositions, but are records of information and most often refer to previous commentaries. I would like to point, however, to two papyri that contain corrections and notes written for school use. Both are autographs, that is, written by the author himself. Autographs are worthy of close attention because they refer to a text before it has been emended and show an author and his mind at work. One of these papyri is *P.Lit.Lond.* 138, a rhetorical exercise from the second century that was entirely written by a teacher or a student. The papyrus shows marginal signs, corrections, and interlinear notes that point to a didactic use. Another papyrus from the fourth century CE consists of two encomia written in honor of a deceased professor at Berytus, where there was a famous school of law.[18] A different professor at the school wrote two versions of the exercise. He did not need to dictate a text to a scribe but penned his composition himself, adding in the margin corrections, additions, deletions, and more verses to be inserted. In both formal or less formal texts, marginalia might be written by the original writer, but often informal texts were annotated by readers in or out of school.

Marginalia refer mostly to poetic authors, especially to Homer, Euripides, Menander, Aristophanes, and Pindar, who are cited very often. Prose is rarely annotated, with some exceptions from Demosthenes.[19] While texts from the school of the grammarian take the lion's share,[20] oratorical texts are rarely represented, probably because observations on language in these texts were of lesser interest. One exception

---

17. Cribiore 2020a. "Instead of," for example, refers to another term that was more current, a gloss
18. Cribiore 2020a.
19. Cf. Gibson 2002.
20. Marginalia in texts studied at elementary levels are nonexistent.

is a papyrus with notes jotted down during a lecture.[21] It preserves some theory but also the personal contributions of a teacher or a student. Though one suspects that most of the notes originated from a scholastic context, sometimes it is difficult to be certain. The handwriting of students beyond the elementary level might be informal but not necessarily so clumsy as to constitute a clear marker. The fact that marginalia usually occur on the verso—that is, the back of a papyrus—is also an unsure clue.[22]

Yet in some cases other evidence corroborates the suspicion that some annotated papyri likely originated in schools.[23] Such is the case of *PSI* VII 747, with the first book of the *Iliad*. The text and the notes are written by the original writer in an informal and not accomplished hand. The writer may have been a student.[24] Another papyrus shows fragments from Euripides's *Hypsipyle*, a play that was a favorite in education.[25] The text is written by a scribe who occasionally added notes to dialogues regarding the speaker. Another hand, smaller and cramped, made alterations and additions in the text and added notes in the margin. The editors of this magnificent papyrus (*P.Oxy.* XXXIV 2694) remark that the scribe, who had a very accomplished and elegant hand, had probably been commissioned to write the text of Book 4 of Apollonius's *Argonautica* on the recto and on the verso a commentary on the text. Though this elegant specimen was, because of its formality, not supposed to have annotations in the margins, notes were written on both sides in handwriting different from the main hand. This text was therefore probably read and annotated in school.[26] Many marginalia reproduce the format of commentaries with lemmata and explanations, as in the commentaries of Didymus and Olympiodorus. Many of them are extracts from the scholarly tradition, either directly or in a brief form. They always deal with issues from the commentaries of the Alexandrians and focus on the exegesis of the authoritative texts of the classical period and on language.

---

21. *P.Oxy.* XVII 2086; see Cribiore 2001b, 144. On a papyrus of Plato's *Republic* annotated during a lecture, see Part I.
22. Cf. Cribiore 1996.
23. I will mention only a few of these papyri with notes from a school context.
24. McNamee 2007, 25.
25. *P.Oxy.* VI 852; Cribiore 2001c.
26. McNamee (2007, 55) observes that the text is reminiscent of *scholia minora*, that is, elementary glossographical material.

CHAPTER 8

Notes from Athens
Philodemus On Frank Criticism

Between 1752 and 1754, a Roman villa was discovered at the buried town of Herculaneum (now Ercolano) in southern Italy, on the ancient coastline below the volcano Vesuvius, close to Naples.[1] In an eruption in 79 CE, the temperatures around the villa reached 310–330° Celsius, and the town was destroyed. It was covered by the thick layer of volcanic material deposited by Vesuvius. The villa was luxurious, as its architecture and the numerous works of art, including frescoes, marble sculptures, and bronzes, testify.[2]

Most of the villa has not been excavated yet, in part for reasons of safety. It is now known by the name Villa dei Papiri because its library contained many hundreds of carbonized book rolls.[3] The owner of the house was probably from the family of the Pisones and might have been Lucius Calpurnius Piso, son-in-law of Julius Caesar; Philodemus of Gadara was his protégé. Cicero (*In Pisonem* 68–72, 74) alludes to Philodemus, without mentioning him, as being in constant company

---
1. See the comprehensive introduction to the subject by Longo Auricchio et al. 2020.
2. Many are now housed in Naples, in the Museo Archeologico Nazionale.
3. See Sider 2005. The numerous attempts to unroll the carbonized volumes started in the eighteenth century with Father Piaggio, a genius technician who constructed a useful machine that was used by modern scholars like Richard Janko and David Blank.

of the senator.[4] The library contained philosophical works that were already packed in cases when the volcano erupted.[5] There are several copies of the same work, and it is unclear whether there was a scriptorium in the villa or whether the volumes were copied somewhere else. This extraordinary Epicurean library was probably assembled in Athens first and attested to the activity of the Garden of Epicurus with works of Epicurus and his disciples.

The volumes were assembled from the third century BCE to the beginning of the first century BCE. The library was then transported from Athens to Campania, where it acquired a great quantity of volumes written by the Epicurean Philodemus that affirm his own incredible scholarly activity. It is still not certain if Philodemus resided in the villa. Only a connection with Naples can be found. Why transport a library?[6] Philodemus seemingly meant to transmit the Hellenistic doctrine of Epicurus and of his teacher Zeno to Italy and transplant it there. He must have realized that the center of Epicurean philosophy was not Athens anymore and so moved part of that book collection to Italy.[7] The Garden was in a crisis and seems to have been attacked by detractors. Perhaps the work *Peri Parrhesias* was a sign of that. The simplest and more natural explanation of Philodemus's conduct, however, is that the library in the Villa dei Papiri was his personal collection to which, after his death, other works of his were added, together with books of Epicurus and Epicureans like Demetrius Lacon.

On Frank Criticism

Philodemus's Περὶ παρρησίας (in Latin, *De libertate dicendi*; *On Frank Criticism*) belongs to a group of Philodemus's works on ethics. This was the part of philosophy that attracted him most. Other books on this subject include a major work on vices and virtues in ten books, a vast inquiry into passions, and toward the end of his life a work on death.

---

4. Philodemus was born in 110 BCE and died circa 30 BCE. At that time Piso was about thirty years old.
5. The papyri in the cases (*capsae*) were in worse condition than the others because of water. My first visit to the villa was about twenty years ago. The archaeologist who took me around said that some of the cases were transported on the seacoast and found on the beach. That showed, he said, that books were considered more valuable than people.
6. If he surely did that.
7. There was, for example, a work titled *On Epicurus* and another that consisted of Epicurean memoirs.

This last contained personal reflections but showed that Philodemus never lost his Epicurean serenity, even in the face of mortality. The Περὶ παρρησίας was written when the philosopher was young and wanted to meaningfully express his debt to his teacher Zeno. It originated as lecture notes he had taken in Athens. In this case, therefore, Philodemus is our student, and from that vantage point we will inspect the notes he took. The titles of papyri 1003, 1389, and 1471 from Herculaneum indicate that those texts also derived from *ek ton Zenonos scholon* (ἐκ τῶν Ζήνωνος σχολῶν).[8] Other works too seem to have to do with Zeno's school.

The *Peri Parrhesias* is usually called a treatise or a handbook but is rather a notebook, a collection of annotations that Philodemus based on his teacher's lectures. The true voice of Zeno or of his class appears in the questions and answers. The unusually long subscription at the end of the roll that contains it (*P.Herc.* 107) says, "Among books composed in an abbreviated way; on characters and types of life, from the lectures of Zeno." It seems therefore that the comparatively short work is what remains of a longer ethical treatment.[9] It was not unusual to take down notes during philosophical lectures, as we have seen. Philodemus was very devoted to Epicurus and to his intermediary Zeno, who probably was the most important Epicurean philosopher after Epicurus himself. This papyrus is not the only one to contain notes of Philodemus. Some of Philodemus's works are also transcripts of lectures of Zeno and other philosophers. In *On Signs* (*P.Herc.* 1065), for example, Philodemus put together a few sets of notes: his own notes on a lecture of Zeno as well as transcripts of a different lecture of Zeno that had been taken down by Bromius, a fellow pupil.[10]

The papyrus roll of *Peri Parrhesias* (*P.Herc.* 1471) was found in very lacunose condition, and its startling loss of continuity should be attributed to its deteriorated state. A short history of the publication of this fragmentary roll, though, is necessary to explain why scholars struggled to resolve a text that is incomplete and consists of fragments whose order cannot be established with certainty. Only recently did definite improvements occur. The mediocre edition of Olivieri was adapted by a team of scholars (Konstan et al. 1998, ii) in preparing their translation of the text, which provoked much criticism because no attempt

---

8. Del Mastro 2004, 34–35.
9. The text was found in Herculaneum; see Fitzgerald et al. 2004, 78.
10. See Obbink 2004.

was made to order the fragments or to consult the original papyrus in Naples.[11] In addition, the translation itself leaves much to be desired. In 2004 Michael White revisited the question of the text and with the aid of multispectral images gave a lucid description of the situation; in 2009 he made new observations on the roll.[12] In two articles Daniel Delattre considered the order of fragments and columns.[13] His conclusions agree with those of White, although the two scholars were not in contact. This provides some assurance that the decipherment of the papyrus and the order of the columns is correct. Delattre also published a short but comprehensive work on the papyri of Philodemus in the Villa dei Papiri in 2006 that is still very useful and balanced in his criticism of the author.[14]

Daniel Delattre is also working on the Greek text and translation of the fragments that he has put in order. While he has worked on the multispectral images and on the *disegni* for many years, his work remains unpublished. However, with great generosity, he has shared his Greek text, translation, and interpretation with me, and I have compared the Greek and the French translations.[15] This serves as an important example where further work will be necessary to prepare a good edition of this exciting but difficult papyrus roll.[16]

Hypomnematikon

Before looking at the Περὶ παρρησίας in some detail, we need to consider an intriguing issue, amply discussed by scholars, which might have a further impact on our view of the functioning of the school.[17]

---

11. Cf. note 1. At the same time, this translation of a difficult text is still useful, since nothing was done from 1914 to 1998. It has raised interest in the papyrus.

12. White 2004, 2009.

13. Delattre 2010 studied the roll and its reconstruction. See also Delattre 2015.

14. See Delattre 2006. I thank Daniel Delattre for sending me this work, especially because the book is no longer in print. It derived from lectures at the University of Liège.

15. I have translated into English the French notes of Delattre and will use my translation when citing passages. Delattre's French translation covers col. 135–181, that is, the readable part of Olivieri-Konstan. When possible, I have maintained the numbering of the fragments in the 1998 text, but sometimes I will cite fragments that were not in that edition or were present there but much abbreviated. I will also include in the translation passages that contain conjectures and try to follow their sense. In my translation I will not include many parentheses and dots because this is a preliminary edition and for the sake of convenience.

16. Dirk Obbink and Giovanni Indelli promised some time ago a new edition that so far has not materialized.

17. See Cavallo et al. 1983 and Blank 1998. Dorandi (2007, 66–81) examined the question in its entirety from the beginning, providing some conclusion of the debate. It is necessary to

The papyrologist Holger Essler recognized four steps in writing a literary text.[18] In the first, an ancient writer would read his sources and write notes or annotate interesting passages in them, which he would put together without concern for order. Next, the author or his assistant would order and connect the notes to produce a first draft, called *hypomnema*. This running text would still need stylistic embellishments and a formal presentation. Third, therefore, the author would reconsider the ensemble with a critical eye, clarify obscure points, refine the presentation, and introduce rhetorical adornments. The result was the final version that could be handed to scribes and reproduced in multiple copies. Some of the rolls found in Herculaneum present a distinct typology. Some are written with care, while the handwriting of others leaves something to be desired. These rolls have led to the formulation of the hypothesis that the former belonged to texts that were published, while the others circulated freely but only in the school.

A number of these works have the title *hypomnematikon*, which is a rare term that denotes, as discussed elsewhere, the form in which some literary works in the Greek and Roman world, especially in late antiquity, were disseminated in drafts.[19] Usually an author produced a work that he either left unfinished or chose not to edit, with the intention of avoiding its circulation among the general public. As in the case of Arrian, however, other people, sometimes collaborators, obtained the text and disseminated it. Then the author, who was not ready to make this work public, denounced the appropriation. At other times it was the author himself who produced and disseminated a book that was incomplete and abridged but was meant to reach friends, acquaintances, or students. Galen, in a commentary on a work of Hippocrates, makes a sharp distinction between complete work (*syggrammata*) and incomplete, which he calls *hypomnematika*. This distinction has some weight with regard to what follows.[20]

Guglielmo Cavallo, examining rolls in the Villa bearing the title *hypomnematika* and others without it, remarked that the former presented a handwriting considerably different from the latter as well as irregular margins, corrections, additions between the lines and in the

---

follow this debate in detail because of its relevance. I will consider the views of these scholars adding to the discussion.

18. Essler 2017.
19. Cribiore 2019.
20. Galen, *In Hipp. artic comm.* III 32 (XVIIIA, pp. 529, 13–530, 2 Kühn).

top margin, and transposition of parts. He therefore advanced the hypothesis that these texts (the *hypomnematika*) were destined to have a limited circulation in the school. I think that these papyri have much in common with some autograph texts written by teachers and students of rhetoric that were not formal copies, were not penned by scribes, and originated in schools.[21] David Blank's conclusion, however, is that the term *hypomnematikon* (together with *hypomnema*) did not serve to designate a version of a work that was not finished, but instead distinguished texts (often shorter) that were basically identical. The term was a reference to a genre, and a scribe had the option to add it or not to a roll as he was requested to produce copies of varying degrees of formality. In discussing this view Tiziano Dorandi took up the question from the beginning, basically following Cavallo's opinion but accepting in the end Blank's view that those books were not incomplete.[22] They had particular characteristics that needed to be explained but were complete rolls that had been conceived as such. They were not formal texts written in clear and elegant characters but complete copies with some shortcomings destined to have a limited circulation within the school.

Philodemus had a strong respect and affection for his master Zeno, who was regarded as the epitome of the wise man and was the head of the school in Athens. He took down some lectures, produced some works deriving from them when he was there, and then completed them after he left. In Athens he started his important text *On Rhetoric*, which supposedly amounted to at least ten books and is regarded as both educational and political. It points to the conditions of rhetoric and whether or not it was an art. Philodemus's aim was to defend Zeno from attacks of other Epicureans, who claimed that rhetoric was not an art. While Philodemus argued that forensic and political rhetoric were *not* an art, he did regard sophistic and epideictic oratory as an art and argued that rhetoric disappointed its young proponents because it could not make good politicians out of them.

The first three books of *On Rhetoric* contain additions and corrections and bear the title *hypomnematika*. They could be compositions or copies of lectures. Dorandi concluded that these books, which were complete, were meant to circulate within the school. It appears that

---

21. See Cribiore 2019, 13–16. Among them there are, for example, *P. Oxy.* XLV 3135 and 3136 with *meletai*, that is, rhetorical exercises. Consider also a medical text, *P.Lond.Lit.* 165, the *Anonymus Londiniensis*.

22. Delattre 2006 also subscribes to this view.

Philodemus had a special and privileged relationship with the library. If all these works were completed before Philodemus arrived in Italy, he may have used them in teaching. All these copies, moreover, were kept there, even after Philodemus had died, indicating that an interest in the school remained. Some may have been commentaries on traditional works, as we will see in the schools of Didymus and Olympiodorus. The identification of some texts with the title *hypomnematikon* will reappear in late antiquity in the commentaries to Aristotle of the Neoplatonic philosophers, which we will take into account subsequently. Some of them, including Ammonius, Olympiodorus, Philoponus, and Simplicius, called some works of Aristotle *hypomnematika* in the sense of personal copies not meant to be disseminated widely.[23] According to Ammonius, a new text derived from an ensemble of general notes and observations taken from ancient books. In this he was not very far from Lucian. He considered texts that included only the principal points to be *hypomnematika*.

One question remains: who made these formal and informal copies, some of which were transcripts of the lectures of Zeno and others which were Philodemus's own compositions? Was this task considered the exclusive prerogative of scribes with different handwriting, according to their abilities? It is possible to venture an opinion. Some of the rolls with corrections and additions might have been recorded by students at the school and not by professionals. In this way some of the copies were twice removed from Zeno's lectures. We do not know what Philodemus did with his transcripts from the actual lectures. Did he deposit these rolls only with the intention to preserve them at the Villa, or did he use them to lecture again, wishing that his students could hear Zeno's own words?

Among the papyri that were better preserved and could be more easily dated, Guglielmo Cavallo commented on the differences between those written by uneven hands and those with competent handwriting.[24] It seems plausible that, as Philodemus communicated Zeno's lectures to his students, his words were taken down by various students, who perhaps compared their versions and corrected errors and omissions. More uncertainty remains, though, about the person who wrote the version in expert handwriting. He could have been a scribe or even a

---

23. Dorandi 2007, 68–70; Ammonius, *In Cat.*3.13; Olympiodorus, *In Cat.* 21–35.

24. So, for example, he has identified at least eight writers engaged in making copies of *On Rhetoric*.

very competent pupil to whom the philosopher had assigned this task. What is clear, in any case, is that these texts ultimately derived from the annotations of Philodemus.

The prior observations are significant because they allow us to glance a bit at Philodemus's classes. The informal copies of lectures that the philosopher had taken in Athens circulated among the students and might have been read, studied, and copied again when young men cared to have individual texts. Alternatively, students recorded them *dal vivo*. Cavallo has discovered a large number of different hands among the manuscripts, which might occasion various hypotheses.

The Text of *Peri Parrhesias*

An outline of the structure of col. 154–181 provides an overview of how the text was ordered, making it possible to identify a continuous narrative and avoid chopping up the text too much. This has never been done before and allows one to see the various arguments strung together in a rational way.[25] The questions addressed to Zeno, somewhat abbreviated, will be in bold. Thus one can listen to the voices in the class. We have questions from interlocutors (students and others), Zeno's responses, and Philodemus taking down the text and delivering it to his own class.[26] The question and answer of Point 6 (col. 181, the end of the papyrus) suggests that Philodemus was aware of the difficulties raised by the practice of frank criticism but accepted it and supported it.

1. (155–157, 160). A question to Zeno which he answers. **Should we submit no one to frank criticism? This for sure deprives them of the goods that the criticism brings, which is so important.** It is always good when friendship is present, but it is essential to use the group with some caution.
2. (162, 163). **Will the sage tell his friends about what concerns him when he is the subject of *parrhesia*?** If he does that, on the one hand he is guilty of egocentrism, but on the other Epicurus approved of that.

---

25. I am using the structure devised by Delattre. The structure in Konstan et al. 1998: 8–10 is manifestly wrong.
26. In what follows I will identify as **col.** the chapters in Delattre, and as **fr.** those in the 1998 publication.

3. (165, end of 169). **What to do if the sage, thinking incorrectly, administered frank criticism to those who were not guilty of anything bad? Does this damage frank criticism?** No, it does not impair it.
4. (172, 174). **Will he use frank criticism for those who cannot stand it?** The teacher knows what is good for the youth who is agreeable and friendly toward his friend. The students are aware that the life in the community will be strengthened. He will use frank criticism several times on those who disobey.
5. (178). **How should we treat those who are angry with the sage because of his frank criticism?** If their anger can be tolerated, his own anger will not be full of hate. He knows that it is natural for young people to shake the yoke.
6. (181). **How can we understand if the one who seems to approve the method is sincere or not?** We have to pay attention to the situation to see if someone is an impostor, but sometimes he can be trusted. Those who are pretending need to be investigated (fr. 88).

Due to the fragmentary status of the papyrus, it is difficult to establish the order of the large fragments and to place the innumerable small ones.[27] It is possible to see in the text a continuous treatment of the topic in all its aspects and come to firm general conclusions regarding its pedagogic methods, but not in great detail. Judging from features like words of encouragement, teachers' tirades, mortification of individuals, frequent invective, and students' lamentations, rhetoric pervades *Peri Parrhesias*. One also has to consider an additional factor—when Zeno fielded questions from his audience, his lectures were filtered through both a live performance and the notes taken by the philosopher.

On reading the text, one can perceive questions and answers that enliven it and set it apart from a regular philosophical essay. Some of these are direct questions, while others are indirect and introduced by "if," but all testify to a reality of teaching and learning, as we shall see in the other texts we will examine.[28] The many repetitions may also be attributed to its nature: points were hammered in over and over,

---

27. See the reconstruction of Delattre 2010.
28. Issues of this kind emerged from Epictetus. I will discuss the existence of questions and answers with regard to the commentaries of Didymus and Olympiodorus.

rendering them so effective that even after centuries the modern reader can feel Zeno's arguments, insistence, and refrain. These characteristics are typical of notes taken down from lectures that were not really emended. They transmit the rhythm of a class where students asked for clarifications and asked to return to points treated before. In some respects, in any case, the description of the pedagogical methods implied by *Peri Parrhesias* may cause some surprise, and the protestations of the teacher-sages and the bewilderment of the students appear authentic.

This text, which was written two hundred years after Epicurus, has been considered from many points of view. Studies have centered on the concept of friendship that is stressed frequently, on students' confessions, on the existence of different schools of thought concerning punishment or in any case of other philosophical schools, on the psychagogue's method of exhortation, and, consequently, on its similarities to Paul's methods of conversion.[29] It was also studied as an example of the care for moral conscience that existed in Epicureanism two centuries after the life of Epicurus: conscience was developed through confession and criticism. Most importantly, in his notes Philodemus wanted to communicate the arguments of his master Zeno regarding the views of the Garden of Epicurus on *parrhesia*, a fundamental concept for the school. In the text, there are still visible traces of allusions by Philodemus to Epicurean rivals of Zeno. *Parrhesia* involved the courage and attempt to speak freely for the improvement of another. It especially concerned the relationship between teachers and students but also had a broader role. *On Frank Criticism* is not only a pedagogic text but also regards a way of establishing bonds of friendship and loyalty among Epicureans in general and the members of the school in particular. Frank speech was also a political virtue that citizens needed to practice in the Assembly in order to fulfill their roles, and the concept of freedom of speech distinguished free men from slaves. For Philodemus, however, the traditional political connotation was lost. The philosopher's self-control, lack of fear, knowledge of human sentiments, and moral freedom permitted him to exercise *parrhesia* as a means to discharge his duty to improve his comrades and students. This rigorous practice should not acquire negative connotations of rivalry or jealous competition. Frank speech within the group was an expression of friendship and served to better other people. It had to be accepted with

---

29. Glad 1995.

gratitude. "He will not consider a slanderer one who desires that his friend obtain correction, since he is not such, but he will consider him a friend of friendship, for he understands exactly the difference between these. If instead he cannot distinguish, he will call a friend even a friend of vice."[30]

Most interestingly, Glenn Holland has shown that Lucian extended *parrhesia* beyond philosophical circles to indicate satirical attacks among the educated public.[31] The idea of *parrhesia* was usually connected with Cynics and Stoics as well as with the practice of diatribe. Epictetus associated it with the Cynics in *Diss*. 3.22.94, but Arrian's mention in the letter to Gellius is more meaningful and personal. In it he lists Epictetus's "frankness of speech" as one of the reasons why he treasured Epictetus's message.[32] Part II pointed to the reasons for which the philosopher could exercise frank speech with impunity. Epictetus practiced his harsh criticism not only with his students but with others too, such as visitors. His moral superiority, self-control, and freedom from any fear, including the fear of death, gave him the right to speak freely and to accuse his students. While in the *Discourses* one can see a rigorous application of *parrhesia* directed at students, criticism of young men toward their peers is almost absent, and much vain boasting, together with some solidarity with one's classmates, can be seen circulating in class. A much later example of frank criticism is reported by the philosopher Marinus,[33] who destroyed his two commentaries on Plato after receiving sharp criticism from the philosopher Isidorus. Isidorus exercised *parrhesia* here, but its effects were painful and drastic, and for us regrettable. Marinus should not have burned his books.

We are first in Athens, where Zeno is lecturing to his audience, and then in Naples with Philodemus. Parts of the roll put into relief the general setting of administering *parrhesia*; other passages point to the situation of the teacher-sages who are in charge of that, and others again show the reactions of the students. Before inspecting *Peri Parrhesias* to look at the educational methods applied and the ethical principles that governed them, I would like to see if we find traces of the further instruction that was imparted. Gregory Snyder remarked that

---

30. Col. 157 D. (Konstan et al. 1998).
31. See Holland 2004.
32. See Part III. See also Epictetus fr. 36: "Freedom of speech cannot be taken away."
33. Marinus succeeded Proclus as the head of the school in Athens in 485. Damascius, *Vita Isidori* fr. 90 Zintzen; Edwards 2000, 55–57. Cf. Cribiore 1999, 280.

in the work of Philodemus the background noise of the classroom has been removed, and *On Frank Criticism* contains almost nothing that points directly to the substance of instruction.[34] A few references, however, are still visible beneath a text that has a completely different agenda. Though *On Frank Criticism* insists on truthfulness, openness, and moral instruction but also refers to coercion and a lack of trust, here and there it contains some veiled allusions to activities that were not simply ethical. So far, commentators have not paid attention to these but instead have concentrated on self-disclosure, suppression of flattery, and criticism of peers.

Among the fragments of *On Frank Criticism* that might refer to pedagogy, fr. 10 presents a teacher "practicing the art." We are also told immediately after that at times he only practiced frankness so that students would pay attention. It appears that the two activities are distinct. Epicurus's text may have been involved.[35] Another fragment (3) mentions "memorizing."[36] Epicurus insisted that all his pupils should study and memorize summaries and epitomes of the most significant Epicurean conclusions. In this way, a young man could see the entire structure of the system. The problem was, however, that in this way the student did not use his rationality and imbibed ready-made philosophy. This injunction was directed not only at those who did not stay for the length of the instruction but also at those who did. An allusion to "not believing the gods" attributes that to Epicurus (fr. 6). Epicurus was opposed not to a belief in the gods but to the idea that they watched human conduct. This was the origin of a reproaching conscience. Col. IXa mentions toil: "Weakness or [dislike] for toil has befallen him and are the causes for which he has reasoned [falsely]." The word *ponos* in reference to schoolwork and apathetic behavior and issues of laziness and insufficient dedication to studies appear in some educational texts.[37] In Col. XIVb the students explore a topic and its causes, after which the class "moves on from the larger issues" to "other things." Lastly Col. XXa brings an interesting issue to the fore. It presents weaker students who recognize that they "are surpassed only in regard to theoretical arguments" but are acceptable concerning character and judgment. It seems that the school taught the philosophy of predecessors and how

---

34. Snyder 2000, 59–60.
35. It is possible, however, that here the text refers to the art of medicine.
36. The reading is by Gigante 1975, 55n41.
37. Cf. numerous examples in Libanius.

to reform one's personality. We are in an Epicurean context, but the observation corresponds to what we have noticed with Epictetus, Musonius, and other Stoics. Ethical issues had priority over theoretical ones, which were introduced later and to a limited extent. From texts and knowledge people should not derive a vain belief in themselves but should aim at improving their conduct.

Moving now to frank criticism itself, it is clear that the new fragments of the roll studied by Daniel Delattre show a preponderance of passages regarding the teacher-sages. Some contain admonitions to them to apply *parrhesia* correctly and follow the rules. Others point to important issues in their conduct. They stress that the sage has to pay extreme attention not to be wrong and unjust. While sometimes he will catch a guilty person in the very act, at other times he will have to use his reason and intuition.

In a volume on the ethics of Philodemus, Voula Tsouna has concentrated on the *Peri Parrhesias* in an attempt to make sense of the whole text.[38] In 2007, of course, this scholar could consider only the Greek fragments and the translation that were included in the 1998 publication and could not base her assessment on the new text put together by Daniel Delattre and its interpretation. She concentrated on the fragments that illuminated the position of the teacher-sage versus that of a student. As I said, the text has survived as an ensemble of short fragments that constitute about half of the original papyrus.[39] Thanks to Daniel Delattre more fragments are now at our disposal. We should discuss if those teachers who used disputable methods of chastising were really enlightened figures as was claimed. Several fragments hint at educators who appear confused, violent, unforgiving, and vengeful. Does the text convey an altogether optimistic view of ancient education? According to Tsouna, "The method of *parrhesia* represents a pragmatic as well as optimistic approach to human fallibility and to the possibility of correction and salvation."[40] Most likely this is true only in theory. The Epicureans and Zeno had devised a system of moral education that could work if it was applied correctly. Of course, most often educational practices implicitly aim to improve pupils' knowledge and moral

---

38. Tsouna 2007, altogether a valuable book.

39. According to Delattre (2010) there are about a hundred fragments. Most consist of a few lines; those longer than that are very rare.

40. "It has humanitarian and philanthropic dimensions, involving as it does elements of empathy, compassion, and forgiveness." Tsouna 2007, 103.

progress, but the ways to achieve that need to be taken into account to obtain a balanced view.

Peri Parrhesias offers many elements of discontinuity. As we examine some of the passages that concern the teacher-sages, we are confronted with only a few that praise them indiscriminately and laud the subtle ways in which they conduct their inquiries. Frank criticism is called an "artistry" that was difficult to exercise (fr. 666). Students' criticism touches the teachers in a superficial way, and the latter's position of power seems at first unassailable. Little that happens is shown from young men's point of view. Most often, we see their comportment through the admonitions of a superior power and through Zeno and Philodemus. They govern the narrative and appear very conscious of the pitfalls implied in the practice and the cracks in the whole edifice.

Can we imagine that those passages became part of the *Peri Parrhesias* at the very beginning, when the practice had been recently instituted and Zeno wanted to make it known to other Epicureans? Can we suppose that Zeno delivered his lectures to a public ignorant of the phenomenon? In my opinion, the *Peri Parrhesias* was delivered when the practice was established to a degree and some people contemplated questionable elements. Zeno and other Epicureans had seen Epicurus's recommendations for a thorough cleansing of the conscience. Some were utterly loyal to the philosopher, but others were perplexed and maybe hoped for changes and even a removal of frank criticism. The text is replete with warnings, which came only after *parrhesia* was administrated, was put to the test, and people became aware of undesirable effects. The negative sides of the practice are reflected sharply in the composition of the text. When Zeno pointed to the innumerable pitfalls inherent in the power of the teacher-sages, he was referring to a current practice that was working only to a point. Examples of bad behavior, violence, arrogance, admonishments that could be friendly or biting, self-consciousness, timidity, cowardice, and unjust display of force had probably become part of common experience. "An optimistic approach to correction and salvation" had been perhaps at the origin of frank criticism, but the picture that the text transmits is now replete with doubts and distrust that are reflected in the admonitions.

It seems that the application of frank criticism was done in public in front of several people. The practice is justified by the approval of Epicurus: "We will obey Epicurus who has dictated our life choices" (col. 151). And in col. 156: "We know that Heracleides was praised because he had denounced his faults to Epicurus since he considered the accusations coming from the revelation of his faults secondary to its helpfulness. Polyaenus was a man who went to visit Epicurus, when Apollonides proved his nonchalance."[41] "He (Epicurus) launched some accusations against Apollonides" (col. 180).[42]

The practice of *parrhesia* consisted of the denunciation of one's faults; it had to be made not only by students but also sometimes by teacher-sages in the presence of an audience. After that, the subject had to reform his behavior. It was a difficult practice; a few times the text mentions "bites," wounds, and piercing accusations. The following passage, however, gives a general account of frank criticism. It stands close to the beginning of the roll and gives a glowing view of *parrhesia*, where the sage is presented as a savior of the young man who will assist him in everything. We will see that other fragments will show less enthusiasm from the students and will sow doubts about the behavior of some sages. The practice was not always smooth and done with kindness. Sometimes the treatment was sharp, and violence against those who did not pass the test occurred. We can venture that the question may have sounded rhetorical, even to the participants who were aware of some opposition.

> The student must immediately express his faults, that is, his weak points, to the sage. He considers this man as his unique guide in terms of right reason, regards him as his only savior, and speaks of him saying "this man follows my steps."[43] He has entrusted himself to him to be cured. How could it happen that he is not ready to show him those of his faults that require a treatment?

We are told that the practice could not take place before people who were there by chance; that is, only those belonging to the school could be present. A few passages show that the audience did not entirely agree with this rule. Some of the people who were present were not in favor and hesitated to approve it openly. Zeno in Athens and Philodemus in Athens and Naples confronted other groups of dissenting Epicureans, and these fragments likely allude to them.

> And there, in front of friends, while a great number of them are hesitant, he (the sage) will persist in frank criticism, and again in

---

41. Apollonides and Polyaenus cannot be identified. Heracleides was perhaps Heracleides of Pontus.
42. The text mentions again Epicurus in fr. about Leontheus, who was against belief in the gods.
43. Col. 146. A reference to Odysseus following Diomedes, *Il.* 10.246–247.

the opposite way. And with some who do not need it, he will omit the admonition before people who are there by chance, he will not, even when among those who are present someone was lost or was left on the side without care.[44] . . . And although he (i.e., the student) disobeyed earlier disdaining the reproach as foreign to himself, later he will obey the rebuke. He will be afflicted by passions that make one conceited and arrogant and constitute an obstacle, but when he is free, he will pay heed. And as he encountered passions that distort one, now he will not encounter them anymore. (Col. 173)

A curious fragment shows that during frank criticism some people who were in love were very fond of chatting about their passions, as those close to them shied away from that kind of talk. Anger and severity were in proportion to an error, whether it was major or mild. In the latter case, when the fault was bearable, a milder kind of criticism and punishment had to be inflicted. "Toward those who were stronger than the tender ones and more in need of treatment . . . he will employ the harsh form of frankness" (fr. 7). And again, he will criticize severely those who are stronger and presumably arrogant and sure of themselves:

Most often the teacher will practice the art in such a way. But sometimes he will also practice frank criticism, even if there were risks because he believed that students would not obey. He will criticize with passion those who are extremely strong both by nature and because they are successful. (fr. 10)[45]

A fragment may refer to the rejection of non-Epicurean methods and knowledge, that is, to a different type of philosophical education or a student's previous notions (rhetoric) before he encountered philosophy. It mentions spitting out bad, disgusting food and nourishing oneself with good. Laziness and procrastination (*argia* and *anabolai*) elicit an aggressive response from the teacher, even though we do not know the details.[46]

---

44. Probably a confused young man.
45. Those students may have been there for long and progressed in their knowledge. Cf. also fr. 7: frank criticism will intensify with them because "they are hardly changing, even when they are shouted at."
46. Col. Va. Fr. 18. Another interpretation could be that the student is spitting out the *parrhesia* "just like food that repels." He is not content with the food and assistance that he has received and tries to abuse the sage. See also my discussion of Epictetus in part II.

There were apparently definite rules that the teacher-sage had to respect, even though he sometimes tried to evade them, and they were there to prevent abuses. The teacher-sage should try not to express personal reasons for disliking the method or some persons. To justify his behavior with students, he should point to the fact that he too would have to confess.[47] Not all teachers were well qualified for the practice, but some were better than others.

> He should not start from personal grievances as happens to most scholars[48] and should not practice frank criticism with arrogance and excessive fervor . . . despising and denigrating. . . . When they are angry, they remind the others that they themselves have to stand frank criticism often and will tolerate remonstrances from others. . . .. It is shameful to restrain from hurling to the teachers and only to them everything that concerns them, since this did not regard the preparation of the gifts.[49] . . . When (the teachers) are under the judgment of the same people, if these do not like them or are unable to correct them or will not be able to persuade those who are better than them instead of someone who does not have any fault, who care for them, who is better and knows how to heal them . . . And even this is accompanied by "bites" beyond the fact that they will receive beautiful recompenses.

And again, in a different part of the roll, speaking of the treatment that the student will receive by a sage or one of his classmates, the sage "should not do that continuously and to everyone, should not mention every fault whatever it is and not in the presence of people who have nothing to do with the affair and not in an excessive way but with compassion and no violence" (col. 160).

The concept that frank criticism needed to be repeated (several times) when it has been unsuccessful is stressed in two fragments (col. 171 and 172). It is compared to the behavior of a doctor who insists on purging when he has not attained any results.

If the horse trainers accept not to be obeyed by their horses,[50] the sage, who is a trainer of men, cannot tolerate the disobedience of

---

47. I am putting together parts of three adjacent fragments, col. 143, 144, and 145, with col. 150.
48. Maybe "cultivated people."
49. These were the "goods" that an allegiance to Epicurus would bring.
50. Students were sometimes called *poloi*, young horses.

a young man when he is excessive.... He will use a harsh, frank criticism and in fact it will be effective in this way but sometimes in the opposite way. In any case, since frank criticism sometimes has been effective once, he will try a second time and perhaps even a third. And if the young man has refused to obey when he was in the midst of his passion, now that it has diminished, he will change.

The practice appeared implacable and relentless. It would continue, even if no results take place initially. Compared to the horse trainer, the teacher-trainer did not tolerate disobedience. It appears that when frank criticism was applied several times, an interval elapsed between occurrences to give the young man the possibility to reform his behavior.

Some of the young men are very irritated, even if they are dressed with the Greek garb. They find difficult to accept what the man says when practicing frank criticism. Since this is an occasion for people to laugh at them, they cannot dare listen to a schoolmate with good will.... (col. 137) It is not only that he calumniates us, but we want to avoid blushing out of shame. (col. 157)

In this passage, another reason students were opposed to the practice is stated. They felt self-conscious and resented the possible reactions of others. Besides the pain they might suffer, they felt that the bystanders and their classmates did not listen to the accusations with goodwill and that they might become an object of ridicule.

Other fragments look at the way the sage should administer frank criticism:

Every fault should be addressed after examining it with attention. Some people have reproached them directly because of the affection they feel for them and some of these reproaches were strong because of their ignorance.... We do not think that the sage will make mistakes if he has an awareness of the perfection of the argument and also of caution. But it is possible that he will commit mistakes in applying frank criticism if he does not wait for the end[51] and does not leave aside things that cannot be always imputed to the man. (col. 163) ... If he finds in the act those who are in love or have certain vices but using reasonable probabilities

---

51. This may mean that the sage interrupted the student and did not let him finish. He was impatient and abrupt.

to reach a judgment. On the other hand, if the actions that aim at success do not have the result that he really hoped for, even when plausible chances derive especially from reasonable probabilities it is necessary, even by agreement, to reach an accord because reason demands to treat the issue deeply.[52]

Several fragments admonish the sage and try to guide him on a road that is fraught with problems, accidents, prevarication, and even hate.

> They [the students] regard the fact that they have to submit to the despotic power of other men intolerable . . . and difficult to endure. . . . If the rebuke is not very similar to that of a sage and a philosopher; if the sage has overlooked one of the misdeeds, we do not refuse to blame him. But we think that it is not correct that he [the student] would be indicted purely and simply on all charges, even though he has acted badly only once.[53]

The Epicurean community was isolated from the rest of the world, with students insulated from their original families, and adopted an expectation that teachers were supposed to ignore students' life circumstances for the instruction to be successful (fr. 8).[54] The usual pedagogic practice in antiquity, however, was for teachers to communicate with families. In the school of Epictetus, the young men's living conditions, social backgrounds, and affection for those at home were well in view.[55] In the Garden of Epicurus, teachers were detached from their pupils to create a void around them. That void could stimulate students to learn and possibly make them more able to tolerate. Teachers were also uninterested in how students would fare later in life (fr. 21). Thus a pupil had to refrain from confronting a teacher with his own affairs and had to concentrate solely on his instruction (fr. 39). And yet life intruded and could not be ignored. There was not only philosophy. Some students apparently took more than average care of their bodies. These beautifying measures were considered shameful when a doctor

---

52. A combination of col. 161, 166, and 164.
53. Col. 140–141.
54. I use the singular to refer to instructors. Fr. 45 seems to point to the existence of some assistant teachers called *kathegetai*, like in Egypt.
55. Cicero exercised control over his son studying rhetoric in Athens. In the fourth century Libanius shows instances when families were in Antioch to supervise students. He also wrote to them regularly to inform them of progress in conduct and issues of learning. Cf. Cribiore 2007a.

had not ordered them.⁵⁶ Students were prone to disobedience when they were in the midst of intense (erotic) passions and appetites distorted their feelings; they felt strong and invincible (65-66).⁵⁷ Teachers were watching the signs and were ready to act, even when they were not sure (col. 166).

> The sage was not able to convince people that he would benefit them in all circumstances.... There are occasions when the student will abandon philosophy and, perhaps, he will hate the sage in some way. And if sometimes he submits to frank criticism, it will not be useful to him because he has decided that it will not benefit him.

Students were encouraged to apply frank criticism to schoolmates: "Although many good things result from friendship, there is nothing better than having one to whom one will say what is in one's heart and who will listen when one speaks."⁵⁸ But students' reactions could be mixed. It could happen that some of them ran to the teachers to ingratiate themselves. To show their goodwill they reported what a friend had said or done against them (fr. 52). A student who was censured by young men in the same position found their criticism more painful than when he was corrected by a teacher and would suspect envy or scorn from "contemptible" fellow students. In those cases, trust would become lack of trust. Frank criticism was not useful because the young man suspected his classmate and hid his secrets.

> The classmates surely know all the good qualities that we possess and they present themselves to correct them and in that case frank criticism is not useful at all.... The youth who does not give a report to the most special of his friends is clearly trying to hide his faults and that one who has little secrets will not have more because, as everyone knows, nothing passes unnoticed. (col. 147)⁵⁹

Distrust of the teacher-sage and his systems is very noticeable. The Epicurean Lucretius, who was a contemporary of Philodemus, adds his

---

56. We can guess massages, or excessive exercises. It is unclear where these distractions took place. Were they part of the life in the community or when the young men returned home for a period?
57. Compare Libanius on *aidoia* (private parts) in *Or.* 3. His students had great interest in love affairs.
58. See fr. 28. This applies to teachers and classmates.
59. A condemnation of the one who hides his secrets occurs in fr. 41-42.

voice to those who upheld a strong discipline, showing how to mortify his patron Memmius with harsh words. Memmius was apparently indifferent to a mention of the death of Epicurus, leading Lucretius not only to attack his resistance at the idea of dying in the future but to say that in any case he seemed already dead. Memmius wasted his life in sleeping and dreaming, and his mind was plagued by vain terrors. "You cannot discover what is your pain, poor drunken wretch, oppressed as you are by many cares on all sides, as you wonder drifting with uncertain mind."[60] This is a grim rebuke.

It is often remarked that *On Frank Criticism* testifies to two different manners of punishment advocated by two currents of Epicurean thought: harsh castigation or gentle rebuke.[61] It is impossible, however, to identify the specific names of proponents of the harsh system of correction, and no text mentions such a dispute unequivocally. I wonder, therefore, whether there was in fact such a stark difference within the Epicurean school, or whether *On Frank Criticism* attests simply to natural reactions to and by students with challenging dispositions. Educators in antiquity used both methods of correction.[62] Harsh discipline was common in education in the Greek and Roman world, both then and later. Libanius's letters and orations advocate both methods, often refraining from harshness and preferring to inspire a sense of reverence into the students, but at times using words of anger and violently throwing students out of the class.[63]

What the text of *Peri Parrhesias* clearly shows is that besides its proponents there were others who entertained some doubts, particularly because the teacher-sages might insist on punishment when their measures were excessive and counterproductive. In Philodemus's text both types of correction appear at random, administered by different types of teachers and applied to students of different temperaments. One passage (Col. IIIb) juxtaposes two teachers of different dispositions, attributing their methods to their personal natures: "One teacher is

---

60. *De rerum natura* 3.1040–1050.
61. See Glad 1995, 123–24; Konstan et al. 1998, 11–12.
62. Cribiore 2001b, 65–73.
63. *Or.* 2.20, where Libanius asserts that he is gentle with students and does not have a cane to beat them; *Or.* 58.1 and 38, where he asserts that he has refrained from beating and flogging them on the grounds that that treatment obtains the opposite effect. He prefers to convince them with argument and not with the lash (*Or.* 3.15), where the maximum punishment for a student is to be thrown out of the class. Only in *Ep.* 1330.3, addressed to a father, he contemplates the possibility of beating an idle student.

irascible and snappish toward everyone, while another is always mild; one speaks frankly about everything in a good way, but another does so deficiently on some matter." The irascible philosopher contradicted his philosophic upbringing. Falling into ignorance, he appeared unwilling to accept his mistakes and insisted on a harmful practice. He would have used gentle and convincing arguments at the beginning, but then his anger prevailed in the face of a lack of success. We do not know how large the community was; it may have included a limited number of students so that a multiplicity of teachers was not necessary. Friendship was central to all relations. One wonders whether at times we are seeing the same teacher reacting differently to different situations and showing a gamut of reactions, as is suggested by the following fragment. When "he is not disappointed in some people or indicating very vehemently his own annoyance, he will not, as he speaks, forget 'dearest' and 'sweetest' and similar things" (fr. 14).

The text shows that frank criticism was administered at the beginning with goodwill and amiable words, using the language of friendship. The sage had two different attitudes toward a student. If the teacher-sage felt that he was not seriously deficient, he approached the pupil with a friendly attitude. If the teacher-sage was dissatisfied with the pupil, he became aggressive. Fr. 21 mentions malediction, insults, and madness. The deficient teacher, in any case, was supposed to submit to the criticism of others in the community. And yet every time the pupil was urged to put himself in the teacher's hands.

There could be consequences, as an interesting fragment reveals, such as that students would be enticed to leave the school by certain men who would take them away: "Men who are charlatans divert many, seizing them after some stress and enchanting them with their subtle kindness" (fr. 60), a passage that recalls Epictetus.[64] It is unclear who these men were. Perhaps they were teachers of rhetoric, who could offer pupils a competing type of education, or perhaps they were non-Epicurean philosophers. The first case is more likely because, as we have seen, some distressed students felt they had to abandon philosophy (col. 166). We have seen that, in Musonius's and Epictetus's times, many people, including parents, disliked philosophical education on the grounds that it was theoretical and did not open many doors in the

---

64. Cf. Epictetus 1.22.18; the man with rings perhaps was just someone deriding philosophy. In Lucian many philosophers are described as "charlatans." It is possible that here there is an allusion to other philosophers.

future. This is what a student laments: "He does not labor over how one will fare in life" (fr. 21).

It is when harsh criticism is meted out without reason that students' voices rang loudest, manifesting an open frustration that comes alive many centuries later and that differs from simple descriptions in educational texts. Here we witness an aggressive attack on personal dignity:

> He says: "If I did not err, (the sage) is going to say that I deserve frank criticism now that he came upon me." Unless, by Zeus, fear does not make him say: "In fact yesterday I have not erred at all, I say. But I committed [a mistake] of my own will as many young people do and for this I have to be whipped." (col. 171)[65]

At this point the text conveys the sense of outrage of the young man who felt mistreated. Among those students in need of treatment, some were able to correct themselves, but others felt that the punishment was unjust. "Their stubborn persistence gives them trouble and the fact that they are not aware of their errors and, though they reproach others, that they believe that for the most part they have not erred."[66] Not all students had to receive frank criticism. Teachers were not infallible, and they might have at times administered frank criticism even when no mistakes were committed. What to do with some teachers who throw "maledictions and insults" through madness (fr. 21)? We are told that sharp frankness in fact bears a similarity to insult.

Medicine and Philosophy

Central to Epicurean doctrine was the belief that sickness of the soul needed to be cured. The analogy of medicine and philosophy was used quite frequently. There was an open asymmetry between the sick needing a cure and the doctor providing it and between the active doctor and the passive man afflicted by disease. Epicurus states that philosophy was hopeless when it did not help a diseased soul, just as an art of medicine that did not cure bodily suffering could not have any use.[67] The analogy of medicine and philosophy was not only a metaphor but

---

65. Cf. about the sage in fr. 9: "He will also sometimes transfer to himself an error that occurred in his youth." In Dobbin 1998 *aneton*, referring to "error," should not be translated as "intemperate." This is an error of "relaxation" that the young teacher made when he was young and loosened up.
66. Col XVb.
67. Epicurus 221 Us.

also was a strong tool, because an understanding of it brought a philosopher to search for ways to cure the soul and inspired the sick to undergo treatment for the cure. Thus the central interest of philosophy became taking care of diseased humanity. The idea that curing the illness of the soul was analogous to using medicine to prevail over bodily sickness was old and present already in Homer.[68]

In Epicurean philosophy, the philosopher became a diagnostician who developed a cure, starting from signs like the doctor and interpreting them for the benefit of the sick ". . . even if he recognizes that the student had not committed any wrongs. It is more or less as if a doctor, judging from probable signs, gave a patient in need another purge and then, since he was wrong in interpreting the signs, refrained forever from purging again this man when he had another disease; exactly for this reason he will use again *parrhesia*."[69] In this case the teacher had an advantage over the physician. When the signs of misbehavior were not sufficient to make a sure diagnosis, by submitting the student to frank criticism he would have sure proofs.[70]

Peri Parrhesias shows that the Garden was a therapeutic community. The patient had to ask the philosopher for help, and the latter listened and planned a remedy. Like a doctor, the philosopher had to develop the type of cure and find the ways in which it became effective. Yet doctors, like philosophers, were not infallible. With the Stoics and Epictetus in particular, the cure was devised through an accurate observation of a pupil, but with Epicurus curing the individual was insufficient; the whole community had to derive an advantage. The Epicurean teacher had to observe symptoms that plagued humanity, such as anger, vanity, arrogance, insolence, flattery, and other negative traits. All the members of the community participated in the correction and development of the pupil. Though it was him and not the community that was the center of observation, the student had to be aware of the welfare of humanity. For the Stoic philosophers, the pupil was the protagonist of the dialogues, and the confrontations in Epictetus's *Discourses* were always between one single pupil and the philosopher. The latter started from signs of indifference, laziness, and misbehavior and determined an

---

68. See Nussbaum 1994, 49. Nussbaum explores the analogy of philosophy and medicine throughout her book. She wonders if this idea was more developed in the Garden than in Epicurus himself, though of course Epicurus's words have been transmitted only in part (116).
69. Delattre has put together in col. 171 two previous fragments (86 and 64).
70. Col. 170 (fr. 64 K).

individual therapy just as the physician used fever and other symptoms to beat the disease. The Epicureans especially condemned flattery as the opposite of trustworthiness and considered it a communal danger because of the confusion it created when trying to identify faults. In theory, a teacher should not attack the personality of a pupil as it appears in *Peri Parrhesias*. Errors of a pupil differed in terms of magnitude, and the cure differed from case to case as the doctor reacted to various illnesses. As a doctor could not apply the same method indiscriminately, the philosopher needed to be flexible when treating particular faults. Anger and severity were in proportion to an error, whether it was major or mild. In the latter case, when the fault was bearable, a milder kind of criticism and punishment would be inflicted. "Toward those who were stronger than the tender ones and more in need of treatment . . . he will employ the harsh form of frankness" (fr. 7). And again, he would criticize severely those who are stronger and presumably arrogant and sure of themselves. "Most often the teacher will practice the art in such a way. But sometimes he will also practice frank criticism, even if there were risks, because he believed that students would not obey. He will criticize with passion those who are extremely strong both by nature and because they are successful" (fr. 10).[71]

The analogy of medicine with philosophy existed in all Hellenistic schools and later was particularly stressed by the Stoics.[72] As we have seen, Epictetus uses it frequently.[73] He remarks that sometimes patients entrusted their body to a physician, begged him to give them a cure, and were serene in front of pain and death so that the doctor-philosopher could help and guide them. More often the reality was complicated. In rebuking an ambitious student who planned to open a school of philosophy, Epictetus remarks that the lad put his hand to an inappropriate task. He intended to open a medical office (*iatreion*) without knowing the art profoundly. He was in possession of drugs, yet not only did he not know how to use them, he also never made an effort to learn (3.21.20). A school of philosophy was a hospital, but those who entered should not expect to feel pleasure when they left. Instead, they would get out in pain (3.23.30). Philosophers advised those who were looking for a new beginning to leave their country and not fall back into old

---

71. Or because they had belonged to the community and had progressed in education.

72. See, e.g., Plutarch, *Mor. On the Education of Children* 7d–e. Plutarch regards philosophy as the most important discipline that should be at the center of education.

73. I will document only a few occurrences of this analogy.

habits (3.16.11-12). In the same way, doctors advised the patient with a chronic disease to find a different climate, but the advice was not always followed.

Epictetus remarks that teachers did not invite people to lectures, just as doctors did not offer their services to those who did not call them (3.23.27). There is no information in Philodemus's work regarding how the students joined the community. Did they choose to embark on philosophical education out of youthful enthusiasm? Did they experience parents' resistance? Certainly, it seems that they encountered some disillusionment. Help was available but success could be difficult to attain. *Parrhesia* was a flexible method used to punish actual errors of the moment, not to predict future outcomes. Likewise, a doctor had to decide case by case, but the physician's task was easier than that of the philosopher, who had to confront and diagnose defects of the soul that might be invisible. A question to which Zeno responds is what to do if the teacher-sage is wrong and applies *parrhesia* with no need (col. 170). This seems to be a dominant issue in the text. The doctor who read the signs wrongly purged a patient twice and then, aware of the mistake, refrained from purging the same man suffering from a different malady. Both the doctor and the philosopher, however, could misread the signs because of their ignorance of the circumstances and the character of the pupil. Like the doctor, moreover, a teacher could act irrationally. As Epictetus remarks, the good surgeon counseled a patient and invited him to undergo surgery but there were also bad and inexperienced surgeons.

The "therapy" implicit in the much later text of Epictetus's *Discourses* reminds one of the students' treatments in Philodemus's work. But a clear difference should be noticed. In both works, the relation between a student and a teacher is at the center, but in Philodemus the whole community is affected. In Epictetus, moreover, the voice of the pupils is mostly silenced. Although in one passage, tears and a runny nose accompany the harsh denunciations of the teacher, in most cases we can only imagine students' reactions, if there were any. Epictetus was entirely aware of the fact that some students regretted leaving their home and families and missed a system of education based on easy-to-follow rules. Yet his harshness was apparently justified by their seeming indifference, and their voices of protest were suffocated. It is possible that Arrian was not interested in those conflicts that had caused the teacher's rage. In the letter to Gellius, Arrian manifests his desire to communicate to others the philosopher's frank speech, one of the reasons why he admired Epictetus, but one cannot rule out that the philosopher's authority had stifled any dissent so that only the philosopher's voice was audible.

Philodemus's notes succeed in transmitting some of the realities of learning and the sacrifice and suffering for its sake. The fact that in Athens he had seen that type of paideia in action and recorded lectures at which he was present gives vividness to his notes. One wonders if he knew that type of education from close up, if he had been subjected to it, and if he completely approved of it. It is likely that he did and that he was sincere. There were such people "who do not speak from their entire heart but rather by forming an image of themselves that they are truly lovers of frankness, but when the rebuke comes, they have their pretense exposed" (*ekkoptein*, cut out). In col. 181 (fr. 94), Zeno replies to someone who had asked him how to recognize an impostor. After some surveillance, however, if this person manifested friendship, he could be forgiven.

There were positive aspects of *parrhesia*, especially the courage to speak freely to improve oneself and others and its connection to friendship. A philosopher who practiced it would acquire the right of frank speaking, along with the duty to apply it, because of his superior morality and personal freedom. The transmitted doctrine was only Epicurean, and students were not exposed to other doctrines in Athens and in Italy, where individuals were saturated with Epicurean principles without having the possibility to debate rationally alternative views. On the contrary, Stoic education admitted the possibility of consulting the works of predecessors in order to have a complete view of philosophy.

Peri Parrhesias, on the other hand, testifies that the practice involved some danger, to the point that students sometimes felt that they were the subject of violence, enmity, and rancor. It is clear that their self-esteem was greatly diminished, and some realized that philosophy was not their calling. Some of the passages reveal that they had lost their confidence and felt insignificant. They admitted rather humbly that the teacher-sages might be brighter than they and so that they had to accept the maltreatment. "Sometimes they believed that their teachers were misled, punishing them when they had not erred, or they had disregarded some of the things that even a wise man disregards or that they are more intelligent when they do not like them or hate them or envy them" (col. XXIa). The student was aware that the teacher had abused his authority but tried to justify the instructor's actions with inculcated concepts, such as the superior intelligence of the sages.[74] The latter were then absolved, even when possessed by hate and envy.

Richard Sorabji, in a powerful and wide-ranging publication, inquired about the various views on moral conscience and included *Peri Parrhesias*.[75] He looked at the roles the Greeks and Romans played versus Christian views. The idea of awareness of knowledge of oneself was well expressed in the verb *suneidenai*, with a reflexive pronoun in the dative.[76] Epicurus had a view of self-awareness of one's faults that led to fear and punishment, and much later Christians adopted a concept of confessions and penitence. Plato often presented Socrates as aware of a *daimon*, a spirit who advised him. Epicurus also developed an idea of watchers contributing to the individual's reform. The Stoics and Epictetus derived their concept of a guardian from him. We have seen that Epictetus had a strong belief in Zeus, who was able to oversee all the world and all humanity. In *Discourse* 1.14 Epictetus shows that Zeus included conscience as something present in every man. In one of his solo dialogues, he maintains that each man has within himself a *daimon* as a guardian to whom he was supposed to listen and obey.[77] In *On Frank Criticism* students and teachers must confess their faults. Criticism was accompanied by corporal punishment, ridicule, and mortification. Anxiety, fear, and revulsion for the irascible teacher were palpable here. In theory this system of education could have positive results when the teacher-sages were monitored closely. In practice this appears a closed, almost suffocating world.

Philodemus did not just repeat the lessons of his predecessors but manifested himself as a man of significant literary culture. He was far from being averse to traditional paideia. He had an authentic interest in, and knowledge of, literature, and his poetic epigrams achieved considerable distinction.[78] He believed that an Epicurean had to know not only contemporary texts but also the classical works of poetry, rhetoric, and philosophy.[79] Some training in reading and writing was available,

---

74. In Col. XVIa, however, "the most intelligent reproach their pupils gently and to their liking but for the most part they are rebuked sharply."
75. Sorabji 2014a. Here I am following Sorabji's book.
76. Sorabji (2014a, 25) makes an important correction in fr. 67, reading *syneidesis* "conscience" in place of *synoidesis* "swelling."
77. Epictetus 1.14.11–15. The Stoics had argued for the same idea. Cf. Seneca, *Ep.* 41.2, where the *sacer spiritus* is *observator* and *custos*.
78. Sider 1997.
79. See Angeli 1988, 61–70.

and people were encouraged to take advantage of it and reach a level of competence.[80] The literary references in *On Frank Criticism* are few, yet they are present: Homer, some mythology, such as the labors of Heracles, and little more. Another of Philodemus's works, *The Good King According to Homer*, regards situations based on Homeric texts with an impressive quantity of exact references unusual in most literary texts. The work addresses Calpurnius Piso and in essence is political, pointing not only to the positive aspects in the Homeric texts that a politician must consider but also to the negative ones. It was meant to be useful to a consul and senator in difficult times. Some of the characteristics of a government, according to Homer, could even be regarded as detrimental to the consideration of the good conduct and power of a sovereign. Though scholars have regarded *On the Good King According to Homer* as a text meant to strengthen Philodemus's relation with Piso, the philosopher also puts in relief virtues and vices observed by a good Epicurean.[81] A powerful man had strong obligations and could not ignore a difficult reality. In this moment, however, Philodemus does not lose his basically optimistic outlook. A brief consideration of a beautiful epigram may complete a view of the philosopher as a man interested in poetry and the cultural heritage of the Greeks. In *Anthologia Palatina* 11.41 he presents his life at a moment when he was turning thirty-seven and looking at the future with dismay. His existence was like a papyrus roll that was slowly losing its columns. Desire still inflamed him, but the madness was going to cease, so that the female figure of the moment would be its *koronis*, the beautiful sign at the end of a text on papyrus.[82]

It is difficult to assess properly the originality of Philodemus as a philosopher because details of Epicurean activity before him are not well known. Moreover, his statements that some of his works derived from the lectures of Zeno are problematic from this point of view, because it is uncertain how much of his work comes directly from his master. However, one cannot deny his vast and diverse production and his enthusiastic admiration for Epicurus. His bond with his old teacher Zeno, even beyond death, is evident from his desire to take with himself the lectures that he had recorded. Philodemus was a clear and

---

80. Snyder 2000, 57–60, on the basis of *P. Herc.* 1005.
81. See Philodemus's approval of Homer in Fish 2022.
82. See Sider 1997, 72–78 no. 4. Xanthippe appears in a cycle containing poems 1–8. She evokes Socrates's wife and represents an ideal image of marital love that is far from being negative. The *koronis* was a beautiful, decorative sign at the end of a literary papyrus text.

systematic philosopher who arranged his works according to categories and perhaps from the beginning had devised a plan on how to proceed. He was also a sensitive man who respected the works of others even though he engaged with alternative views, and his polemical works attacking rivals are not numerous.[83] Deeply convinced of the validity of Epicurus's doctrine, he was aware of his role in transmitting it at the end of the Republic and the beginning of the principate.

---

83. Or at least he did not attack his contemporaries but only philosophers of the past.

Chapter 9

Taking Notes in the School of Didymus the Blind

The Continuous Value of a Traditional Literary Culture

It has been widely recognized that classical education had several shortcomings.[1] From a contemporary standpoint, observance of rigid rules and formulas, reliance on the same authoritative texts, and a narrow curriculum risked stifling creativity, individual thinking, and resistance. In contrast to the way intellectual inquiry flourished under Athenian democracy, the development of education in the imperial period apparently did not have much to do with social and political change, remaining the elite pagan aristocracy's exclusive patrimony.[2] And yet the same education also provided a rigorous system of training, a tendency to scrutinize ancient texts to assimilate their fabric and beauty, and a genuine admiration for, and cultivation of, rhetorical excellence; all these elements deeply impacted young minds.[3] It is sometimes forgotten that this "imperfect" education produced superb literary figures. While it is surprising that paideia spread equally across the East and West and lasted uniformly over the centuries, I argue that paideia's

---

1. Morgan 2007.
2. See Barrow 2015.
3. Lendon 2022, 14–25. Lendon argued that parents must have been satisfied by what paideia offered. Ancient students learned what was offered to them deeply. Cf. Cribiore 2001b.

enduring presence signifies that it was still vibrant and that stereotyped ideas and contents had not congealed its spirit.

Recent work by Stenger on late antique education has explored the "dynamism and innovations of educational ideologies," providing a detailed analysis of educational ideas while trying to define new trends. Stenger considered questions of upbringing, educational identity, self-transformation, and the intersection of education and ideologies.[4] Stenger concentrates on some Christian thinkers' educational theorizations: that is, on educational philosophy, noting that ancient paideia had reached such a state of inertia that it became easy prey for religion, the Christian Church, and textual communities. However, when we explore the appropriation of traditional education by Christian figures such as Didymus the Blind and Olympiodorus, we will ask ourselves whether they did successfully incorporate classical paideia, which had not ceased to satisfy them.

Christians established a strong notion of religious education—a departure from traditional ideas that were also entrenched in their late antique minds. Once that had happened, religious formation was always present in the philosophical curriculum. While morals and ethical concepts jumped to the foreground in ancient Christian education, we should recognize that these ideas had previously been cultivated, even if with less intensity. Moral formation and the attainment of ethical excellence were already at the center of Quintilian or Plutarch's educational projects. In addition, we have also explored the ethical concerns of Stoic philosophers such as Musonius and Epictetus. Epictetus aimed to instill a moral conscience in his students, guiding them to become better human beings. Stenger rightly insists on the concept that Christian education was a tremendous force that affected a person's whole existence. It offered an individual a path to proper behavior and a new "way of life." But this was not truly an innovation; long ago Pierre Hadot insisted that philosophical education at all times meant to follow and practice a way of life. Epictetus too had wished for his students a transformation that affected their entire existence.[5]

Stenger also treats postclassical education as a monolithic and immutable system. He manifests no desire to go beyond what he defines as the usual and tired examinations of the classroom, the curriculum,

---

4. Stenger 2022. See also Stenger 2019.
5. Stenger 2022, 141–88 passim. As usually happens, the book basically ignored Hadot and did not mention Epictetus and his promotion of teaching a way of life.

and students' life. These are the issues with which I am concerned in these sections—issues that in contrast I find to offer new and exciting perspectives. Late antique appropriation of an earlier culture took different forms. The Christian Didymus in the fourth century and the pagan Olympiodorus in the sixth adopted to some extent (though in different ways) a traditional literary culture with its lore of divinities. From the third century CE on, the cultural opposition between Christians and pagans becomes considerably less marked. It leaves very few traces in grammatical and philosophical works, to the point that the closing of the Athenian school of philosophy is never mentioned in all the late commentaries.

Initially, Christian communities resisted the notion that traditional education could also address spiritual understanding and therefore was not in opposition to Christian values. Christian writers created the model of the illiterate saint who was only inspired by God, a model that is sometimes still taken at face value by scholars who use in their arguments the fourth-century *Vita Antoni*, written by the Alexandrian bishop and theologian Athanasius. Recently that notion has been strongly challenged, but an incorrect understanding of illiteracy continues to characterize treatments of other Christian charismatic figures.[6] At that time, the boundaries between pagan and Christian allegiance to the classical culture became more fluid and were less of a divisive force. Educated Christians who felt part of the traditional literary culture had argued that "it was a culture of the tongue, not of the heart" and could serve the common good.[7]

In the fourth century and later, higher education, with its traditional curriculum that went back to the Hellenistic period, remained the norm also among Christians, at least in some domains.[8] Grammatical and rhetorical studies were still followed with enthusiasm. But, as usual, philosophy was studied more rarely, with a concentration of activity in Athens and Alexandria. It is meaningful to remember that in the second century, Epictetus had identified Zeus with God, the *theos* whom he worshipped fervently and who was crucial in his ethical system. Other Olympians are present in the *Discourses*, but they belong to

---

6. See Rubenson 1995; Rubenson and Larsen 2018. Brakke (1995, 253–55) maintained that the reference in Athanasius regarded higher schooling and not primary education, and Cribiore (2013, 66–69) reinforced that argument.

7. See Kaster 1988, 71.

8. Of course, there was not a definite equivalent of Christian grammatical and rhetorical culture.

a secondary tier and are never identified with a higher divinity.[9] While we see here an authentic belief in God, the other gods are relegated to a mythological space.

There is much evidence that at that time, Christians and pagans did not belong to bounded, opposed groups but rather were more flexible. There were various degrees of intensity inherent in religious allegiance. In many respects, Christianity was not too far from a traditional mindset that accepted the Olympians in a literary context. The *dipinto* in one of the rooms of the fourth-century school discovered in Egypt's Dakhla Oasis, at Amheida, testifies to some syncretism.[10] Its first column contains an invocation to a God (line 4), whose name should be capitalized to distinguish him from the mythological gods that are then mentioned. "May God grant my wishes that you learn the Muses' honeyed works with all the Graces and with Hermes son of Maia reaching the summit of rhetorical knowledge." This teacher, imparting some grammatical and rhetorical precepts to the students, was evidently a Christian who did not refrain from mentioning the Homeric gods.

Didymus the Blind in his commentaries on biblical books mentioned traditional pagan education centered on the usual authors. His aim, however, was not to discuss mythology and the pagan gods but only to allude to or mention them in the course of his exegesis of the Bible. He took it for granted that young men would be able to identify those traditional passages and authors from past schooling. Certainly the emperor Julian would not have approved of his teaching, though Didymus's very limited reliance on pagan notions was not threatening, and Didymus had all the pedagogic and moral qualifications that the *Codex Theodosianus* 13.3.5 considered mandatory. The hidden intention of Julian's school law, with its perverse logic, was to ostracize Christian educators who regularly used traditional literature.[11] Julian meant to form an exclusive group that had access to the canonical texts. That became manifest in Julian's *Epistle* 61c, in which the emperor openly opposed Christian teachers of higher education. The latter could not engage with traditional paideia and with the pagan gods unless "they

---

9. Epictetus believed in a divine law according to which people should not desire what they did not have but needed to be content with what they did have; one had to conduct oneself honestly and obey God in everything. *Diss.* 2.16 and 28; Bénatouïl 2009, 39, 179–94.

10. Cribiore et al. 2008, 183. This *dipinto* is on a wall of the most important room in the school, room 15, which had pillars. See also Cribiore and Davoli 2013; Cribiore 2015.

11. On the various phases of the opposition to Julian, see Van Nuffelen 2020. See also Stenger 2022, 32–42; Stenger 2009.

carried them in their souls." The contradiction of believing in a Christian God but continuing to teach mythology led in his view to an ethical crisis. The gods "were the guides of all learning" and deserved total allegiance. Christian teachers had to either stop teaching the traditional paideia or prove they were sincere in expounding on Homer and Hesiod. Clear evidence of allegiance was necessary. That probably consisted of a public pagan sacrifice, a very difficult testimony for a Christian.[12] Illustrious educators like Prohaeresius[13] stopped teaching, even though Julian made an exception for them.

However, another side of allegiance to the traditional gods needs to be taken into account. Just as some Christians did not refrain from mixing their religious ideology with aspects of pagan beliefs or culture, so too some pagans were so more in culture than in religious fervor. They cultivated close relations with Christians and were not as strongly absorbed in the cult of the traditional gods as Julian seemed to be. I have argued elsewhere that Julian's rescript not only was aimed at Christians who operated somewhat in both camps but also cautioned "gray pagans," who to some extent distanced themselves from the religious content of the Greeks' cultural heritage.[14] Libanius was one of these; he taught Christian students like Amphilochius of Iconium and Optimus, who became rhetorician bishops.[15] Tradition claimed that he also taught John Chrysostom.[16] The Edict and the letter, in my opinion, sent pagans a controversial message: that they too had to reform their views.

Didymus: A Christian Philosopher

Several ancient historians have provided details on the life of Didymus the Blind, who was hailed as a renowned Christian teacher in fourth-century Alexandria.[17] Rufinus reports that Didymus lost his eyesight as a child but through strenuous work and prayer achieved a high level

---

12. See Vössing 2020, 18; Germino 2004. On the reaction of some Christian authors, such as Gregory of Nazianzus, see Elm 2012.
13. Eunapius, *VS* 101.1–108.4 485–93. Cf. Cribiore 2007a, 52–54.
14. See Cribiore 2013, 229–37.
15. Cribiore 2007a.
16. John Chrysostom may have been his student in Antioch, but there is no trace of him in Libanius's letters.
17. See, e.g., Palladius, *Historia Lausiaca* 4.9; Sozomen, *Historia ecclesiastica* 9.15; Socrates Scholasticus, *Historia ecclesiastica* 4.25; Rufinus of Aquileia, *Historia ecclesiastica* 2.7; Jerome, *Chronicon* 8. 812. Rufinus and Jerome took classes from Didymus. His dates are ca. 313–398.

of learning. He had a vast knowledge of grammar, rhetoric, logic, music, arithmetic, and geometry, and a complete familiarity with the Holy Scripture, which he knew by heart. Didymus followed the doctrines of Origen and was eventually condemned as a heretic together with Origen and Evagrius in the sixth century in a synod convened by Justinian. His works, however, show that he was flexible within his circle. Though he was loyal to the exegetical and theological views of Origen, he did not show theological conformity.[18]

Didymus's students regarded him as an ascetic master, and he regarded his instruction as a form of Christian philosophy, a school for virtue. At that time, as Richard Layton remarked, "The study of philosophy, unlike other educational disciplines in antiquity, relaxed the boundaries between human and divine."[19] It is very unlikely, in any case, that Didymus's students had attended privileged schools of philosophy before. Didymus resided in Alexandria his entire life, and because teachers were usually itinerant it was said that "his sedentary existence was imposed by his blindness."[20] This is not a necessary inference, even though Didymus had a further motivation not to leave the city, namely, his health. Teachers traveled when they did not have steady commitments, but when a school became established, they would reside in that place for the rest of their lives, as the examples of Epictetus in Epirus and Libanius in Antioch show. Didymus needed time and tranquility to teach his students and to write. It is possible that his blindness influenced Didymus in a different sense. In his works he never mentioned or alluded to current events. Alexandria was then a major center of pagan intellectuals, philosophers, mathematicians, physicians, and literary figures. It was also a turbulent city at the time, but Didymus apparently kept himself away from everything.[21] In these commentaries and lectures he never actually cites Origen, who continued to be a controversial figure. Didymus's lack of mentioning current events was probably due to his desire to concentrate on his studies and teaching, closing himself within his classroom, and not on any uncertainty about his allegiance to Origen.

---

18. Origen probably started as a pagan and then converted to Christianity. He presented himself as a Christian Platonist, which his adversaries considered a contradiction in terms. He was criticized during his life and afterward. See Ramelli 2009.
19. Layton 2004, 13.
20. Layton 2004, 7.
21. See Watts 2006, 2010.

Although sometimes called a university, Didymus's school was probably a Christian group meeting in Alexandria. It is not clear what a church school was. The instruction may have taken place either in an imposing setting similar to that of Kom el-Dikka in Alexandria or in Didymus's own private rooms, where he offered advanced instruction in biblical interpretation.[22] A very productive writer, he became an authority in biblical exegesis and left treatises and several commentaries on the Bible. These contain no biographical information but illuminate his teaching. The Christian literary tradition put him in contact with the ascetic Antony.[23] Jerome, Athanasius, and Didymus referred to the figure of Antony as an admired basis for their approach to culture and practical Christian life. Socrates of Constantinople, Sozomen, Jerome, and Rufinus testified to an encounter of Didymus and Antony in which the latter told Didymus that his eyes were those of angels: they put him in contact with God.[24] This was a recognition that asceticism and Christian intellectualism had to be regarded as complementary. Didymus represented the type of Christian intellectual deeply immersed in an education and culture that were not only Christian. His type of Christian philosophy was intellectually driven.

Blending classical culture and his deep knowledge of the scriptures, Didymus wrote two books on the Trinity and compendia of his understanding of the Christian faith, drawing on Origen's works *On First Principles* and *Against Celsus*. He also produced treatises on some theological issues and commentaries on the scriptures, just as contemporary followers of Plato and Aristotle did on the works of their predecessors. Many are not extant or are severely lacunose, but their style differs sharply from that of the two school commentaries that I discuss in this section. These commentaries, devoted to Psalms and Ecclesiastes, stand out because they contain students' questions interspersed with exegesis and represent class lectures of Didymus that were taken down as notes.[25]

---

22. See Derda et al. 2007. On the use of these halls, see Watts 2010. Marrou (1956, 328) thought of Didymus's school exclusively as a private relationship between a lecturer and a listener, but now it is possible to go further than that. About the location of the school, cf. Libanius at the beginning of his career.

23. Socrates, *HE* 4.25; Sozomen, *HE* 3.15; Jerome, *Ep.* 68.2; Rufinus, *HE* 11.7.

24. On a balanced view of the encounter between Didymus and Antony, see Layton 2004, 19–26. See also Watts 2006, 182–83. It is unlikely that, even if the encounter took place, Antony would refer to Didymus in those terms.

25. *Patrologia Graeca* 39. The five commentaries on papyrus (about one thousand leaves of papyrus) were discovered deep in a cave in a monastery near Cairo in 1941 and are usually referred to as "the Tura papyri." They should be dated to the late sixth century. For publication and translation of these texts, see Kehl 1964, 43–47; Gesché 1962, 400–417. The commentaries

Didymus' commentaries, written mainly in the third quarter of the fourth century, have survived to us in five papyrus codices. Discarded in the sixth century, in 1941 they were found in a cave in Tura, close to Cairo. What follows concerns these notes and attempts to ascertain who recorded them. The surviving commentaries cover the whole of Ecclesiastes, while those on the Psalms are incomplete. In contrast to other commentaries such as those on Zechariah and Genesis, the lemmata and the exegesis are shorter here.

In what respects are the transcripts of Didymus's classes significant? These notes are so valuable because they illuminate ancient Christian teaching and learning and the differences from pagan education. Since notes are proverbially disorderly, a scribe copied them after they were redacted—as happened for Arrian's notes—but maintained the texts with their apparent shortcomings. We should compare the evidence they offer against what exists for other ancient schools and evaluate what they show of the exegesis of Christian texts in the early Christian period. Libanius, who lived in the same period as Didymus, left abundant testimonies of his own teaching. From these we can derive much information about the composition of his classes, the social and economic backgrounds of his students, and the curriculum they followed. All this material is of a different tenor from what comes to light through Didymus's commentaries, however, because it consists of orations and exercises that were edited and published. Even in the letters, Libanius's voice is muffled by the need to observe some conventions, work in favor of student recruitment, and enlarge his political and religious circles. Both his students' voices and his own are often conventional and are far from constituting direct testimonies, while through Didymus's comments the pedagogic setting is direct and authentic. The *Discourses* of Epictetus feel more vivid than the works of Libanius, permitting us to perceive otherwise unknown sides of his personality and pedagogy. For this reason, I sometimes call on Epictetus for comparison, even though he lived more than two centuries before Didymus and was a Stoic philosopher rather than a Christian.[26]

---

on the Psalms and Ecclesiastes have been published in the series Papyrologische Texte und Abhandlungen, together with a German translation (Binder and Liesenborghs 1979, *Lage 1*; Liesenborghs 1965, *Lage 22 und 23 des Tura-Papyrus. Kommentar zum Ecclesiastes* Bonn I/VI). Didymus's commentary covered the whole of Ecclesiastes but only a portion of the Psalms. See the magisterial publication of the text on the *PsT* by Blumell et al. 2019, 26:10–29:2 and 36:1–3.

26. Dionisotti 1982, 83–125, at 98–99 lines 18–19 and 24; Dickey 2012, 2015; Cribiore 2001b, 15–16.

Levels of Teaching in Early Christianity

The commentaries on Psalms and Ecclesiastes, unlike Didymus's other commentaries, contain roughly three hundred questions (or observations) and corresponding answers. The level of the questions is not uniform. The students might ask about the meaning of a phrase or term, or they might venture into more advanced material. Didymus might reply with a straight answer or by showing the different meanings of a word in the singular and plural or in the passive voice, or by postponing his answer with some impatience. The questions are about numerology, points of grammar, and interpretation. Most of the questions are introduced by a sign επερ followed by an abbreviation sign that has been interpreted as representing various forms of ἐπερωτάω (to ask). To these I would also add the possibility of ἐπεργάζομαι (to discuss, to inquire about and elaborate).[27] From the beginning these commentaries were identified as Didymus's lectures to rather advanced students, but signs of the presence of students of various levels of learning are visible. The evidence shows that Didymus addressed students who were not mere catechumens, interested not only in grammar and lexical issues, but also in some logic, rhetoric, philosophy, numerology, geometry, and astronomy.[28] In these disciplines, however, their level was not very sophisticated. Throughout, moral exhortations and emphasis are present, suggesting that some ascetics and monks attended the classes in addition to the students of various levels.[29] Though these are not commentaries in the traditional sense, the term *commentarii* is aptly used for them as a term applied to notes.[30] With their various formats, the students' questions let us see the mechanics of a teacher's delivery of lectures and generation of responses.

Didymus's Tura transcripts, like Arrian's notes, reveal how classes were conducted and guide us helpfully through school routines.

---

27. Menander Rhetor Treatise II 442.19. Cf. Blumell et al. 2019, 133n14.

28. Nelson 1995. Nelson's excellent dissertation, which she did under the guidance of Ludwig Koenen, was never published but is available. Its detailed examination of the texts that illuminate Didymus's classes has proved a useful reference for scholars. She attempts to calculate the length of the lectures and when they were given (19–24). The fact that the class met in the morning and then after an interruption continued in the late afternoon is logical. It seems that Epictetus did the same. Layton (2004, 5, 7, 160) argued that Didymus aimed at consolidating tradition and presided over an academy modeled on Greek philosophical schools.

29. Blumell et al. 2019, 18. Apparently some women were also present.

30. On nomenclature, see part I. Olympiodorus's texts, which we will consider in the next chapter, were also called *commentarii*.

Plutarch discusses this topic at length in his essay *On Listening to Lectures* (42F–43F), which contains abundant references to students' questionable behavior during lectures. He distinguishes between questions asked by students and auditors interrupting the lecturer and those that he allows them to ask at the end of the lecture. An audience should be silent and avoid asking questions while a lecture is being delivered, but even those questions asked at the end should be appropriate; the ethical philosopher should not be plagued by "those in natural science or mathematics."[31] The commentaries of Didymus on the Psalms and Ecclesiastes, however, are not proper lectures delivered continuously to the public along the lines prescribed by Plutarch. They cite lemmata, that is, verses and passages from the Bible, and comment on them in front of a lively audience of students who ask clarifications and further questions. Apparently Libanius did not permit questions at his lectures, but he certainly responded to them during teaching.[32] We have seen above that not so many questions by students are present in Epictetus's *Discourses*. Arrian presents many solo performances of the philosopher where the words of Epictetus contain both questions and answers. His students are behind the text, but their recorded interventions are very few. Occasionally one can hear Didymus's voice uttering a student's question, as Epictetus did. The rhythm and frequency of the questions in Didymus's text is another indication that it reproduces the spontaneous unfolding of the teaching that is captured by notes. Questions can be very brief or long and detailed, or they can be reproduced in a series.[33] Some are at the end of a session as in Plutarch's essay, but others occur throughout a session and sometimes allude to material done previously. They can even occur at the beginning of a session and recapitulate issues encountered before.

In order to understand in which respects Didymus's school corresponded to a traditional system of liberal studies in the Greek and Roman world and specifically covered material in a grammarian's context, it is necessary to review and also challenge what we know about ancient education. Years ago, I attempted to show that a primary level of learning was generally followed by literary studies under the grammarian

---

31. *Physikas* and *mathematikas*, 43C.
32. In *Or.* 3.12–14 he listed all possible misbehaviors by students without including questions of any kind.
33. See *PsT* 104.7; Nelson 1995, 23.

and the rhetor.[34] While elementary education might be acquired informally in cities and the countryside alike, teaching at subsequent levels traditionally took place in cities and was limited to students who could afford the expense. Philosophical education was not part of the *enkyklios paideia*; it was restricted to smaller circles. I want to emphasize now that these divisions were not rigidly observed in all cases, as students of various ages could be admitted to higher levels, and education could be adapted to local circumstances.[35] In late antiquity especially, education was changing. The situation was much more fluid than what exists in the modern world, although one might be tempted to find some parallels. In the Roman and late antique periods, the traditional divisions in circles of learning were beginning to be effaced according to circumstances, localities, and the availability of specialized teachers.

In earlier centuries, educational theory certainly did not favor such blurring. Writing in the first century in the city of Rome, Quintilian denounces those grammarians who were then encroaching on the territory of rhetoric teachers by introducing *progymnasmata* in their classes.[36] He maintains that each educational level has its proper sphere, but his protests show that these different models of teaching were already established. Quintilian puts up a passionate defense of his field, rhetoric, but different models were in existence not only in the countryside but also in urban settings, with teaching of the rudiments going hand in hand with that of higher disciplines. In second-century Rome, Fronto was a lawyer, had a political career, and tutored the emperors Marcus Aurelius and Lucius Verus in rhetoric.[37] He was a supporter of Latin literature, and his lessons were often permeated by his passion for obscure and archaic words, with a focus on how they should be chosen and arranged, using examples selected from poets such as Ennius.[38] He taught rhetoric but had a fervent interest in literature and attempted to inculcate in Marcus Aurelius the skill of writing beautiful epistles. His model was Cicero, and he sent some excerpts of his letters to Marcus,

---

34. Cribiore 2001b.
35. I fear that what I wrote especially in 2001 was taken too literally. At that point I was considering traditional education. I was striving to delineate the functions of the teachers at the various educational levels and did not take into account that the diversity was more nuanced.
36. Quintilian 2.1.
37. Champlin (1980) is still the best book.
38. An example among many, e.g., *De eloquentia* 3, Haines 1929, 73–81: on attention to synonyms and terms of old writers, see 77.

who had asked him for a selection of them to improve his language skills.³⁹ Teaching epistolary skills was traditionally a task for the grammarian, but since it was needed, Fronto took it over.

Later on, other schools in the East would try to follow this same model in which certain disciplines coexisted with others.⁴⁰ Some of these schools were large and specialized and catered to students who came from all over the Roman East to learn rhetoric. Necessity, however, sometimes dictated different arrangements. In Antioch, Libanius was "the sophist of the city," and we can surmise that the other local rhetorical groups did not attract the same crowds as his school, which counted eighty students in its best years. Libanius's school was exclusively for rhetoric, a subject in which he was the ultimate authority, but he employed a number of assistants. For years these assistants were considered grammarians employed by the school, but I have shown more recently that they were rhetors who functioned below their levels of expertise.⁴¹ The school included some very young students and others who were married adults, and so different types of teaching were required.⁴² The curriculum itself was rooted in traditional poetry and literature, and the assistants' task was to guide students through literary texts, especially the Homeric poems.

In Egypt, private teachers called *kathegetai* offered their services to young men who could not attend advanced classes in cities like Oxyrhynchus and Alexandria.⁴³ These were teachers of higher education, and they covered levels above the elementary, including subjects up to rhetoric. The letter that the student Neilos wrote to his father in the first or second century indicates that in Alexandria, the teaching of rhetoric was organized in small groups around private teachers.⁴⁴ In the fourth-century *dipinto* found on the wall of a Greek school in Amheida, the ancient Trimithis in Egypt, literary texts by Homer and Plutarch would suggest the teaching of the grammarian, while another text hints at moving up to the next level, that of the rhetor.⁴⁵ It is

---

39. See, e.g., *Ad Antoninum Imp.* ii.4 and ii 5, Haines 1929, 156–59. Fronto declared that there was nothing more perfect than the letters of Cicero.
40. Cribiore 2007a, 42–84.
41. Cribiore 2007a, 30–37.
42. It was necessary to cater to some students such as the young son of Libanius Cimon.
43. Cribiore 2001b, 53–54, 57; *P.Oxy.* VI 930, with a *kathegetes* teaching grammar. For a *kathegetes* instructing a girl, see Cribiore 2001b, 87, 94–96.
44. *P.Oxy.* XVIII 2190, Cribiore 2001b, 57.
45. Cribiore et al. 2008, 170–91; Cribiore and Davoli 2013, 1–14; Cribiore 2015, 179–92.

absurd to think that two different teachers were involved in a small school in a remote location. Rather, a competent *kathegetes* with knowledge in both areas must have left the Nile valley to serve those privileged young men in the Dakhla Oasis whose parents cared to offer them a competitive education. The schools I have described above are examples of institutions where subjects were not strictly separated, but where instead the same people covered some of each of them according to necessity.

The size of the school where Didymus taught as *doctor scholae ecclesiasticae* is unclear. According to Rufinus, the school was not under the authority of bishop Athanasius but rather an urban study group meant to promote personal growth through the reading of the scriptures. As was customary, exegetical lessons were given in the morning and the afternoon was devoted to "a largely transient group of students."[46] Students of various ages and backgrounds came and went, and Didymus had to adapt to their different levels. It is not very significant that in the first century Philo of Alexandria probably had only three students in his class, as the dialogue *On Animals* reveals.[47] It is likely that Philo, who came from a prominent family and did not have to earn a living from teaching, was not working in an institutional context, but the diversity of students must have been a challenge. One should not be surprised by the lack of uniformity of Didymus's pedagogic message. At times, in any case, context suggests the presence of more than one student, even if Didymus never uses the second person plural in reference to his audience.[48]

Tradition has attributed to both Origen and Didymus an important role in the catechetical school in Alexandria, so it is worthwhile to try to understand what kind of a school that was. The two commentaries we must consider show that Didymus's teaching did not in fact address catechumens. For centuries scholars have discussed the catechetical school in Alexandria: its existence, characteristics, and especially the kind of instruction that was imparted there. Both Knauber (1968) and Crouzel (1970) argued for elementary notions being given to the younger ones while older students received some philosophical and ethical teaching.[49]

In a 1977 study by van den Hoek, the account of Eusebius of Caesarea in the *Church History* was strongly criticized, because he depicted

---

46. Bayliss 2015, 16.
47. Philo of Alexandria, *Alexandria, vel de ratione quam habere etiam bruta animalia*. Translated from Armenian by A. Terian, Paris, 1988.
48. Nelson 1995, 25.
49. Knauber 1968; Crouzel (1970) critiques in detail Knouber's argument. Stenger (2022) does not consider the young catechumens but focuses his attention on older individuals.

an actual school continuing across time, but more recently it has attracted less criticism.⁵⁰ In 6.3.8-9, Eusebius portrayed the school as something unified, but this seems his own creation.⁵¹ Several times Eusebius referred to a *didaskaleion*, a term that is rather ambiguous and would indicate a place of teaching or instruction. In one instance, however, he referred directly to a "catechetical" school and said that Origen when he was eighteen years old had become the head of the catechetical school in Alexandria (6.30.1).⁵² Eusebius says that when Origen realized that he had too many students, he asked his student Heraklas to conduct the elementary classes for the youngest of them, keeping for himself the teaching of the older students. Origen's teaching in Alexandria and Caesarea gave his more advanced students some philosophical and ethical precepts that could strengthen them in learned discussions, but it is unclear whether these were mostly notions deriving from general advanced paideia to help them understand the Scriptures.⁵³

The Schooling of Origen

A good case from which to appreciate the variety of Christian learning experiences in Didymus's time is the course of studies that Origen followed before teaching in Alexandria and later in Caesarea Maritima.⁵⁴ In the *Homilies on the Psalms* there is a remark about himself as grammarian and philosopher.

> Ὁ διδάσκαλος καὶ κύριος ἡμῶν τοσαῦτα ἔχει μαθήματα ὡς ἀπαγγέλλειν οὐκ ἐπὶ δέκα ἔτη, ὡς ἀπαγγέλλει γραμματικὸς καὶ οὐκ ἔχει τί διδάξει οὐδὲ ὡς φιλόσοφος ἀπαγγέλλει παραδιδοὺς καὶ οὐκέτι ἔχει καινότερόν τι εἴπῃ, ἀλλὰ τοσαῦτά ἐστι τὰ μαθήματα τοῦ Χριστοῦ ὥστε αὐτὸν ἀπαγγέλλειν εἰς ὅλον τὸν αἰῶνα.

Our teacher and Lord has these teachings to proclaim not for 10 years as the grammarian teaches, who then does not have anything new to teach, neither as the philosopher who expands and

---

50. Van den Hoek (1997, 85-87) argued that what Eusebius had remarked was not fundamentally wrong and was worthy of more attention. Though he can be criticized in some respects it is important not to dismiss him.
51. See Heine 2010, 26-64.
52. Both Origen and his teacher Clement of Alexandria mention a *didaskaleion*.
53. Harmless 2014.
54. See Heine 2010.

proclaims and then does not have anything new to say, but these are the teachings of Christ so that he proclaims them for whole ages. (*Homilia in Psalmum* 74.6)[55]

This passage has troubled scholars of Origen very much because it seems to indicate that Origen studied with a grammarian for ten years, a really long time—as people have objected—and then passed to the guidance of a philosopher without studying rhetoric. There are three solutions for the dilemma. We will see in what follows that in sixth-century Alexandria, Philoponus was called a grammarian and actually had a formal appointment as such but was also teaching philosophy. Another scenario is also possible: Origen studied with a primary teacher for about five years and then with a grammarian for five more. In this way his schooling would have followed the usual protocol, but teachers' titles would be different from usual. The primary teacher could be called *grammatistes*, and sometimes the titles *grammatistes*, the teacher of elementary letters, and *grammatikos*, the teacher of liberal letters, were considered together and their titles were mixed. It is indicative that in the fourth century, authors like Libanius and Themistius called the *grammaticus* by the name *grammatistes*. Robert Kaster has shown that a more fluid notion of literacy could be expected especially away from the large educational centers, with grammarians entrusted with a variety of teaching.[56] So a third solution for the dilemma about Origen's schooling is that the passage above is correct and he might have learned all subjects before philosophy from a grammarian, including some rhetoric. Whatever solution we adopt, what precedes confirms that the boundary between different types of teachers could be porous.

Was Didymus a Grammarian?

Blossom Stefaniw has argued that "Didymus was a fourth century Christian grammarian," asserting that Didymus as a true classical grammarian taught only the traditional subjects that were part of his sphere.[57] Though this statement surprised many scholars, no one has

---

55. Perrone 2015 ed. *Origenes* vol. 13, p. 279, lines 11–15. The Homilies were found seventy years after the finding of the Tura Papyri in 1941. There are twenty-nine Homilies, four of which are new and have the Greek text.
56. See Kaster 1988, 45–47 and 447 with the appendix.
57. Stefaniw 2018, 181. Stefaniw wrote a valuable book, but I disagree with her on her position that Didymus was a grammarian and taught the subjects traditionally attributed to grammarians.

argued against it systematically, so the question deserves some probing. It not only clarifies Didymus's role but also allows us to glean information about an ancient Christian classroom. Stefaniw's argument is that Didymus was a grammarian because "he exhibited all the symptoms of a grammarian."[58] His students often raised questions on points of grammar, forcing him to linger on explanations, and as a consequence there were many interruptions and repetitions. While Stefaniw rightly maintains that Didymus did not offer catechetical or purely ethical instruction, he did cover so many other subjects that it seems unnecessary to imprison him in a grammarian's cage. Some of his "illustrious" students, such as Rufinus or Jerome, joined his class after learning history, rhetoric, and some philosophy and could not be satisfied with simple questions. Others may have spent only a year or two in a grammarian's class and would still have needed help reading the Bible and guidance to avoid committing errors of interpretation. Didymus was able to respond to all occasions.

The activities of a grammarian had many facets related to reading and writing, but in the Tura commentaries these are mostly confined to clarifying the exegesis of a text.[59] Lemmata varied, but most of them were short and were followed by explanations intended to facilitate reading comprehension. Though this activity corresponded to the first of the six parts that traditionally constituted the expertise of a grammarian, most of the other domains of the grammarian, such as prosody, explanation of literary devices, and the studies of language and orthography, are almost absent from the commentaries.[60] Didymus's principal aim was to help some students overcome the obscurities of the narrative and properly understand the literal meaning before all else. Because Didymus was not teaching his students how to write, he gave them a minimum of "historical" notes, that is, the minutiae and whereabouts of biblical figures according to the grammarian's method. Only the minimum amount of information necessary to facilitate their understanding was deemed worthwhile. Unlike the pedantic grammarians, who indulged in these minutiae and inundated their students with all of their knowledge of mythological and historical lore, Didymus uses the *historiae* at a minimal level, and his commentaries are far from swollen with trivia.

---

58. Stefaniw 2019, 43–91 at 79 and passim.
59. Cribiore 2001b, 185–219.
60. This according to Dionysius Thrax, Cribiore 2001b, 185.

Many of the students' questions and Didymus's explanations concern the speaker of a passage, the *prosopon*. Identifying this figure was arduous in some passages. Readers of Latin and Greek literature, and not only students of the Bible, might be confused at times. In the margins of some school papyri containing Homeric passages, readers marked the names of the speakers to facilitate reading. Thus, in *P.Oxy.* II 223, which contains Book 5 of the *Iliad* and is replete with lectional signs, a second hand added the speakers' names, including the general voice of the poet. The Psalms were particularly difficult in this respect because they might be uttered by either a divine or a human voice.[61] When he helped his students, Didymus was not wearing his grammarian's hat but was simply a concerned teacher who perceived that his students were inadequately prepared. In explaining points of grammar, nuances in meaning, differences in prepositions, the singulars or plurals of verbs, or unknown words, Didymus was trying to remedy the gaps in the cultural baggage of those of his students who were not yet ready for Christian exegesis.

We have seen that the philosopher Epictetus had to confront students who were nostalgic for their gymnasia and past friends and who requested explanations of words. At their previous levels of studies, they had become habituated to the method of minute explanations that Epictetus referred to with disdain. In this case habit was compounded with the need to clarify some words used in philosophy, as also happened with Didymus. Epictetus argued with some contempt that the explanation of "little words" (*lexeidia*) should not take place in the school of a philosopher.[62] Didymus was usually more patient when confronting the same needy students, because their comprehension of the Scriptures was also at stake. It is very clear that the school of Didymus included students of more varied levels of learning and preparation and was less specialized than the school of Epictetus, which revolved around Stoic philosophy. And yet in both can be perceived the need to satisfy the requests of diverse students. Didymus was not a grammarian, but he knew grammar well, and when necessary he could act like one. Some of his students used uncertain language and needed to strengthen their grammar and comprehension of the text, but there is no need to assign Didymus only a grammarian's role. The frequency

---

61. Nelson (1995, 32–33) examines various occurrences.
62. *Diss.* 3.21.6–8. Cf. his identical dislike for *logaria* a diminutive of "words" in 2.18.26. See 2.1.31–33.

of linguistic explanation in the two *Commentaries* indicates that the average student in the class did not possess a high level of knowledge, but the texts also refer to aspects of rhetoric and philosophy to which other students had been exposed.

Another concern of Didymus was to impart to his most advanced students some notions of numerology, natural science, and logic, including the study of syllogisms.[63] This is a further indication that Didymus was not specifically a grammarian but instead a teacher who was flexible, like all good teachers, and responded to the needs of his students. If he appears more engaged with grammar than with other disciplines, it is only because the level of learning of his students was mostly lower, and they had not previously had a formal education in philosophy. For Didymus the absolute philosophical authority was Aristotle. Didymus quoted from some works of Aristotle, alluded to specific points in his commentaries and lectures, and incorporated Aristotelian logic in his instruction. He mentioned some syllogisms, including the one about the liar that was popular in the schools.[64] This syllogism has the following form: "If a person says, 'I am lying,' does he lie or tell the truth? If he is lying, he is telling the truth; if he is telling the truth, he is lying."[65] Apparently the Stoic Chrysippus had written six books on this exercise, and Epictetus repeatedly refers to him in connection to syllogisms.[66] Syllogisms were part of an education in philosophy, but they were often practiced at the early stages, judging from their appearances in Epictetus. He presents some of his students joining his school and proudly showing off their skill in these puzzles. Such students' philosophical ideals consisted of speaking fluently on philosophical principles, showing them off to others, and talking glibly without working on their knowledge of themselves or introspection. It appears that syllogisms were amusing philosophical exercises that Didymus found necessary for giving his best pupils a taste of philosophy. These notions were certainly not included among the subjects taught by a grammarian.[67] Didymus was very competent in various fields, and he dipped into his diverse stores of knowledge to serve his most advanced students.

---

63. Nelson 1995, 132–80. Stefaniw (2019) recognized the various subjects he taught.
64. Nelson 1995, 132–39; Gellius, *NA* 18.2. Adults too practiced on them with some enjoyment.
65. von Arnim 2004.
66. *Diss.* 2.17.34 and 2.21.17 on the syllogism of the liar. About syllogisms in general, see 2.23.44, 2.1.39, and 4.6.
67. Stefaniw (2019, 146–47 and 166) forces them under "the intellectual patrimony."

Adrian's Introduction to the Sacred Scriptures

It is useful to consider here as an example of a properly grammatical commentary a very interesting text that is not well known: *Adrian's Introduction to the Sacred Scriptures: An Antiochene Handbook for Textual Interpretation*. This text exemplifies the Christian use of traditional education and confirms that Christian grammatical practice followed the traditional one and was confined to properly grammatical notes.[68] Thus this text is very different from that of Didymus and very informative about how a grammatical commentary would look and what the functions of grammarians were. The text is customarily dated to the beginning of the fifth century and is of great importance because it is the only surviving handbook of biblical interpretation that issued from the fourth and fifth centuries. It purports to address teachers who needed to instruct students and is set in the schoolroom, as Adrian says, in an Antiochene context of biblical scholarship, especially on the Psalms.[69] In early Christian times, lexica, commentaries, and glossaries were inspired by classical texts but were centered on a new classic, the Sacred Scriptures. The text is influenced by John Chrysostom and by the exegetical works of Theodore of Mopsuestia that preceded it.[70] Theodore's commentaries on the Psalms and on the Minor Prophets are also a source. Adrian cites and mirrors especially the latter, showing little difference between early Christian texts and the tradition of Greek grammarians and rhetors.

We do not know for sure whether Adrian was a grammarian, but his only surviving work is entirely concerned with the practices of grammar in elucidating texts, looking at style, figures, and tropes and explaining unfamiliar words. It is not fundamentally dissimilar from Quintilian. The commentary is short and is not designed to comment on a particular book, but instead is intended to show a set of instructions that a beginner needs to follow. It is divided into three parts: message (content), diction, and word arrangement. Adrian felt that the text of the Sacred Scriptures was difficult, and so it was imperative for a beginner to know its peculiarities. The type of exegesis that Christian texts followed was

---

68. See Martens 2017, a welcome new edition, translation, and commentary of this text. The text was never translated into English and is not present in the TLG. In the following, I am faithful to Martens's text.

69. Martens (2017, 14n29) cites the words of Theodoret on the prevalence of the Psalms in Christian education. He argues that commentaries on those were much needed.

70. On Theodore of Mopsuestia (350–428), see Becker 2006.

modeled on that of the Homeric poems, which presented many difficulties to a reader in style and content. The Christian teacher should first instruct the student about the content of a work, but before embarking on a line-by-line commentary he had to aim at exegetical precision by teaching the student the peculiarities of the biblical language such as figures and the various kinds of tropes.[71] Adrian was familiar with the tradition of commentaries in Antioch. In an important part of appendix 3 (75), Adrian refers to the fact that Christian exegesis must use the same interpretive principles as the classical tradition. He argues that Christian exegesis needs to model itself on the interpretation of Homeric epics and should not venture into unnecessary conjectures. Adrian's book does not touch on rhetoric and philosophy, but exclusively concerns grammatical material. By examining Adrian's work, one realizes that Didymus could not be only a grammarian.

Are Didymus's Texts a Conglomeration of Notes?

In some respects, the Tura commentaries match the notes that Arrian took in the classes of Epictetus, and they are also not dissimilar from the lectures of Olympiodorus taken down by a student.[72] While the content is different, all the annotations contain a degree of spontaneity that is typical of notes; they let us hear the voices of those who recorded them. This is what constitutes their strength, authority, and fascination. There is no doubt that these were rough annotations of Didymus's teaching. Mistakes, confusions, and chaotic questions are sure indications of that. The Tura commentaries also show that some students might become confused and fall behind, remaining stuck on and requesting explanations of a previous passage.[73] The students sometimes challenged their teacher, but more often they followed along with some reluctance. Didymus's responses to questions might be rapid, and he often used the expression *amelei* ("come on, of course, no doubt") when he felt impatient to move ahead. At times, however, the students would settle on a certain passage, and he would be forced to linger more or less patiently. "We have already said that frequently!" Didymus

---

71. First there will be a short biography of the author, information, and content and then the commentary. We will see that Olympiodorus will follow this division.

72. Stefaniw (2019, 41) argues that the Tura commentaries do not match other lecture notes because she is concentrating on the grammatical aspects of Didymus's teaching. She also does not take into accounts Epictetus's *Discourses*.

73. *PsT* 83, 21; Stefaniw 2019, 63.

would sometimes protest to no avail, and sometimes he would refuse to explain a second time. His impatience at being asked to repeat a point is at times palpable, and he can be seen avoiding answering some questions, perhaps because he considered them problematic or redundant.[74] In certain respects the similarity of these notes to those that are evident in some works of Aristotle is striking.[75]

Evidence of Didymus's veiled anger at students of different levels is not surprising in a text that originated in class and was not intended to be published. We can compare with this Epictetus's fury that arose at the sluggish and unethical behavior of some of his pupils. In this case too, notes allow us to look behind a text and comprehend Didymus's teaching strategies. As in the case of Epictetus, annotations taken by others present in the class can put us in direct contact with the raw feelings of the protagonists. The beginning of an important passage about Job, centered on Job's rightfulness, is lost.[76] In this long disquisition and dialogue about the biblical figure, Didymus is far removed from the persona of a grammarian: for instance, he is not concerned with Job's genealogy or with discussing the minute details of his story. The student who was Didymus's interlocutor in this dialogue was far beyond needing grammatical help, knew the Bible well, and needed to delve immediately into the meat of the discussion.

Richard Layton has recognized this as one of the most enlightening pedagogic passages of the Tura commentaries.[77] Here, Didymus engages a well-prepared student who confronts him in a heated debate with the question of whether Job was righteous when he cursed the day he was born. The student reacts with indignation to the apparent reproof of the teacher because he sees a weakness in the argument and does not want to be silenced. The introduction and discussion of the opinion of Protagoras, who is defined as a sophist and whom perhaps the student had never encountered, serves to support the impossibility of mental certainty. The debate is only loosely philosophical, but Protagoras makes it dialectical.[78] After a debate on the equal validity of

---

74. *PsT* 222, 12; Nelson 1995, 48.
75. Cf. part I: the school of Aristotle.
76. *PsT* 222, 15-29.
77. Layton (2004, 29-35) explores the "scholastic dynamics" of the passage. See also Nelson 1995, 43-47.
78. Stefaniw (2019, 71) rightly recognizes that the most advanced lessons of Didymus cannot be properly categorized as philosophical. Yet they belong to high stages of education such as rhetoric. Some philosophical and ethical questions are also treated.

contradictory statements, the student finds he has depleted his ammunition but is also left without the conclusive answer he feels he deserves. This must have been a letdown; he was up to the challenge and had insisted on an intellectual confrontation. Centuries later the philosopher Philoponus found himself in a similar situation. Rather than replying to one of his objections, his master Ammonius cut off the discussion and said that otherwise they would surpass the time allotted. In the next lecture Ammonius did not take up the subject and declined to continue discussing it.[79]

One of the values of the Job passage is that it shows how notes are useful in portraying the dynamics of a real classroom. They allow us to move beyond the rigidity of pedagogic texts that had been emended and transmitted in the regular fashion. In this interchange between teacher and student, Didymus appears to be on the defensive and does not fully dispel his pupil's doubts. Didymus here is a less than sympathetic pedagogue and seeks to escape from the discussion. This passage also exemplifies how uneven Didymus's answers were and how perceptible (and authoritarian) his voice was. He treats some questions abruptly and very briefly, and others by impatiently confronting students' insistence or inquiries. Sometimes he refuses to answer altogether. Questions could arise at unpredictable moments, sporadically or all at once. They followed the ups and downs of teaching and learning, evoking the natural movements of lessons, as notes reveal. Didymus refers to his lectures as *praxeis*, as in the philosophical lectures of late antiquity.[80]

Models held a central position in ancient education. They existed for writing and style, providing students a guide when they produced their texts. As Plato's Protagoras said, elementary teachers wrote lines and made students write according to them (*Prt.* 326d). Then, by memorizing poetry and literature, students followed other models. Education also used *exempla* to delve into the pupil's world, appealing to his memory and imagination regarding not only grammar but also rhetoric, philosophy, and other disciplines such as medicine. Epictetus uses examples regarding the fields of medicine, music, and navigation, adding to these a wealth of historical examples, some based on contemporary events that could touch on pupils' concrete situations.[81]

---

79. Sorabji 2016b, 388.
80. Cf. the lectures of Olympiodorus and others that were divided in sections (*praxeis*).
81. Roller 2018.

The notes of the Tura commentaries show that Didymus used examples of every kind to support his exegesis of the Scriptures.[82] He had a personal predilection for *paradeigmata*, which he must have thought had formidable pedagogic value for clarifying a discussion. Most of the time he did not identify their source. Besides biblical examples he also used traditional ones from the everyday world, and especially from rhetoric and philosophy. He had a heterogeneous class. It seems that Didymus's teaching was for this reason highly individualized, even though he strove to observe procedural guidelines. In this endeavor, exempla could serve as links between the various levels in his class. Some students would simply have enjoyed their descriptive texture, while others may have been reminded of previous lessons on Socrates and Plato.

Shorthand *Notae* or Students' Annotations?

As emphasized at the beginning of this chapter, I argue that a text consisting of notes cannot automatically be assumed to be those of students who took them down during class but could also be *notae* of stenographers present at the lectures. Informal notes of stenographers that were never published would still allow us to gain information on how Didymus's class was conducted. In what follows, however, I will show that it is very likely that students rather than stenographers recorded the texts. It is commonly maintained that it was stenographers who took down the commentaries on Psalms and Ecclesiastes, as happened in the case of Didymus's other works. The early commentators who were not familiar with students' texts were unanimous in this respect, and more recent ones such as Bienert, Richard Layton, and Blumell take it for granted that tachygraphers recorded Didymus's classes, without discussing the issue.[83] Grant Bayliss is the only scholar who has declared his uncertainty about whether these texts were the records of a secretary or students' notes.[84] Even though decisive evidence is lacking, the cumulative considerations point in the latter direction. It is necessary to keep in mind the whole question of how stenographers worked, which I have covered in more detail in a previous chapter, to clarify the question. At the time of Didymus,

---

82. Nelson 1995, 51: "The number of such examples is overwhelming."
83. Bienert, 1972. Nelson (1995, 13) argues for a stenographer.
84. Bayliss 2015.

stenographers were very popular in certain circles and occupied prestigious positions. Scholars of Didymus's works often use the terms "stenographer" and "scribe" interchangeably, but some precision is needed: stenographers recorded words directly, while scribes copied from a model.

The historian Rufinus (11.7) is the source of the general conviction that Didymus functioned exclusively with the help of stenographers.

> *Huius aliquanti dicta, vel communiter disputata, vel proponentibus responsa adhibitis notariis descripsere.*[85]
>
> Some took down his words through the use of stenographers when they discussed together or the answers which he gave to those who questioned him.

We should not be certain that Rufinus's text alludes to the back-and-forth of questions and answers that occurred in Didymus's class. First of all, though Rufinus claimed that he had studied with Didymus, he may not have had firsthand knowledge of the functioning of the school as it appears in the Tura papyri, because he did not attend lectures at the same level, but instead followed more sophisticated ones that promoted deeper understanding. One indication that he was not well informed about the school is the fact that he incorrectly portrayed it as very similar to the catechetical school that previously, under Origen, imparted rather elementary notions of doctrine to those preparing for baptism. Moreover, argumentation also took place in other lectures and was probably not transmitted to us because those lectures were written up for publication, polished, and refined, a process during which questions must have been eliminated from them.

The students' questions in the commentaries on the Psalms and Ecclesiastes are of varied tenor and length, but more than a third of them are abbreviated. They show full or partial verses of the Septuagint with requests for interpretation, and sometimes consist of a single participle or word.[86] Questions such as these refer to previous sections of the text and are almost inexplicable without that context.[87] It is absurd to suppose that student questions were so condensed in reality; some interactions would have needed elaboration in a class, but who would have

---

85. Schwartz and Mommsen 1999, XI 7, 1013. Some have emended the late *aliquanti* in *aliquanta*.
86. *PsT* 210.3–5 and 210.16–18.
87. Nelson 1995, 28–29 on abbreviated questions.

shortened them? I have argued elsewhere that stenographers did not frequently take any initiative or intervene in texts to alter them. Instead, they would adhere precisely to a text that was delivered orally without making changes.[88] A student, however, may not have had the same respect for his classmates' voices and therefore may have preserved only what was necessary to introduce Didymus's responses, exactly as we suspect that Arrian had done. Having been unable to see since a very young age, Didymus depended on someone else to read for him the passages of the Bible that he wanted to interpret in class. It is likely that he would have selected one of his best students to perform this service for him and also, I suggest, to jot down class notes.[89] Students and scholars usually did not know stenography, which was a specialized activity. We can surmise that when Didymus lectured in class his pace was rather slow, as was the case in the class of Epictetus; the frequent interruptions and requests for explanation are evidence for this. Didymus was not delivering a ready-made sermon for an audience; he aimed at getting his message through to his pupils. He had no need for fast tachygraphers.

A student notetaker might betray his relative lack of expertise. The commentaries on Psalms and Ecclesiastes include some sentences that are incomplete, subjects or verbs that have to be supplied from the context, thoughts that are unclear, lemmata following answers, frequent anacolutha, abrupt connections between verses, the improper use of pronouns, and frequent parentheses. These are signs of oral delivery, showing that the commentaries on Psalms and Ecclesiastes were lectures given in the classroom. These types of irregularities do not appear in other texts of Didymus, which were certainly recorded by stenographers and then revised, and they may signify that a student recorded them. Since a real professional was not involved and the recording was informal, these notes remain testimonies of teaching and classroom life and were not published. In this respect, the hand is not indicative one way or the other. The documentary hand, which is generally fluent with some irregularities, could have belonged either to a stenographer

---

88. Cribiore 2021.The other texts of Didymus preserved very few signs of oral delivery. Bayliss 2015, 33.

89. Advanced students who had taken the class of a teacher for several years had a position of privilege and could even teach occasionally, such as Eusebius (no. 25 in *PLRE* I) who became a substitute teacher when Libanius was sick and did very well. See Cribiore 2007b, 267, *Ep.* 887 (no. 81). Kehl (1964, 41–43) pointed to the oral quality of the text taken down by a student but also mentioned stenographers.

who "translated" his *notae* or to a scribe who copied the student's notes later on.⁹⁰ The categories of scribes and private writers were not rigid and could be porous; the writer might have been an advanced student.⁹¹

There is another unusual feature of the *Commentaries* on the Ecclesiastes and Psalms that suggests that we are dealing with a student's notes, that is, the frequent occurrence of spaces between words. Spaces are occasionally visible in some documentary texts, but their presence in this case is exceptional because of their frequency and demands explanation. These spaces are less visible in the *Commentary to the Psalms* because the text is more fragmentary, but they are frequently present in the *Commentary to the Ecclesiastes*, for example in *EcclT.* 154.⁹² Underneath the lemmata the rest of the space is divided into easily read units. Shorter sentences are also often introduced by large letters. To say that these interventions made the text easier to read is an obvious observation,⁹³ but why was the text set up in this way and by whom?

We do not know if the commentary was supposed to end up in the hands of students after being taken down and reproduced in many copies or if it was used as a model against which certain passages could be checked. What is clear, however, is that the writer was familiar with a presentation of texts used to facilitate reading in school settings. When a student entered the class of a grammarian, he would still need help decoding passages written in *scriptio continua*, that is, in continuous blocks without division of words or lectional signs. Only a few books with this feature are preserved, mostly of Homer, but models with separated words provided by a teacher would have fundamentally helped beginners.⁹⁴ Thus Homer or Isocrates could be approached with greater confidence. These models formed an indispensable transition to texts written by scribes in continuous blocks. I suggest that it was a student who had learned to read and write with the aid of passages with separated words and was very familiar with this practice who noted down the *Commentaries*.

I have considered several factors that, in my analysis, point to the presence of a student (or students) who recorded two of the *Commentaries* of Didymus. The text's frequent lack of clarity, its mistakes, and its

---

90. Blumell et al. 2019, 3–6.
91. Cribiore 2020a.
92. I thank Gregg Schwendner for this private communication.
93. Blumell et al. 2019, 14–16.
94. Cribiore 2001b, 132–41.

heavily oral flavor should not be attributed to a stenographer, who generally would have reproduced a text *dal vivo* with accuracy. The fact that the students' questions are condensed and compressed beyond what would be reasonable in class also depends on a certain manipulation of the text, the recording of which is more easily attributed to a student than to a professional notetaker. We have seen a similar disregard for students' questions in Epictetus's *Discourses*, which I have attributed to Arrian's relative lack of interest in the voices of his classmates and to his concentration on the message of his teacher. Compounded by the regular spaces between words that appear in the text for easy legibility, all of this indicates a scholastic *mise-en-page*. We are familiar with the regard ancient teachers had for senior students, to whom they even entrusted classes to teach. Didymus was no exception. We should not visualize the school of Didymus as a rigid institution with fixed membership and curriculum.[95] The commentaries give evidence for many levels of learning and refer to students with diverse backgrounds. Ancient schools, especially in late antiquity, were not divided into uniform and discrete groups; teachers could cover various roles, and students learned subjects at several different levels.

---

95. Layton 2004, 159. Contrary to that, see Bayliss 2015, 16.

CHAPTER 10

Listening to Olympiodorus

The commentaries of several philosophers of the late Alexandrian school of philosophy were recorded by students who took notes during lectures *apo phones*, that is, from the voice of a teacher.[1] A huge quantity of philosophical writings survive from the late Roman Empire, when philosophy was embedded in pagan and Christian culture. This work consists mainly of commentaries, especially on Aristotle and Plato. In the Roman Empire and in late antiquity texts from previous times were at the center of philosophical instruction. Even though discussions and dialogues continued to be present in class, teachers paid a lot of attention to reading and interpreting texts. The term "commentary" inevitably suggests a scholarly exercise, but these commentaries were not only about texts per se but were also attempts to search for the "truth" in the ancient philosophers.[2] The Neoplatonic commentaries have not received a lot of attention, because they have not been studied in full but only consulted

---

1. This expression appears in the fifth and sixth centuries and is used in the philosophical schools of Athens, Alexandria, and Gaza. It is also used for Byzantine grammarians and iatrosophists. The lectures of the grammarian Georg Choeroboscus were taken down by his students. The text was simple but very prolix. The classic article is Richard 1950.
2. Cf. Wildberg 2005, 317.

occasionally. Among these I will focus on the *Commentary on the First Alcibiades*, which the philosopher Olympiodorus delivered to his class.

Olympiodorus was one of the last pagans to teach at the school of Alexandria in the sixth century. His students were mostly (or all) Christians from the elite who wanted to embark on careers in the clergy or at the Byzantine court.³ Members of the elite were steeped in classical culture, and philosophy was an important part of that. His life spanned approximately from 500 to 570, embracing the whole reign of Justinian. In the late 530s he apparently disappeared as a philosopher. This was the final period of pagan philosophy, because the emperor took extreme measures against philosophy as a way of pagan learning; these culminated in Justinian's closure of the pagan school of philosophy in Athens in 529, an event that strangely did not leave any traces in the commentaries.⁴ At that time, in Alexandria and elsewhere, philosophy was strong and producing many commentaries.

A short history of the school is necessary. The first significant representative of the school of Alexandria was Hermeias in the fifth century. When he died, before 470, his widow Aedesia took her son Ammonius to Athens to study with the philosopher Proclus. Proclus revived Neoplatonism and composed, among many other works, a *Commentary on the First Alcibiades* that is centered on the types of love in Platonic literature. It differs significantly from the commentary of Olympiodorus, which was taken down by students and will be considered next. Ammonius was the teacher of at least four of the most prominent philosophers of late antiquity: Philoponus, Simplicius, Asclepius, and Olympiodorus. It was they who edited his lectures, because Ammonius apparently refrained from writing.⁵

When Ammonius died, before 526, it was not Philoponus, the most brilliant of his students, who succeeded him; instead, Olympiodorus, who revered Ammonius and considered him as the final authority, held the chair of philosophy.⁶ Philoponus had an official post as grammarian

---

3. On the atmosphere in the city with pagan and Christian students, see Watts 2010.
4. General information on Olympiodorus and his times in *The Stanford Encyclopedia of Philosophy*, "Olympiodorus," https://plato.stanford.edu/archives/sum2018/entries/olympiodorus/. In this introductory part I follow Wildberg (2005) and the many works of Richard Sorabji.
5. Cf. Richard 1950, 192: "Ammonius did not like to write." Cf. Cribiore 2017. The Christian Zacharias painted a portrait of the philosopher teaching from his high chair. On Ammonius see Verrycken 2016b.
6. Sorabji 2010.

and was always given the title of *grammatikos*. It has been suggested that he may have occupied a position in the school as editor of Ammonius's lectures, but others would have collaborated too.[7] Olympiodorus in his writings never mentions Philoponus and apparently ignored or pretended to ignore what was happening in Alexandria so close to himself. Some hostility and rivalry can be read in his attitude. Koenraad Verrycken has tried to define the complex career of Philoponus, but some of his claims might be conjectural.[8] The philosopher had the Christian name "John" from his birth in Alexandria around 490. Yet even if he was born a Christian, his philosophy was not necessarily Christian for the rest of his life. In fact, Verrycken conjectures two phases, I and II: Philoponus I adhered to Neoplatonism, but Philoponus II later abandoned his philosophical past.

We have seen in part I that in Plato's *Theaetetus* (143a), Euclid had to take several steps in order to jot down a sufficiently correct version of a speech he had heard from Socrates. Socrates did not teach in a closed environment resembling a class, and yet this example of note-taking, the first to my knowledge, can be envisioned in an educational setting. The late antique Neoplatonic commentaries that students took down in Alexandria from the lectures of their teachers of philosophy are not very different. The impulse to consolidate one's memory is not surprising, and texts escaped their authors and circulated on their own.[9] In *Oration* 11.6 Dio Chrysostom comments that "the text must be delivered before other audiences and many will come to know it." Von Arnim saw in this an explanation for the dissemination of different versions of the same text.[10] People in the audience, and probably students as well, took down texts in the form they remembered them, and there was no way to control quality or circulation. In the same oration of Dio, sections 22-24 concerning the language of Homer is followed by a similar version with several modifications.

At times, commentaries did not originate from scholars' conscious will. A curious incident involving notes emerges from the *Life of Proclus* by Marinus.[11] It seems that the fifth-century philosopher Proclus was

---

7. Westerink 2016, 353. At that time Asclepius became the editor, but later on Philoponus filled that place and became the leading figure of the school.

8. Verrycken 2016a.

9. Cribiore 2019.

10. von Arnim 1898, 170-71. The discussion expands to 181-82; see also 281-82; Praechter 1909 (2016), 43.

11. *Life of Proclus* 27; Edwards 2000, 99.

initially very reticent to write a commentary, refusing to do so because of certain visions that had forbidden him from it. His disciple Marinus asked him to make a note in appreciation of a book of Orpheus's that needed a commentary and devised a stratagem: Proclus's disciples would ask him to make notes in the margins of commentaries, after which they "then made a single collation of them all." Again, a new book was created. According to this anecdote, which is difficult to take at face value because Proclus actually wrote a lot, Proclus made a sharp distinction between notes and a finalized text, but perhaps it is more likely that, "having a good nature," he gave in to the requests of his students.

Even though only one version of each of the late antique philosophical commentaries is now known, there may have been more in circulation. The same lectures may have been given again over subsequent years, and in theory multiple students may have attempted to take down a single one. Most of the commentaries only contain the phrase *apo phones* (from the voice of someone). Certain philosophers made limited claims to their texts and allowed their ideas to circulate freely, with some inevitable alterations and mistakes. We are not well informed about the students who annotated the lectures. In the case of Didymus, I surmise that the notetaker was an advanced young man of the caliber of the student who interrogated Didymus on the story of Job. In late antiquity too, it is likely that the role of notetaker would have been assigned by the instructor, or at least sanctioned by him. A philosophical anecdote relating to Proclus shows the mechanics of dictation and recording within a student-teacher relationship. Marinus reports that the old Plutarch of Athens was so taken by the young Proclus's determination and enthusiasm for philosophy that he included him in his study circle, which was reading Aristotle and Plato. It was Plutarch himself who exhorted Proclus to take notes recording what was said in the group, saying that they would eventually form a treatise on the *Phaedo* under Proclus's name.[12] A story reported by Photius shows the student Theosebius taking down a single text several times.[13] The same student twice recorded the Alexandrian philosopher Hierocles's lectures on the *Gorgias*, with confusing results, since a comparison of the versions shows notable discrepancies. But was Theosebius entirely

---

12. Marinus, *Proclus or on Happiness* 12. Translation by Edwards 2000. The treatise on the *Phaedo* is lost.
13. Photius *Bibl.* 338b35-36b.

to blame for the details surrounding the fundamental exegesis and its inconsistencies? Tradition has preferred to blame the student, but it is possible that Hierocles had actually delivered different accounts at different times.

The ancient commentators exhibited a notable indifference to intellectual property in allowing their students to write down and circulate notes from their lectures.[14] Their reasons for this attitude were partly due to the state of publication in antiquity. The commentators would have been aware, as we have already seen in other cases, that copies of some lectures might be disseminated without their consent and beyond their control, and they would have had to accept the inevitable and even take some distance from their teaching lectures. Below I investigate one further reason for their acceptance of the status quo. These notes were "class" copies produced by several students in collaboration. We have seen that in the third century the philosopher Plotinus refrained from writing for ten years, with the result that his students, especially Amelius, wrote massive amounts of notes. Ammonius, we are told, did not like writing either and had to rely on others. One wonders whether in both cases Plato's negative attitude toward writing was so influential that it established a trend.[15] Longinus in any case talked about this very topic, saying that in all schools some philosophers preferred to write but others did not for complex reasons.[16] In the case of Ammonius and Plotinus an important reason was to keep their teachings private.

Philosophers like Olympiodorus, who wrote several works on Plato and Aristotle, surely distinguished between the formal texts they wrote for publication and those they shaped more informally from the words they spread in class. The former were carefully organized and composed, while the latter were transcripts. In their lectures to students, philosophers were aware of the needs of their audience and supplied information of every kind. Like all good teachers they cared to plant seeds of knowledge in their students. In his *Commentary on Gorgias*, Olympiodorus considers the merits of teachers, from whom all our knowledge comes.[17] The teacher proceeds calmly, telling the pupils that just as an "apprentice potter first shapes something little," they should not begin

---

14. Praechter 1909 (2016), 44, also reporting the above episodes. See below.
15. Plato, *Phdr.* 274b–277a.
16. Cf. part I where Longinus explores this issue.
17. Jackson et al. 1998, 257–58, lecture 40.6.

by learning to make a wine jar, but should avoid being too ambitious. Rather than considering their commentaries true "intellectual property," philosophers would have regarded their lectures as schoolwork. In the commentaries, pedagogy was paramount. Critics have objected to the limited attention Olympiodorus devoted to theoretical philosophy, but he seems to have had different aims.

We shall consider the caution with which Olympiodorus presented his message in his commentary on the *First Alcibiades*, but there is no direct evidence of his comportment in class. A fragment from Philoponus, however, lets us see the philosopher scrutinizing the faces of his students in an attempt to assess the reception of his message. In order to learn, says Philoponus, young people need to be endowed by nature or receive instruction. Otherwise, those who frequently attend lectures might become annoyed and frustrated. Without the changes that nature or instruction bring, the teacher "might not be able to explain the expressions in the face of someone showing that he has understood what we say and the other expressions showing that he has not understood us."[18] We glimpse the philosopher going around the class interrogating his students' faces in order to fine-tune his message. Every philosopher had to assure himself that his class was following him, particularly in an introductory course. Students would have arrived with a baseline preparation in grammatical notions and generally would have been exposed to rhetoric, as the *Discourses* of Epictetus show. Olympiodorus had an interest in rhetoric. He possibly taught this discipline, or at least tried to encourage it because it was a good source of revenue, but philosophy was not part of the *enkyklios paideia*, and only some privileged young men chose to be exposed to it.[19] They were mostly novices and needed guidance.

Olympiodorus on the *First Alcibiades*

The order in which Plato's dialogues were taught was discussed throughout antiquity with mixed opinions,[20] and in late antiquity it became commonly accepted that the *First Alcibiades* served as an introduction, followed by *Gorgias* and *Phaedo*.[21] The topic of the *First*

---

18. Sorabji 2014b, 771.21-772.3, 125.
19. Jackson et al. 1998, 20 and 17-20 and 37-44 on Olympiodorus and rhetoric.
20. Cf. Diogenes Laertius 3.62.
21. Festugière 1969, 281-96. On the curriculum, see Jackson et al. 1998, 11-15.

Alcibiades was perfect for the late antique student, who would have known that after some years of rhetoric he would need to meet civic responsibilities, even if these did not any more involve crucial decisions of war and peace. A confused student feeling uncertain about his future would have been able to identify with the young Alcibiades, who was admired for all his qualities, both physical and cultural.[22] He had teachers for every subject, such as arithmetic, poetry, grammar, and rhetoric. In his teachers' classes, Alcibiades sometimes played games, speaking out confidently against cheating classmates.[23] He felt self-assured and did not care to apply effort in the proper directions, claiming that all the other men in politics were uneducated anyway. Alcibiades was sometimes reluctant, but Socrates claimed that he was at the ideal age to learn. Sections 129–135 of the dialogue concern knowing oneself in order to manage city affairs and impart virtue to the citizen. Virtue was becoming for a free man, and vice was proper for a slave. At the end of the dialogue, Alcibiades appears convinced and ready to be educated.

The commentary of Olympiodorus is structured differently from those of Didymus. In Didymus's commentaries, lemmata are elucidated and students' questions receive answers. The commentaries on Ecclesiastes and especially the Psalms dealt with popular texts that students probably already knew in part. The *First Alcibiades* may not have been as well known to beginners, and we can expect that the participants in the seminar would have been asked to read it before or that they would have had the text in their hands. In Kom el-Dikka, one of the fifth- or sixth-century Alexandrian classrooms excavated in 2005 shows a high *thronos* surrounded by four tiers of seats in a horseshoe shape.[24] A stone in the middle of the space was probably the base of a lectern that could have been used by a student to read. The teacher may have used it too, to rest his text before expounding while walking around the classroom.

---

22. See, e.g., the beginning of Plato's *Protagoras* and the *Symposium* (212e 1–2), where the beauty of Alcibiades is emphasized.

23. *First Alcibiades* 110B, an attractive vignette.

24. See in Plato *Prt.* 315c the representation of a class, with Hippias sitting on a high chair and the other philosophers on benches around him. On teachers' imposing chairs in antiquity (*thronoi*), see Cribiore 2001b, 28–34. On Kom el-Dikka, see Cribiore 2007b; Libanius *Or.* 5 and *Chria* 3 (Foerster vol. 8). Plutarch *Mor. Whether an Old Man Should Engage in Public Affairs* 796 represents philosophers sitting on high chairs and lecturing. An image that is not well known on a stele at the Musée d'Art et d'Histoire in Geneva represents a teacher of math sitting on a large chair with a small boy in front of him; see Chamay and Schärlig 1998. The figure of the boy is tiny to show his relative unimportance.

Olympiodorus organized the content of his commentary into twenty-eight *praxeis*, that is, lessons of various length, each one divided into two parts. The *theoria* provided an exegesis and discussion of some of the text, while a shorter section (*lexis*) concentrated on elucidating phrases and words. Internal evidence gives the reader a sense of the passage of time during teaching and shows the movement of the commentary toward the end, with Olympiodorus using expressions such as "we must proceed to the subject," "we said yesterday," "we observed before," "as we said at the beginning," and "as we stated already."[25] Together with the many repetitions, these statements confer authenticity on the text and give the reader a sense of how the class was conducted. Attempting to calculate how much time it would have taken Olympiodorus to deliver the whole seminar, scholars have estimated a duration of about ten weeks.[26]

The Life of Plato

The commentary starts with a brief reference to Aristotle, suggesting that the previous curriculum would have covered his work in part.[27] After some paragraphs in which Olympiodorus promises his students that they will be enchanted by Plato's fountain and inspirations, he briefly engages in narrating a "Life of Plato." Why did Proclus not include a similar narrative in his commentary? The most likely answer is that Olympiodorus's "Life of Plato" was an encomium more related to rhetoric than to philosophy.[28] I have already remarked on Olympiodorus's knowledge of and partiality to rhetoric. To some of his students, this piece must have sounded familiar. Encomia were the most popular of the *progymnasmata* (preliminary rhetorical exercises), because on leaving a rhetorical school a young man would be expected to write panegyrics of political figures and of his city.[29] This "Life of Plato" has all the ingredients of the exercise as described by Menander the Rhetor,

---

25. 3.2; 34.8; 48.14; 54.17; 55.12.
26. Griffin 2015. Griffin 2020, a continuation covering the translation and commentary of 10–28, is equally masterful.
27. All Neoplatonist commentators accepted the harmony of Aristotle and Plato; see Sorabji 2016b, 3–5.
28. On the life of Plato in this text, see the good interpretation of Griffin 2015, 43–46. I think, however, that the consideration of this life as an encomium is indispensable.
29. Cribiore 2007, 144–46, on Libanius.

Theon, Aphthonius, and Libanius.[30] According to the fourth-century rhetor Aphthonius:

> This is the division of encomium. You will develop it under the following heads (*kephalaia*). You will have a prologue referring to the subject. Then you will place birth, which you will divide into nation, homeland, ancestors, and parents. Then education, which you will divide into pursuits, competence, and customs. Then you will adduce the most important head of encomium, achievements, which you will divide into soul, body and fortune (soul: e.g., courage, practical wisdom; body: e.g., beauty, speed, strength; fortune: e.g., power, wealth, friends). After these, the comparison, attaching greater weight to the subject of the encomium through juxtaposition. Then an epilogue, more akin to a prayer.

In this "Life of Plato," after a prologue, the headings of the encomium follow Plato's ancestors and parents (*genos*), his education, teachers, and achievements in various subjects, and most importantly, his deeds: his closeness to powerful people; his trips to Sicily; his journeys to Egypt and Phoenicia, where he learned priestly skills and the lore of the Magi; and, especially, the founding of the Academy. A short comparison with Homer then leads to a prayer. This "Life of Plato" is constructed like a perfect encomium, with the proper *kephalaia*. Olympiodorus must have delivered it as a transition to the Alcibiades text.

Westerink, who edited this commentary superbly and had to face tough decisions, made specific choices, as we shall see.[31] The text was full of every kind of mistake: grammatical, syntactical, oral, and phonetical. In editing, Westerink resolved not to correct any error that he felt was a blunder on the part of the notetaker, but he also had to decide whether some of them could ultimately be attributed to Olympiodorus himself.

Plato's dialogues are imaginary accounts of conversations in which exchanges involving students and teaching often take place. In the late antique commentaries we hear the voice of the teacher expounding on his exegesis, but not those of students who ask questions. The presence of the student is revealed by his notes, marginalia, and mistakes, and perhaps by the fact that the exegeses of certain passages may reflect

---

30. Patillon and Bolognesi 1997, 83–86 and 131–32 with Aphthonius's text; Patillon 2008; Russell and Wilson 1981, 2–6.
31. Westerink 1956.

students' requests for explanations. It would be wrong, I think, to envision a class with only one voice. In this case, the questions may be hidden because the notetaker chose not to copy them as part of simplifying his rendition of the text, as happened with Epictetus and Didymus. In published accounts of lectures, some aspects of the oral texts were effaced, such as references to the members of the audience as *hetairoi* and the use of the address in the second person. I believe that in Olympiodorus's *First Alcibiades* these aspects are still visible, but one must actively look for them.

The philosopher was responsible for the *theoria* in which he expounded on the parts of the text he had chosen, but what exactly was the place of the *lexis* in the economy of the whole? How did he isolate certain portions that needed clarification? Was Olympiodorus retracing his steps and rereading the dialogue in order to focus on certain ambiguous expressions? Or was he, like Philoponus, in the habit of studying the faces of his students for signs that they were uncertain and unconvinced? This must have been so in some cases, but not in all. I suggest that the various explanations often addressed students' questions and doubts, which were then made to disappear from the commentary in order that only the philosopher's voice could be heard.[32] Some of the *lexeis* refer to elementary expressions, such as, in 25.1.9-10, distinctions between words like "one," "first," "only," "multitude," and "mob," or the explanation that "in so many years" means "such a long time" in 26.1. In 35.10 the comparison of "you do not know with precision" with "you only surmise" is a response to a simple question. At 37.14-19 Olympiodorus retorts "it is certainly fair to wonder" at an expression used by Socrates—this too is a response to a question. At 50.15 someone must have asked about the meaning of the text "among the Hellenes and not only among them," which the philosopher explained as a reference to all Europe, to foreigners, and to people across the earth. This is only a small sample of the *lexeis* that show attention to issues of grammar and basic comprehension of the text. They must have originated from students' direct participation. Gellius explains that his teacher, the philosopher Taurus, allowed almost everyone to ask questions.[33] Classes were full of life. Quintilian mentions rivalry, noise, jumping,

---

32. I will examine only some instances in the first part of the commentary.
33. *NA* 1.26. Taurus too asked questions after a reading of Plato's *Symposium*, *NA* 17.20; Snyder 2000, 111-12.

and standing up.³⁴ He considers questions integral parts of a class: the teacher "must answer questions readily and himself question those who do not ask any."

At the end of the "Life of Plato," the philosopher is compared to Homer, who is broadly present throughout the commentary. In late antique Alexandria, the philosophers relied on knowledge of the traditional curriculum based on classical literature and myths. Olympiodorus was openly pagan, but he worked within a Christian environment, although one that was not particularly hostile. His aim was to keep alive those Greek cultural achievements of the fifth and fourth centuries BCE that were not considered offensive to Christianity. Though he did not accept certain tenets, such as those concerning eternal punishment and suicide, his students were not particularly challenged by his paganism. They could get along easily with Socrates, Plato, and the pantheon of the Olympians.³⁵ Of course the Christian students of Olympiodorus could not accept traditional religion and mythology, but the philosopher usually omitted the names of the Greek gods and did not consider their individual features. He only spoke of a general God. Classical paideia was one of his concerns, so that Homer, Demosthenes, Aelius Aristides, and Plutarch were often mentioned in class. When he said at the beginning of his *First Alcibiades* that his students had to learn Plato because he could be useful to them, he referred mostly to that classical learning that was still considered some kind of passport in cultural contexts that could open many doors.

Regarding the *First Alcibiades* commentary, Westerink remarked, "There is a quotation from Homer for almost any occasion, but they are often no better than confused reminiscences pieced together."³⁶ We must evaluate this criticism and put it in perspective. We have seen that, in the second century, Epictetus's quotations from Homer often consisted of half lines, popular verses that freely circulated, and short paraphrases. In a few cases he referred to verses that were rarely quoted by others but would appear in much later literature, mostly in grammarians' works.³⁷ The fact that those lines were cited correctly must have been due to Arrian's competence in literary matters and his impeccable schooling. In the second century, the Second Sophistic had

---

34. Quintilian 2.2.
35. See Jackson et al. 1998, 8–11.
36. Westerink 1956, ix.
37. Cf. chapter 6.

revived Homer.³⁸ And yet Epictetus, a philosopher, not having an intrinsic literary interest, did not quote him for the beauty of his poetry but to bend him to his own purpose, reinterpreting the poet to show how useful he could be to the budding philosopher and how nefarious some of his lines were when taken literally.³⁹

An interest in Homer survived in the sixth century, but rather than concentrating on accuracy, philosophers now only wanted to evoke situations and concepts. In terms of tastes, Olympiodorus cited the *Iliad* more than the *Odyssey*, which was generally the less well known of the two in antiquity.⁴⁰ His reading choices conformed to the Homeric quotations preserved in the papyri, and also matched those of literary individuals in antiquity.⁴¹ He quoted from the whole of the *Iliad* and not just the first half, although as usual Books 1 and 2 attracted most of his attention. Though he quoted less from the *Odyssey*, it is interesting that he cited Book 11, which concerns the underworld, only twice, preferring other lines instead.⁴² He often referred to Homer traditionally, as *ho poietes*, the poet par excellence. Euripides, whom he called *ho tragikos*, is the only tragic poet to survive in the commentary. Olympiodorus paid attention almost exclusively to his *Hippolytus* and *Orestes* and reported short verses or allusions to them.

It is interesting to glance at his use of literature and at the lengths of his citations, keeping in mind that in Plato he had found some justification for quoting short poetic lines. Three times he quotes the same short line 352 of *Hippolytus*, in which Phaedra replies that the nurse herself had mentioned the name of Hippolytus: "you heard it from yourself, not me."⁴³ Olympiodorus also cites a passage from Epictetus, *Encheiridion* 5: "And as Epictetus the Stoic, who became a true Stoic in his mind, says: an uneducated person blames others for his own faults; one whose education has just begun blames himself and not others; but one whose education is complete blames neither another nor himself." Alcibiades, who here lacks education, has blamed Socrates by saying "as

---

38. On Philodemus's positive attitude toward Homer, see Fish 2022; Kim 2010; Kim 2022; Manolea 2022.

39. One might compare Dio's *Oration* 11 where he criticizes Homer from many points of view. On various views of Homer, see Lamberton 1986.

40. Cf. Cribiore 2001b, 195–96.

41. Cribiore 2001b, 197.

42. Book 11 and specifically the underworld were extremely popular because readers could return to characters of the *Iliad*. Cribiore 2001b, 196.

43. The whole passage I am looking at is 101.1 to 104.6.

you say." As his education progresses, he will not blame anyone. Like Phaedra, Socrates says, "You said this, not me." In *First Alcibiades* (113 C), Plato alludes briefly to the same verse of the *Hippolytus*. Olympiodorus comments to his students: "Plato teaches us how one ought to paraphrase poetic passages, namely, that one should not cite the passages themselves because that is tedious and weakens the words but rather should excerpt some phrases."[44] Citing a rather long passage from the philosopher Epictetus was acceptable, but half lines of poetry, short allusions, and paraphrases served the student of philosophy well.

The Mistakes

Errors of various kinds appear in the philosophical and poetic quotations and in the commentary to the *First Alcibiades*. While some are due to misheard words, phonetic spelling, or even the introduction of faulty verses that a student had never heard before and with which he struggled, we also have to allow for the possibility that in some cases Olympiodorus himself may have been the source of the confusion. Scholarly attention has focused on the student, who is deemed "less competent than usual" and "none too brilliant," and has considered his ignorance and hearing impediment with consternation.[45] Was he really an exceptionally unprepared young man? Dodds even deemed it suspicious that the commentary became shorter as it proceeded, which he attributed to the fact that "the student's interest flags."[46] In reality, all teachers in antiquity began by covering a text in detail and little by little proceeded much more quickly, with the consequence that the first books of Homer, for example, were much better known.[47]

The papyri have sensitized us to the fact that Greek was a language in evolution and that over time its speakers lost sensitivity to certain linguistic phenomena.[48] They could no longer clearly perceive the distinction of vowel length, they interchanged liquids (lambda/rho) and sibilants (sigma/zeta), and they were not sensitive to aspiration. Together with iotacism, these are only some of the phonetic changes that could significantly alter the appearance of a word. Two occurrences might

---

44. *Commentary* 104.4.
45. Tarrant 1999, 24; Westerink 1956, viii.
46. Dodds 1957, 357.
47. Cribiore 2001b, 194–97.
48. Gignac 1976. On linguistic changes, see Evans and Obbink 2010.

take place. Scholars agree that all the errors in Olympiodorus's *Commentary* are due to faulty hearing, and therefore the student must have had trouble taking down a text in a sort of dictation. This, however, is not the only possible scenario; another variation is also likely. Even if Olympiodorus had pronounced words in a traditional way and the student had heard them correctly, when writing them down he could have committed phonetic errors.[49] Of course, this type of mistake does not exhaust the whole gamut of possible blunders that show that the "editor," as Westerink called the notetaker, had confronted a challenging task. In previous centuries, phonetic errors were commonplace only in documentary texts, but in the sixth century they could affect people in cultured milieus. The "editor" would have brought his own writing habits to school.

Olympiodorus was probably not exempt from mistakes, but scholars have generally tended to forgive him and to refuse to admit the possibility that he himself was responsible for some big blunders in his text.[50] Thus two important errors have been usually attributed to the "editor." The erroneous mention of Thrasymachus as a character of the *Gorgias* and the misattribution of a famous quotation from the *Republic* to the *Timaeus* are errors that have seemed hardly ascribable to a professor of Platonic philosophy.[51] And yet, if the student had been guilty of making those names up, it is strange that he would have taken the initiative to change the text while taking notes. Those were factual errors and not phonetic ones. It is possible that the student left blank spaces here that he or someone else filled in later. We should also reflect on the fact that teachers might not be always infallible. We have considered in the introduction the mistakes that appear in the treatises of Aristotle that reproduced his live lectures to students. In that case too, Aristotle's faulty use of the sources could be attributed to the philosopher himself. Tarrant may be the voice of reason: "One has to force oneself to recall the greater fallibility of the modern academics within the class-room (even when well prepared) than within their private study."[52] Just as the notes of modern students appear quite unruly and may be compared with

---

49. Cribiore 1996, 92–93.
50. Most recently, Griffin 2015, 47.
51. 61.8 and 45.2; Westerink 1956, ix; Dodds 1957, 357. See, however, Griffin 2015, 199n297. Griffin removes from Olympiodorus some of the blame for the last instance.
52. Tarrant 1999, 24. Tarrant shows examples of transpositions in the text when Olympiodorus's comments were given at a different time.

those of the *Commentary*, so too a modern professor may sometimes be absent-minded when lecturing to a class.

Another perplexing feature of this text is the presence of two different *praxeis* commenting on *First Alcibiades* 126c–127e, an intriguing occurrence that needs explanation.[53] It seems bizarre that Olympiodorus would have commented twice in class on the same passage of Plato, and in a quite different way both times. It appears more plausible that one of the two lectures had been given at a different time and in a different venue. The "editor" must have found the second version somewhere, maybe among Olympiodorus's papers, and decided to include it. After *praxis* 21 the new text formed *praxis* 22, and probably the numbers of the lectures were adjusted not while Olympiodorus was lecturing but later, by someone who was reading the whole text. In the margin at 192.10 a student added, "I wrote a double version of this lecture because the explanations were different." But this raises a doubt. Is the picture of a single student taking down the commentary still realistic, or did the "editor" work together with others?

Notes on Notes: The Manuscript's Marginalia

The manuscript of Olympiodorus's lecture taken down by his students, the archetype of all other copies, is *Marcianus graecus* 196, which dates to the later ninth century and also contains commentaries on the *Gorgias* and *Phaedo*.[54] The manuscript is in excellent condition and includes all the notes, corrections, and doodles along with a good number of mistakes. This was one of the earliest works of profane literature to be transliterated into minuscule, and it does not show many errors of transmission.[55] Its margins are crowded with written observations, summaries of arguments, and lists of items, all of them things that look like school exercises. Westerink rightly included these jottings in his edition of the *Commentary* because they appeared contemporary, but they were otherwise ignored and left untranslated, on the grounds that a student had been "fully" responsible for them. These marginal notes are not uniformly of the same kind and level of expertise. As we consider them, we should ask ourselves some basic questions. Would a student have been able to do drawings and make lists in the margins at the same time

---

53. *Commentary* 183.15 to 192.9 the first lecture; 192.10 to 197.6, the second one.
54. For observations on the manuscript, see Duke 1990, 19–29; Tarrant 1999, 23–40.
55. Dodds 1957.

that he was recording Olympiodorus's words? Were additional students involved in adding these notes at the same time? May these notes sometimes reflect further explanations that the philosopher gave in class, but that did not become part of the main text?

In trying to give a reader an idea of how these marginal notes look, I will divide them into three overlapping types: lists of words, geometric drawings with sporadic words inserted, and longer passages of poetry and prose that refer to single lines in the text. Thus the marginalia at 42.10–43.3 appear rather elementary. Commenting on Socrates mentioning human experiences, a student listed adjectives and nouns referring to *pathe* in three columns, in what looks like an exercise at the grammatical level. Likewise, at 58.7–11 the student listed four nouns, "God, Socrates, Alcibiades, and the citizens" in a line, and underneath each one placed adjectives such as "better" and "worse" (*cheiron* and *kreitton*). The young man who at 73.12–74.7 wrote in two columns nouns such as rhetor, soldier, captain, and citizen paired with their corresponding aims (getting rich from spoils, persuading through speech, triumphing over enemies, and making the citizens good) also seems to be at a lower level than that implied by the reading of Plato.[56] In similar exercises the words are sometimes recorded in alphabetical order.

The drawings in the margins are attractive. At times one has the impression that this young man, like others nowadays, enjoyed producing stylized doodles and considered the actual notes secondary.[57] At 195.11–196.3 he wrote only a few phrases and single letters about just people (the *dikaioi*), instead devoting all his attention to a geometrical drawing. Here and in other schematic drawings he used the adjective *asystaton* (incoherent) to show the lack of correspondence between some terms.[58] At 179.10–20 he placed terms that do not correspond in a kind of box formed with horizontal, vertical, and oblique lines. Four spaces are defined and *asystaton* is repeated. At 156.9–12 he wrote in five lines the genealogy of Zeus, Danae, and their descendants, whose names are separated neatly by various lines, in what must have been a memory exercise.

The last type of marginal notes raises some issues of attribution. Again, I note only a few examples. In one, Olympiodorus quotes a single line from Aristophanes's *Acharnians*, 531, but in the margin of 29.13 a

---

56. There are many more exercises at this level.
57. See 81.26–82.4; 118.18–22.
58. 65.10–19; 195.11–196.3.

student has added additional verses, 530–34. When and from where did he get them? Was he able to remember the lines himself, or did Olympiodorus supply them in response to someone in class asking for the passage? At 216.4, a bare allusion to the *moly* in the *Odyssey* leads to a longer explanation about the plant.[59] At another point in the commentary, Olympiodorus mentions the term *Metragyrtes*, a priest of Cybele, without adding any explanation. A long marginal note at 159.16 fills in the details. This *historia* mentions a man who went to Attica and bewitched the women of the goddess. After the Athenians killed him, a plague came to the city. Apollo made expiation to pacify the dead. The Athenians built an edifice in the man's honor and dedicated it, along with a statue of him, to the Mother of the Gods. It seems inconceivable that Olympiodorus had solely cited the exotic name of this priest of Cybele without expanding on the background when in the rest of the text he can so often be seen adding elementary explanations. Did his class ask for clarification? At 174.5 the adjective *philochremosyne* is explained in a marginal note that mentions a proverb and the story of an oracle of Apollo. When the student adds to the story that "Aristotle mentioned this oracle in the *Athenaion Politeia*," it appears likely that Olympiodorus must have told the story of the oracle to the class as an aside but then found it superfluous to introduce it in the commentary.

What precedes suggests an intriguing picture of Olympiodorus and his class. First of all, I think that students should not be blamed for every mistake present in the text. The philosopher might have made some slips himself in the heat of the lecture or in the ennui of the delivery. He would have commented more than once on the *First Alcibiades*, as the presence of two different *praxeis* at 126c–127e reveals. This dialogue may have been the foundation of a recurring series of lectures. I have also suggested that some extensive marginal notes may be attributed to him, having derived from some further clarifications requested by his class. These were loosely related to the Platonic text and issued from students' questions. I have said above that questions are not directly visible in this commentary, unlike occasionally in the notebooks of Epictetus and Didymus; but they must have taken place, because they were a mandatory ingredient of classroom life at all times. I have proposed that some of the *lexeis* may have issued naturally from students' requests for explanations. Likewise, the longer *historiai* present in the

---

59. *Od.* 10.305. The word is cited often in antiquity, for example, by Galen and Gregory of Nazianzus.

margins probably represented Olympiodorus's responses to students' demands for elucidation.

An issue that demands attention is how many students were involved in writing the commentary and in adding the marginal notes. We have seen that so far scholars have referred to a single person, the "editor" who was responsible for taking down the lectures, but in light of what we have ascertained this scenario seems impossible. There were too many activities to cover. Taking down the main text would have required much care, the provision of a different version at 126c–127e would have had to be done by a different student, and the marginal notes seem to show various levels of expertise. The notetaker did not have sufficient time to both write the text and add the marginal notes, and probably someone else did so.

Praechter commented on the generosity of the ancient philosophical commentators, who allowed students to write down their lectures *apo phones* and to circulate them among the public.[60] This scholar argued that these philosophers exhibited "a remarkable indifference to intellectual property." I have already commented on some of the reasons philosophers such as Olympiodorus did not mind the status quo and showed this apparently unselfish behavior. And yet, now that we have glanced at the students who may have collaborated to write the whole commentary, Olympiodorus's lack of resentment is clear and reasonable. The recording of the commentary on the *First Alcibiades* was not the product of a single student but was instead a class endeavor. Looking at the work of Olympiodorus through the eyes and interventions of his students allows us to glean information on the activities of teachers of philosophy and their students that would be otherwise unreachable. In part III we have witnessed the pedagogical methods of a variety of philosophers who aimed at instilling in young men knowledge and a new way of life. The ancient philosophical classroom has now acquired not only definite instructors and pedagogical methods unknown before but also students who listened to lectures and played an indispensable role in recording their teachers' voices.

---

60. Praechter 1909 (2016).

Conclusion
The Authentic Philosopher's Voice

This volume on note-taking in education serves as an important "window" into the scholarly life taking place in ancient philosophical classrooms, examining the connections between note-taking, recording, and listening during philosophical lectures that have shaped and molded our perspectives of education in antiquity. Class annotations have provided us with a unique opportunity to examine pedagogic themes and the issues they raised. In the preceding chapters, I described significant discoveries and revelations on ancient note-taking and pedagogy that make it possible to recognize the central traits of an education in philosophy. Some questions still remain: Were these notetakers forming a cache of discourses for a personal library? Did they intend to use their notes to write commentaries? Or instead, did they discard their notes after a certain period of time? While we do not have access to extant, complete books that were compiled using notes, we do have the fabric of these texts. We also have initial evidence that students compiled notes to be used later when composing their own books and lectures, as they, in some cases became philosophers, as is the case of a student of Epictetus who left that school to start one of his own.

CONCLUSION

In the previous chapters, I have also illustrated how ancient classes were conducted, examining not only how teachers of philosophy communicated and shaped their educational messages but also how students received and reacted to them. Of great value are the words of ancient authors, such as Porphyry or Iamblichus, regarding pedagogical concerns, the makeup of classes, the curricula followed, and students' and educators' reactions. Their personal experiences concerning schooling complement our existing scholarly discourse. However, the notes taken down during classes of philosophy that we have studied provide direct testimonies of pedagogical aspects that were mostly unexplored before. The resulting picture is vivid, providing pivotal access to the ancient philosophy classroom and revealing the choices students made when they took notes, their conflicts with teachers, the occasional dialogues they reported, and the writing mistakes they committed.

At the beginning of this note-taking journey, we encountered the lectures Theodor Mommsen gave in Berlin at the end of the nineteenth century, which two of his students recorded with great enthusiasm. Though Mommsen never published a history of the imperial period, for which scholars had waited impatiently, historian Alexander Demandt published an account of the age of the emperors by using the two students' notes, found serendipitously in 1980. No doubt this event and its consequences are exceptional, but can we compare in some respects those nineteenth-century notes to those that students jotted down so many centuries before? Can we interpret the past in presentist terms?[1] Although the issue of presentism has never been solved satisfactorily with common agreement of all commentators, it is clear that antiquity cannot be used as a straightforward stepping stone to the modern world. Yet past events can reveal meaningful connections to modern events, and in turn the modern world can illuminate the past, providing a more detailed picture. Using the examples throughout this volume, we have confirmed this connection through the phenomenon of students taking notes in both ancient and modern settings.

Mommsen certainly knew that his two students were taking down notes during his lectures, especially because they apparently were sitting in the front rows of the classroom. But did he find this gratifying? Teachers at every level of education were surely aware that often their

---

1. See what the *New York Times* of September 21, 2022, says about the math prodigy and logician Saul Kripke. Most of his research is unpublished and survives only in notes and private transcriptions.

words were preserved because their students recorded them faithfully. While many reasons prevented Mommsen from writing and publishing his book about the imperial age, would he have been pleased that his views about this history did not remain completely and entirely with him? Furthermore, was he inspired and encouraged that his students jotted down notes as a memory aid? Finally, how similar was notetaking in his lectures to that in the classes of Philodemus, Arrian, and the students of Didymus the Blind and Olympiodorus? The investigations in the various chapters provide a necessary first step to understanding these connections, but more could and should be done in future pedagogical research.

In antiquity, people generally employed notes in their writing endeavors in attempts to structure their work, assist their memories, and organize their lives, such as when traveling or teaching. In higher education, annotations might be copious and lengthy, but generally such notes exhibited limited length as a common characteristic. The notetaker would produce a text consisting of points to remember and his observations, with a view toward using it in a different, personal creation. The preceding material shows that notes were not limited to scholars and scholarly practice but instead had a richer function and may comprise a genre of their own.[2]

The longest text we have examined in this research is the *Discourses* of Epictetus, as taken down by his disciple Arrian, who declared that on his own initiative he had preserved the philosopher's free voice (*parrhesia*). The question of whether Arrian himself had jotted down the notes can be resolved by considering factors that previous scholars overlooked. Arrian was an enthusiastic disciple who aimed to communicate the significance of Epictetus's ideas while also rendering the atmosphere in his classes. In doing so, he also reported some traits of the philosopher's teaching style that did not show Epictetus in the best light. A compiler of a finished account not relying on notes would have probably toned down his rendition of Epictetus's "therapy." Though Arrian may have made revisions or shortened accounts while taking down the philosopher's words, he certainly did not compose the text entirely, as some have claimed. Questions by students that occur naturally during teaching are rarely represented, though we have Epictetus's responses. Perhaps Arrian did not consider them essential, had

---

2. Arnould and Poulouin 2008.

some difficulties in keeping up with the philosopher's pace, or omitted some details and repetitions. Regardless, the text as we have it transmits Epictetus's authentic voice to us. We are exposed to Epictetus's oral style, his use of unusual expressions and contemporary language, and the vocabulary of philosophical teaching. The *Discourses* show that Arrian's notes transmit not only the content and the ethical message of the lectures but also the essence of Epictetus's class, the behaviors of students, their resistance and arrogance, and the philosopher's disappointment at his pupils' indifference. Students' emotions, such as envy, regret, and feelings of loneliness, are revealed too.

Notes from other texts, taken in the classes of Philodemus, Didymus the Blind, and Olympiodorus, have helped us fill in details regarding not only the mechanics of note-taking but also teaching methods, student engagement and level of ability, and school attendance in different periods. School texts written on papyrus are rather static objects, and their messages and lessons can become muffled. With some exceptions, these texts do not provide the insight desired beyond their materiality. Educational texts by authors such as Quintilian are prescriptive and descriptive—the orator himself was engaged with them, writing, and sometimes dictating in his old age in the privacy of his room, and his students emerged from his memory. Furthermore, the letters of Libanius offer more concrete information on educational environments, but everything is filtered through the rhetor's voice, so his students recede into the background.

The texts we have looked at, however, allow us a glimpse of teaching methods in classes and illuminate the background. The notes of Olympiodorus, and to a lesser extent those of Didymus, permit us to appreciate the passage of time in a learning environment, with the teacher moving back and forth, looking back at the past and forward to the future. With Olympiodorus, the scene becomes even brighter, with students taking down notes from the philosopher, completing them, and transcribing different versions. I have shown that in the past scholars have surmised that *apo phones* texts were jotted down by a single notetaker who was guilty of all imperfections. These assumptions have been proven wrong. The marginal notes that emerged from Olympiodorus's explanations allow us to understand how classes were conducted and how young men simultaneously sought accuracy in their notes while also wanting to distract themselves.

In examining these notes, we have focused on their content and powerful immediacy. Philodemus's annotations display some striking aspects of Epicurean paideia and show the reactions of those who were immediately involved. The voice of Didymus the Blind has come alive to us through the annotations of students, allowing us a glimpse at a Christian group in Alexandria. They illuminate a religious background of the texts in which Christian teachers functioned alongside pagans. We have focused on Epictetus's *Discourses*, concentrating on his teaching strategies and his ambiguous opposition to rhetoric and literature. In all these texts, we have tried to determine who spoke and who was receiving the message.

In general, ancient texts are the products of long elaboration and resist being restored to their original condition. Any attempt to return to the past and reconstitute the original, foundational version of a text ultimately makes us aware of the necessity of recognizing a multiplicity of versions, each consisting of many layers that are often unreachable. Even with the evidence of manuscripts at hand, readers have trouble reconstructing changes and alterations.

Notes, though, lie at the crossroads of the history of the book and the reception of works. Our endeavor has focused on notebooks that originated from singular sources, texts, events worthy to be recorded, and lectures delivered in class or to the public—a rich source base in which communication is central. A fundamental characteristic of these texts that are grounded in notes is the direct connection between the message source and its receiver. In our case, meaning is also created through the reactions of those who took notes; these individuals filtered through their own minds the words they received *apo phones*.

As we discern and examine the inner workings of how these texts were created, we become aware of the great value of annotations. Readers usually gravitate toward so-called definitive texts that offer more or less fixed written contents and pose fewer challenges of interpretation. The classical tradition chooses what is canonical, and those texts immediately become privileged, with annotations remaining in the periphery. And yet, texts consisting of notes allow us to sometimes focus on the writer's intentionality, the teacher lecturing, and the students receiving their message, and as a result notes permit us to venture somewhat beyond speculation.

References

Adler, Ada, ed. 1935. *Suidae Lexicon* I.4. Stuttgart.
Alföldy, Géza, and Johannes Straub. 1972–74. *Bonner Historia-Augusta-Colloquium*. Bonn.
Algra, Keimpe, Jonathan Barnes, Jaap Mansfeld, and Malcolm Schofield, eds. 1999. *The Cambridge History of Hellenistic Philosophy*. Cambridge.
Allen, Ansgar. 2020. *Cynicism*. Cambridge.
Amato, Eugenio, Aldo Corcella, and Delphine Lauritzen, eds. 2017. *L'école de Gaza: Espace littéraire et identité culturelle dans l'antiquité tardive*. Leuven.
Amato, Eugenio, and Jacques Schamp. 2005. *Ethopoiia: La représentation des caractères entre fiction scolaire et réalité vivante à l'époque impériale et tardive*. Salerno.
Andrieu, Jules. 1954. *Le dialogue antique: Structure et présentation*. Paris.
Angeli, Anna, ed. 1988. *Agli amici di scuola (P.Herc. 1005)*. Naples.
Antoni, Agathe, Graziano Arrighetti, M. Isabella Bertagna, and Daniel Delattre, eds. 2010. *Miscellanea Papyrologica Herculanensia*. Vol. 1. Rome.
Arnould, Jean-Claude, and Claudine Poulouin, eds. 2008. *Notes: Études sur l'annotation en littérature*. Rouen.
Arns, Paulo Evaristo. 1953. *La technique du livre d'après saint Jérôme*. Paris.
Aubenque, Pierre. 1983. "Sur l'inauthenticité du livre K de la Métaphysique." In Moraux and Wiesner 1983: 318–44.
Avenarius, Gert. 1956. *Lukians Schrift zur Geschichtsschreibung*. Meisenheim am Glan.
Bagnall, Roger S. 2011. *Everyday Writing in the Graeco-Roman East*. Berkeley.
Bagnall, Roger S., Nicola Aravecchia, Raffaella Cribiore, Paola Davoli, Olaf E. Kaper, and Susanna McFadden, eds. 2015. *An Oasis City*. New York.
Bagnall, Roger S., and Raffaella Cribiore, eds. 2006. 2nd ed. 2015. *Women's Letters from Ancient Egypt, 300 BC–AD 800*. Ann Arbor.
Barigazzi, Adelmo, ed. 1966. *Favorino di Arelate: Opere*. Florence.
Barnes, Jonathan. 1995. "Life and Work." In *The Cambridge Companion to Aristotle*. Cambridge.
———. 1997. *Logic and the Imperial Stoa*. Leiden.
Barrow, Robin. 2015. "The Persistence of Ancient Education." In Bloomer 2015: 281–91.
Basil. 1934. *Letters, Volume IV: Letters 249–368. On Greek Literature*. Translated by Roy J. Deferrari, M. R. P. McGuire. Loeb Classical Library 270. Cambridge, MA.
Bayliss, Grant, D. 2015. *The Vision of Didymus the Blind: A Fourth-Century Virtue-Origenism*. Oxford.

Becker, Adam H. 2006. "The Dynamic Reception of Theodore of Mopsuestia in the Sixth Century. Greek, Syriac, and Latin." In S. Johnson 2006: 29–47.

Beer, Beate. 2020. *Aulus Gellius und die Noctes Atticae: Die literarische Konstruktion einer Sammlung*. Berlin.

Behr, Charles Allison, ed. 1986. *P. Aelius Aristides: The Complete Works*. Vol. 2. Leiden.

Bénatouïl, Thomas. 2009. *Les stoïciens III: Musonius—Épictète—Marc Aurèle*. Paris.

Beresford, Adam. Translated 2020. *Aristotle: The Nicomachean Ethics*. London.

Berti, Emanuele. 2007. *Scholasticorum studia: Seneca il Vecchio e la cultura retorica e letteraria della prima età imperial*. Pisa.

Bienert, Wolfgang. 1972. *Allegoria und Anagoge bei Didymos dem Blindem von Alexandria*. Patristische Texte und Studien 13. Berlin.

Billerbeck, Margarethe. 1978. *Epiktet: Von Kynismus*. Leiden.

———. 1996. "The Ideal Cynic from Epictetus to Julian." In Branham and Goulet-Cazé 1996: 205–21.

Binder, Gerhard, ed. 1983. *Didymos der Blinde. Kommentar zum Ecclesiastes (Tura-Papyrus). Teil I,2: Kommentary zu Ecclesiastes (2.), Kapitel 1,1–2,14*. PTA 26. Bonn.

Binder, Gerhard, and Leo Liesenborghs, eds. 1965. *Didymus der Blinde. Kommentar zum Ecclesiastes, Lage 1 des Tura-Papyrus*. Cologne.

———, eds. 1979. *Didymos der Blinde. Kommentar zum Ecclesiastes (Tura-Papyrus), Teil I.1: Kommentar zu Eccl. Kap. 1,1–2,14*. PTA 25. Bonn.

Binder, Gerhard, Leo Liesenborghs, and Ludwig Koenen, eds. 1969. *Didymos der Blinde: Kommentar zum Ecclesiastes (Tura-Papyrus); Teil 6: Kommentar zu Ecclesiastes, Kapitel 11–12*. PTA 9. Bonn.

Blair, Ann. 1999. "The Problemata as a Natural Philosophical Genre." In *Natural Particulars : Nature and the Disciplines in Renaissance Europe*, edited by Anthony Grafton and Nancy Sirasi, 171–204. Cambridge, MA.

———. 2004. "Note Taking as an Art of Transmission." *Critical Inquiry* 31:85–107.

———. 2008. "Student Manuscripts and the Textbook." In Campi et al. 2008: 39–74.

———. 2010. *Too Much to Know: Managing Scholarly Information before the Modern Age*. New Haven, CT.

Blank, David. 1998. "Versionen oder Zwillinge? Zu den Handschriften der ersten Bücher von Philodems *Rhetorik*." In Most 1998: 123–49.

———. 2010. "Ammonius Hermeiou and His School." In Gerson 2010: 654–66.

Bloomer, W. Martin. 1997. *Latinity and Literary Society at Rome*. Philadelphia.

———. 2015. *A Companion to Ancient Education*. Malden, MA.

Blumell, Lincoln H., Thomas W. Mackay, and Gregg Schwendner, eds. 2019. *Didymus the Blind's Commentary on Psalms 26:10–29:2 and 36:1–3*. Turnhout, BE.

Boge, Herbert. 1974. *Griechische Tachygraphie und Tironische Noten*. Hildesheim.

Bohle, Bettina. 2020. *Olympiodors Kommentar zu Platons "Gorgias": Ene Gegenüberstellung seiner modernen und seiner antiken Interpretation*. Studien zu Literatur und Erkenntnis 11. Heidelberg.

Bonhöffer, Adolf Friedrich. 1890 (2018 rpt.). *Epictet und die Stoa. Untersuchungen zur Stoischen Philosophie*. Stuttgart.

Borges, Cassandra, and C. Michael Sampson. 2012. *New Literary Papyri from the Michigan Collection: Mythographic Lyric and a Catalogue of Poetic First Lines*. Ann Arbor.
Boud'hors, Anne. 2013. "Apprendre à lire et à écrire: Deux documents Copte Revisités." *Journal of Juristic Papyrology Suppl.*: 1027–39.
Boudon-Millot, Véronique. 2007. *Galien. 1: Introduction générale, Sur l'ordre de ses propres livres, Sur ses propres livres, Que l'excellent médecin est aussi philosophe, texte établi, traduit et annoté*. Paris.
Boudon-Millot, Véronique, and Jacques Jouanna, eds. 2010. *Galien. Tome IV. Ne pas se chagriner*. Paris.
Bourdieu, Pierre, and Jean-Claude Passeron. 1990. *Reproduction in Education, Society and Culture*. 2nd ed. Translated by R. Nice. London.
Bowersock, Glen Warren. 1967. "A New Inscription of Arrian." *GRBS* 8:279–80.
———. 1969. *Greek Sophists in the Roman Empire*. Oxford.
Brakke, David. 1995. *Athanasius and the Politics of Asceticism*. Oxford.
Branham, Robert Bracht, and Marie-Odile Goulet-Cazé, eds. 1996. *The Cynics: The Cynic Movement in Antiquity and Its Legacy*. Berkeley.
Brisson, Luc, ed. 1982. *Porphyre, la vie de Plotin*. Paris.
Brooke, Christopher. 2012. *Philosophic Pride: Stoicism and Political Thought from Lipsius to Rousseau*. Princeton.
Brunt, Peter A. 1977. "From Epictetus to Arrian." *Athenaeum* 55:19–48.
———. 1994. "The Bubble of the Second Sophistic." *BICS* 39:25–52.
Bryant, John. 2002. *The Fluid Text: A Theory of Revision and Editing for Book and Screen*. Ann Arbor.
Cagnazzi, Silvana. 1997. *Nicobule e Pamfila: Frammenti di storiche greche*. Bari.
Cameron, Alan. 2004. *Greek Mythography in the Roman World*. Oxford.
———. 2011. *The Last Pagans of Rome*. Oxford.
Campi, Emidio, Simone De Angelis, Anja-Silvia Goeing, and Anthony Grafton, eds. 2008. *Scholarly Knowledge: Textbooks in Early Modern Europe*. Geneva.
Cannon, Garland. 1989. "Abbreviations and Acronyms in English Word-Formation." *American Speech* 64:99–127.
Capasso, Mario. 2020. "Philodemus and the Herculaneum Papyri." In Mitsis 2020: 378–429.
Cardullo, Loredana. 2012. *Asclepio di Tralle: Commentario al libro Alpha Meizon (A) della Metafisica di Aristotle*. Acireale, IT.
Caserta, E. 2012. *Notizie degli scavi*. Ser. 9, vol. 21–22:53–19.
Cavallin, S. 1945. "Saint Génès le notaire." *Eranos* 4:150–76.
Cavallo, Guglielmo, Mario Capasso, and Tiziano Dorandi. 1983. *Libri, scritture e scribi ad Ercolano: Introduzione allo studio dei materiali greci*. Naples.
Chamay, Jacques, and Alain Schärlig. 1998. "Répresentation d'une table de calcul." *Antike Kunst* 41:52–55.
Champlin, Edward. 1980. *Fronto and Antonine Rome*. Cambridge, MA.
Chen, Anne Hunnell, and William Vernon Harris, eds. 2021. *Late Antique Studies in Memory of Alan Cameron*. Leiden.
Chin, Catherine M. 2008. *Grammar and Christianity in the Late Roman World*. Philadelphia.

Chroust, Anton. 2015 (1973). *Aristotle: New Light on His Life and on Some of His Lost Works. Some Novel Interpretations of the Man and His Life*. Vol. 1. London.
Clark, Gillian. 1989. *Iamblichus; On the Pythagorean Life*. Translated Texts for Historians 8. Liverpool.
Colardeau, Théodore. 1903 (2004 rpt.). *Étude sur Épictète*. Paris.
Coles, Revel A. 1966. *Reports of Proceedings in Papyri*. Brussels.
Colesanti, Giulio, and Manuela Giordano, eds. 2014. *Submerged Literature in Ancient Greek Culture: An Introduction*. Berlin.
Collette, Bernard. 2021. *The Stoic Doctrine on Providence: A Study of Its Development and of Its Major Issues*. New York.
Comeau, Marie. 1932. "Sur la transmission des sermons de Saint Augustin." *Révue des Etudes Latines* 10:408–22.
Conti, Eleonora Angela. 2013. "Orazione giudiziaria." *Comunicazioni dell'Istituto Vitelli* 11:20–38.
Contini, Gianfranco. 1974. "Come lavorava l'Ariosto." In *Esercizi di lettura sopra autori contemporanei*, 232–41. Turin.
Coope, Ursula, and Barbara Ann Sattler, eds. 2021. *Ancient Ethics and the Natural World*. Cambridge.
Cooper, John M. 2012. *Pursuits of Wisdom: Six Ways of Life from Socrates to Plotinus*. Princeton.
Costa, Cosimo. 2008. *La paideia della volontà: Una lettura della dottrina filosofica di Epitteto*. Rome.
Costamagna, Giorgio. 1990. "Dalla tironiana alla tachigrafia sillabica." In Ganz 1990: 83–89.
Courtonne, Yves. 1961. *Saint Basile Lettres*. Vol. 2. Paris.
Cribiore, Raffaella. 1996. *Writing, Teachers, and Students in Graeco-Roman Egypt*. Atlanta.
———. 1999. "Greek and Coptic Education in Late Antique Egypt." In Emmel 1999: 279–86.
———. 2001a. "School Papyri and the Textual Tradition of Homer." *Atti XXII Congr. Pap.* 279–86.
———. 2001b. *Gymnastics of the Mind: Greek Education in Hellenistic and Roman Egypt*. Princeton.
———. 2001c. "The Grammarian's Choice: The Popularity of Euripides' *Phoenissae* in Hellenistic and Roman Education." In Too 2001: 241–60.
———. 2007a. *The School of Libanius in Late Antique Antioch*. Princeton.
———. 2007b. "Spaces for Teaching in Late Antiquity." In Derda et al. 2007: 143–50.
———. 2013. *Libanius the Sophist: Rhetoric, Reality and Religion*. Ithaca.
———. 2015. "Literary Culture and Education in the Dakhla Oasis." In Bagnall et al. 2015: 179–92.
———. 2017. "The Conflict between Rhetoric and Philosophy and Zacharias' *Ammonius*." In Amato et al. 2017: 73–84.
———. 2019. "Genetic Criticism and the Papyri: Some Suggestions." In Reggiani 2019: 173–92.
———. 2020a. "Autographs Again." *Segno e Testo* 18:45–55.
———. 2020b. "Classical Decadence or Christian Aesthetics? Libanius, John Chrysostom, and Augustine on Rhetoric." In Flower and Ludlow 2020: 99–113.

———. 2021. "Stenographers in Late Antiquity: Villains or Victims." In Chen and Harris 2021: 220-32.
Cribiore, Raffaella, and Paola Davoli. 2013. "New Literary Texts from Amheida, Ancient Trimithis (Dakhla Oasis, Egypt)." *ZPE* 187:1-14.
Cribiore, Raffaella, Paola Davoli, and David M. Ratzan. 2008. "A Teacher's Dipinto from Trimithis (Dakhleh Oasis)." *JRA* 21:170-91.
Crouzel, Henri. 1970. "L'école d' Origène à Césarée: Postscriptum à une édition de Grégoire le Thaumaturge." *Bulletin de Littérature Ecclésiastique* 71:15-27.
Damschen, Gregor, and Andreas Heil, eds. 2013. *Brill's Companion to Seneca, Philosopher and Dramatist*. Leiden.
Décarie, Vianney. 1983. "L'authenticité du livre K de la Métaphysique." In Dumoulin et al. 1983: 295-317.
Deferrari, Roy Joseph. 1922. "St. Augustine's Method of Composing and Delivering Sermons." *AJP* 43.2:97-123.
Delattre, Daniel. 2006. *La villa des papyrus et les rouleaux d'Herculanum: La bibliothèque de Philodème*. Cahiers du Cedopal 4. Liège.
———. 2010. "Le franc-parler de Philodème (*Pherc.* 1471): Reconstruction bibliologique d'ensemble du rouleau." In Antoni et al. 2010: 97-109.
———. 2015. "La pratique maîtrisée du franc-parler: Philodème de Gadara, Le Franc Parler (Col. 151-162D)." In Loubet et al. 2015: 435-53.
Del Corso, Lucio E. 2005. *La lettura nel mondo ellenistico*. Rome.
———. 2022. *Il libro nel mondo Antico. Archeologia e storia (secoli VII a.C-IV d.C)*. Rome.
Del Mastro, Gianluca. 2004. *Titoli e annotazioni bibliologiche nei papiri greci di Ercolano*. Naples.
Deppman, Jed, Daniel Ferrer, and Michael Groden, eds. 2004. *Genetic Criticism: Texts and Avant-Texts*. Philadelphia.
Derda, Tomasz, Tomasz Markiewicz, and Eva Wipszycka, eds. 2007. *Alexandria: The Auditoria of Kom el-Dikka: Journal of Juristic Papyrology Supplement*. Warsaw.
Desideri, Paolo. 1978. *Dione di Prusa. Un intelletuale Greco nell'impero romano*. Messina.
———. 1992. "Tipologia e varietà di funzione comunicativa degli scritti dionei." *ANRW* 2.33.5:3903-59.
Deubner, Ludwig, ed. 1937. *Iamblichi de vita Pythagorica liber*. Leipzig: Teubner.
Devresse, Robert. 1954. *Introduction à l'étude des manuscrits grecs*. Paris.
De Wet, Chris L., and Wendy Mayer, eds. 2019. *Revisioning John Chrysostom: New Approaches, New Perspectives*. Leiden.
Dickey, Eleanor. 2007. *Ancient Greek Scholarship: A Guide to Finding, Reading and Understanding Scholia, Commentaries, Lexica and Grammatical Treatises from Their Beginnings to the Byzantine Period*. Oxford.
———, ed. 2012, 2015. *The Colloquia of the Hermeneumata Pseudodositheana*. Vols. 1-2. Cambridge.
———. 2016. *An Introduction to the Composition and Analysis of Greek Prose*. Cambridge.
Diels, Hermann. 1904. "Laterculi Alexandrini aus einem Papyrus Ptolemäischer Zeit." *Abhandlungen der Preussischen Akademie der Wissenschaften* 2:3-36.
———, ed. 1952. *Fragmente der Vorsokratiker*. Vol. 2. Berlin.

Diethart, Johann, and Klaas W. Worp. 1986. *Notarsunterschriften im Byzantinischen Ägypten*. Vienna.

Dionisotti, Anna Carlotta. 1982. "From Ausonius' Schooldays? A Schoolbook and Its Relatives." *JRS* 72:83–125.

Dobbin, Robert, ed. 1998. *Epictetus: Discourses Book 1*. Oxford.

———, ed. 2008. *Epictetus: Discourses and Selected Writings*. London.

Dodds, Eric Robertson. 1957. "Review of L. G. Westerink, ed. *Olympiodorus: Commentary on the First Alcibiades of Plato* (Amsterdam 1956)." *Gnomon* 29:356–59.

Dominguez, Adolfo J., ed. 2018. *Politics, Territory and Identity in Ancient Epirus*. Pisa.

Donini, Pierluigi. 1994. "Testi e commenti, manuali e insegnamento: La forma sistematica e i metodi della filosofia in età postellenistica." *ANRW* II 36.7:5027–100.

Dorandi, Tiziano. 2000. *Le stylet et la tablette*. Paris.

———. 2007. *Diogenes Laertius: Lives of Eminent Philosophers*. Cambridge.

———. 2013. *Nell'officina dei classici: Come lavoravano gli autori antichi*. Rome.

———. 2020. "Epicurus and the Epicurean School." In Mitsis 2020: 13–42.

Doutreleau, Louis, Adolphe Gesché, and Michael Gronewald, eds. 1969. *Didymos der Blinde: Psalmenkommentar (Tura-Papyrus); Teil 1: Kommentar zu Psalm 20–21*. PTA 7. Bonn.

Duke, E. A. 1990. "Evidence for the Text of Plato in the Later 9th Century." *Revue d'histoire des texts* 19:19–29.

Dumoulin, Bertrand, Andreas Graeser, Paul Moraux, Hans Strohm, and Jürgen Wiesner, eds. 1983. *Zweifelhaftes im Corpus Aristotelicum: Studien zu einigen dubia*. Berlin.

Düring, Ingemar. 1966. *Aristoteles: Darstellung und Interpretation seines Denkens*. Heidelberg.

Dürrenmatt, Jacques, and Andreas Pfersman, eds. 2004. *L'espace de la note*. Rennes.

Dusil, Stephan, Gerald Schwedler, and Raphael Schwitter, eds. 2017. *Exzerpieren, Kompilieren, Tradieren: Transformationen des Wissens zwischen Spätantike und Frühmittelalter*. Millennium-Studien/Millennium Studies 64. Berlin.

Eddy, Matthew Daniel. 2016. "The Interactive Notebook: How Students Learned to Keep Notes during the Scottish Enlightenment." *Book History* 19:87–131.

Edwards, Michael. 2000. *Neoplatonic Saints: The Lives of Plotinus and Proclus by Their Students*. Liverpool.

———. 2019. *Aristotle and Early Christian Thought*. Studies in Philosophy and Theology in Late Antiquity. London.

Edwards, Michael, and Christopher Reid, eds. 2004. *Oratory in Action*. Manchester.

Egberts, A., Brian Paul Muhs, and Joep van der Vliet, eds. 2002. *Perspectives on Panopolis: An Egyptian Town from Alexander the Great to the Arab Conquest*. Leiden.

Eller, Meredith Freeman. 1949. "The *Retractationes* of Saint Augustine." *Church History* 18.3:172–83.

Elm, Susanna. 2012. *Sons of Hellenism, Fathers of the Church*. Berkeley.
Emmel, Stephen, ed. 1999. *Ägypten und Nubien in spätantiker und christlicher Zeit: Akten des 6. Internationalen Koptologenkongresses*. Wiesbaden.
Epictetus. 2018. *How to Be Free: An Ancient Guide to the Stoic Life : Encheiridion and Selections from Discourses*, transl. A. A. Long. Princeton.
Essler, Holger. 2017. "P.HERC. 152/157—An Author's Master Copy." *Segno e Testo* 15:57–80.
Evans, Trevor Vivian, and Dirk Obbink, eds. 2010. *The Language of the Papyri*. Oxford.
Fairweather, Janet. 1981. *Seneca the Elder*. Cambridge.
Favreau-Linder, Anne-Marie, Sophie Lalanne, Jean-Luc Vix, Gérard Freyburger, and Laurent Pernot, eds. 2022. *Passeurs de culture: La transmission de la culture grecque dans le monde romain des Ier–iVe siècles après J.-C.* Turnhout, BE.
Festugière, André-Jean. 1965. "L'Autobiographie de Libanius." *REG* 78:623–34.
———. 1969. "L'ordre de lecture des dialogues de Platon au Ve/vIe siècles." *Museum Helveticum* 26.4:281–96.
Finkelberg, Margalit. 2019. *The Gatekeeper: Narrative Voice in Plato's Dialogues*. Leiden.
Fiorani, Francesca. 2020. *The Shadow Drawing: How Science Taught Leonardo How to Paint*. New York.
Fish, Jeff. 2022. "An Epicurean Evaluates the Practical Wisdom of Homer: Philodemus on the Good King." In Manoela 2022: 259–74.
Fitzgerald, John T., Dirk Obbink, and Glenn Stanfield Holland, eds. 2004. *Philodemus and the New Testament World*. Leiden.
Flower, Richard, and Morwella Ludlow. 2020. *Rhetoric and Religious Identity in Late Antiquity*. Oxford.
Foat, F. W. G. 1902. "Sematography of the Greek Papyri." *JHS* 22:135–73.
Fowler, Ryan C., ed. 2014. *Plato in the Third Sophistic*. Berlin.
Franchina, Duilio. 2010. "I *notarii* in Agostino." In Milanese et al. 2010: 1003–20.
Ganz, Peter, ed. 1990. *Tironische Noten*. Wiesbaden.
Garelli, Marie-Hélène. 2007. *Dancer le mythe: La pantomime et sa réception dans la culture antique*. Louvain.
Geerlings, Saint Wilhelm, ed. 2005. *Possidius Vita Augustini*. Paderborn.
Genette, Gerard. 1997. *Paratexts: Thresholds of Interpretation*. Cambridge.
Gera, Deborah Levine. 1997. *Warrior Women: The Anonymous Tractatus de Mulieribus*. Leiden.
Germino, Emilio. 2004. *Scuola e cultura nella legislazione di Giuliano l'Apostata*. Naples.
Gerson, Lloyd P., ed. 2006. *The Cambridge Companion to Plotinus*. Cambridge.
———, ed. 2010. *The Cambridge History of Philosophy in Late Antiquity*. Vols. 1 and 2. Cambridge.
———, ed. 2018. *The Enneads*. Translated by G. Boyd-Stones et al. Cambridge.
Gesché, Adolphe. 1962. *La christologie du "Commentaire sur les Psaumes" découvert à Toura*. Gembloux.
Giardina, Andrea. 2001. "Conclusioni." *Antiquité Tardive* 9:289–95.
Gibson, Craig A. 2002. *Interpreting a Classic: Demosthenes and His Ancient Commentators*. Berkeley.

Gigante, Marcello. 1975. "'Philosophia medicans' in Filodemo." *CErc* 5:53–61.

Gignac, Francis T. 1976. *A Grammar of the Greek Papyri of the Roman and Byzantine Period*. Vol. 1. Milan.

Gill, Christopher. 2000. "Stoic Writers of the Imperial Era." In Rowe and Schofield 2000: 597–615.

———. 2003. "The School in the Roman Imperial Period." In Inwood 2003: 33–58.

———. 2005. "Competing Readings of Stoic Emotions." In Salles 2005: 445–70.

———. 2022. *Learning to Live Naturally: Stoic Ethics and Its Modern Significance*. Oxford.

Gill, Mary Louise, and Pierre Pellegrin, eds. 2012. *A Companion to Ancient Philosophy*. Chichester, West Sussex, UK.

Glad, Clarence E. 1995. *Paul and Philodemus: Adaptability in Epicurean and Early Christian Psychagogy*. Leiden.

Gleason, Maud W. 1995. *Making Men: Sophists and Self-Presentation in Ancient Rome*. Princeton.

Goldhill, Simon, ed. 2008. *The End of Dialogue in Antiquity*. Cambridge.

Goodall, Blake. 1979. *The Homilies of St. John Chrysostom on the Letters of St. Paul to Titus and Philemon*. Berkeley.

Goulet, Richard. 1982. "Porphyre. La vie de Plotin. Text, Traduction et Notes." In Brisson 1982, 2:131–87.

Goulet-Cazé, Marie-Odile. 1982. "L'arrière-plan scolaire de *La vie de Plotin*." In Brisson 1982, 229–328.

———. 1986. "Introduction Général." In *L'ascèse cinique: Un commentaire de Diogène Laërce VI 70–71*. Paris. 11–28.

———. 2017. *Le cynisme, une philosophie antique*. Textes et Traditions 29. Paris.

Grant, Robert M., and Glen W. Menzies. 1996. *Joseph's Bible Notes (Hypomnestikon)*. Texts and Translations 41. Atlanta.

Graver, Margaret R. 2007. *Stoicism and Emotions*. Chicago.

———. 2013. "Ethics II: Action and Emotion." In Damschen and Heil 2013: 257–75.

Griffin, Michael J. 2014. "Pliable Platonism? Olympiodorus and the Profession of Philosophy in Sixth-Century Alexandria." In Fowler 2014: 73–100.

———. 2015. *Olympiodorus: Life of Plato and on Plato First Alcibiades 1–9*. London.

———. 2016. "Ammonius and the Alexandrian School" In *Brill's Companion to the Reception of Aristotle in Antiquity*, edited by Andrea Falcon, 394–418. Leiden.

———. 2020. *Olympiodorus: On Plato: First Alcibiades 10–28*. London.

Gronewald, Michael, ed. 1968. *Didymos der Blinde: Psalmenkommentar (Tura-Papyrus); Teil 2: Kommentar zu Psalm 22–26,10*. PTA 4. Bonn.

———, ed. 1969. *Didymos der Blinde: Psalmenkommentar (Tura-Papyrus); Teil 4: Kommentar zu Psalm 35–39*. PTA 6. Bonn.

———, ed. 1970. *Psalmenkommentar (Tura-Papyrus); Teil 5: Kommentar zu Psalm 40–44,4*. PTA 12. Bonn.

———, ed. 1977. *Didymos der Blinde: Kommentar zum Ecclesiastes (Tura-Papyrus); Teil 2: Kommentar zu Ecclesiastes, Kapitel 3–4*. PTA 22. Bonn.

———, ed. 1979. *Didymos der Blinde: Kommentar zum Ecclesiastes (Tura-Papyrus); Teil 5: Kommentar zu Ecclesiastes, Kapitel 9,8–10,20*. PTA 24. Bonn.

Gronewald, Michael, and Adolphe Gesché, eds. 1969. *Didymos der Blinde: Psalmenkommentar (Tura-Papyrus); Teil 3: Kommentar zu Psalm 29–34*. PTA 8. Bonn.

Gurd, Sean. 2012. *Work in Progress: Literary Revision in Classical Antiquity*. New York: Oxford University Press.

Guthrie, William Keith Chambers. 1981. *A History of Greek Philosophy*. Cambridge.

Hadot, Ilsetraut. 1996. *Commentaire sur le Manuel d'Épictète. Introduction & édition critique du texte grec*. Leiden.

Hadot, Pierre. 1979. "Les divisions des parties de la philosophie dans l'antiquité." *Museum Helveticum* 36:201–23.

———. 1990. "Forms of Life and Forms of Discourse in Ancient Philosophy." *Critical Inquiry* 16:483–505.

———. 1995. *Philosophy as a Way of Life: Spiritual Exercises from Socrates to Foucault*. Oxford.

———. 2002. *What Is Ancient Philosophy?* Translated by J. M. Chase. Cambridge, MA.

Haines, Charles Reginald. 1929. *Fronto's Correspondence*. Cambridge, MA.

Hall, Edith, and Rosie Wyles, eds. 2008. *New Directions in Ancient Pantomime*. Oxford.

Harmless, William. 2014. *Augustine and the Catechumenate*. 2nd ed. Collegeville.

Hartmann, William K. 1905. "Arrian und Epiktet." *Neue Jahrbücher für das klassische Altertum, Geschichte und deutsche Literatur und für Pädagogik* 8:252–75.

Hartney, Aideen. 2004. "Transformation of the City: John Chrysostom's Oratory in the Homiletic Form." In Edwards and Reid 2004: 83–98.

Haslam, Michael W. 1994. "The Homer Lexicon of Apollonius Sophista, I: Composition and Constituents." *CP* 89:1–45.

Heath, Malcolm. 1995. *Hermogenes on Issues: Strategies of Argument in Later Greek Rhetoric*. Oxford.

———. 2004. *Menander: A Rhetor in Context*. Oxford.

Heine, Ronald E. 2010. *Scholarship in the Service of the Church*. Oxford.

Hellweg, Rainer. 1985. "Stilistische Untersuchungen zu den Krankengeschichten der Epidemienbücher I und III des corpus Hippocraticum." PhD diss., Bonn.

Henry, René, ed. 1959–67. *Photius bibliothèque*. Vol. 2. Paris.

Hense, Otto, ed. 1905. *C. Musonii Rufi reliquiae*. Stuttgart.

Hershbell, Jackson. 1989. "The Stoicism of Epictetus." *ANRW* 2.36.3:2148–63.

Hoffman, Philippe. 2012. "What Was Commentary in Late Antiquity? The Example of the Neoplatonic Commentators." In Gill and Pellegrin 2012: 597–622.

Holford-Strevens, Leofranc. 2020. *Aulus Gellius: Attic Nights, Preface and Books 1–10 (Auli Gelli Noctes Atticae: Praefatio et Libri I–X)*. Oxford.

Holiday, Ryan. 2014. *The Obstacle Is the Way: The Timeless Art of Turning Trials into Triumph*. London.

Holiday, Ryan, and Stephen Hanselman, eds. 2017. *The Daily Stoic Journal: 366 Meditations on Wisdom, Perseverance, and the Art of Living*. London.

Holland, Glenn Stanfield. 2004. "Call Me Frank: Lucian's (Self-) Defense of Frank Speaking and Philodemus' περὶ παρρησίας." In Fitzgerald et al. 2004: 245–67.

Horster, Marietta, and Christiane Reitz, eds. 2003. *Antike Fachschriftsteller: Literarischer Diskurs und sozialer Kontext*. Stuttgart.
Howley, Joseph. 2018. *Aulus Gellius on Roman Reading Culture*. Cambridge.
Hutchinson, D. S., and Monte Ransome Johnson. 2005. "Authenticating the *Protrepticus*." *Oxford Studies in Ancient Philosophy* 29:193–294.
———. 2014. "Protreptic Aspects of Aristotle's *Nichomachean Ethics*." In Polansky 2014: 383–409.
Inwood, Brad, ed. 2003. *The Cambridge Companion to the Stoics*. Cambridge.
———, ed. 2014. *Ethics after Aristotle*. Cambridge.
Jackson, Henry. 1920. "Aristotle's Lecture-Room and Lectures." *Journal of Philology* 35:191–200.
Jackson, Robin, Kimon Lycos, and Harold Tarrant, eds. 1998. *Olympiodorus Commentary on Plato's Gorgias*. Leiden.
Jacob, C. F. 2004. "Questions sur les questions: Archéologie d'une pratique intellectuelle et d'une form discursive." In Volgers and Zamagni 2004: 25–54.
Jaeger, Werner. 1948. *Aristotle, Fundamentals of the History of His Development*. 2nd ed. Translated by R. Robinson. Oxford.
Jagu, Amand. 1946. *Épictète et Platon*. Paris.
Jocelyn, H. D. 1982. "Diatribes and Sermons," *Liverpool Classical Monthly* 7: 3–7.
Johnson, Maxwell E. 2007. *The Rites of Christian Initiation: Their Evolution and Interpretation*. 2nd ed. Collegeville, MN.
Johnson, Scott Fitzgerald, ed. 2006. *Greek Literature in Late Antiquity: Dynamism, Didacticism, Classicism*. Aldershot, UK.
Johnson, William A. 2010. *Readers and Reading Culture in the High Roman Empire: A Study of Elite Communities*. Oxford.
Johnson, William A., and Holt N. Parker. 2011. *Ancient Literacies: The Culture of Reading in Greece and Rome*. Oxford.
Jones, Arnold Hugh Martin. 1973. *The Later Roman Empire 284–602: A Social, Economic, and Administrative Survey*. Oxford.
Jones, Christopher P. 2001. "Apollonius of Tyana's Passage to India." *GRBS* 42:185–99.
Jouanna, Jacques. 2009. "Médicine et philosophie: Sur la date de Sextus Empiricus et de Diogène *Laërce* à la lumière du *Corpus* Galénique." *REG* 122:359–90.
———. 2016. *Hippocrate tome IV Épidémies I et III*. Paris.
Juynboll, Gualtherüs Hendrik Albert. 1973. Review of U. Sezgin, *Abū Mihnaf: ein Beitrag zur Historiographie der umaiyadischen Zeit* (Leiden, 1971). *Bibliotheca Orientalis* 30.1/2:102–3.
Kaster, Robert. 1980. "Macrobius and Servius: Verecundia and the Grammarian's Function." *HSCP* 84:219–62.
———. 1988. *Guardians of Language: The Grammarian and Society in Late Antiquity*. Berkeley.
Kehl, Aloys, ed. 1964. *Der Psalmenkommentar von Tura, Quaternio IX (Pap. Colon. theol. 1)*. Cologne.

Kelly, John Norman Davidson. 1995. *Jerome: His Life, Writings, and Controversies.* New York.

Ker, James. 2004. "Nocturnal Writers in Imperial Rome: The Culture of *Lucubratio.*" *CP* 99.3:209-42.

Kim, Lawrence Young. 2010. *Homer between History and Fiction in Imperial Greek Literature.* Cambridge.

———. 2017. "Atticism and Asianism." In Richter and Johnson 2017: 41-66.

———. 2022. "Homer in the Second Sophistic." In Manolea 2022: 164-88.

Kincheloe, Joe L., Shirley R. Steinberg, and Patricia H. Hinchey, eds. 1999. *The Post-Forman Reader: Cognition and Education.* London.

Kloeters, Gert. 1957. "Buch und Schrift bei Hieronymus." PhD diss., University of Münster.

Knauber, Adolf. 1968. "Das Anliegen der Schule des Origenes zu Cäsara." *Münchener Theologische Zeitschrift* 19:182-203.

Koniaris, George Leonidas. 1983. "On Maximus of Tyre: Zetemata (II)." *CA* 2:212-50.

König, Jason, Katerina Oikonomoboulou, and Greg Wolf. 2013. *Ancient Libraries.* Cambridge.

König, Jason, and Tim Whitmarsh. 2007. *Ordering Knowledge in the Roman Empire.* Cambridge.

Konstan, David. 2011. "Excerpting as a Reading Practice." In Reydam-Schils 2011b: 9-22.

Konstan, David, Diskin Clay, Clarence E. Glad, Johan C. Thorn, and James Ware, eds. 1998. *Philodemus on Frank Criticism.* Atlanta.

Kramer, Johannes, and Ludwig Koenen, eds. 1970. *Didymos der Blinde: Kommentar zum Ecclesiastes (Tura-Papyrus); Teil 3: Kommentar zu Ecclesiastes, Kapitel 5 und 6.* PTA 13. Bonn.

Kramer, Johannes, and Bärbel Krebber, eds. 1972. *Didymos der Blinde: Kommentar zum Ecclesiastes (Tura-Papyrus); Teil 4: Kommentar zu Ecclesiastes, Kapitel 7-8,8.* PTA 16. Bonn.

Lamberton, Robert D. 1986. *Homer the Theologian: Neoplatonist Allegorical Reading and the Growth of the Epic Tradition.* Berkeley.

Lamberton, Robert D., and John J. Keaney, eds. 1992. *Homer's Ancient Readers: The Hermeneutics of Greek Epic's Earliest Exegetes.* Princeton.

Law, Vivien, and Ineke Sluiter, eds. 1995. *Dionysius Thrax and the Technē grammatikē.* Münster.

Layton, Richard A. 2004. *Didymus the Blind and His Circle in Late-Antique Alexandria.* Urbana.

Lefebvre, Jules Joseph. 2004. "'Note' et 'Note': Proposition de défrichage linguistique." In Dürrenmatt and Pfersman 2004: 27-35.

Legras, Bernard. 1997. "L'enseignement de l'histoire dans les écoles grecques d' Égypte (III BCE-VI CE)." *Archiv für Papyrusforschung* 21 Congr. Pap. Beiheft 3. Berlin: 586-600.

Lendon, J. E. 2022. *That Tyrant, Persuasion: How Rhetoric Shaped the Roman World.* Princeton.

Leon-Ruiz, Daniel William. 2021. *Arrian the Historian: Writing the Greek Past in the Roman Empire*. Austin, TX.

Lettinck, Paul, ed. 2014. *On Aristotle Physics 5–8 with Simplicius: On Aristotle on the Void*. London.

Lewis, Naphtali. 2003. "Shorthand Writers." *Comunicazioni dell' Istituto Papirologico G. Vitelli* 5:19–27.

Liapes, Vayos, and Antonis K. Petrides, eds. 2018. *Greek Tragedy after the Fifth Century: A Survey from ca 400 BC to ca AD 400*. Cambridge.

Liesenborghs, Leo, ed. 1965. *Kommentar zum Ecclesiastes: Lage 22 und 23 des Tura-Papyrus*. Cologne.

Lightfoot, J. L. 1999. *Parthenius of Nicaea*. Oxford.

Liotsakis, Vasileios. 2019. *Alexander the Great in Arrian's Anabasis: A Literary Portrait*. Berlin.

Long, Anthony A. 1992. "Stoic Readings of Homer." In Lamberton and Keaney 1992: 41–66.

———. 1999. "Stoic Psychology." In Algra et al. 1999: 560–84.

———. 2002. *Epictetus: A Stoic and Socratic Guide to Life*. Oxford.

———. 2006. "Roman Philosophy." In Sedley 2006: 184–210.

Longo Auricchio, Francesca, Giovanni Indelli, Giuliana Leoni, and Gianluca Del Mastro. 2020. *La villa dei papyri: una residenza antica e la sua biblioteca*. Rome.

Loubet, Mireille, Didier Pralon, and Gilles Dorival, eds. 2015. *Poïkiloï Karpoï. Exégèses païennes, juives et chrétiennes: Etudes réunies en homage à Gilles Dorival*. Aix-en-Provence.

Luce, T. James. 1977. *Livy: The Composition of His History*. Princeton.

Lutz, Cora E. 1947. *Musonius Rufus, "The Roman Socrates."* New Haven.

Lutz, Cora E., and Gretchen Reydam-Schils. 2020. *That One Should Disdain Hardships: The Teachings of a Roman Stoic: Musonius Rufus*. New Haven.

Lynch, John Patrik. 1972. *Aristotle's School: A Study of a Greek Educational Institution*. Berkeley.

Maas, Michael, ed. 2005. *The Cambridge Companion to the Age of Justinian*. Cambridge.

Macris, Constantinos, Tiziano Dorandi, and Luc Brisson. 2021. *Pythagoras Redivivus: Studies on the Texts Attributed to Pythagoras and the Pythagoreans*. Academia Philosophical Studies, 74. Baden-Baden.

Manetti, Daniela. 1990. "Doxographical Deformation of Medical Tradition in the Report of the Anonymus Londinensis on Philolaus." *ZPE* 83: 219–33.

———. 1999. "Aristotle and the Role of Doxography in the Anonymus Londinensis." In *Ancient Histories of Medicine*, edited by P. J. van Eijk, 95–141. Leiden.

Manolea, Christina-Panagiota, ed. 2022. *Brill's Companion to the Reception of Homer: From the Hellenistic Age to Late Antiquity*. Leiden.

Mansfeld, Jaap. 1994. *Prolegomena: Questions to Be Settled before the Study of an Author, or a Text*. Leiden.

Mansion, Augustine. 1958. "Philosophie première, philosophie seconde et Métaphysique chez Aristote." *Rev. Philos. de Louvain* 56:165–221.

Marchesi, Ilaria. 2008. *The Art of Pliny's Letters: A Poetics of Allusion in the Private Correspondence*. Cambridge.
Maresch, Klaus, and Isabella Andorlini. 2006. *Das Archiv des Aurelius Ammon (P. Ammon)*. Band 2, A. *Papyrologica Coloniensia* vol. 26/2. A. Munich.
Marincola, John. 1997. *Authority and Tradition in Ancient Historiography*. Cambridge.
Markovich, Daniel. 2022. *Promoting a New Kind of Education: Greek and Roman Philosophical Protreptic*. International Studies in the History of Rhetoric 16. Leiden.
Marrou, Henri-Irénée. 1956. *A History of Education in Antiquity*. Translated by G. Lamb. New York.
Martens, Peter W., ed. 2017. *Adrian's Introduction to the Divine Scriptures: An Antiochene Handbook for Scriptural Interpretation*. Oxford.
Martin, Jean. 1974. *Antike Rhetorik, Technik und Methode*. Munich.
Martin, Jean, and Paul Petit, eds. 1979. *Libanios: Discours I, Autobiographie*. Paris.
Matthews, John. 2006. *The Journey of Theophanes: Travel, Business, and Daily Life in the Roman East*. New Haven.
Mayer, Wendy, and Pauline Allen. 2000. *John Chrysostom*. London.
Mazzarino, Santo. 1988. *L'impero romano*. 3rd ed. Bari.
——. 1989. *Storia sociale del vescovo Ambrogio*. Rome.
McDermott, William C. 1972. "M. Cicero and M. Tiro." *Historia* 21:259–86.
McNamee, Kathleen. 1981. *Abbreviations in Literary Papyri and Ostraca*. Ann Arbor.
——. 2001. "A Plato Papyrus with Shorthand Marginalia." *GRBS* 42:97–116.
——. 2007. *Annotations in Greek and Latin Texts from Egypt*. New Haven.
McNamee, Kathleen, and Michael L. Jacovides. 2003. "Annotations to the Speech of the Muses (Plato *Republic* 546B–C)." *ZPE* 144:31–50.
McPhee, John. 2017. *Draft No. 4: On the Writing Process*. New York.
Menci, Giovanna. 1992. "Il commentario tachigrafico." *Pap.Congr.* 19:451–65.
——. 2001. "Echi letterari nei papyri tachigrafici." *Atti XXII Int. Congr.Pap.*: 927–36.
——. 2019. "Terminologia tachigrafica in alcune similitudini del *De virginitate di Basilio d'Ancira*." In Reggiani 2019: 227–34.
Migliario, Elvira. 2007. *Retorica e storia: Una lettura delle Suasorie di Seneca padre*. Bari.
Milanese, Marco, Paola Ruggeri, and Cinzia Vismara, eds. 2010. *L'Africa romana. I luoghi e le forme dei mestieri e della produzione nelle province africane*. Rome.
Milne, Herbert, and John Mansfield. 1934. *Greek Shorthand Manuals*. London.
Mitsis, Phillip, ed. 2020. *Oxford Handbook of Epicurus and Epicureanism*. Oxford.
——. 2021. *Ratio certe cogit: Studi sulla teoria etico-politica degli Stoici*. Translated by E. Piergiacomi. Rome.
Montiglio, Silvia. 2011. *From Villain to Hero: Odysseus in Ancient Thought*. Ann Arbor.
Moraux, Paul, and Jürgen Wiesner, eds. 1983. *Zweifelhaftes im Corpus Aristotelicum*. Berlin.

Morgan, Teresa. 1998. *Literate Education in the Hellenistic and Roman World.* Cambridge.
———. 2007. *Popular Morality in the Early Roman Empire.* Cambridge.
Moscadi, Alessandro. 1970. "Le lettere dell'archivio di Teofane." *Aegyptus* 50:88–154.
Most, Glenn W., ed. 1998. *Editing Texts / Texte edieren.* Aporemata 2. Göttingen.
Müller, Gernot Michael. 2021. *Figurengestaltung und Gesprächinteraktion im antiken Dialog.* Stuttgart.
Müller, Gernot Michael, and Sabine Föllinger, eds. 2013. *Der Dialog in der Antike. Formen und Funktionen einer literarischen Gattung zwischen Philosophie, Wissensvermittlung und dramatischer Inszenierung.* Berlin.
Naas, Valérie. 1996. "Réflexions sur la method de travail de Pline l'ancient." *RPh* 70:305–32.
Natali, Carlo. 1991. "Aristotele professore?" *Phronesis* 36:61–73.
———. 2013. *Aristotle: His Life and School.* Princeton.
Nelson, Anne Browning. 1995. "The Classroom of Didymus the Blind." PhD diss., University of Michigan.
Norman, Albert Francis, ed. 1992. *Libanius: Autobiography and Selected Letters.* Vol. 1. Cambridge, MA.
Nussbaum, Martha. 1994. *The Therapy of Desire: Theory and Practice in Hellenistic Ethics.* Princeton.
———. 2004. "Emotions as Judgements of Value and Importance." In Solomon 2004: 183–99.
Obbink, Dirk. 2004. "Craft, Cult, and Canon in the Books from Herculaneum." In Fitzgerald et al. 2004: 73–84.
O'Connell, Mark. 2012. "The Marginal Obsession with Marginalia." *New Yorker*, January 26.
Oldfather, William Abbott. Translated 1926. *Epictetus: The Discourses as Reported by Arrian, The Manual and Fragments.* The Loeb Classical Library. 2 vols. London.
Olivieri, Alessandro, ed. 1914. *Philodemi Περὶ παρρησίας libellus.* Leipzig.
Opsomer, Jan. 2010. "Olympiodorus." In Gerson 2010, 2:696–710.
Papadoiannakis, Yannis. 2006. "Instructions by Question and Answer: The Case of Late Antique and Byzantine *Erotapokriseis.*" In S. Johnson 2006: 91–105.
Parsons, Peter. 1982. "Facts from Fragments." *G&R* 29:184–95.
Patillon, Michel. 2008. *Corpus rhetoricorum.* Vol. 1. Paris.
Patillon, Michel, and Giancarlo Bolognesi, eds. 1997. *Aelius Théon, Progymnasmata.* Paris.
Patillon, Michel, and Luc Brisson, eds. 2002. *Longin, Fragments. Art Rhétorique, Rufus, Art Rhétorique.* Paris.
Pecere, Oronzo. 2010. *Roma antica e il testo.* Rome.
Peirano, Irene. 2012. *The Rhetoric of the Roman Fake: Latin Pseudepigrapha in Context.* Cambridge.
Pelling, Christopher B. R. 1979. "Plutarch's Method of Work in the Roman Lives." *JHS* 99:74–96.

———. 2002. "The *Apophthegmata regum et imperatorum* and Plutarch's Roman Lives." In *Plutarch and History: Eighteen Studies*, 65–90. London.
Pepe, Cristina. 2018. "The Rhetorical Commentary in Late Antiquity." *Aion* 40:86–108.
Pernot, Laurent. 1993. *La rhétorique de l'éloge dans le monde gréco-romain*. Paris.
Perrone, Lorenzo, ed. 2015. *The New Homilies on the Psalms. A Critical Edition of Codex Monacensis Graecus 314*. Origenes vol. 13. Berlin.
Pettine, Emidio. 1984. *La tranquillità dell'animo di Plutarco*. Salerno.
Pignot, Matthieu. 2020. *The Catechumenate in Late Antique Africa (4th–6th Centuries): Augustine of Hippo. His Contemporaries and Early Reception*. Suppl. to *Vigiliae Christianae* 162. Leiden.
Pinto, Pasquale Massimo. 2013. "Men and Books in Fourth-Century Athens." In König et al. 2013: 85–95.
Polansky, Ronald M., ed. 2014. *The Cambridge Companion to Aristotle's Nicomachean Ethics*. Cambridge.
Pradeau, Jean-François. 2019. *Plotin qui est-tu?* Paris.
Praechter, Karl. 1909. Translated 2016. "Review of the *Commentaria in Aristotelem Graeca*." In Sorabji 2016a: 35–60.
Prentice, William Kelly. 1930. "How Thucydides Wrote His History." *CP* 25.2:117–27.
Pretzler, Maria. 2004. "Turning Travel into Text: Pausanias at Work." *G&R* 51.2:199–216.
Puech, Bernadette. 2002. *Orateurs et sophistes grecs dans les inscriptions d'époque impériale*. Paris.
Raiola, Tommaso. 2015. *Nel tempo di una vita: Studi sull'autobiografia in Galeno*. Pisa.
Ramelli, Ilaria. 2009. "Origen, Patristic Philosophy, and Christian Platonism: Rethinking the Christianization of Hellenism." *Vigiliae Christianae* 63:217–63.
Rees, Bryn Roderick. 1968. "Theophanes of Hermoupolis Magna." *Bulletin of the John Rylands Library* 51:164–83.
———, ed. 1964. *Papyri from Hermopolis and Other Documents of the Byzantine Period*. London.
Reggiani, Nicola, ed. 2019. *Greek Medical Papyri: Text, Context, Hypertext*. Berlin.
Reverdin, Olivier, and Bernard Grange, eds. 1993. *La philologie grecque à l'époque hellénistique et romaine*. Entretiens sur l'Antiquité Classique. 40. Geneva.
Reydams-Schils, Gretchen. 2010. "Philosophy and Education in Stoicism of the Roman Imperial Era." *Oxford Review of Education* 36.5:561–74.
———. 2011a. "Authority and Agency in Stoicism." *GRBS* 51:296–322.
———. 2011b. *Thinking through Excerpts: Studies in Stobaeus*. Turnhout, BE.
Ricciardetto, Antonio, ed. 2016. *L'Anonyme de Londres (P.Lit. Lond. 165, Brit.Libr. inv. 137). Un papyrus médicale grec du Ier siècle après J-C*. Paris.
Richard, Marcel. 1950. "ΑΠΟ ΦΟΝΗΣ." *Byzantion* 20:191–222.
Richter, Daniel S., and William A. Johnson, eds. 2017. *The Oxford Handbook of the Second Sophistic*. Oxford.

Rist, John. 2006. "Plotinus and Christian Philosophy." In Gerson 2006: 386–413.
Roberts, Colin H., ed. 1952. *Catalogue of the Greek and Latin Papyri in the John Rylands Library*. Vol. 4. Manchester.
Roller, Matthew B. 2018. *Models from the Past in Roman Culture: A World of Exempla*. Cambridge.
Ronchey, Silvia. 2000. "Les process-verbaux des martyres chrétiens dans les *Acta Martyrum* et leur fortune." *Mélanges de l'école française de Rome* 112.2:723–52.
Rose, Herbert Jennings. 1933. *Hygini Fabulae*. 2nd ed. Leiden.
Rosenbaum, Stephen E. 2020. "Death." In Mitsis 2020: 118–40.
Roskam, Geert. 2004. "From Stick to Reasoning: Plutarch on the Communication between Teacher and Pupil." *Wiener Studien* 117:93–114.
Ross, William David. 1923. *Aristotle*. Oxford.
Rowe, Christopher J., and Malcolm Schofield, eds. 2000. *The Cambridge History of Greek and Roman Political Thought*. Cambridge.
Rubenson, Samuel. 1995. *The Letters of Saint Antony: Monasticism and the Making of a Saint*. Minneapolis.
Rubenson, Samuel, and Lillian Larsen, eds. 2018. *Monastic Education in Late Antiquity: The Transformation of Classical Paideia*. Cambridge.
Runia, David T. 2016. *Ancient Doxography*. New York.
Russell, Donald Andrew. 1996. *Libanius: Imaginary Speeches: A Selection of Declamations*. London.
Russell, Donald Andrew, and Nigel Guy Wilson, eds. 1981. *Menander Rhetor*. Oxford.
Sacks, Oliver. 2015. *On the Move: A Life*. New York.
Saffrey, Henri Dominique. 1982. "Pourquoi Porphyre a-t-il édité Plotin. Réponse provisoire." In Brisson 1982, 2:33–64.
Salles, Ricardo, ed. 2005. *Metaphysics, Soul, and Ethics in Ancient Thought: Themes from the Work of Richard Sorabji*. Oxford.
Sandys, Gerald N. 1997. *The Greek World of Apuleius: Apuleius and the Second Sophistic*. Leiden.
Scaltsas, Theodore, and Andrew S. Mason, eds. 2007. *The Philosophy of Epictetus*. Oxford.
Scheck, Thomas T., ed. 2010. *St. Jerome's Commentaries on Galatians, Titus, and Philemon*. Notre Dame.
Schenkeveld, Dirk Marie. 1991. "Figures and Tropes: A Border Case between Grammar and Rhetoric." In *Rhetorik zwischen den Wissenschaften: Geschichte, System, Praxis als Probleme des "Historischen Wörterbuchs der Rhetorik,"* edited by Gert Ueding, 149–57. Berlin.
———. 1993. "Scholarship and Grammar." In Reverdin and Grange 1993: 263–301.
Schenkl, Heinrich, ed. 1916. *Epicteti Dissertationes ab Arriano digestae*. 2nd ed. Leipzig.
Schlumberger, Jörg. 1972–74. "Non scribo sed dicto (HA, T 33, 8): Hat der Autor der Historia Augusta mit Stenographen gearbeitet?" In Alföldy and Straub 1972–74: 221–38.

Schoeler, Gregor. 2010. *The Oral and the Written in Early Islam*. London.

Schofield, Malcolm. 2007. "Epictetus on Cynicism." In Scaltsas and Mason 2007: 71–86.

Schulz, Fritz. 1946. *History of Roman Legal Science*. Oxford.

Schwartz, Eduard, and Theodore Mommsen, eds. 1999. *Die Kirchengeschichte*. 2nd ed. Vol. 2. Berlin.

Sedley, David Neil, ed. 2006. *The Cambridge Companion to Greek and Roman Philosophy*. Cambridge.

Seiler, Hanspeter. 2013. "Eine erneute Revision des die Platonische Hochzeitszahl betreffenden Papyrus Oxyrhynchos 1808." *ZPE* 185:63–81.

Sellars, John. 2014. *Stoicism*. Hoboken, NJ.

———. 2021. *Marcus Aurelius*. London.

Setaioli, Aldo. 2013. "Philosophy as Therapy, Self-Transformation, and 'Lebensform.'" In Damschen and Heil 2013: 239–56.

Sharples, Robert W., trans. 2014. *Alexander of Aphrodisias Quaestiones*. 2.16–315. London.

———. 2016. "The School of Alexander?" In Sorabji 2016a: 89–118.

Shields, Christopher John. 2014. *Aristotle*. In "Aristotle: Life and Works," 8–42. London.

Sider, David. 1997. *The Epigrams of Philodemus: Introduction, Text, and Commentary*. Oxford.

———. 2005. *The Library of the Villa dei papiri at Herculaneum*. Los Angeles.

Smith, Robert R. R. 1990. "Late Roman Philosopher Portraits from Aphrodisias." *JRS* 80:127–55.

Snyder, H. Greg. 2000. *Teachers and Texts in the Ancient World: Philosophers, Jews, and Christians*. London.

———, ed. 2020. *Christian Teachers in Second-Century Rome: Schools and Students in the Ancient City*. Leiden.

Solomon, Robert C., ed. 2004. *Thinking about Feeling: Contemporary Philosophers on Emotions*. Oxford.

Sonnino, Maurizio. 2014. "Comedy outside the Canon: From Ritual Slapstick to Hellenistic Mime." In Colesanti and Giordano 2014: 128–50.

Souilhé, Joseph. 1948. *Épictète: Entretiens*. Paris.

Sorabji, Richard. 1994. *Philoponus: On Aristotle Physics 5–8 with Simplicius on Aristotle on the Void, Ancient Commentators on Aristotle, Phys.* 7. Translated by P. Lettinck and J. O. Urmson. 771.21–772.3. London.

———. 2000. *Emotion and Peace of Mind: From Stoic Agitation to Christian Temptation*. Oxford.

———, ed. 2010. *Philoponus and the Rejection of Aristotelian Science*. 2nd ed. London.

———. 2014a. *Moral Conscience through the Ages: Fifth Century BCE to the Present*. Chicago.

———, ed. 2014b. *Philoponus on Aristotle Physics 5–8 and Simplicius on Aristotle on the Void, Ancient Commentators on Aristotle, Phys.* 7. Translated from Arabic by P. Lettinck and J. O. Urmson. London.

———, ed. 2016a. *Aristotle Transformed: The Ancient Commentators and Their Influence*. 2nd ed. London.

———, ed. 2016b. *Aristotle Re-Interpreted: New Findings on Seven Hundred Years of the Ancient Commentators*. London.
———. 2016c. "The Ancient Commentators on Aristotle." In Sorabji 2016a: 1–34.
———. 2016d. "Dating of Philoponus' Commentaries on Aristotle and of His Divergence from His Teacher Ammonius." In Sorabji 2016b: 367–92.
Spinelli, Emidio, and Francesco Verde. 2020. "Theology." In Mitsis 2020: 94–117.
Stadter, Philip A. 1980. *Arrian of Nicomedia*. Chapel Hill.
———. 1989. *A Commentary on Plutarch's Pericles*. Chapel Hill.
———. 2014. "Plutarch Compositional Technique: The Anecdote Collections and The Parallel Lives." *GRBS* 54:665–86.
Stefaniw, Blossom. 2018. "The School of Didymus the Blind in Light of the Tura Find." In Rubenson and Larsen 2018: 153–81.
———. 2019. *Christian Reading: Language, Ethics, and the Order of Things*. Oakland, CA.
Stellwag, H. W. F., ed. 1933. *Epictetus Het Eerste Boek der Diatriben*. Amsterdam.
Stenger, Jan R. 2009. *Hellenische Identität in der Spätantike. Pagane autoren und ihr Unbehagen an der eigenen Zeit*. Berlin.
———, ed. 2019. *Learning Cities in Late Antiquity: The Local Dimension of Education*. London.
———. 2022. *Education in Late Antiquity: Challenges, Dynamism, and Reinterpretation, 300–550 CE*. Oxford.
Suits, David B. 2020. *Epicurus and the Singularity of Death: Defending Radical Epicureanism*. London.
Summers, Walter Coventry, ed. 1910. *Select Letters of Seneca*. London.
Swain, Simon. 1991. "The Reliability of Philostratus' Lives of the Sophists." *CA* 10.1:148–63.
———. 1996. *Hellenism and Empire*. Oxford.
Tarrant, Harold. 1999. "Observations on the Text of Olympiodorus *on Plato's Gorgias*." *Mnemosyne* 52:23–40.
te Heesen, Anke, and Emma C. Spary, eds. 2001. *Sammeln als Wissen: Das Sammeln und seine wissenschaftsgeschichtliche Bedeutung*. Göttingen.
Teitler, Hans C. 1985. *Notarii and Exceptores: An Inquiry into Role and Significance of Shorthand Writers in the Imperial and Ecclesiastical Bureaucracy of the Roman Empire (From the Early Principate to c. 450 A.D)*. Amsterdam.
———. 1990. "Notae und Notarii: Tachygraphie und Tachygraphen im 5. und 6. Jahrhundert." In Ganz 1990: 3–13.
———. 2007. "Kurzschrift." *RAC* 22:518–45.
Theocharidis, Georgios J. 1940. *Beiträge zur Geschichte des byzantinischen Profantheaters im IV und V Jahrhundert, hauptsächlich auf Grund der Predigten des Johannes Chrysostomos Patriarchen von Konstantinopel*. Thessaloniki.
Too, Yun Lee, ed. 2001. *Education in Greek and Roman Antiquity*. Leiden.
Torallas Tovar, Sofía, and Klaas A. Worp. 2006. *To the Origins of Greek Stenography*. Barcelona.
Trapp, Michael B. 1997. *Maximus of Tyre: The Philosophical Orations*. Oxford.
———. 2007. *Philosophy in the Roman Empire: Ethics, Politics, and Society*. London.

Tsouna, Voula. 2007. *The Ethics of Philodemus*. Oxford.
van den Hoek, Annewies. 1996. "Techniques of Quotation in Clement of Alexandria: A View of Ancient Literary Working Methods." *Vigiliae Christianae* 50:223–43.
———. 1997. "The Catechetical School of Early Christian Alexandria and Its Philonic Heritage." *Harvard Theological Review* 90:59–87.
van den Hout, Michel P. J. 1999. *A Commentary on the Letters of M. Cornelius Fronto*. Leiden.
Van Hoof, Lieve. 2013. "Performing Paideia: Greek Culture as an Instrument for Social Promotion in the Fourth Century AD." *CQ* 63.1:387–406.
van Minnen, Peter. 2002. "The Letters and Other Papers of Ammon: Panopolis in the Fourth Century." In Egberts et al. 2002: 177–99.
Van Nuffelen, Peter. 2020. "The Christian Reception of Julian." In Wiemer and Rebenich 2020: 360–97.
Verrycken, Koenraad. 2016a. "The Development of Philoponus' Thought and Its Chronology." In Sorabji 2016a: 251–94.
———. 2016b. "The Metaphysics of Ammonius Son of Hermeias." In Sorabji 2016a: 215–50.
Volgers, Annelie, and Claudio Zamagni. 2004. *Erotapokriseis: Early Christian Question-and-Answer Literature in Context*. Leuven.
von Arnim, Hans Friedrich August. 1898. *Leben und Werke des Dion von Prusa. Sophistik, Rhetorik, Philosophie in ihrem Kampf und die Jugendbildung*. Berlin.
———. (1903) 2004. *Stoicorum Veterum Fragmenta*. Vol. 2. Leipzig. Reprint, Munich.
Vössing, Konrad. 2020. "The Value of a Good Education: The School Law in Context." In Wiemer and Rebenich 2020: 172–206.
Waterfield, Robin. 2022. *Epictetus' Complete Works: Handbook, Discourses, and Fragments*. Chicago.
Watts, Edward J. 2006. *City and School in Late Antique Athens and Alexandria*. Berkeley.
———. 2010. *Riot in Alexandria: Tradition and Group Dynamics in Late Antique Pagan and Christian Communities*. Berkeley.
Webb, Ruth. 2001. "The *Progymnasmata* as Practice." In Too 2001: 289–316.
———. 2008. *Demons and Dancers: Performance in Late Antiquity*. Cambridge.
———. 2018. "Attitudes towards Tragedy from the Second Sophistic to Late Antiquity." In Liapes and Petrides 2018: 297–323.
Wehner, Barbara. 2000. *Die Funktion der Dialogstruktur in Epiktets Diatriben*. Stuttgart.
Westerink, Leendert Gerrit, ed. 1956. *Olympiodorus: Commentary on the First Alcibiades of Plato*. Amsterdam.
———. 2016. "The Alexandrian Commentators and the Introductions to Their Commentaries." In Sorabji 2016a: 349–76.
White, Michael L. 2004. "A Measure of Parrhesia: The State of the Manuscript of *P.Herc.* 1471." In Fitzgerald et al. 2004: 103–30.
———. 2009. "Ordering the Fragments of *P.Herc.* 1471: A New Hypothesis." *Cronache Ercolanesi* 39:29–70.
Wiemer, Hans-Ulrich, and Stefan Rebenich, eds. 2020. *A Companion to Julian the Apostate*. Leiden.

Wildberg, Christian. 2005. "Philosophy in the Age of Justinian." In Maas 2005: 316–40.
Williams, Megan Hale. 2006. *The Monk and the Book: Jerome and the Making of Christian Scholarship*. Chicago.
Willis, William H. 1978. "Two Literary Papyri in an Archive from Panopolis." *Illinois Classical Studies* 3:140–53.
Willis, William H., and Tiziano Dorandi. 1989. "Lista di scolarchi." P.Duk inv.178." *Corpus dei Papiri Filosofici*. I 1. Florence. 81–84.
Wilson, Peter. 2007. *The Greek Theaters and Festivals: Documentary Studies*. Oxford.
Winsbury, Rex. 2009. *The Roman Book*. London.
Wirth, Theo. 1967. "Arrians Erinnerungen an Epiktet." *MH* 24:149–89.
Wiseman, Timothy Peter. 2008. "'Mime' and 'Pantomime': Some Problematic Texts." In Hall and Wyles 2008: 146–57.
Wolfsdorf, David Conan. 2020. *Early Greek Ethics*. Oxford.
Wouters, Alfons. 1979. *The Grammatical Papyri from Graeco-Roman Egypt: Contributions to the Study of the "Ars Grammatica" in Antiquity*. Brussels.
———. 1995. "The Grammatical Papyri and the *Techne Grammatike* of Dionysius Thrax." In Law and Sluiter 1995: 95–109.
Xenophontos, Sophia. 2013. "Imagery and Education in Plutarch." *CP* 108.2:126–38.
———. 2016. *Ethical Education in Plutarch: Moralizing Agents and Context*. Berlin.
Yaeczko, Lionel. 2021. *Ausonius Grammaticus, the Christening of Philology in the Late Roman West*. Piscataway, NJ.
Yates, Frances Amelia. 1966. *The Art of Memory*. Chicago.
Zanker, Paul. 1995. *The Mask of Socrates: The Image of the Intellectual in Antiquity*. Berkeley.
Zetzel, James. 1980. "The Subscriptions in the Manuscripts of Livy and Fronto and the Meaning of Emendation." *CP* 76:38–59.
———. 2018. *Critics, Compilers, and Commentators: An Introduction to Roman Philology, 200 BCE–800 CE*. Oxford.

Index

abbreviations used in notetaking, 93–94, 93n21
Achilles, 144n119, 148, 150, 153, 155–57, 159
Adrian's Introduction to the Sacred Scriptures: An Antiochene Handbook for Textual Interpretation, 218–19
Aedesia, 228
Aedesius, 103
Aelius Aristides, 214, 237
Aeschylus, 39
Agamemnon, 128, 147, 153, 155–57, 159
Albinus of Smyrna, 62; *Introduction to Plato's Dialogues*, 62; *Sketch of Platonic Doctrines*, 20n12, 62
Alcibiades, 32n65, 53, 162, 228, 232–44
Alexander (sophist), 71
Alexander the Great, 11, 87n2
Alexander of Aphrodisias, 58–59, 134n70, 135
Alexandria: catechetical school in, 212–13, 223; classroom configuration in, 233–34, 233n24; Didymus's school in, 161, 204, 205–6; history of school of philosophy in, 228–29; Kom el-Dikka classrooms, 98n36, 99, 206, 233; Olympiodorus (fifth century) teacher in, 92; Olympiodorus (sixth century) teacher in, 135, 228; Origen's school in, 213; philosophers and scholars in, 65, 164–66, 169; Plotinus attending school in, 65; teaching of rhetoric in, 211
allegories, Homer's works treated as, 146–47
alphabetical order, 22
Alypius, 63
Amelius, 62, 66–67, 231
Ammon, 32
Ammonius, 20, 59, 65, 176, 221, 228–29, 231
Amphilochius of Iconium, 204

Andocides, 74n26
annotations. *See* notes and annotations (*notae*)
Anonymous Londiniensis, 33
Antioch: Christian schools in, 219; Libanius's school in, 98n30, 99, 99n41, 99n45, 104, 118n1, 134n73, 188n55, 205, 207, 211
Antiphanes, 26n42
Antisthenes, 29, 109n97
Antony's encounter with Didymus, 206, 206n24
Aphthonius, 235
Apollonides, 184
Apollonius of Perga, 94
Apollonius of Rhodes: *Argonautica*, 169
Apollonius of Tyana, 60–61, 71
Archimedes, 94
Aristarchus, 166, 166n10
Aristides, 34, 35, 133, 141
Aristophanes, 111, 168; *Acharnians*, 242; *Clouds*, 85n17, 102n61
Aristotelian school, 47–57; teachers lecturing from their notes, 68
Aristotle, 10, 47–57; addressing mature students who possessed *phronesis*, 53; commentaries on, 176, 227; compared with works of late antiquity's Platonists and Aristotelians, 59; Didymus teaching from, 217, 220; editing and revising earlier lectures, 54–55; free classes given by, 48n4; inconsistencies in works of, 59; lectures of, 4; mistakes in works of, 52–53, 57, 240; Olympiodorus and, 59, 234; *paradeigmata* (examples) used in philosophy by, 143; personal notes of, 49–50; personal voice difficult to identify in commentaries on, 5; Plato using logic of, 62; speed of speaking, 51–52; students recording treatises

271

INDEX

Aristotle (*continued*)
of, 2, 48–50, 53; works divided into exoteric and esoteric, 48; writing style of, 52. *See also* School of Aristotle
Aristotle, works of: *Athenaion Politeia*, 243; *Eudemian Ethics*, 50; *Metaphysics*, 48, 49, 54; *Nicomachean Ethics*, 50–51; *Problems*, 55–57; *Protrepticus*, 51; *Rhetoric*, 143
Arns, Paulo Evaristo, 73n17
Arrian (Lucius Flavius Arrianus): abbreviations used when notetaking, 93–94; Attic as language of works of, 90, 96; classroom of Epictetus described by, 121–23, 159, 209, 247–49; compared to Didymus, 224; dissemination of texts without assent, 94–95, 174; Epictetus' character revealed through, 159; Epictetus' curriculum not fully revealed in notes of, 134; Homer references in work of, 237; life of, 87; memory and, 28; stenographers, use of, 11, 92; stenography, use of, 11, 74, 89; as student of philosophy, 2, 87, 129. *See also Discourses* (Epictetus) *for work created from his student notes*
ascetism, 206
Asclepiades, 40
Asclepius, 228, 229n7
askesis (spiritual exercises), 5, 140–42
Athanasius, 206, 212; *Vita Antoni*, 202
Athens: Epicurean school in, 171–72, 175, 180, 184; Zeno's school in, 175–76
athletes, imagery of, 85, 133, 141–43, 160
Attic language, 90, 90n8, 96
Aubenque, Pierre, 54
Augustan Age, commentaries written during, 166
Augustine: marginalia of, 8, 18, 73n18; stenographers and scribes, use of, 36, 73, 77n40; works circulating without approval of, 94
Augustine, works of: *Adnotationes in Iob*, 37; *Explanation of the Epistle of James*, 37; *On the Trinity*, 73; *Retractationes*, 36–37
Avenarius, Gert, 26n40

Barnes, Jonathan, 50, 136
Basil of Caesarea, 71, 73; *Address to Young Men on Greek Literature*, 38
Bayliss, Grant, 222
Bénatouïl, Thomas, 141
Beresford, Adam, 50, 52

Bible, commentaries on, 78, 163, 164, 169, 176, 203, 206–9, 217, 222, 225. *See also* Didymus the Blind *for commentaries on Ecclesiastes and Psalms*
Bienert, Wolfgang, 222
Blair, Ann, 18, 23n25
Blank, David, 175
Blumell, Lincoln H., 222
Boethus, 72
Bonhöffer, Adolf, 82
books and texts: circulating prematurely or without authors' approval, 94–95, 95n26, 174, 229, 231, 244; cost of, 135; Epictetus finding inferior to *viva vox* teaching, 129–36, 138; in late antiquity becoming of prime importance, 161; notes as basis of, 29, 58–59, 64, 68; strategies for writing from notes, 23–27; what constitutes, 13. *See also* commentaries; *specific authors*
Borges, Cassandra, and C. Michael Sampson, 39n7
Bowersock, Glen Warren, 124n27
Brakke, David, 202n6
Briseis, 155–56
Bromius (Zeno's student), 172

Caesarea Maritima, Origen's school in, 213
Carneades, 61
Cassius Severus, 44
Cavallo, Guglielmo, 174–77
chalinos (tongue-twister exercise), 39
Christians and early Christianity: accepting Olympians in literary context, 203; Adrian's exegesis of Christian texts, 218–19; ascetism and, 206; Didymus's commentaries and teaching of, 204–9, 212; educational development of, 201–2; Homer used as exegesis model, 219; illiteracy of charismatic figures, 202; Julian's ostracizing, 203–4; levels of teaching, 208–13; on moral conscience, 197; Origen's teaching of, 212–13; similarities to Greek grammarians and rhetors, 218; stenographers at Christological conferences, 74, 77; syncretism of beliefs, 203–4
Chroust, Anton, 47
Chryseis, 155–56
Chrysippus: depiction of, 107, 115n133; Epictetus on, 137–38; on Homer, 147;

purpose of philosophical instruction for, 4, 5–6; students, relationship with, 108, 115; on syllogisms, 217; texts ascribed to, 134

Cicero, 20, 45, 76n33, 188n55, 210; *In Pisonem*, 170

classical education (paideia), 200–204; change from argumentation to authoritative texts, 4; city as location of advanced learning, 210; as easy pray for Christian Church, 201; endurance and spread of, 200–201; in late antiquity, 201; limited group of texts used in, 138, 200; models used for writing and style, 221; Olympiodorus's teaching of, 3, 210, 237; Philodemus's knowledge of, 196–97; in philosophy, 3, 210, 245; shortcomings of, 200; sophists on, 140; students of philosophy having prior education in, 129–30, 132, 137–38, 144, 158, 232. *See also* students; *specific teachers and their schools*

Cleanthes, 134

Clement of Alexandria, 19–20; *Stromateis*, 19

Codex Theodosianus, 203

Colardeau, Théodore, 90, 100n48, 114, 122n20

comedies, 154

commentaries, 163–69; grammatical, 164–66; *hypomnematikon* as title of, 176; name of commentator concealed, 167; popularity of, 138; purpose of writing, 166; textual, 166–67; use of term, 20–21, 22, 208n30. *See also specific authors*

Conference of Carthage (411), 74

Constantius II (Roman emperor), 77

Cooper, John M., 5n6

Costa, Cosimo, 124n26

Crouzel, Henri, 212

Cynics and Cynic philosophy: Epictetus's *Discourses* associated with, 81, 126–28; Homer and, 148n138; *parrhesia* connected with, 180; *Problemata* in works of, 55; theater metaphors, use of, 153; unkempt appearance and, 85n16

Damascius, 63n57

Damis of Nineveh, 60–61

Delattre, Daniel, 173, 182

Demandt, Alexander: *History of the Empire* published from Mommsen's notes, 1–2, 4, 246

Demosthenes, 8, 39, 168, 237

Desideri, Paolo, 35n81

dialogues: as art of daily instruction, 4; Epictetus's use of, 11, 122–24, 159; Musonius rarely using, 121–22; philosophers' use of, 4

Dicaearchus, 98

Dickey, Eleanor, 166

dictation, 3, 35–36, 65, 71–73, 158, 240. *See also* stenographers

Didymus Chalcenterus, 166

Didymus the Blind: appropriation of traditional education by, 201, 202; Aristotle as influence on, 217, 220; background of, 204–5; Bible commentaries by, 163, 164, 169, 176, 203, 206–9, 216–17, 222, 225, 233; catechetical role of, 212; as Christian intellectual, 204–7; classes structured like Greek philosophical schools, 208–9, 208n28; class size, 212; compared to Adria, 219; compared to Arrian, 224; compared to Epictetus, 216, 220, 226; compared to Olympiodorus, 233, 243; curriculum of, 216–17; Ecclesiastes commentary, 78, 206–9, 222–25, 233; as grammarian, 214–17; memory of students of, 28; notes and notetakers of, 3, 10, 51, 64, 162, 230, 248–49; Origen and, 205; Psalms commentary, 78, 206–9, 216, 222–24, 225, 233; school of, as Christian group meeting, 206; spaces in work suggesting students as writers, 225; stenographers and, 70, 222–26; teaching style of, 221–22; texts as conglomeration of notes, 219–22; Tura papyri and, 161

Didymus the Blind, works of: *Against Celsus*, 206; *On First Principles*, 206

Diels, Hermann, 33

diminutives, use of, 119, 127, 136, 139–40, 157n169, 158, 216

Dio Chrysostom: antithesis form of argument used by, 125; as champion of rhetoric, 119, 123; on dictation, 73n16; Homer and, 139, 148; Musonius as teacher of, 91, 91n13, 119n2; on mythological themes in theater,

Dio Chrysostom (*continued*)
154; notes, use of, 35n81; *Oration* 11 (*The Trojan Discourse*), 139, 154, 229, 238n39; on schools of philosophy, 98
Diocletian (Roman emperor): *Edict of Maximum Prices*, 76
Diodorus Siculus, 94
Diogenes Laertius (Diogenes the Cynic): on Antisthenes and loss of notes, 29; citing older doxographical texts, 9; Epictetus and, 113, 124, 126–28, 216, 220, 226; impersonation of, 128; Pamphila references in, 31; on School of Aristotle, 47; on Socrates as prolific writer, 136; Stoics and, 81n3; on Theophrastus's students, 53; on Timon's writing habits, 26–27, 26n42; on Zeno's interpretation of Homer, 147
Dionysius of Halicarnassus: *Opuscula*, 8
Dionysius of Miletus, students of, 41
Dionysius Thrax, 164, 215n60
Discourses (Epictetus): ancient deities in, 202; Arian's notes used for, 3, 5, 11, 51, 80, 86, 87–93, 95, 97, 99, 108, 123, 134, 157–60, 219, 247; Arian's lack of interest in student questions evident in, 209, 226, 243, 247–48; Arian's letter to Lucius Gellius as preface to, 88–89, 91, 94–97, 158, 159, 180, 195; Arian's use of abbreviations when notetaking, 93–94; athletes, imagery of, 85, 133, 141–43, 160; behavioral guidance offered by, 82–84; on books as inferior to live teaching, 129–36, 138; on Chrysippus, 137–38; classroom depiction in, 121–23, 159, 209, 247–49; compared to Didymus, 216, 220, 226; compared to Libanius, 207; compared to Musonius, 91, 96, 122; on the Cynic, 81, 126–28; dialogues used in, 11, 122–24, 159; as *diatribai*, 81; diminutives, use of, 119, 127, 136, 139–40, 157n169, 158, 216; on ethics, 81, 83, 105, 116, 132, 138, 147, 159, 201; excerpts from, 79–80; on father-son relations, 102–4; on faulty judgment as cause of mistakes, 143; on Homer, 111–12, 125n33, 128, 147–51, 155, 157, 158, 237–38; humor in, 85, 100, 111, 116n139, 140, 142, 157; on "impressions" from history and myth, 142–46, 153; on logic, 136–37; Marcus Aurelius on, 20; on moral conscience, 197, 201; myths, use of, 146–52, 158; *onoma*, change in meaning of, 140; on *parrhesia*, 88–89, 180; questions in class, 209, 243, 247–48; on reason as guide, 146; refutation by, 139–42; on rhetoric and rhetorical schools, 118–29, 131; scholars debating authorship of, 90–91, 97; shipwreck, imagery of, 143; spiritual progress as goal of lectures, 5, 81, 83; Stoics and, 11, 80–82, 108, 116, 123, 129, 197, 216, 238; student-philosopher relationship, 193; students at Epictetus's school, 99–101, 104–17, 144, 216, 232; on teaching responsibilities, 105–7; on theater, 152–57; titles of essays in, 95–97, 95n29; *To One of Those Whom He Did Not Consider Worthy* (book 2, section 24), 111–12; volumes surviving from original eight, 80; on wars, 150; Xenophon as influence on, 90. *See also* Arrian *for notes used to write*

Dobbin, Robert F., 91, 123n23, 127n41, 130n52
Dodds, Eric Robertson, 239
Donatus, Aelius: *Life of Vergil*, 34
Donini, Pierluigi, 59
Dorandi, Tiziano, 22n20, 175
doxography, 9
Düring, Ingemar, 49–50
dysgraphia, 65, 65n66

early Christianity. *See* Christians and early Christianity
Ecclesiastes, 78, 206–9, 222–25, 233
Eddy, Matthew, 68
Edwards, Michael, 66n70
Egypt: Dakhla Oasis's Greek school, 203, 211–12; private teachers (*kathegetai*), 211–12; Tura papyri, 161, 207–9, 215, 219–20, 222. *See also* Alexandria
emotions, 107–17
encomium, writing of, 235
Ennius, 210
Epaphroditus, 80
Epictetus: analogy of medicine with philosophy, 109, 194–95; books lacking in intrinsic value for, 138; choosing to lecture and not to write, 63–64; class structure of, 208n28; compared to Libanius, 207; compared to Olympiodorus, 97, 243; compared to Seneca the Elder, 109; compared to Socrates, 85, 109, 114; Didymus

INDEX 275

and, 113, 124, 126–28, 216, 220, 226; on ethics, theology, and freedom, 83; frankness of, 86, 89, 114, 180; God's importance for, 112, 202, 203n9; histories held in low regard by, 130, 165; Koine as language of works of, 90, 96; life of, 80; on moral conscience, 197, 201; Musonius as teacher of, 91, 110, 111, 114n124, 136; no writings extant of, 86; Olympiodorus citing, 238–39; overlooked among the Stoics, 97–98; overview of, 82–86; Philodemus echoing, 191; philosophical instruction's purpose for, 5n5, 51, 83, 85, 132, 136, 141, 182, 193; Plato and, 124, 129, 137, 151; practicality of, 83; *Problemata* and, 55; promoting philosophical training, 98; reputation and popularity of, 82, 85; at School of Aristotle, 47; self-deprecation of, 79, 83, 109; Socrates and, 83, 85, 109, 114, 124, 139, 143n115, 151; stenographers vs. students as recorders of, 10–11; on study of philosophy, 51, 193; teaching responsibilities of, 105–7; Theosebius as scholar on, 64. *See also* Arrian; *Discourses*; Epirus, Epictetus's school in

Epictetus, works of: *Categories*, 20; *Encheiridion (Handbook)*, 80, 146, 238; *On Freedom*, 126. *See also Discourses*

Epicureans and Epicureanism: consulting other schools of philosophy not allowed by, 196; flattery condemned by, 194; isolation of Epicurean community, 188; moral conscience as focus of, 179, 183; moral education devised by, 182; *parrhesia* as unique to, 196; school in Athens, 171–72, 175, 180, 184; school in Naples, 161, 171, 180, 184; on sickness of the soul, 192–99. *See also* Philodemus of Gadara

Epicurus, 171, 181, 183–84, 193, 197; Philodemus and, 172, 198–99

epideixeis, 10, 45, 46, 124, 175

Epiphanius of Salamis, 36

Epirus, Epictetus's school in, 11, 80, 87–117; books possibly used in classes, 134; choice of location, 98; classroom interaction with students, 123n25, 124–25; curriculum of, 134; distinguished from schools teaching rhetoric, 118–19; students, relationship with, 11, 66, 80, 99–101, 104–5, 108–17, 188; students residing in Epirus for rest of their lives, 205; teaching divided into two daily portions, 49n10

Eros (Vergil's secretary), 34

Erotapokriseis, 55

Essler, Holger, 174

ethics: in Christian education, 201; in educational curriculum of Greek philosophers, 201; Epictetus and, 81, 83, 105, 116, 132, 138, 147, 159, 201; Philodemus's works on, 171, 172, 182; Stoics on, 5, 132n62; works on

ethopoiia, 103, 127–28

Euclid, 29, 229

Eudemus of Rhodes, 50

Eumenius, 66

Eunapius of Sardis, 20, 44n26, 63, 103

Euripides, 40, 168, 238; works of: *Atreus*, 153; *Hippolytus*, 153, 238, 239; *Hypsipyle*, 169; *Medea*, 153; *Orestes*, 238

Eusebius of Caesarea, 24n28, 66n70, 212–13, 224n89

Eustathius of Thessalonica, 148

Eustochius, 66

Evagrius, 205

excerptors, role of, 17, 17n2

father-son relations, 102–4, 104n72, 111, 111n115

Favorinus of Arles, 32, 153; *Memorabilia*, 32; *Notebooks*, 32

Foat, F. G. W., 93

food compared to culture and vomiting of knowledge, 54, 106, 133–34, 185n46

Foucault, Michel, 7

frank criticism. *See parrhesia*

French scholarship, notes as focus in, 18

Fronto, Marcus Cornelius, 119n2, 124, 210–11

Gaius, 20n12, 62

Galen: Albinus of Smyrna as teacher of, 62; on Aristotle, 51–52; on Carneades's students, 61–62; on Hippocrates, 21, 22n17, 174; Homer and, 148n135; *hypographai*, used for set of notes, 20n12, 21; *hypomnema*, used for monograph, 21; language choice of, 90n8; lectures and scientific demonstrations of, 4, 59; marginalia by, 8, 18, 36; opposed to publications

Galen (*continued*)
circulating without his approval, 4, 94, 95n26; stenographers and, 72
Galen, works of: *On Fallacies*, 51; *Peri alypesias*, 146
Gallus, 27
Gellius, Aulus, 19, 30–32, 68, 120, 164, 236; *Noctes Atticae*, 30
Gellius, Lucius, 88–89, 88n3, 91, 94–97, 158, 159, 180
Genesis, commentary on, 207
Genesius, Saint, 73
genetic criticism, 7, 7n14, 54
Genette, Gerard, 17, 17n1
Gera, Deborah Levine, 33n73
German students in early modernity, using *Schreibechor* as notetaking technique, 68
Gibson, Craig, 166
Gill, Christopher, 108n91
God: Epictetus identifying Zeus with, 202–3; favoring those who appreciate their good fortune, 100; fourth-century Egyptian school mentioning, 203; Olympiodorus on, 237; Stoics' view of, 112; teachers of philosophy endowed by, 106; virtuous life owed to, 112–13
Goulet-Cazé, Marie-Odile, 66
grammateia (writing on wooden tablets), 21
grammatical commentaries, 164–66
Greek language, evolution of, 239–40
Greek writers as focus of study, 8–9

Hadot, Ilsetraut, 90
Hadot, Pierre, 5n6, 6, 103, 201
hand gestures of orators, 45
handwriting: late antiquity, professional writing hands in, 73; in Philodemus's works, 40, 176–77; Plotinus's dysgraphia, 65, 65n66; of students, 169. *See also* scribes
Hartmann, Karl, 89–90
Hellweg, Rainer, 22n18
Hensel, Paul, 2
Hensel, Sebastian, 2
Heracleides, 183–84
Heracles, 79, 151, 153, 198
Heraklas (student of Origen), 213
Herculaneum, 170, 172
Hermeneumata (bilingual Greek and Latin handbooks), 76–77
Hermogenes of Tarsus, 125, 147
Hermotimus, as student in Lucian's work, 60
Herodes Atticus, 71
Hershbell, Jackson, 97
Hesychius's *Lexicon*, 39, 77n41
Hierocles's lectures on the *Gorgias*, 64, 230
Hippias, 139
Hippocrates, 21, 22n17, 56, 139n95, 174
Holland, Glenn, 180
Homer: in ancient education, 138, 146–49, 237–38; Aristotle's mistakes in citing and quoting, 52–53; Christian exegesis modeled after interpretation of, 219; Cynics and, 148n138; Dio disputing reverence of, 139; Epictetus's references to, 111–12, 125n33, 128, 147–48, 155, 157, 158, 237–38; extracts from (*P.Yale* II 135), 39; first books most thoroughly studied, 239; grammatical instruction using, 165; Libanius's students studying, 211; Lucian's references to, 60; marginalia to, 168; medical analogy in, 193; models to teach students grammar from, 225; Olympiodorus's references to, 237–38; Philodemus's *Peri Parrhesias* references to, 198; Plato's references to, 235, 237; standardization of, 166; Stoics' references to, 146–48; traditional paideia on, 204
Homer, works of: *Iliad*, 41, 138–39, 147–50, 169, 216, 238; *Odyssey*, 40–41, 138–39, 147–49, 151, 238, 243
horses and horse races, analogies to, 83, 100–101, 112, 142, 186–87
Hutchinson, D. S., 51
Hyginus: *Fabulae*, 33
hypomnema: meaning of term, 20–21, 174; as postscripts, 21
hypomnemata, 166–67; abbreviations, use of, 93; Aristides and, 34; Aristotle and, 50; Chrysippus's student and, 5; Euclid and, 29; Hermotimus and, 60; Lucian and, 26; meaning of term, 20–22, 25n35; Philodemus of Gadara and, 163; Plutarch and, 20, 25–26; *scholia* distinguished from, 167
hypomnematica, 20
hypomnematikon, 163, 174–76; intended for limited circulation, 175; Philodemus's *On Rhetoric* and, 175–76; used as title for commentaries, 176

Iamblichus of Chalcis, 51, 61–63, 65, 246; *Life of Pythagoras*, 61
imperial period: commentaries written during, 166; education's development in, 200; Mommsen intending to write history of, 1–2, 246–47; notetaking as common educational practice in, 68
indexing, 22–23, 30
Inwood, Brad, 58
Isidorus, 63n57, 180
Islamic historians, storage of annotations by, 23
Isocrates, 47

Jackson, Henry, 48
Jacobs, C. F., 56
Jaeger, Werner, 49
Jerome (of Stridon): annotating letter of Epiphanius of Salamis, 36; on Didymus and Antony encounter, 206; as Didymus's student, 215; stenographers used by, 73, 74
Jews: conflicts with Syrians, Egyptians, and Romans, 155; as visitors to philosophical schools, 100
Job (biblical), 220–21, 230
John Chrysostom, 154, 204, 218
Johnson, Monte Ransome, 51
Jouanna, Jacques, 22, 22n18
Julian (Roman emperor), 23n23, 77, 203–4
Justinian (Roman emperor), 205, 228

Kaster, Robert, 164, 214
Kehl, Aloys, 224n89
Knauber, Adolf, 212
Koine language, 90, 90n8, 96, 159
Kom el-Dikka classrooms (Alexandria), 98n36, 99, 206, 233

Lampriskos, 113n123
late antiquity: annotation becoming common in, 167; Aristotle compared to works of Platonists and Aristotelians in, 59; classical education in, 201; fluidity of ancient education in, 161, 164; notetaking as common educational practice in, 68; Platonic school in, 64–65; professional writing hands in, 73; rarity of actual examples of notes from, 69, 230; stenographers in, 71, 76; traditional literary culture in, 202, 237

Laterculi Alexandrini, 33
Layton, Richard, 205, 220, 222
lectures: memory of, requiring notes, 63; published accounts of, 236; repeated with variations, 53–55, 64; some philosophers choosing to only lecture instead of writing, 61; students recording in notes, 61–62. *See also specific philosophers and notetakers*
legal cases, 45, 75n30
Leonardo da Vinci's notebooks, 9
Lewis, Naphtali, 76, 76n33
Libanius: antithesis form of argument used by, 125; books used by students of, 135; compared to Epictetus, 207; encomium, writing of, 235; on *grammatistes* (or *grammaticus*), 214; Greek cultural heritage and Christianity of, 204; handwritten speeches by, 3n4; on Homer, 148; letters revealing school environment, 248; memorizing speeches of, 42; notes, used while declaiming, 45–46; parents of students and, 103n65, 188n55; questions during lectures by, 209; rhetoric as exclusive focus of, 211; on rhetors who vomit forth knowledge, 133–34; school in Antioch, 99, 99n41, 99n45, 118n1, 134n73, 205, 207, 211; stenography and, 72n5; on storage and retrieval of notes, 23; on student discipline and punishment, 190, 190n63; students and, 104, 106, 106n81, 110, 111, 211; students reconstructing orations from notes, 29
librarius to copy notes, 42
lists, compilation of, 32–33, 68–69
Livy, 25n32
logic, study of, 136–37
Long, Anthony A., 82, 90, 123n23, 124, 146, 154
Longinus, Cassius, 62–63, 67, 231
Lucian: on Epictetus, 85–86; extending *parrhesia* to educated public, 180; on *grammateia*, 21; on *hypomnema*, 9, 20, 176; mocking unworthy philosophers, 60, 103; notes, use in writing of, 9, 25–26; philosophers described as charlatans, 191n64; on rhetoric, 141; stenographers and, 71–72; theater metaphors, use of, 153–54
Lucian, works of: *De historia conscribenda*, 26; *Dialogues of the Dead, of the*

278 INDEX

Lucian, works of (continued)
　Courtesans, of the Gods, and of the Sea
　Gods, 155; Hermotimus, 60, 141; The
　Ignorant Book Collector, 86; Professor of
　Rhetoric, 21, 120n11; Toxaris, 21
Lucius (pupil of Musonius), 91, 115
Lucius Verus, 44–45, 210
Lucretius, 189
Lyceum, 47. See also school of Aristotle

Mansfeld, Jaap, 52
Marcellinus's biography of Thucydides, 26, 26n39
Marchesi, Ilaria, 22
Marcus (Cicero's son), 42, 42n18, 188n55, 210
Marcus Aurelius, 6n9, 20, 82, 91, 97, 100n47, 129n50, 143, 153n150, 210
marginalia: in ancient papyri, 163–64, 167–69; Augustine and, 8, 18, 73n18; on back (verso) of papyri, 169; in contemporary scholarship, 7, 8; defined, 167; Galen and, 8, 18, 36; geometrical drawings in, 242; Homer and, 168; lists in, 242; in *Marcianus graecus* (manuscript of lecture recorded by Olympiodorus's student), 241–44; notes in margins of notes, 35–37, 241–44; oral sources of, 167; poetry most commonly found with, 168; prose rarely found with, 168; referring to previous commentaries, 168; school origination of, 169
Marinus of Neapolis, 63, 66, 180, 180n33; *Life of Proclus*, 63, 92, 229–30
Maron (on *P.Köln* III 125), 38
Marrou, Henri-Irénée, 206n22
Martin, Jean, and Paul Petit, 46n29
Maximus of Tyre, 101, 110, 153
McNamee, Kathleen, 166n10, 168
McPhee, John, 24
medicine: doctors advertising for patients, 120n11; Epicurean doctrine on sickness of the soul, 192–99; healing imagery applied to philosophy, 109, 144, 192–95, 221; memory and *exempla* required for education in, 221; students recording in notes their teachers of, 68; writing in Koine, 90n8
melete, meaning of, 140–42, 146
Memmius, 190
memory: enhancement strategies for, 28–29; mnemonics and, 41; notes as aid for, 8, 19–20, 24, 28–32, 59, 63, 68, 247; Seneca the Elder and, 43–44, 43nn21–22
Menander, 168, 234
mistakes: in Aristotle's works, 52–53, 57, 240; faulty hearing as cause of, 239–40; faulty judgment as cause of, 143; in Olympiodorus's commentary to *Alcibiades*, 239–41; by scribes, 62; students blamed for, 64, 231, 243
mnemonics, 40–41
Mommsen, Theodor: Demandt using notes of Mommsen's lectures to write imperial history, 1–2, 4, 246; intending to write history of imperial period, 1–2, 246–47
moral conscience: Epictetus on, 197, 201; Epicureans' focus on, 179, 183; Greek/Roman vs. Christian views, 197
Musonius Rufus: advising student on dealings with father, 102; choosing location of where to lecture, 98; choosing to lecture and not to write, 63; compared to Epictetus's text, 91, 96, 122; compared to Socrates, 91; curriculum of, 132; dialogue rarely used in works of, 121–22; as Epictetus's teacher, 91, 110, 111, 114n124, 136; on faulty judgment as cause of mistakes, 143; Homer and, 148; philosophical instruction's purpose for, 182; on rhetors, 120–21; Stoic principles applied by, 115, 201; on study of philosophy, 51, 141
myths, use of, 33, 111, 120, 128, 130, 138–39, 143–44, 146–52, 158, 198

Naas, Valérie, 23n22
Natali, Carlo, 47–48, 48n4, 56
Neilos (student), 211
Neoplatonism and Neoplatonists, 62, 65, 167, 176, 227–29, 234n27
Nicomachus, 48, 50
notes and annotations (*notae*): as basis of later publications, 29, 58–59, 68; categorizing types of, 9; classroom environment depicted in, 121–23, 159, 209, 221, 233–34, 233n24, 247; compilation of, 32–33, 68–69, 174; in context, 15; in margins, 35–37; as memory aid, 8, 19–20, 24, 28–32, 59, 63, 68, 247; physical storage of, 23; placement of, 18; pointing to works only partially known, 31; as record

of actual teachings, 6; as record of annotations no longer extant, 18; scholarly disdain for, 17; in school anthologies, 38–39; in schools of rhetoric, 41–43; selection of, 18–19; sharing of, 27; storage and retrieval of, 22–23; strategies for writing from, 23–27, 247; taking on a life of their own, 37; terminology used for, 19–23; of travelers, 33–35, 68–69. See also marginalia; notes; stenographers; *specific notetakers*

notetakers: Amelius as more fervent of, 66; Didymus's students vs. stenographers as, 222–26; females as, 31–32, 31n62; publishing in their own names, 4, 28

notetaking, 17–37; abbreviations used in, 93–94, 93n21; as aid to declaiming, 43–46; in class, 10, 29, 38–46, 58–59, 61–62, 245; contemporary methodologies for, 7, 68n75; differences in antiquity from modern era, 7–8; in Middle Ages and early modern period, 18, 68; mistakes due to faulty hearing, 239–40; orality linked to, 2; personal flavor of notetaker in, 7; routines for, 68; surfaces used for, 22–23; tablets used for, 22, 24

Numenius, 66n70

Nussbaum, Martha, 144, 193n68

O'Connell, Mark, 7

Odysseus, 148–49, 151

Oedipus, 130, 152n148, 153

officials: actors compared to, 152; competence of, 106n81; Epictetus talking to, about relationship with children, 82–83; Olympiodorus's students entering careers as, 228; study of *First Alcibiades* well suited for, 232–33

Oldfather, W. A., 90, 112n117, 130n52

Olivieri, Alessandro, 172

Olympiodorus: on Aristotle's works, 176; background of, 228; Christian elite as students of, 228; circulation of lectures by, 12; commentaries of, 176; compared to Aristotle, 59; compared to Didymus, 233, 243; compared to Epictetus, 97, 243; compared to Plotinus, 67; distinguishing between writing formal texts and from class notes, 231–35; errors of attribution by, 53; incompetent and untidy students of, 49; lists written by students of, 32; *Marcianus graecus* (manuscript of lecture recorded by student), 241; memory of students of, 28; mistakes in commentary to *Alcibiades*, 239–41; as Neoplatonist, 167–68, 228; as pagan working in Christian environment, 237; philosophical commentary by, 163, 165–66; rhetoric taught by, 232; speed of speaking, 52; students' notes on, 2, 3, 51, 59, 61, 67, 135, 219, 244, 248; as successor of Ammonius, 228; traditional literary culture and, 201, 202, 237; urging students to take notes, 64

Olympiodorus, works of: *Commentary on Gorgias*, 231, 232, 241; *Commentary on the First Alcibiades*, 53, 228, 232–44; "Life of Plato," 234–39; *Phaedo* commentary, 232, 241

Olympiodorus (of fifth-century Alexandria), 92–93

onomata (expressions), 140, 140n99

Optimus, 204

orality, 2–4

Origen, 205, 205n18, 212–13, 223; *Homilies on the Psalms*, 213, 214n55; schooling of, 213–14

Orpheus, 230

Oxyrhynchus, 45, 211

paideia. *See* classical education

Pamphila (Egyptian), 31–32, 68; *Notebooks*, 31

pantomimes, 154

Papias (church writer), 24n28

papyri: informal rhetorical notes on, 45; legal cases recorded on, 45; notetaking on, 23, 24; Pliny the Elder's volumes of notes on, 22; space left for notes on, 45; students' difficulty in obtaining, 39; verso used for schoolwork, 39–40; of Villa dei Papiri, 170–71, 173. *See also* Tura papyri (Egypt)

papyri fragments: *P.Köln* III 125 (Ptolemaic fragment), 38; *P.Lit.Lond.* 138, 35, 168; *P.Mich.* inv. 3498 and 3250a, b, and c, 39; *P.Oxy.* XXXIV, 169; *P.Yale* II 135, 39

paradeigmata (examples) used in philosophy, 143, 222

INDEX

parrhesia (frank criticism), 180–97; courage and speaking freely for improvement of another, 179, 196; doubts about effectiveness of, 190–91, 197; Epictetus and, 88–89, 180; Isidorus and, 180; non-Epicurean method used in, 185; in Philodemus's *Peri Parrhesias*, 177–79; public denunciation of one's faults, 184, 187, 197; repetition when unsuccessful, 186–87; rules governing, 186, 188; students applying to each other, 189; students' opinion of, 184, 187, 189–90, 192, 196–97; teacher's application of, 183–84, 187–88, 191, 195, 197; unique practice of Epicurean community, 193, 196. See also Peri Parrhesias

Parthenius of Nicaea, 27

Pasicles, 49

Paul: collection of *Responsorum libri XXIII*, 37n89; compared to Zeno, 179

Pausanias, 34, 35

Pepys, Samuel, 72n6

Peri Parrhesias (*On Frank Criticism*, Philodemus), 12, 89n4, 101, 163, 171–73, 177–94; frank criticism as educational system, 177–78, 190–91, 196–97; literary references in, 198; medical analogy for philosopher-student relationship, 193–94; moral conscience as focus of, 179; pedagogical methods revealed by, 179, 194; repetition in, 178–79; rhetoric in, 178; on teacher-sages, 183; Zeno's responses to questions, 177. See also *parrhesia*

Philo of Alexandria, 212

Philodemus of Gadara: on Aristotle teaching rhetoric, 47; background of, 170–72, 171n4, 197; classes of, 177, 195; commentaries by, 163; compared to Epictetus, 97; criticizing Epicureans who dissent from frank criticism, 184–85; Epicurus and, 172, 198–99; epigrams of, 40; ethical focus of, 179, 182; frank criticism and, 183; handwriting varying in, 40, 176–77; Homer and, 198; losing students to charlatans, 101, 191; notes from Zeno's lectures and their transmission to Philodemus's students, 3, 12, 161, 172, 177, 198; notes taken by students of, 176–77; originality of, difficulty of assessing, 198; possible personal experience of *parrhesia* in his education, 196; on punishment of students, 190–91; as transmitter of Epicurus's doctrine, 199; as Zeno's student, 172, 175, 198

Philodemus of Gadara, works of: *Anthologia Palatina*, 198; *The Good King According to Homer*, 198; *On Frank Speech*, 179–80; *On Rhetoric*, 175; *On Signs*, 172. See also Peri Parrhesias (*On Frank Criticism*)

Philoponus, 59, 92, 176, 214, 221, 228–29, 229n7, 232, 236

philosophy: benefits of young men learning, 102; Christians studying, 202; closing of pagan schools of, 228; logic vs., 136–37; *melete* in studies of, 140–42; memory and *exempla* required for education in, 221; as most important of all disciplines, 194n72; purpose of education in, 4, 5–6, 83, 85, 131, 132, 141; religious education and, 201; rivalry with rhetoric, 119; students recording in notes their teachers of, 68; teachers' physical characteristics, 106–7, 107n87; teachers' responsibilities, 105–6. See also specific teachers of philosophy and schools of philosophy

Philostratus, 41, 71, 120n9, 133; *Life of Apollonius of Tyana*, 60

Photius, 31, 31n62, 64, 230

Pindar, 168

Piso, Lucius Calpurnius, 170, 198

Plato: Aristotle's logic in, 62; commentaries on, 227; dialogues of, 235; Epictetus and, 124, 129, 137, 151; Homeric references in, 235, 237; on *hypomnema*, 20; on knowledge as food of the soul, 133; lectures by, 4; Marinus's commentaries on, 180; negative view of writing and preferring lectures, 65; Olympiodorus's commentaries on, 232–34, 241; Olympiodorus's "Life of Plato," 234–39; Olympiodorus's students referring to text of, 135, 239; personal voice difficult to identify in commentaries on, 5; purpose of philosophical instruction for, 4; on rhetoric, 119, 141; Socrates and, 197; tachigraphical signs in text of, 74

INDEX

Plato, works of: *Cleitophon*, 128; *First Alcibiades*, 12, 162, 232–44; *Gorgias*, 64, 102, 124, 230–31, 232, 240, 241; *Phaedo*, 64, 230, 232, 241; *Protagoras*, 131, 233n24; *Republic*, 38, 74, 74n25, 240; *Theaetetus*, 29, 229; *Timaeus*, 240

Platonic school: in late antiquity, 64–65; teachers lecturing from their notes, 68

Pliny the Elder, 22, 23n22, 24–25, 30, 34

Pliny the Younger, 22, 22n20, 24

Plotinus, 62–67; Ammonius as teacher of, 65; books "written by" likely from students' notes and scribes' dictation, 65; compared to Olympiodorus, 67; *Enneads* based on students' recordings of lectures, 66; Longinus and, 62–63; optics as interest of, 65n65; Porphyry writing life of, 61, 63n54, 64; refraining from writing, 231; School of, 64–67; as treatise writer, 63; vision problems and dysgraphia of, 65

Plutarch: in ancient education, 237; Egyptian schools teaching texts by, 211; on *hypomnema*, 20, 25–26; on moral and ethical attainment, 201; notes, use in writing of, 9, 25–26; on orators using notes, 45; on philosophy as most important of all disciplines, 194n72; on practice in virtue, 141; Proclus and, 63–64, 230; on *propatheia* (premonitory reaction), 115; questions during classes of, 209; on rhetorical declamations as spectacles, 121; on School of Aristotle's decline, 48; on student behavior during classes, 209; on teacher-student relations, 108–9; as teacher who urged student notetaking, 64

Plutarch, works of: *How to Study Poetry*, 38; *On Listening to Lectures*, 2, 121, 209; *On the Control of Anger*, 25n34; *On Tranquility of Mind*, 25

Polyaenus, 184

Polybius, 25n32

Porcius Latro, 44

Porphyry of Tyre, 65–67, 246; *Life of Plotinus*, 61, 63n54, 64

Possidius, 73n18

Praechter, Karl, 244

Prentice, William Kelly, 26n41

Priam, 130

Proaeresius, 44n26

Problemata, 55–57

Proclus: Ammonius as student of, 228–29; *Commentary on the First Alcibiades*, 228, 234; Marinus succeeding, 63n57, 92n19, 180n33; memorizing his teacher's words, 92–93; Neoplatonism revived by, 228; Plutarch and, 63–64, 230; reticent to write a commentary, 131, 230; as student of Olympiodorus (of fifth-century Alexandria), 92–93; students of, 66; student-teacher relationship and notetaking, 230

progymnasmata (exercises in rhetoric), 126, 126n28, 138, 210

Prohaeresius, 204

propatheia (premonitory reaction), 115, 115n134

prose: marginalia rarely found with, 168; notes, use of, 26

Protagoras, 47n2, 139, 220–21

Psalms: in *Adrian's Introduction to the Sacred Scriptures*, 218; Didymus's commentaries on, 78, 206–9, 216, 222–24, 225, 233; Origen's *Homilies on the Psalms*, 213, 214n55; prevalence in Christian education, 218n69; Theodore's commentaries on, 218

Pseudo-Longinus: *On Memory*, 28

Pythagoras, school of, 61

questions in philosopher's class, 67, 124, 209, 236–37, 243, 247–48

Quintilian, 8, 28, 41–46, 73n20, 108n94, 134n73, 164–65, 201, 210, 218, 236, 248

refutation, 139–42

Reydams-Schils, Gretchen, 132n62

rhetoric and oratory: annotating in schools of, 41–43; Epictetus's views on, 118–29, 131; hand gestures, use of, 45; hard work to master, 120; *melete* from studies of, 140–41; memory and *exempla* required for education in, 221; Musonius on, 120–21; notes as aid to, 43–46; Olympiodorus as teacher of, 232; Plutarch on, 121; *progymnasmata* (exercises in rhetoric), 126, 126n28; rivalry with philosophy, 119; schools catering to, 211; students recording in notes their teachers of, 68; writing vs. improvisation, 45

Roman Empire: educational texts used during, 227; mimes and pantomimes

INDEX

Roman Empire (*continued*)
    as popular theatrical forms in, 155;
    Odysseus as popular figure in, 148;
    philosophy embedded in pagan and
    Christian culture in, 227; philosophy
    vs. rhetoric in, 227; teachers with small
    student groups replacing philosophical
    schools, 61
Roman Republic: shorthand used in, 72;
    stenographers in, 71
Ross, William David, 49
Rufinus, 204, 206, 212, 215, 223

Sacks, Oliver: *On the Move: A Life*, 8
Saffrey, H. D., 65
Sarpedon (*Iliad*), 150–51
scholia distinguished from
    hypomnemata, 167
school of Aristotle. *See* Aristotelian
    school
schools of other philosophers. *See specific
    philosopher or location of school*
schoolwork: *chalinos* (tongue-twister
    exercise), 39; grammatical commentaries,
    164–66; lectures as, 232; on papyri
    fragments, 38–41. *See also* students
scribes: distinguished from
    stenographers, 223; earnings of,
    76n37; Euripides's *Hypsipyle* written
    by, 169; formal handwriting of, 73–74;
    mistakes by, 62
Second Sophistic, 11, 32, 124, 237–38
Sellars, John, 6n9
Seneca the Elder: on acceptance of
    misfortunes, 131; on assimilation
    of knowledge, 133; distinguishing
    between true anger and preliminary
    to anger, 117; Epictetus compared to,
    109; Homer and, 148; on logic, 136;
    notetaking and, 43–44; oratory and,
    46; Stoics and, 82, 97, 115; on students
    living with philosophical teachers, 99;
    on written texts, 129
Seneca the Elder, works of: *Controversiae*,
    43; *Suasoriae*, 43
Seneca the Younger, 102
Servius, 164
Setaioli, Aldo, 115
Sharples, Robert, 58
shipwreck, imagery of, 143
shorthand, 72, 76–77; *Commentary*
    (stenographic signs), 75, 77
Simplicius, 176, 228

slaves: as stenographers, 42–43, 70, 72,
    76n33; term "slave" used for student,
    79, 110, 111, 113–14
Smith, Robert R. R., 107
Snyder, Gregory, 58–59, 86n22, 132,
    134n70, 180–81
Socrates: on Alcibiades at ideal age to
    learn, 233; on books as unresponsive,
    133; compared to Musonius, 91;
    depictions of, 107; on Didymus and
    Antony encounter, 206; Epictetus and,
    83, 85, 109, 114, 124, 139, 143n115,
    151; Euclid and, 29; modesty of, 109;
    in Olympiodorus's commentary on
    Plato, 236–39; Plato and, 197, 229;
    purpose of philosophical instruction
    for, 4; question-and-answer format of
    discourses, 124; role of philosopher
    and, 103; as writer, 136; on written
    word's inferiority to spoken, 131;
    Xenophon and, 11, 96
Socrates, works by: *Apology*, 119;
    Phaedrus, 131
Sopater, 31
Sorabji, Richard, 197
Soteridas of Epidaurus, 31
Souilhé, Joseph, 68n75, 120n8
Sozomen, 206
Stefaniw, Blossom, 214–15, 219n72,
    220n78
Stellwag, H. W. F., 91
Stenger, Jan R., 201, 212n49
stenographers, 10, 70–78: accuracy
    and credibility of, 77–78; Aristotle's
    era without, 52; Arrian and, 89;
    Commentary (stenographic signs),
    75, 77; Didymus's students vs.
    stenographers as his recorders, 222–26;
    Epictetus and, 11, 70; Gellius and,
    30; philosophers using, 70–72; Pliny
    the Elder and, 25; process used by, 74;
    religious conferences and sermons
    recorded by, 74, 77–78; scribes
    distinguished from, 223; shorthand,
    terms for, 72; shorthand used by,
    72; slaves as, 42–43, 70, 72, 76n33;
    social position of, 75–78, 223; special
    training of, 70, 74, 75–77, 77n39;
    students using, 42; terms for, 71n2;
    texts and letters, dictation of, 35
Stobaeus, 91
Stoics and Stoicism: analogy of medicine
    with philosophy, 194; Arrian and, 87;

consulting other schools of philosophy allowed by, 196; on death and destiny, 150–51; Diogenes Laertius and, 81n3; distinguishing between theoretical instruction and philosophy, 5; emotions defined by, 107; Epictetus and, 11, 80–82, 97–98, 108, 116, 123, 129, 197, 216, 238; ethics as field of study for, 5; on God's existence, 112; on Homer, 146–48; little extant of, 81–82; Musonius Rufus and, 91; *parrhesia* connected with, 180; past learning of students and, 144; philosophical instruction's purpose for, 182, 193; present-day popularity of, 97; *Problemata* in works of, 55; as system to cope with emotions, 115–16; teacher's relationship with students, 115–17, 193; theater metaphors, use of, 153; written word deemed inferior to personal communications by, 132

Strabo, 48

students: arrogance of, 84, 112, 137, 143, 159, 183, 185, 194, 233; attachment to their teachers of philosophy, 63; behavior of, 2, 82–85, 100–101, 106, 111, 137–38, 193, 209, 236–37, 248; benefits of joining school of philosophy, 103; blamed for errors in notes, 64, 231, 243; citizens of the world, learning to become, 83, 119, 127; compiling publications from their notes, 58–59, 64, 231; confusion created as lectures revised and edited, 53–55; depictions of, 107; discipline and punishment of, 108–9, 110n109, 111, 113n123, 114–15, 190, 197; disobedience of, 178, 183, 185–87, 189; disorientation upon leaving their past lives, 144, 144n119; dull and weak like "stones," 110, 112; father-son relations, 102–3; home lives of, 101–5; illnesses of, 104–5; incompetence and laziness of, 49, 110–12, 141; mocking of, 60–61, 106, 112, 127, 138; papyri and manuscripts used by, 3; parents' punishment of, 108; parents' view of paideia, 200n3; parents' view of philosophical education, 103, 191–92, 195, 212; past education and life prior to entering school of philosophy, 118, 129–30, 132, 137–38, 144, 158, 232; as recorders of ancient philosophers, 2, 60–64; term "slave" used for, 79, 110, 111, 113–14; *zelotai* vs. *akroatai*, 66. *See also specific schools and teachers*

Suda lexicon, 31
Suetonius, 44
Sulpicius Severus, 94
Summers, Walter Coventry, 102n59
Swain, Simon, 90n8
syllogisms, teaching of, 217
Synesius, 23
syntagmatica, 20
Syrianus, 64

tachygraphical signs, 74–76, 75n26, 75n30
Tacitus, 44
Tarrant, Harold, 240
Tatian, 154
Taurus (philosopher), 236
Teitler, H. C., 77
Tertullian, 94
texts. *See* books and texts
Theaetetus, 54
theater, 152–57
Theodore of Mopsuestia, 218
Theon, 41, 166–67, 235; *Progymnasmata*, 41
Theophanes of Hermopolis, 34–35
Theophrastus, 48, 50, 53–57
Theosebius, 64, 230–31
Thessalos: *Epidemics*, 21–22, 22n17
Theuthras, 72
Third Sophistic, 121
Thucydides, 20, 26nn40–42, 29–30; *History*, 26, 29
Timon, 26–27, 26n42
Tiro (Cicero's secretary), 42, 45, 76n33
traditional literary culture, continuous value of, 200–204; in late antiquity, 202–4
tragedies, 130, 153–54, 238
travelers' annotations, 33–35, 68–69
Trojan War, 150, 155. *See also* Homer, works by: *Iliad*
Tsouna, Voula, 182
Tura papyri (Egypt), 161, 207–9, 215, 219–20, 222. *See also* Didymus the Blind

van den Hoek, Annewies, 212
Vergil, 27; Servius's commentary to, 164
Verrycken, Koenraad, 229

Villa dei Papiri (Herculaneum), 170–71, 173
vocabulary of philosophical teaching, 140, 159
von Arnim, Hans Friedrich August, 35n81, 43n21, 229

Wehner, Barbara, 122, 155n165
welfare of humanity, 193, 197
Westerink, Leendert Gerrit, 235, 237, 240–41
White, Michael, 173
Wirth, Theo, 90, 140n99
women as students, 31–32, 65
written texts: dictation and orality of, 3–4; formation process of, 3, 174; philosophers choosing to only lecture instead of writing, 61, 63, 65; students, not teachers, engaging in writing, 62

Xanthippe, 198n82
Xenophon, 11, 90, 96, 140n99, 157

Zanker, Paul, 107, 115, 115n133
Zechariah, commentary on, 207
Zeno: Athens school of, 175–76; compared to Paul, 179; criticizing Epicureans who dissent from frank criticism, 184–85; Epictetus influenced by, 124, 134; on Epicurians, 178–79; frank criticism and, 183, 196; on Homer, 146–47; moral education devised by, 182; notes taken by Bromius, 172; notes taken by Philodemus of Gadara, 3, 12, 161, 172, 177, 198; Philodemus as student of, 171, 172, 175, 198; Stoics and, 82
Zeus, 102, 113, 197, 202

www.ingramcontent.com/pod-product-compliance
Lightning Source LLC
Chambersburg PA
CBHW030526230426
43665CB00010B/783